POPULAR CULTURE
IN FRANCE

STANFORD
FRENCH AND ITALIAN
STUDIES

volume III

ANMA LIBRI

The Wolf and the Lamb

POPULAR CULTURE IN FRANCE

FROM THE OLD REGIME
TO THE TWENTIETH CENTURY

EDITED BY

JACQUES BEAUROY
MARC BERTRAND
EDWARD T. GARGAN

1977
ANMA LIBRI

Stanford French and Italian Studies is a collection of scholarly publications devoted to the study of French and Italian literature and language, culture and civilization. Occasionally it will allow itself excursions into related Romance areas.

Stanford French and Italian Studies will publish books, monographs, and collections of articles centering around a common theme, and is open also to scholars associated with academic institutions other than Stanford.

The collection is published for the Department of French and Italian, Stanford University by Anma Libri.

© 1976 by ANMA LIBRI & Co.
P.O. BOX 876, Saratoga, Calif. 95070
All rights reserved.

LC 76-16899
ISBN 0-915838-31-1

Printed in the United States of America.

Preface

When the great English poet T.S. Eliot published in 1948 his *Notes towards the Definition of Culture* he very modestly intimated that he did not have an adequate approach to the subject of popular culture. On this question he suggested that his readers consult the American moralist and democratic socialist Dwight Macdonald's brief essay "A Theory of Popular Culture," which appeared in the first issue of *Politics* in February 1944. Dwight Macdonald's essay was a significant call for reflection on "the meaning of Popular Culture as a historical phenomenon." For Macdonald every consideration of popular culture was "basically a political question" and this political concern was understandably urgent at the close of the Second World War. Yet scholars more reticent about their political convictions than either the Tory poet or the radical political philosopher have in the years since the War increasingly discovered that the study of popular culture is central to all consideration of literature and history, of language and art. Starting from different positions, traditions, and academic commitments literary scholars, historians of ideas, ethnographers, social historians and students of literature have arrived at a common agreement on the importance of popular culture to their particular inquiries. French scholarship inspired by Jules Michelet and the contemporary example of the work of Robert Mandrou has played the pre-eminent role in forming this consensus.

When in 1974 preparations began for the twenty-first annual conference of the Society for French Historical Studies to be held at the University of Wisconsin, Madison, in April 1975, it seemed right and proper that this scholarly *fête* devote its major attention to the theme of popular culture and collective mentalities. The contributions of Clarke Garrett, Robert Kreiser, Robert J. Bezucha, Barnett Singer, and Timothy J. Clark were presented at the Madison conference. Lucienne A. Roubin gave her *"Savoir et art de vivre campagnard"* at Madison and Michael R. Marrus his "Folklore as an Ethnographic Source: A *Mise au point.*" At the same time, Professor Marc Bertrand of the Department of French and Italian of Stanford University was organizing a Symposium on *Popular Culture and Learned Culture in France: The Seventeenth to the Twentieth Centuries*, also to be held in April 1975. Professor Natalie Zemon Davis of the University of

California, Berkeley, and Jacques Beauroy, the Attaché Culturel de France à San Francisco, participants in the planning at Madison and aware of the project at Stanford, urged that all those involved exchange their ideas and plans. This was quickly done and resulted in the inclusion in this volume of the essays by Robert Mandrou, Marc Soriano, Lucienne A. Roubin, and Eugen Weber from the Stanford Symposium. While this book was being edited, two other contributions took form: Michael R. Marrus' essay on modernization and dancing in rural France and Edward Shorter's "The *Veillée* and the Great Transformation," both read at the Pacific Coast Branch Meeting of the American Historical Association in Berkeley in August 1975. As the volume took final shape, Susan J. Delaney, a young scholar in art history at the University of Wisconsin, Madison, offered her essay on "*Atala* and the Arts" to complement that of Timothy J. Clark on art and popular culture.

The cooperation that has made this collection possible was characterized by both theoretical and practical accord on the questions that matter and has resulted in discourse that happily transcends the usual barriers between disciplines. In this territory shared alike by historians, literary scholars, ethnographers, and art historians the study of popular culture has found the voice and language which, if not that of the poet or philosopher, is yet appropriate to the human science.

Any edited volume is necessarily a joint venture and in this instance the task has greatly benefited from the work and counsel of Mary T. Anglim who served on the original committee at Madison which fashioned the conference of the Society for French Historical Studies on the popular culture of France since the Old Regime. Thanks are especially due to Professor Alphonse Juilland, editor of *Stanford Studies in French and Italian*. Stanford University, through Professors Halsey Royden, Dean of Humanities and Sciences, and W. Bliss Carnochan, Dean of the Graduate Division, has generously contributed to the publication of this volume.

Edward T. Gargan	Marc Bertrand	Jacques Beauroy
University of Wisconsin	*Stanford University*	*Cultural Attaché*
		San Francisco

Contents

INTRODUCTION

The Historian and Popular Culture*

NATALIE ZEMON DAVIS

Students of popular culture in France readily think of Jules Michelet's *Le peuple* (1846) and Charles Nisard's *Histoire des livres populaires* (1854-64) as early stages in the history of their subject. In fact, its study stretches back in some forms to the late fifteenth century, with clerical treatises on "superstitions" and learned collections of popular proverbs; and surely back to the opening years of the nineteenth century, with the publications of antiquarian societies on rural customs and beliefs.[1] Even if they have such precursors, however, Michelet and Nisard are a useful starting point for this discussion. They suggest to us not only the range of feeling with which scholars have approached popular culture — from sympathetic identification to critical disapproval — but also two alternative conceptions of what "popular culture" means. Each of these words has a long history of ambiguity, and neither man used the precise term. But their work implies both a definition and a way to go about the task.

For Michelet, the concept refers to the values, beliefs, customs, rituals and associations of peasants or of artisans and working people of the city. Here culture is characterized, as anthropologists might, by its relation to the lives and purposes of a specified social group. To unearth it, one starts with a community and studies it, or one starts with some institution or form of behavior *known* to be part of that community. Thus Lucienne Roubin, herself an ethnographer, contributes to our collection an essay on the general characteristics of rural culture and its transmission, and an essay on the varied purposes of the Provençal *chambrette*, an organization of male villagers, heads of families outside the circle of the local notables. Thus the cures and curses of cunning men in the seventeenth century, the *bourrée* and other group dances of young villagers in the nineteenth

* The author wishes to acknowledge the assistance of a Faculty Research Grant from the University of California, Berkeley.
[1] I have described this early development in N.Z. Davis, *Society and Culture in Early Modern France: Eight Essays* (Stanford, Ca., 1975), ch. 8.

century, and the evening village gathering or *veillée*, become means by which Clarke Garrett, Michael Marrus and Edward Shorter can show the uncertainties and constraints of rural life.[2]

For Nisard, on the other hand, popular culture seems to designate certain kinds of literature, art, religious practice or festivity, which either are widely dispersed in a society or are intended for a broad public. Here popular culture is characterized by its differences from learned or high culture. Further developed by sociologists and literary critics,[3] this usage often sorts popular culture into folk, popular and mass — the first the creation of a local and unlettered world, the second the product of a social system with more interchange between oral and literate culture, the third a commodity diffused throughout industrial society.

To get at popular culture in this sense, one starts with a cultural artifact, trys to locate it in a network of relationships — who created it? who communicated it? who hears, reads, sings, sees or acts it? — and then tries to assess its meaning. This was the tack taken by Robert Mandrou in his pioneering book of 1964 on the *Bibliothèque bleue* of Troyes. So too a few years ago, Jacques Le Goff and Emmanuel Le Roy Ladurie considered the fairy story of Mélusine from the twelfth to the seventeenth centuries and were able to relate certain changes in motif to the time, place and audience for the tale.[4] And so in this collection several papers begin with a form of "popular" cultural expression and then move to its context, uses and significance: a fable of La Fontaine (Marc Soriano); the ecstasies of the *Convulsionnaires* in Paris in the 1720's and 1730's (Robert Kreiser); the virgin Atala in nineteenth-century art (Susan Delaney); and a Manet painting of The Bar at the Folies-Bergères and its source, the *café-concert* (Timothy J. Clark). Eugen Weber raises the question of cultural form and context in his very title, "Who Sang the Marseillaise?" How national and

[2] For a study of associational life rooted in one region, see Maurice Agulhon, *Pénitents et Francs-Maçons de l'ancienne Provence* (Paris, 1968).

[3] See, for instance, Leo Lowenthal, *Literature, Popular Culture and Society* (Englewood Cliffs, N.J., 1961); Harold L. Wilensky, "Mass Society and Mass Culture: Interdependence or Independence," *American Sociological Review*, 29 (1964), pp. 173-197; Herbert J. Gans, *Popular Culture and High Culture: An Analysis and Evaluation of Taste* (New York, 1974); Rosalie L. Colie, "Literature and History," in James Thorpe, ed., *Relations of Literary Study: Essays on Interdisciplinary Contributions*, (New York, 1967), pp. 1-26; Robert Escarpit, ed., *Le littéraire et le social: Eléments pour une sociologie de la littérature* (Paris, 1970); and Russel B. Nye, *Notes on a Rationale for Popular Culture* (Publication of the Popular Culture Association, n.d.).

[4] Robert Mandrou, *De la culture populaire aux XVIIe et XVIIIe siècles: La Bibliothèque bleu de Troyes* (Paris, 1964; new ed., 1975); and Jacques Le Goff and Emmanuel Le Roy Ladurie, "Mélusine maternelle et défricheuse," *Annales: économies, sociétés, civilisations*, 26 (1971), pp. 587-622. For two exemplary studies providing context for cultural artifacts, see Svetlana Alpers, "Bruegel's Festive Peasants," *Simiolus: Netherlands Quarterly for the History of Art*, 6 (1972-73), pp. 163-176; and Maurice Agulhon, "Le problème de la culture populaire en France autour de 1848" (Princeton Univ., Shelby Cullom Davis Center Seminar, May 13, 1974).

popular could the song be when several decades after the Revolution "French was a foreign language for a large minority of the country's inhabitants"?

Clearly there is some overlap between the anthropological definition and the narrower literary or sociological definition of popular culture. At their best, both procedures have the same ultimate goals: the careful explication of values, beliefs, and customs and their relation to social milieu. Furthermore, we need both approaches to the study of *mentalités*. If we start with a group or community, as did Gérard Bouchard in his interesting portrait of an eighteenth-century village in the Sologne, we may find that our sources seem to go stubbornly silent on certain matters, such as carnival festivity and female gossip circles.[5] It is then we envy the tired anthropologist in the field who can wait for the next transvestite festival or the next childbirth to come around. But we are not without recourse, we can turn to research focussed on popular play and recreation and on popular medicine to help us reinterpret our sources and perhaps fill in the gaps. Similarly, students of artisanal life in the sixteenth and seventeenth centuries may be disappointed when inventories *post mortem* turn up virtually no books among their subjects' belongings. Then monographs on patterns of publication, book distribution and prices and thematic analyses of book content may come to their aid; or even better, the original books themselves, with prefaces that give clues about reader-ship and signatures on the fly-leafs and title pages.[6]

If we start with a cultural artifact, on the other hand, we may find it is not special to peasants or to some urban grouping, but has a wide social spread and a structure and support staff to perpetuate it. It is then that community studies can help us see the way the same cultural form may function in different milieus. For example, Keith Thomas discovered that magical assumptions, ritual and practitioners existed in abundance at all levels of English society in the sixteenth and first half of the seventeenth centuries. The explanatory uses of magic had to be related not only to the worries of village life, but also to the cares of the city and the intellectual ambitions of the learned.[7]

So, too, several of the cultural forms described in this collection were sustained by persons of diverse social origins and require for their in-

---

[5] Gérard Bouchard, *Le village immobile: Sennely-en-Sologne au XVIIIe siècle* (Paris, 1972). Reflection on both the areas of festivity and the informal association among the village women might well have affected M. Bouchard's assessment of the weaknesses in village integration and processes of socialization.

[6] Further discussion and bibliography in Davis, *Society and Culture*, ch. 7 ("Printing and the People").

[7] Keith Thomas, *Religion and the Decline of Magic: Studies in Popular Beliefs in Sixteenth and Seventeenth Century England* (London, 1971).

terpretation considerable knowledge of context and community. The convulsionary men and women in Paris in the 1730's who preached to each other in tongues, were many of them from shopkeepers' families, but also from the families of nobles and professionals. The men who crowded into the *café-concert* in the center of Paris in Manet's day were, as Timothy Clark says, "a mixture of *bourgeois* and *populaire*." The chaste or dying Atala appeared both on expensive dessert plates and in cheap prints on the walls of country inns; possibly the engraved narratives of the farm daughter, stealing away with her aristocratic lover, then returning repentant with her baby, had a similarly wide range in viewers. Delaney remarks that to understand these images fully, one would need to learn much more about the interiors of lower-class homes and about contemporary attitudes toward family and sexuality.

It is clear from these examples that we must not legislate one sense for "popular culture," but that we must know which of its meanings applies to our work. Each approach — what I have dubbed the "anthropological" approach and the "literary-sociological" approach — has some limitations and some advantages for the historian. The value of this collection is that the two appear side by side. Their complementarity is evident, and we may be able more readily to move toward a synthesis.

A second concern in the study of popular culture has been its relations with other forms of culture. Robert Mandrou has given us here, as in his other work,[8] a masterful survey of the possible connections between rural and learned cultures of the Ancien Régime: the dissemination of medieval learning and stories out to the peasants through the printed books in the peddlers' packs; the movement of fairy tales upward through the words of rural wet nurses and servants; and the assault on peasant superstitions by the post-Tridentine clergy and by the trial of village witches. Other essays in this volume illustrate and add to these relations, carrying the story on into the twentieth century. Lucienne Roubin paints a picture of little interaction: the peasant world and the world of the upper classes side by side in mute and fearful incomprehension; and even within the same village space, the new bourgeois recreation *cercle* indifferent to the old solidarity of the *chambrette*. In contrast, Robert Bezucha maps out the campaign of mid-nineteenth-century civilizers to reform the "cruel customs" of the masses, to get them to slaughter their cattle more humanely, to stop beating their horses and stop amusing themselves with cock fights.

Next it was the turn of the village schoolteachers, as education became universal and obligatory. M. Mandrou and Barnett Singer describe the

---

[8] For instance, Robert Mandrou, *Des humanistes aux hommes de science (XVIe et XVIIe siècles)* (Paris, 1973). On the movement of fairy tales, the central work is, of course, Marc Soriano, *Les contes de Perrault: Culture savante et traditions populaires* (Paris, 1968).

position, accomplishments and limitations of those key figures in the transformation of local rural culture into French national republicanism. Even then, peasant culture did not bend easily, as rural lads showed suspicion of technical innovations preached by men who refused to speak their patois, and peasant mothers set impossible standards for the behavior of schoolmistresses. Michael Marrus discusses the cultural conflict not only in terms of what came into the village — the dance halls, with those who knew the latest steps for couples to dance — but also in terms of the railroad which took people away. Finally, the folklorists arrived to record a vanishing village life.

Nor do these images exhaust the possible ways of relating popular culture to other cultural forms. One can look at the variation in learned and upper-class attitudes toward rural culture. In the sixteenth century, for instance, a lawyer at the Parlement of Paris was marvelling at "how many learned Physicians had been outdone by a simple old peasant woman . . . with a single plant or herb," while Doctor Laurent Joubert was trying to correct the "ignorant routines" of the village midwives; a humanist prelate of Beaujeu was demanding that all pagan and ethnic mumming be stamped out, while a Rouen religious, Noel Taillepied, was allowing that a little Druid gaming on New Year's Day would not hurt the salvation of souls.[9]

One can look for features of peasant culture other than fairy tales which have moved up the social scale in some suitably modified form (remedies, proverbs, dances); and especially in this collection, one will find cultural encounters in which class lines appear to be jumped or temporarily to melt away. Marc Soriano's exploration of La Fontaine's "The Wolf and the Lamb" reveals the sources of the fable to be not merely bookish, but also political: the lamb eaten "sans procès" has as its background the *procès* Fouquet; Colbert is the target as well as the angry, vengeful wolf. The poet speaks with Aesop's voice and also with the voice, freely chosen by La Fontaine, of the gifted story-teller of the village.

Another kind of freedom is found in the gatherings of the *Convulsionnaires* and in the *café-concert*. Mixing social classes, as we have noted; "popular" in expression (glossolalia in the one; vulgar, slangy singing in the other), these were occasions when social roles were reversed. Clerics among the Convulsionaries were outranked by simple Sisters with spiritual gifts; officials and business agents at the Folies-Bergères played at being apprentices, and vice versa. Here were "rites of status reversal," in Victor Turner's phrase; here was carnival topsy-turvy — but dangerous, rather than allowable, leading to dissolution, not to renewal.[10] The *café-*

---

[9] Davis, *Society and Culture*, pp. 120, 258-262, and 261 n.; and Noel Taillepied, *Histoire de l'Estat et Republique des Druides* (Paris, 1585), p. 120^r.

[10] Victor Turner, *The Ritual Process: Structure and Anti-Structure* (Chicago, 1968), chs. 3-5; also Davis, *Society and Culture*, chs. 4-5.

concert was seen as sinister. It was partly the smell of money, the sale of sex. But Clark concludes, "It seems as though one class, the dominant class, was obliged to exploit the forms of another, the class it dominated. In the process it was forced to include and imitate *too much* of the culture it aimed to domesticate."

Plainly the essays in this volume present us with a more complex picture of social processes than is usually expected in the study of this subject. And this is only the beginning. Like cultural conflict, cultural adoption and cultural imitation are not just chance fads, but are connected with social, economic and political matters. The ambivalence of the learned in the sixteenth century, wanting both to adopt and to correct features of popular culture, had as its concomitants a certain fluidity in the social structure; a concern for the French tongue, stirred by humanist, Calvinist and political interests; and provincial loyalties not yet in intolerable tension with national loyalty. In the nineteenth century, upper-class attitudes toward popular culture evidently ranged from terror to fascination. Some of the sources for these feelings are traced in this collection.

A third question posed by these essays is the thorny one of interpretation. We are dealing with a subject where, for the period before the twentieth century, words like "backward" and "primitive" have been readily supplied to interpret what we find; where traditions of our craft, some of them going back to the sixteenth century, provide a descriptive vocabulary like "naive," "spontaneous," "concrete," "irrational," "escapist," "violent," "passive," "unchanging." Some of these characterizations emerge also from the essays here. The picture of peasant culture presented by Lucienne Roubin, Michael Marrus and Edward Shorter does stress its unchanging, or at least very slowly changing character, until in Shorter's phrase it was "shattered under the hammer blows of modernization." Robert Kreiser's urban *Convulsionnaires* are surely "spontaneous,"[11] and the violence at the *café-concert* always simmered just below the surface.

Do our essays also broaden the choice of adjectives (as might anthropologists working on pre-literate or non-European peasant societies) to include, say, "ordering," "planned," "mindful,"[12] "critical," "artful," "flexible"? I would even like to add the possibility of "innovative." Ordered and ordering, yes, from several portraits (Roubin, Marrus, Shorter)

[11] Though even here, a thematic and linguistic analysis of the long "sermons" of the Convulsionaries, still preserved in manuscript, might reveal regularities in social and religious criticism. Alfred Métraux' observations on the utterances and gestures of persons in Voodoo trance suggest that it is insufficient to explain them in sexual and psychological terms; the person in the trance says something that he or she cannot say at ordinary times.

[12] On the use of this term in regard to Japanese peasants of the nineteenth century, see Irwin Scheiner, "The Mindful Peasant: Sketches for a Study of Rebellion," *Journal of Asian Studies*, 22 (1973), pp. 579-591.

in which village institutions mesh nicely to control the behavior of everyone in the community and guarantee the transmission of values to the young. But "flexible," evidently not, as our authors stress the power of prescription against the possibility of individual choice, introduced only with "modernization." "Innovative" rarely, if at all, as most of these studies describe novelty as coming in from outside, whether in the form of books with blue wrappers, schoolteachers, or railroad lines. Edward Shorter does speculate, however, on the importance of new forms of family sentiment which, if they did not originate in the village in the late nineteenth century, had to have genuine roots there if they were to transform local life.

On the matters of rationality and criticality in popular culture, our essays give diverse views. Robert Mandrou remarks that rural folk medicine had some empirical basis and was on occasion efficacious; Clarke Garrett wonders if there might even be some reason to magical techniques for curing sexual impotence. At the same time, M. Mandrou points to a whole area of peasant culture which was "escapist," that is, the medieval lore of the *Bibliothèque bleue*, with its representation of an aristocratic society long since gone and "absolutely not open to the problems of the time." Edward Shorter takes a like view of these tales, still being recited at the *veillée* in the nineteenth century: "rules of the game derived from the adventures of Saint Innocence or Fairy Fanfreluche could not have been all that applicable to village society."

Marc Soriano might respond to these assessments: "And why not applicable?" He insists upon the political and moral resonance of an age-old tale with animals as characters, its impact depending in part on the cultural and social context in which the tale is heard, on the teller and his or her audience. Might the same point be made about the fairy story? (I urge readers to test this out on Mélusine as I did recently with students and a colleague, and see with what residue of feeling you are left and whether you all agree with Jacques Le Goff that Mélusine is the victim of that tale and her husband its hero.) It is agreed that fairy stories can teach traditional values and also offer free play for erotic and private fantasy, but is that all? The author C. S. Lewis has argued that fairy tales are not necessarily "compensatory, running from the disappointments of the real world"; but can rather arouse a special discontent and a new yearning, and add a critical dimension to the everyday world. Perhaps this was sometimes true in the European past we have been considering. There are tales in the old Celtic repertory that were supposed to confer special powers on those who heard them. And as fairies could use their power, if they wished, to act on humans benevolently, so male peasants in eighteenth-century Ireland and France sometimes blackened their faces and put on female garb and resisted their rent-raising landlords — all "under sanction of being fairies," who could hardly be arrested.[13]

These episodes bring us to a final interpretive issue, that of the staying power and vitality of popular culture. In his "Who Sang the Marseillaise?" Eugen Weber has given an elegant realization of his own earlier programmatic statement: to show how "the variety of local, traditional, popular cultures inherited from the past gave way before an official . . . . national culture. . . ." Quoted in this volume by another essayist,[14] these words could stand as the organizing principle for most of the chapters in this collection. The "popular culture" left in the wake of national victory may then be seen as little better than the pandering pictures of Atala described by Susan Delaney. Without a doubt, this program and this perspective are essential. But another perspective is available as well, one suggested by E. P. Thompson in his *Making of the English Working Class* (1963); and by Richard Hoggart, who despite the onslaught of the mass media can still find some local culture with bite and flavor in the working-class quarters of Leeds.[15] A perspective suggested, too, by M. Soriano's poet, for whom popular culture is always an essential resource, and by Timothy Clark's painter, whose explorations of "modernity" leave one unsure what victory has been won.

[13] C.S. Lewis, "On Three Ways of Writing for Children," in *Of Other Worlds: Essays and Stories* (New York, 1966), pp. 26-30; Alwyn Rees and Brinley Rees, *Celtic Heritage: Ancient Tradition in Ireland and Wales* (London, 1961), ch. l; and Davis, *Society and Culture*, pp. 147-149. See also Bruno Bettelheim, *The Uses of Enchantment. The Meaning and Importance of Fairy Tales* (New York, 1976), Introduction.

[14] See Robert Bezucha's essay below, and its note 8.

[15] See also E.P. Thompson, "Patrician Society, Plebeian Culture," *Journal of Social History*, 7 (1974), pp. 382-405; and Richard Hoggart, *The Uses of Literacy: Aspects of Working-Class Life with Special Reference to Publications and Entertainments* (London, 1957).

1

Cultures Populaire et Savante: Rapports et Contacts

ROBERT MANDROU

La présentation de ce sujet présente une difficulté préalable d'identification qu'il importe de lever avant tout autre propos: l'expression culture populaire a certainement droit de cité dans le vocabulaire socio-culturel français, mais sous des acceptions pour le moins contestables. Pour les tenants d'un certain populisme, il n'y a de culture populaire que celle créée par le peuple, celui des Compagnons du Devoir ou des traditions artisanales les plus solides. Dans cette ligne, les animateurs de l'association *Peuple et Culture* entendent conserver ces traditions, mais en même temps enrichir les classes populaires des apports de la culture savante, implicitement reconnue comme supérieure.[1] Pour les spécialistes de folklore, espèce en voie de disparition à l'heure actuelle, la culture populaire se définit comme culture de la société traditionnelle, entité quelque peu mythique dans la mesure où elle est présentée comme immobile et immuable pendant des siècles: culture en voie de disparition depuis la fin du XIXe siècle, menacée, gommée par la société industrielle, elle aurait été détentrice de la sagesse de l'humanité.[2] Enfin de façon plus commune encore, pour ce qu'il est convenu d'appeler le public cultivé, la culture populaire n'est jamais que le reflet dégradé d'une culture savante par un phénomène d'acculturation à l'intérieur d'une société globale qui passe par la diffusion des valeurs dominantes, l'enseignement, les mass media dans le monde contemporain. Toutes ces définitions qui font référence à la reproduction plus qu'à la contestation de la hiérarchie sociale ne sont

---

[1] Les animateurs de *Peuple et culture* sont actuellement le sociologue J. Dumazedier, l'autodidacte B. Cacérès, le journaliste J. Rovan. Les publications de l'association sont tout à fait significatives, de même que l'oeuvre romancée de B. Cacérès (*L'Espoir au coeur, Le bourg de nos vacances*) et son *Histoire de l'Education populaire* (Paris, 1964).
[2] Cf. A. Varagnac, *Civilisation traditionnelle et genres de vie* (Paris, 1948), et les différentes introductions données par G.H. Rivière aux expositions du Musée national des Arts et Traditions Populaires, pendant le quart de siècle où il a dirigé cet établissement.

assurément pas satisfaisantes pour l'historien qui se soucie d'explorer et reconstituer des structures socio-culturelles.[3] Nous leur préférons une définition ethnologique, qui reconnaît à tout groupe social homogène à l'intérieur d'une société donnée une originalité et une unité culturelle: la civilisation française est faite d'une combinatoire complexe de cultures variées dont aucune ne peut prétendre représenter la totalité de la culture française; communautés rurales, villes et provinces, "pays" au sens géographique du terme tout comme groupes socio-professionnels ou classes ont leurs cultures, qui ont ensemble à la fois contacts et rapports de différenciation. Il n'existe certainement pas, dans quelque société que ce soit, de culture étanche, et pas plus de culture populaire "authentiquement pure" que de culture savante présentant ce caractère. Mais les processus historiques selon lesquels se sont réalisés ces contacts et échanges n'ont guère été étudiés par les spécialistes jusqu'à maintenant: nous voudrions en donner deux exemples, l'un touchant la société d'Ancien Régime, l'autre concernant la IIIe République et son école.

*   *   *

Reconstituer les cultures populaires au sein de l'Ancien Régime n'est certes pas une tâche insurmontable: l'obstacle essentiel est la dispersion et l'hétérogénéité des sources qui constituent rarement des séries cohérentes et d'interprétation aisée. Ainsi en va-t-il des procès verbaux de visites épiscopales, dont nous possédons de grandes séries pour quelques diocèses au moins, les relations des fêtes dans les communautés urbaines et rurales, celles des pèlerinages et des processions qui constituent les temps forts de la vie religieuse. Jusqu'à maintenant, seules des explorations monographiques ont pu rendre compte des quelques aspects les plus significatifs.[4] Dans l'état actuel de ces recherches, mieux vaut encore raisonner sur le seul ensemble cohérent qui ait été exploité jusqu'à maintenant, la littérature de colportage destinée à une clientèle populaire dont un fonds important est conservé à la Bibliothèque Municipale de Troyes: sans rappeler dans le détail ce qu'a été cette littérature d'évasion, puisque cette étude est maintenant connue et a suscité des travaux complémentaires non négligeables,[5] nous argumenterons sur les données fournies par

[3] Cf. quelques mises au point plus détaillées dans la récente réédition de mon ouvrage de 1964: *De la culture populaire en France aux XVIIe et XVIIIe siècles.*

[4] Signalons ici la remarquable étude de G. Bouchard, *Le village immobile, Sennely en Sologne* (Paris, 1972). En outre, bien sûr, nombre de mémoires de maîtrise qui ne peuvent prétendre à l'édition et qui sont utilisés par ceux qui les ont dirigés, comme J. Delumeau et moi-même.

[5] Ouvrage cité à la note 3. Ajouter quelques travaux qui complètent plus ou moins heureusement cette analyse: G. Bollème, *Almanachs populaires aux XVIIe et XVIIIe siècles* (Paris, 1969);

cette étude et sur les prolongements qu'il est possible de lui reconnaître dans la perspective qui est la nôtre aujourd'hui, soit quatre points d'égale importance.

En premier lieu, la littérature de colportage marque fortement le passage de la culture savante médiévale au niveau populaire: ce transfert, à quelques siècles de distance, a été réalisé par des imprimeurs-libraires en mal de publication, alors que, au début du XVIIe siècle, le monde de l'imprimerie passait pour une crise de sous-production catastrophique, décrite notamment par Montchrestien.[6] Puisant dans les fonds savants qui avaient constitué l'essentiel de leur activité pendant la période antérieure, ces imprimeurs ont réalisé une réduction des contenus suivant des schèmes que seuls des médiévistes seraient en mesure d'identifier et qui ne peuvent être décrits, même sommairement ici. Du moins faut-il indiquer clairement les quatre domaines dans lesquels cette opération est nettement identifiable:

a) les vies de Saints qui correspondent au répertoire de la Légende dorée, pour l'essentiel. Sans nul doute, les livrets de Troyes ont perdu une bonne part de la fantaisie bavarde des récits conservés dans la Légende dorée. Le schéma est réduit à quatre données qui se retrouvent partout, invariables et monotones: le pécheur en sa jeunesse folle, la conversion qui est toujours foudroyante, la vie exemplaire qui s'ensuit et enfin les miracles qui ne peuvent manquer de se produire sur la tombe ou les reliques du Saint. Certes des variantes peuvent intervenir dans la définition des vertus guérisseuses ou dans la description de quelques saints du terroir champenois, Ortaire et autres. C'est peu de choses et cela n'entame en rien le tableau d'ensemble.

b) les cantiques et chants de piété: Bible ou Grande Bible des Noëls anciens et nouveaux, Cantiques de la Passion, etc.; les imprimeurs ont puisé là à pleines mains dans les répertoires qui leur étaient fournis par le diocèse et ne se sont pas trop souciés de la musique: une vague indication donnée sous le titre: "sur l'air de oh ma belle bergère" suffit sans doute pour les citadins; pour les ruraux, il leur est toujours loisible de broder sur un air connu. Ce répertoire "musical" doit beaucoup au récit de la Passion, tout comme l'enseignement religieux habituellement proposé au "menu peuple" par le clergé.

c) les almanachs et les ouvrages d'astrologie qui font référence à la

---

La bibliothèque bleue (Paris, 1971); N. Belmont, *Mythes et croyances dans l'ancienne France* (Paris, 1973); M. de Certeau, *La culture au pluriel* (Paris, 1974). Une place à part doit être faite au bel ouvrage de Marc Soriano, *Les contes de Perrault, culture savante et traditions populaires* (Paris, 1968).

[6] Montchrestien, cité dans la réédition de mon livre, *De la culture populaire*, pp. 36-37. Voire aussi H.J. Martin, *Livre, pouvoirs et société à Paris au XVIIe siècle* (Genève, 1970), Introduction.

science des secrets de nature doivent beaucoup aux savoirs savants répandus dans les deux derniers siècles du Moyen Age sous l'égide d'Albert le Grand, le célèbre dominicain, né en Souabe et maître de l'Université de Cologne. Par un jeu sur les mots bien compréhensible, Le Grand Albert, ouvrage plus savant publié au XVIe siècle a donné naissance au petit Albert, qui compte plus de recettes de guérison que de traités scientifiques. Les almanachs par ailleurs ont repris à leur compte quelques éléments de ce savoir diffus, notamment tout le déterminisme du Zodiaque et des tempéraments, abondamment décrits dans le grand kalendrier des bergers et dans ses imitations.[7]

d) Enfin les romans de chevalerie qui relatent les exploits de Charlemagne, Fierabras, Roland, Ganelon pendant les Croisades contre les Infidèles dérivent directement des chansons de geste médiévales, déjà réduites souvent de moitié lors de leurs premières éditions imprimées du XVIe siècle, et à nouveau diminuées jusqu'à une centaine de pages, quelques dizaines de chapitres de récits édifiants et touchants; ils donnent l'image terriblement passéiste d'une société aristocratique, qui ne ressemble guère à la société française des XVIIe et XVIIIe siècles et qui a été cependant acceptée par les publics écoutant la lecture à haute voix de ces récits à la veillée: tout comme, *mutatis mutandis*, les descriptions de l'existence menée par les stars et les princes qui nous gouvernent dans la presse à sensation du XXe siècle.[8]

Ainsi cette littérature qui ignore pratiquement la production savante contemporaine (Corneille, La Fontaine exceptés) offre aux milieux populaires une représentation du monde qui n'est absolument pas ouverte aux problèmes du temps (ni la Réforme, ni les révoltes populaires par exemple n'ont leur place dans ce répertoire); soit une vision archaïsante par rapport à la culture savante contemporaine, ce qui renvoie en quelque sorte à une société antérieure pour une large part mythique. Offerte au peuple, cette littérature qui a été assurément acceptée — le succès de la formule pendant plusieurs siècles l'atteste — démontre un décalage et un transfert évident entre cultures savante et populaire à l'époque classique.

Au demeurant, la littérature de colportage ne représente qu'une composante des cultures populaires, dont plusieurs éléments ne sont pas reconstituables: ni les tours de main, ni les règles sociales non écrites notamment. Mais l'originalité de ces cultures populaires n'est point contestable pour autant: la preuve en est fournie par les contemporains appartenant aux classes supérieures de la société qui ont exprimé avec vigueur

---

[7] "Le grant kalendrier et compost des Bergiers avecq leur astrologie et plusieurs autres choses," édition "savante" de Nicolas Le Rouge en 1510, reprise et modifiée par la suite.
[8] Une analyse comparée de *Jours de France, Paris Match* (pour ne rien dire d'hebdomadaires moins recommandables) dans cette perspective serait intéressante.

leur mépris. Ce rejet systématique mérite une analyse, qui constituera mon second point. Trois témoignages peuvent être appelés en démonstration:

En premier lieu, les libertins érudits qui, pendant la première moitié du XVIIe siècle, n'ont jamais manqué une occasion de souligner combien les croyances populaires relèvent d'une "inculture" fondamentale. Se proclamant "déniaisés," autant que les gens du peuple sont niais, ils accumulent les preuves: le bon abbé de Villeloin, Michel de Marolles, relate dans ses Mémoires, avec quelque lourdeur, qu'il a eu maintes fois l'occasion de s'agenouiller devant le chef de St Jean Baptiste — allusion aux paradoxes nés du traffic médiéval des reliques.[9] Mieux encore: Gabriel Naudé scandalisé par le succès remporté par la secte des Rose Croix à Paris dans les années 1615-1620, a consacré tout un petit livre à dénoncer la crédulité des Parisiens en face de ces rumeurs et de ces affiches annonçant l'arrivée de ces Rosicrucistes, inventés par J.V. Andreae dans les premières années du siècle.[10] Au milieu du siècle, lorsque ces libertins qui évoluent dans l'entourage du cardinal Mazarin se trouvent pris dans les troubles de la Fronde, ils enragent contre ce ministre qui se laisse chansonner sans réagir: au demeurant, ils sont partisans convaincus de l'absolutisme, parce que seul un gouvernement fort peur tenir en respect les passions populaires c'est-à-dire "la bête" sans cesse en révolte: rude leçon qui n'a pas été oubliée par le jeune roi, après 1661.

Seconds témoins, plus probants peut-être encore, les clercs post tridentins qui ont pris en charge la lutte contre les superstitions: nous savons tous que l'Eglise romaine, dans sa volonté de faire face aux attaques portées par les réformés contre les pratiques peu orthodoxes longtemps tolérées au Moyen Age, a décidé de procéder à une épuration de ces pratiques. La mise en oeuvre de ces décision — retardée en France par les difficultés faites par les Parlements à la "réception du Concile" — a été lente. Elle intervient cependant dans la seconde moitié du XVIIe siècle et n'a cessé de progresser ensuite, à mesure que la fondation des séminaires diocésains a amélioré la formation intellectuelle du bas clergé rural. Un seul exemple peut illustrer ce propos: en 1679, un curé théologien de bonne stature, Jean Baptiste Thiers publie un ouvrage en quatre volumes consacré à la condamnation des superstitions para-sacramentaires, c'est-à-dire attachées aux pratiques des sacrements;[11] ce travail monumental

---

[9] *Les Mémoires de Michel de Marolles, abbé de Villeloin, divisez en trois parties, contenant ce qu'il a vu de plus remarquable en sa vie depuis l'année 1600, les entretiens avec quelques-uns des plus scavants hommes de son temps* . . . (Paris, 1656 [réédition annotée en 1755, à Amsterdam]).

[10] Gabriel Naudé, *Instruction à la France sur la vérité de l'histoire des frères de la Rose Croix* (Paris, 1623).

[11] J.B. Thiers, Docteur en Théologie et curé de Vibraie, *Traité des superstitions selon l'Ecriture sainte, les décrets des conciles et les sentimens des Saints Pères et des théologiens* (Paris, 1679 [une seconde édition, revue et augmentée en 1697]).

qui s'appuie sur les statuts synodaux, les textes des Pères de l'Eglise et une connaissance directe de pratiques répandues au Sud-Ouest de Paris est une belle illustration de ce souci majeur du clergé, qui s'est exprimé à maintes reprises par la suite, en particulier par des plumes oratoriennes, comme Malebranche et le Brun: à travers la condamnation du nouement de l'aiguillette, du baptême des enfants morts, de l'utilisation impie des cimetières, se définit un profil austère de la vie ecclésiale, qui n'a pas toujours reçu l'assentiment des fidèles, manifestement frustrés par la condamnation et la suppression de pratiques qui faisaient partie inté-grante de leur univers mental:[12] la "religion mieux comprise" comme aiment à dire les théologiens (en particulier ceux qui se sont occupés des affaires de possession)[13] est assurément celle des clercs mieux instruits, beaucoup plus que celle de fidèles attachés à quantité de croyances qui peuvent mêler sans malice pratiques païennes, héritées d'un lointain passé mal effacé et prescriptions plus ou moins orthodoxes. Là aussi, le décalage est sensible entre cultures savante et populaire.

Enfin, il suffira de mentionner d'une phrase le mépris que la plupart des philosophes qui ont illustré le siècle des Lumières, professent à l'égard des milieux populaires (exception faite, parmi les plus grands, pour Diderot et Jean-Jacques Rousseau). La plus belle illustration en est four-nie par Voltaire lui-même qui professait sans honte que la religion était nécessaire au peuple pour le retenir dans la déférence et dans le travail et qui reprochait avec véhémence aux Frères des Ecoles Chrétiennes de distribuer dans les classes populaires une instruction élémentaire capable de détourner celle-ci de leurs devoirs essentiels: obéir et travailler. Par une curieuse homologie, Voltaire prince des philosophes retrouvait à ce niveau les arguments de Colbert qui voulait lutter contre la multiplication des collèges, perdition de la bourgeoisie marchande.

Ainsi les cultures populaires sont-elles bien reconnues, identifiées par les milieux savants dans les deux derniers siècles de l'Ancien Régime: ce monde populaire qui s'exprime si fréquemment dans les violences des révoltes, doit être tenu en laisse, "policé" suivant l'expression du temps qui précède celle de "civilisé." Assurément il fait peur, en raison de ces émeutes et des troubles qui scandent la vie quotidienne des villes et des campagnes. Mais il inquiète également, dans la mesure où ces milieux peuvent paraître détenir des savoirs méconnus, ignorés et cependant importants. Ce que nous pouvons maintenant montrer rapidement: ce sera notre troisième point.

---

[12] Une bonne illustration de ces conflits dans le livre de G. Bouchard cité à la note 4.
[13] Cf. mon gros livre *Magistrats et sorciers en France au XVIIe siècle* (Paris, 1968), notamment pp. 187-188, 523-533.

Nul doute que les communautés rurales en particulier aient eu leurs traditions et leurs réussites: les campagnes n'ont eu pendant tout l'Ancien Régime ni médecins, ni sage-femmes et ont cependant assuré leur savoir, grâce aux bergers et aux sorcières qui connaissent les vertus des plantes et maintes recettes éprouvées de génération en génération pour faire face à la maladie. C'est ici le lieu de rappeler le mot de Paracelse, médecin itinérant à travers l'Allemagne occidentale, de Bâle à la basse Rhénanie: "tout ce que je sais, je l'ai appris des sorcières."

La connaissance des secrets de nature, disent d'ordinaire les rédacteurs des almanachs qui ne savent pas exactement d'où vient ce savoir, empiriquement contrôlé, éprouvé par des siècles de pratique expérimentale. Assurément il nous est très difficile de le reconstituer.[14] Dans les écrits qui nous ont été conservés — style grand et petit Albert — il peut être difficile de retrouver ce qui était recette éprouvée et efficace et fantaisie des rédacteurs. Certaines recettes font sourire assurément, lorsqu'il est recommandé de mélanger des pattes de mouche et de la cire d'abeille pour fabriquer une pommade capable de guérir les maux de dents ou de se faire aimer d'une belle indifférente. Par contre, il n'est pas douteux que bergers et sorcières ont pratiqué une connaissance sure des vertus des plantes et des minéraux, qui représente une pharmacopée nullement imaginaire, solidement appuyée sur une pratique réelle et transmise de génération en génération. En attendant une reconstitution à venir de ce savoir et de ces coordonnées essentielles, il est plausible de situer le débat sur un point essentiel: les connaissances chimiques de Paracelse et des médecins arabes se sont transmises à travers quelques facultés de médecine, comme Montpellier et Padoue; leur diffusion a provoqué au milieu du XVIIe siècle un débat très significatif, celui de l'iatrochimie.

Dans le Paris des années 1640-1670, deux écoles s'affrontent sur ce problème, concrétisé sur un point précis: l'utilisation de l'antimoine dans la médicamentation — et accessoirement du quinquina. S'opposent deux camps, Guy Patin, médecin hippocratique traditionnel qui ne connaît d'autres remèdes que la saignée, le lavement et la purgation, qui est fort de son bon droit — la médecine officielle — et qui peut faire respecter le monopole d'exercice des médecins parisiens; de l'autre côté, les iatrochimistes comme Renaudot et quelques autres, médecins montpellierains qui ne craignent pas de faire appel à de nouvelles médicamentations: vin émétique, eaux thermales, et autres médicaments qui agissent sur les

---

[14] Toute recherche entreprise dans cette direction permettrait de faire avancer dans cette perspective: les oeuvres médicales de Paracelse peuvent en constituer le point de départ, notamment: *Von Krankheit und gesunden Leben; Uber das lange Leben; Uber die Tugenden der Kraüter, Wurzeln, Samen; Uber die Grade und Zusammensetzungen der Rezepte und natürlichen Dinge; Uber die natürlichen Warmbäder.*

humeurs et sur la santé des malades. A chaque mésaventure qui échoit aux iatrochimistes, Patin chante victoire dans ses lettres; mais il est légitime de penser qu'il se tait lorsque ces médicamentations nouvelles réussissent. Au surplus, il est bien connu que le cabinet de consultations médicales ouvert par les Renaudot auprès de leur bureau d'adresses a connu un grand succès tout de même que les conférences scientifiques de ce même bureau, où ces problèmes étaient débattus, parmi d'autres.[15]

Ainsi se profile le contact avec un savoir, récupérable pour ainsi dire mais non point accepté par les autorités. Sur ce plan, les médecins parisiens n'ont pas l'ouverture d'esprit que manifestent les savants anglais fondateurs de la Royal Society en 1662: les statuts de la nouvelle société mise sur pied pour assurer l'avancement des sciences comportent un article qui prévoit au contraire la recherche et la mise à l'épreuve des savoirs perdus qui font partie du patrimoine commun aux populations de l'Angleterre.[16] Ce qui est reconnaître aux savoirs populaires une dimension très réelle dans le domaine scientifique lui-même: de cette réalité, le conflit ouvert entre bergers et sorcières d'une part et les autorités en place, judiciaires et religieuses, constitue sans nul doute l'aspect le plus connu, le plus voyant: à travers les milliers de procès faits aux sorcières rurales, s'exprime en filigrane plus que de façon tout à fait claire cette opposition entre le savoir des uns et l'autorité des autres. L'essentiel est peut-être là, plutôt que dans les classiques démonstrations qui mettent en avant le pacte satanique, l'alliance avec l'ennemi du genre humain et les ratiocinations des théologiens et des magistrats.

Il est assez clair que les contacts entre cultures savantes et populaires sont multiples et résultent tout autant d'un souci d'acculturation nourri par les classes supérieures que d'une nécessité sociale reconnue au XVIIIe siècle par les hommes des Lumières. Sur quoi quelques précisions peuvent encore être fournies, qui achèveront d'éclairer cette rapide reconstitution des cultures dans la société d'Ancien Régime. La philanthropie des Lumières, cette charité laïcisée décrite naguère par Michel Foucault[17] s'est tournée vers le peuple, timidement, bien avant les élans populistes du romantisme littéraire. Attitude condescendante à l'ordinaire, qui considère le menu peuple comme une société à éduquer. Bien avant que Michelet en 1847 proclame la nécessité de récupérer les almanachs pour

---

[15] Sur cette question, voir le récent ouvrage de Howard M. Solomon, *Public Welfare, Science and Propaganda in Seventeenth Century France, The Innovations of Theophraste Renaudot* (Princeton, 1972).

[16] Texte (traduit) de l'article en question: "essayer de faire renaître certains arts intéressants dont les secrets sont aujourd'hui perdus."

[17] M. Foucault, *Folie et déraison, Histoire de la folie à l'âge classique*, première édition (Paris, 1961).

assurer l'éducation du peuple,[18] des écrivains de second rang se sont penchés sur cette littérature de colportage pour la moraliser: Madame d'Aulnoye qui écrit elle-même des contes, M. du Tressan qui s'est chargé de réécrire les quelques romans de la Bibliothèque bleue.[19] Au terme de cet effort, mal connu, une nouvelle bibliothèque du peuple a été mise en circulation: en beaux livres, dorés sur tranches, qui étaient inéluctablement inaccessibles à un public populaire, pour de simples raisons financières. L'effort mérite d'être noté, sans plus: il est sans commune mesure avec le mouvement légèrement postérieur en Allemagne du Sturm und Drang.

Plus importants sont, sans nul doute, les échanges dûs aux contacts sociaux; l'essentiel me paraissant ici la fonction socio-culturelle des domestiques dans la société d'Ancien Régime, sur deux plans au moins: en premier lieu, c'est le rôle des nourrices campagnardes qui élèvent les enfants des villes, en un temps où les cités passent pour polluées et néfastes à l'élevage des jeunes enfants. Toute une organisation s'est mise en place dès le XVIIe siècle dans les grandes villes comme Paris, Lyon et Rouen, grâce à laquelle les enfants citadins passent les trois à quatre premières années de leur vie à la campagne, confiés à des jeunes femmes villageoises, surveillées par leur curé et par le meneur qui les a présentées en ville et qui leur apporte périodiquement le prix de la pension. Un système parallèle existant d'ailleurs pour les enfants abandonnés légitimes ou illégitimes, recueillis dans les hôpitaux.[20] Ces enfants — au cours de ces années aujourd'hui reconnues comme décisives pour la formation des personnalités — ont donc été bercé par les histoires et les chansons des villageoises. Et cette influence s'est continuée aussi longtemps que la pratique de la mise en nourrice s'est maintenue: Gérard de Nerval et Proust en ont rendu l'un et l'autre éclatant témoignage.[21] En second lieu,

---

[18] Michelet, "Ce que je rêvais dans l'église d'Engelberg," *Le Figaro*, supplément littéraire, 29 octobre 1892 (cité par G. Bollème, *Les Almanachs populaires*, p. 127: "L'Almanach, bien compris, serait un excellent moyen d'éducation. Il n'y aurait qu'à substituer au vieux calendrier, à ce qu'il a de confus et souvent d'absurde, le calendrier qui donnerait les véritables saints, ceux surtout de la Patrie. Une page pour chacun, ce ne serait ni long, ni difficile à retenir. . . ."

[19] M. le comte de Tressan, de l'Académie française, *Corps d'extraits des romans de chevalerie* (Paris, 1782), avec un discours préliminaire tout à fait explicite. De même sous le titre général Bibliothèque bleue, Les Quatre fils Aymon, suivis de Jean de Calais et Geneviève de Brabant (Paris, Garnier, s.d.).

[20] Cf. pour Lyon, M. Garden, *Lyon et les Lyonnais au XVIIIe siècle* (Paris, 1970; édition abrégée, Paris, 1975); pour Paris, différents mémoires de maîtrise effectués sous ma direction et l'article de J.-P. Aron, "Le régime des nourrices au début du XIXe siècle à Paris," in *Actes du quatre vingt treizième congrès national des Sociétés Savantes, Tours 1968* (Paris, 1971), dont les conclusions sont tout à fait acceptables aussi pour le XVIIIe siècle.

[21] Références in *De la culture populaire*, pp. 187 et 189.

il faut évoquer le rôle plus complexe des cochers, laquais et femmes de chambre que leur travail quotidien met en contact permanent avec les bibliothèques de leurs maîtres et oblige en outre à de longues pauses d'attente pendant lesquelles ils doivent occuper leur temps: ce qu'ils font soit en puisant dans les richesses culturelles de leurs maîtres soit en lisant les ouvrages de l'office, c'est-à-dire précisément le trésor du colportage. Incontestablement, ce personnel domestique, en particulier dans la région parisienne, possède une information culturelle plus large que l'ensemble des classes populaires urbaines, et à plus forte raison rurales. D'où leur rôle, assurément, dans la période révolutionnaire, sur lequel les historiens de la fin de XVIIIe siècle ne se sont sans doute pas assez penchés.

Ainsi peuvent se présenter les tensions et les osmoses qui caractérisent les rapports entre cultures populaire et savante dans la société française d'Ancien Régime — telles que du moins nous pouvons les éclairer dans l'état présent de nos connaissances. Il y aurait encore beaucoup à dire sur ces questions, en particulier sur le problème de l'usage des langues régionales, supports des cultures provinciales qui se sont réfugiées dans les milieux populaires, dès l'instant où les classes supérieures parlent français et sont raliées de fait à la culture dominante. Mais l'exemple est trop lourd pour être présenté maintenant.[22] Mieux vaut passer tout de suite à notre second point.

*   *   *

Le rapport dialectique qui s'est institué en France au XIXe siècle entre les cultures populaires régionales — voire locales — et l'institutionalisation de l'enseignement primaire généralisé, et devenu à partir de 1880 à la fois laïque, obligatoire et gratuit, n'a pas encore fait l'objet d'études approfondies: les étapes politiques et administratives de la scolarisation sont connues, de la loi Guizot aux lois Ferry;[23] les transformations de la société rurale ont été à plusieurs reprises esquissées, de façon magistrale par R. Thabault naguère,[24] de façon plus intimiste et pointilliste par Gaston Bonheur;[25] mais nous n'avons pas encore l'étude historique et

---

[22] Sur cette question, voir Yves Castan, *Honnêteté et relations sociales en Languedoc au XVIIIe siècle* (Paris, 1975).

[23] Une synthèse rapide a été publiée dans la collection U (A. Colin) par A. Prost, *L'Enseignement en France (1880-1967)* (Paris, 1968).

[24] Roger Thabault, *Mon village, ses hommes, ses routes, son école (1848-1914), l'ascension d'un peuple* (Mazières en Gâtine) (Paris, 1945); et le compte rendu de L. Febvre dans les *Annales d'histoire sociale*, VII, pp. 141-146, "Ce grand personnage historique: l'école primaire."

[25] Gaston Bonheur, l. *Qui a cassé le vase de Soissons? L'album de famille de tous les Français* (Paris, 1963); 2. *La République nous appelle, l'album de famille de Marianne* (Paris, 1965); 3. *Qui a cassé le*

sociologique informée qui serait nécessaire pour éclairer ce problème capital.[26] Aussi bien les considérations qui suivent, doivent-elles être comprises plus comme des hypothèses de travail que comme des conclusions à un travail achevé: j'aurai d'ailleurs occasion pour la période de l'entre-deux-guerres d'insérer l'évocation de souvenirs personnels, ce qui accentue encore le caractère subjectif d'une telle synthèse provisoire.

Notre point de départ est d'ordre idéologique et socio-professionnel: l'Ecole primaire française dans sa plénitude d'enseignement obligatoire a été fondée par des hommes politiques qui assumaient pleinement l'idéologie scientiste dans la seconde moitié du XIXe siècle: le savoir est libérateur tant il est vrai que "l'ignorance n'a jamais libéré personne"; et jusqu'aujourd'hui, le journal du Syndicat National des Instituteurs (le SNI) s'intitule *l'Ecole Libératrice*. Les grands fondateurs de l'Ecole primaire, les Jules Ferry, Jean Macé et quelques autres se sont attachés à constituer une école du peuple, construite pour le peuple et animée par lui: le recrutement des Ecoles Normales départementales, où se formait l'immense majorité des instituteurs jusqu'en 1940, ne se faisait-il pas en circuit clos, de l'école primaire aux Ecoles primaires supérieures et ensuite à l'Ecole Normale du département, par l'intermédiaire d'un concours d'entrée dans celle-ci; et accessoirement avec l'aide d'une bourse nationale conquise au terme du Cours Moyen 2e Année pour poursuivre les études audelà de la scolarité obligatoire (douze ans) dans les E.P.S., qui ont été supprimées par le gouvernement de Vichy (de même que les Ecoles Normales d'ailleurs, transférées dans les lycées).[27]

Ce corps enseignant sévèrement sélectionné a été formé pendant plus d'un demi-siècle à une discipline pédagogique solide qui permettait aux instituteurs, exercés dans des classes d'application annexées aux Ecoles Normales, d'assurer pleinement leur tâche, même dans les conditions les plus difficiles, où les classes rurales non homogènes en termes de classes d'âge devaient être conduites simultanément. Pendant la même période, les "séminaires laïques," comme les Ecoles Normales ont souvent été nommées, donnaient au personnel enseignant du Primaire une triple foi

---

pot au lait? *L'album de famille de toutes les Françaises* (Paris, 1970). Le troisième volume est certainement le moins bon, l'auteur tire à la ligne; mais les deux premiers sont essentiels à notre propos.

[26] Il convient de faire des réserves méthodologiques importantes à la lecture de Maurice Crubellier, *Histoire culturelle de la France, XIXe-XXe siècles* (Paris, 1974), qui pose le problème mais le traite dans des perspectives fort discutables. Plus recommandable est la rapide synthèse de Philippe Joutard, dans le chapitre IV du tome III de *l'Histoire de France* publiée par G. Duby en 1972.

[27] La IVe République n'a pas rétabli les E.P.S., mais a remis en place les E.N.D. qui n'ont cependant pas retrouvé tout leur prestige d'antan, pour des raisons qui seront explicitées plus loin.

qui animait assurément, au moins jusqu'en 1914, la plupart des instituteurs et institutrices, pionniers de la science, de la République et de la Libération sociale.

En premier lieu, une foi de charbonnier assurément dans le progrès scientifique comme élément de domination du monde naturel, sinon des hommes. Roger Thabault dans *Mon village* a remarquablement montré comment les instituteurs, surtout lorsqu'ils appartenaient par leurs origines au monde rural, pouvaient exercer sur les adultes comme sur les enfants un véritable magistère scientifique: tenus de pratiquer dans le jardin de l'école une véritable formation expérimentale à l'usage de leurs élèves, ils étaient d'autant plus aptes à conseiller également les parents qu'ils assumaient très fréquemment les fonctions de secrétaires de mairie: celles-ci les mettaient nécessairement en contact avec la totalité de la population et leur donnaient un rôle déterminant dans la gestion de la commune puisqu'ils assuraient le secrétariat du Conseil Municipal, avec une continuité qui n'était pas garantie pour les élus. Mais le plus important — et le plus difficile à reconstituer — est sans doute le prestige attaché à l'homme de savoir, en un temps où la seule concurrence notable était celle du médecin, et celle du journal. L'instituteur qui passait un quart de siècle dans le même poste et enseignait ainsi deux générations de la même communauté rurale, pouvait valablement tenir une fonction de mentor — en dépit de résistances qui seront présentées dans un instant.[28]

En second lieu, l'instituteur enseigne l'amour de la patrie et de la République, l'une et l'autre indissolublement liées: les instructions ministérielles, les visites des Inspecteurs Primaires, les conférences pédagogiques annuelles en portent la marque. Ce faisant l'instituteur reproduit à sa façon une corrélation qui est établie en haut lieu: la Sorbonne d'avant 1914 est à la fois scientiste et républicaine; et dans certaines disciplines comme l'Histoire, avec une touchante naïveté qu'illustre bien Ernest Lavisse. Outre l'enseignement choral et civique que Gaston Bonheur a évoqué avec une pointe de lyrisme,[29] l'école primaire joue son rôle d'autant mieux que les instituteurs ont été utilisés par l'Etat Major avec beaucoup de constance: aiguillés dès l'Ecole normale vers les pelotons d'officiers de réserve (les E.O.R.), la plupart des jeunes instituteurs se sont retrouvés, par milliers, en 1914 aspirants ou sous lieutenants; la première guerre mondiale a été une hécatombe pour cette jeune génération, comme Gaston Bonheur l'a également bien souligné.[30] Assurément,

[28] R. Thabault a montré mieux que personne ce rôle de l'instituteur, notamment avant la guerre de 1914: *Mon village*, passim.

[29] Gaston Bonheur, *La République nous appelle*, passim. Il serait peut-être bon de faire une place, ici, aux "bataillons scolaires"; ceux-ci n'ont pas "fonctionné" également dans toute la France et cette pédagogie attend encore son historien. Louis Pergaud en a traité, à sa façon, dans *La guerre des boutons*.

[30] G. Bonheur, *Qui a cassé le vase de Soissons*, p. 353: "La prétendue grande guerre ne fut pas

l'école où s'apprennent les chants patriotiques, où se confectionnent les cartes d'électeurs, où se préparent les défilés du 14 juillet et du 11 novembre — en tête desquels les écoliers ont leur place désignée — est bien le lieu républicain par excellence — au même titre que la mairie qui la jouxte dans la plupart des villages. Comme dit toujours G. Bonheur, "l'Ecole et la République vivent sous le même toit."[31]

Enfin, pour les instituteurs de la IIIe République, l'école démocratique est un instrument de libération sociale: n'en sont-ils pas eux-mêmes l'exemple vivant; sortis du peuple, ils ont "fait instituteur" comme disent les vieilles gens encore aujourd'hui (alors que sous l'Ancien Régime, la sortie se réalisait en faisant curé), ils nourrissent la conviction que la diffusion des savoirs est un élément essentiel de la démocratisation dans une société qui proclame de grands principes égalitaires depuis 1789 (et qui les fait enseigner), mais qui ne les met guère en application. Aussi bien les instituteurs sont-ils fermement attachés à l'allongement de la scolarité obligatoire qui a été réalisée partiellement et non sans à coups depuis 1936 de même qu'à toutes mesures qui facilitent les cursus scolaires, comme la gratuité de l'enseignement secondaire décidée en 1932. Sur ces thèmes qui sont devenus problématiques et polémiques depuis une quinzaine d'années en France, il n'y a pas d'hésitation sensible jusqu'à la deuxième guerre mondiale: d'aucuns prônent la démocratisation dans une perspective républicaine, d'autres dans la visée d'une révolution prolétarienne. Tous sont d'accord sur le processus: cette stabilité dans les convictions du corps enseignant primaire a été bien montrée par Jacques Ozouf.[32]

Le tableau est cependant incomplet: l'Ecole primaire laïque et républicaine s'est définie de la sorte face à des résistances qui méritent examen: l'une est bien connue — trop peut-être, dans la mesure où le roman et la polémique s'en sont emparés depuis longtemps; l'autre est plus difficile à cerner. L'une et l'autre délimitent la situation sociale et culturelle de l'instituteur dans ce monde encore en majeure partie rural qu'est la France jusqu'à la seconde guerre mondiale.

La première résistance est celle du clergé catholique, qui dans beaucoup de communes a pris une allure "Clochemerlesque": les implications politiques, en termes généraux, sont bien connues, de la IIIe à la Ve République. L'Eglise catholique s'est vue en quelques décennies dépossédée de sa

seulement une hécatombe insensée de paysans, . . . ce fut un massacre d'instituteurs. Pour sauver la révolution allumée dans nos livres par quelques étincelles de la Commune, arrachées au brasier des Tuileries, il eût fallu une paix de Brest Litovsk. C'est à ce prix qu'il y a eu une révolution russe, au lieu d'une révolution française. Quelques veuves, comme ma mère, ne pouvaient suffire à embraser l'horizon — à peine, vestales laïques, à maintenir ces dernières braises qui nous réchauffent."

[31] G. Bonheur, *La République nous appelle*, p. 15.

[32] J. Ouzouf, *Nous les maîtres d'école, autobiographies d'instituteurs de la Belle époque* (Paris, 1967).

fonction éducatrice, qu'elle avait réussi à sauvegarder partiellement jusqu'à la fin du Second Empire. Contre la République qui a renoncé au Concordat et ré alisé la séparation de l'Eglise et de l'Etat en 1905, le haut et le bas clergé français n'a pas ménagé les anathèmes jusqu'à la "divine surprise" de 1940; et même au-delà. Mais cette histoire bien connue importe moins à notre propos que la lutte quotidienne (ou hebdomadaire) menée contre l'Ecole des "Sans Dieu" et contre l'instituteur, mauvais berger et suppôt inavoué du Diable. Péguy a dénoncé dès le début de ce siècle ce que cette aggression permanente avait de ridicule et d'ineffi-cace;[33] il n'a guère été écouté pendant ces années qui précèdent la pre-mière guerre mondiale, par ses coreligionnaires. En réalité, la guerre du clocher et de l'école primaire s'est déroulée sur plusieurs plans, plus ou moins vive suivant les régions: impitoyable en Bretagne et dans une bonne partie du Massif Central, elle s'est vite atténuée dans les villes et les communes suburbaines. Mais elle mérite toute l'attention de l'historien pour comprendre ces fameux clivages sociaux et politiques qui se tradui-sent dans les comportements des groupes:[34] même les aspects les plus cocasses qui ont suscité la verve des romanciers et des cinéastes devraient là être pris en compte, car les propos jetés en chaire le dimanche ont souvent suscité des réactions vives de la part des fidèles et des détachés; en second lieu, vient la concurrence des deux écoles, dans la mesure où les prêtres ont réussi à faire vivre — dans tout l'ouest notamment — avec l'aide d'un personnel souvent mal formé, mais toujours dévoué, des écoles rivales de l'école publique; entrent encore en ligne de compte les oeuvres para-et péri-scolaires, pour lesquelles le curé s'appuie toujours sur le dévouement et la générosité de ses ouailles, cependant que les instituteurs utilisent la puissante Ligue de l'enseignement fondée en 1866 et ses filiales

[33] De Péguy, la célèbre formule opposant les curés respectés et distants et les instituteurs plus aimés que les clercs dit bien à quel point cette opposition systématique a finalement desservi les premiers plus que les seconds. "Nous ne croyons plus un mot de ce que nous enseignaient nos maîtres laïques, et toute la métaphysique qui était dessous eux, est pour nous moins qu'une cendre vaine. Nous ne croyons pas seulement, nous sommes intégrale-ment nourris de ce que nous enseignaient les curés, de ce qu'il y a dans le catéchisme. *Or nos maîtres laïcs ont gardé tout notre coeur et ils ont notre entière confidence. Et malheureusement nous ne pourrons pas dire que nos vieux curés aient absolument tout notre coeur ni qu'ils aient jamais eu notre confidence*" (souligné par nous). Charles Péguy, "L'Argent" (1913), *Oeuvres en prose* (Editions de la Pléiade), p. 1120.

[34] Un témoignage capital concernant la Bresse et le Jura sous l'occupation, où ces comporte-ments pérennes sont analysés avec beaucoup de finesse. Léon Werth, *Déposition, Journal (1940-1944)* (Paris, 1946), où tout est à peser au plus juste et dont on peut détacher quelques formules pour mettre en appétit le lecteur: "la démocratie, quand même, me disait le vieux jardinier, les dents serrées sur sa pipe, la démocratie, c'est quelque chose"; ou encore à propos des usages des pompiers lors des enterrements: "l'Eglise est un des points où le paysan fait l'épreuve de sa liberté" (pp. 145 et 144). Cf. la recension de Lucien Febvre: "Une tragédie, trois comptes rendus," *Annales, économies, sociétés, civilisations* (1948), pp. 51-68.

d'Education physique et artistique. Enfin le conflit s'épanouit, si l'on peut dire, sur le plan politique: ce qui est trop connu pour qu'il y ait lieu d'insister.

Cependant les instituteurs se sont également heurtés à une résistance, plus sourde et plus complexe, de la part des populations paysannes elles-mêmes; le problème peut se définir par ses aspects contradictoires: d'un côté, Roger Thabault souligne fort nettement combien les paysans de Mazières en Gâtine sont réticents face à l'innovation technologique; quels que soient les discours de l'instituteur, c'est l'adoption par l'un d'entre eux de la nouveauté qui crée le mouvement.[35] De l'autre, G. Bonheur souligne avec ferveur et justice le prestige, dont jouissait sa mère: qui lira sans émotion "Le Tour de Ville" par lequel se clôt une carrière (au cimetière) au terme de son premier livre.[36] Mais sa mère était originaire de Barbaira, où elle a enseigné la majeure partie de sa vie: là est sans doute une des clés de notre paradoxe. Car le premier aspect de cette résistance tient au langage: l'Ecole de la République ne parle que le français, le plus pur, celui des grands écrivains qui constituent notre Panthéon littéraire; elle ignore les parlers locaux, traités de patois et les pourchasse non seulement des salles de classe mais aussi des cours de récréation. Alors que les enfants, en famille et au travail, dans les champs et les échoppes, n'entendent et ne parlent que ces patois, auxquels depuis la seconde guerre mondiale le droit à l'existence érudite a été rendu.[37] Dans les nombreux cas où l'instituteur est lui-même fils du pays et parle la langue locale, il semble que cette opposition ait été atténuée de plusieurs façons: à la fois par sa pratique — hors des heures de classe — de la langue du cru et par une tolérance souriante à l'égard des petits écarts quotidiens commis par les écoliers. Il n'en reste pas moins qu'un effort considérable était demandé aux enfants pendant les premières années de leurs cursus.[38] Plus importante est peut-être la résistance à l'intervention de l'instituteur dans les pratiques culturales et à la pression — directe ou indirecte — qu'il pouvait exercer en faveur de conquêtes réalisées par la science agronomique: nouvelles machines perfectionnées, semences sélectionnées, rotations novatrices, protection chimique de la vigne, etc. Les

[35] R. Thabault, *Mon village*, pp. 149 à 160 en particulier.
[36] 'Requiem pour une institutrice," in G. Bonheur, *Qui a cassé le vase de Soissons*, p. 433 et suivantes.
[37] Les mouvements régionalistes qui se sont épanouis dans les années soixante font grand état de cette "répression" linguistique, qui n'est pas niable. Le français est langue de la République une et indivisible, proclamait déjà Grégoire en 1793. Il se mêle à ces analyses des considérants de "lutte de classes ethniques" qui sont plus difficiles à suivre.
[38] Il est vrai que sous l'Ancien Régime, les enfants apprenaient à lire en latin; et que les Frères des Ecoles Chrétiennes qui ont innové en enseignant à lire en français, ont pu connaître des problèmes semblables.

débats que pouvaient susciter de telles interventions, à partir de leçons données en classe ou au jardin d'enfants, sont évidemment très difficiles à reconstituer: seuls des instituteurs mémorialistes pourraient y pourvoir en rappelant de vieux souvenirs.[39] Assurément, l'école primaire n'a pas manqué à sa tâche d'unification culturelle et politique, telle qu'elle avait été définie dans les années 1880; elle était moins attentive sans nul doute aux caractères originaux des régions — voire des "pays," au sens étroit et traditionnel du terme. Une telle constatation ne diminue pas l'importance de son rôle "historique": elle en marque une limite, tout comme l'analyse sommaire des contenus de l'enseignement.

Tout reste à faire, ou peu s'en faut, dans ce domaine: les ouvrages de Gaston Bonheur déjà cités présentent un survol, à la fois pointilliste et orienté par les souvenirs personnels de l'auteur qui n'est certes pas négligeable; mais une analyse systématique serait nécessaire pour rendre compte plus complètement des enseignements à en tirer.[40] Récemment Jean Bouvier, s'interrogeant sur les freinages mentaux qui ont paralysé l'essor capitaliste de la France jusqu'au milieu du XXe siècle, a tiré le meilleur parti d'une analyse du "Tour de France de deux enfants."[41] De façon sans doute plus subtile, il faudrait s'interroger aussi sur le choix des textes et des exercices, qui constituaient l'essentiel des travaux scolaires: à côté des palmarès très étroitement personnalisés de Gaston Bonheur, une étude des thèmes travaillés en mathématiques comme en dessin mériterait d'être faite: les légendaires problèmes de baignoire qui n'en finit pas de se remplir et de trains qui courent à la rencontre l'un de l'autre ont plus d'un sens, s'il faut les considérer comme les symboles du progrès technique. Ces réserves faites, il est permis d'avancer que sur trois points au moins, le message de l'école publique primaire se trouvait assez limité, intrinsèquement parlant; et a pu rapidement poser problème, aux instituteurs eux-mêmes, bien avant 1939.

En premier lieu en ce qui concerne cette éducation civique unanimiste qui était enseignée à l'école et qui s'est trouvée ici et là, remise en question dès le début du siècle par les plus "avancés" des instituteurs, à savoir l'aile

---

[39] Dans mes propres souvenirs auvergnats (aux Martres de Veyre), j'ai trace d'une visite annuelle organisée dans une ferme modèle installée près de l'Allier où la conservation des fourrages et la traite mécanique des vaches faisaient l'objet de longues démonstrations; j'étais certainement plus attentif que les fils de paysans qui m'entouraient, et qui avaient été mis en garde par leurs parents.

[40] A partir de souvenirs personnels conservés particulièrement frais chacun peut refaire le chemin de Gaston Bonheur et arriver à des conclusion comparables. Un tel itinéraire sous-tend largement les notations rassemblées dans les pages qui suivent.

[41] G. Bruno (pseudonyme de Mme Fouillée, femme d'Universitaire), *Le Tour de France de deux enfants* (Paris, 1877; et d'innombrables rééditions: la 411e en 1904, reproduite en 1968); cf. J. Bouvier, "Le mouvement d'une civilisation nouvelle," in *Les temps nouveaux*, T. III de *Histoire de France*, dirigée par G. Duby (Paris, 1972), pp. 57-60.

syndicaliste de la corporation. Certes dans les manifestations solennelles ou quotidiennes, l'ensemble, étayé par des instructions ministérielles rarement remaniées, avait bonne allure: les leçons de morale matinales commentant la devise révolutionnaire et républicaine par excellence, Liberté, Egalité, Fraternité, étaient d'autant mieux reçues que cette courte leçon, discours non commenté ni discuté, qui n'était pas sanctionné par une note ou une leçon à apprendre était toujours accueillie avec faveur, sinon avec ferveur.[42] De la même façon, enfants et maîtres prenaient part avec le même enthousiasme mesuré par les enseignants soucieux de la bonne présentation de leurs élèves aux festivités majeures: le défilé au monument aux morts du 11 novembre, la fête des Ecoles lorsqu'elle était organisée par l'instituteur, en réponse d'ordinaire à la fête patronale du curé et des "bien pensants" et surtout le 14 juillet, la fête par excellence qui coïncidait peu ou prou avec la fin de l'année scolaire: retraite aux flambeaux, défilé du 14 juillet jusqu'à la place de la mairie avec discours du maire (souvent préparé par l'instituteur secrétaire de mairie) et réponse-compliment d'un écolier choisi avec soin; enfin les chants qu'il faut bien appeler patriotiques, où figuraient à côté de La Marseillaise, le chant du Départ, Sambre et Meuse, En passant par la Lorraine; et plus rarement le Temps des Cerises. . . . Mais toute cette éducation civique masquait, c'est bien évident, les tensions et les oppositions sur lesquelles se maintenait, tant bien que mal, l'équilibre de la société française contemporaine: gommant le souvenir de la Commune, les premiers Mais sanglants et les grandes grèves au début du siècle, les mutineries de 1917. . . . Lorsque 1936 arriva, ces contradictions éclataient au grand jour dans une France coupée en deux, où les instituteurs avaient affirmé leur choix; et répudié tout unanimisme fallacieux.[43]

En second lieu, l'école primaire a enseigné un mépris du monde de l'argent qui allait jusqu'au refus du développement économique et de la société industrielle:[44] la morale de La Fontaine, pour une part, illustrée notamment par la fable "Le Savetier et le financier" que tous les enfants

---

[42] Les maîtres que j'ai connus n'en doutaient point: ils alternaient sagement la morale générale, la leçon d'hygiène et l'éducation civique; mais pratiquaient cet exercice comme un dérouillage matinal, une fois toutes choses et êtres mis en place avant de passer aux exercices plus sévères: la dictée ou le calcul.

[43] Le gouvernement de Vichy ne s'y est pas trompé, qui s'est archarné avec obstination contre l'institution et lui a porté des coups dont elle ne s'est pas complétement relevé.

[44] C'est ce que Jean Bouvier a démonté dans le texte cité ci-dessus, note 41; "tout au long du livre, d'ailleurs, sont valorisés les anciens métiers et l'artisanat: sabotiers, serruriers, fromagers, horlogers, chaudronniers, dentellières, mégissiers. . . . Toute la vieille France rurale, mi paysanne, mi industrielle, est passée en revue avec piété. Les fermes encombrent le paysage français et symbolisent le pays. . . . La grande industrie n'est pas à proprement parler oubliée, mais tout à fait minimisée" (p. 57). J. Bouvier consacre également un long développement à la morale de soumission exaltée par Madame Bruno.

ont appris un jour ou l'autre dans ma génération; la définition de l'usine telle que la répandait l'histoire de ces deux enfants, Julien et André, parcourant la France et maudissant les fabriques génératrices de fumées et de déchets polluants qui défiguraient les paysages ruraux et leur naturelle pureté; c'est encore la leçon de maintes dictées, empruntées aux plus grands et aux plus petits écrivains où se trouvaient exaltées la douceur des soirées champêtres, la paix des campagnes et la probité candide des paysans qui ont accompli leur quotidienne besogne. Assurément la société rurale française où dominaient — numériquement — les petits exploitants autoconsommateurs, pouvait se reconnaître aisément à travers ces tableaux et cette morale implicite, nourrie par ailleurs d'aphorismes touchants, du style: "l'argent ne fait pas le bonheur." Mais il est permis de souligner aussi — outre les significations socio-économiques qu'a si bien dégagées J. Bouvier — combien ce refus du monde et de l'argent, cette condamnation du succès matériel se trouvaient continuer, par une permutation laïcisée, une des plus anciennes et des plus désuètes leçons de l'Eglise romaine. Ce faisant, les enseignants, "jansénistes laïcs," avaient assurément d'autres objectifs: les syndicalistes du moins, qui avaient adhéré au syndicalisme révolutionnaire dès avant 1914, visaient moins une démocratie sociale de petits propriétaires qu'un socialisme libéré des contraintes capitalistes:[45] mais la leçon restait encore implicite, ce que Gaston Bonheur appelle le vestibule de la démocratie socialiste.

Il est enfin une troisième limitation qui tient à la définition couramment admise, sous la pression des autorités de tout grade, des Ministres et Directeurs de Ministère, jusqu'aux inspecteurs primaires, de la laïcité, conçue comme une neutralité assortie d'impératifs catégoriques pesants dans la pratique quotidienne du métier. Certes les obligations faites au personnel enseignant, alors que la classe politique se préoccupait au premier chef de désarmer l'hostilité du clergé et de laminer sa clientèle électorale, se comprennent parfaitement dans la période de la IIIe République naissante: dominer par la neutralité les conflits religieux et politiques, c'était une nécessité d'opportunité qui avait pour sens immédiat de gommer ou atténuer les exposés touchant les questions portées sur la place publique par les adultes. Ne point toucher plus avant à la Réforme en pays réformé, glisser sur la Saint Barthélémy et sur les déportations de Communards, sur les misères de Versailles, etc.[46] Il faut pourtant recon-

---

[45] Gaston Bonheur l'a perçu, pour la période antérieure à 1914, à travers l'expérience de ses parents: "La divinité bourgeoise détrônée, que proposait l'école, à la place? Il ne faut pas se voiler la face, l'école préparait, tranquillement, la démocratie populaire, un monde socialiste — et désargenté — dont elle n'était que le vestibule"; *Qui a cassé le vase de Soissons*, p. 353. Sur quoi, G. Bonheur enchaîne à partir de l'interrogation: "Qu'est-ce qui a coupé son élan?" sur le passage cité à la note 30.

[46] Ces "précautions" n'ont pas été le propre du seul enseignement primaire. Marc Bloch se

naître que cette neutralité gouvernementale et répressive avait un inconvé-
nient majeur: limiter la portée de l'enseignement donné dans le domaine
capital de l'initiation aux futures responsabilités du citoyen et de son rôle
dans la cité. Aussi bien il y a longtemps que les enseignants de tous degrés
et leurs syndicats se sont élevés contre cette définition et ont revendiqué
(et mis en pratique, sans attendre l'autorisation officielle) une "laïcité
ouverte" qui délivre l'enseignant de ce carcan dont les limites non plus que
les justification n'ont jamais été clairement définies et précisées par le
législateur.[47]

Ces trois éléments expliquent assez que l'enseignement primaire français se soit trouvé rapidement dépassé par l'évolution politique et sociale
du pays bien avant 1939; ils annoncent aussi la remise en question qui s'est
faite depuis la Libération et qui se poursuit jusqu'aujourd'hui. A l'heure
actuelle, où l'enseignement est devenu obligatoire théoriquement jusqu'à
16 ans, en fait jusqu'à 14 ans, l'enseignement primaire n'est plus que la
première étape d'un cursus qui redouble en temps la durée primitivement
assignée pour constituer le bagage minimum de tout Français. En cela, les
Républiques de l'après guerre ont comblé les voeux des enseignants dans
leur souci de démocratisation. Pourtant l'école primaire qui passait
jusqu'à la seconde guerre mondiale comme un modèle, au moins sur le
plan pédagogique,[48] est maintenant en crise et sa fonction même se trouve
remise en cause aussi bien de l'intérieur que de l'extérieur. Le corps
enseignant primaire s'interroge — et la collection de *l'Ecole Libératrice* en
témoigne[49] — de même que les réformateurs professionnels des Sciences
de l'Education et du Ministère de la rue de Grenelle. Il est bon, là encore,
de situer, énumération plus qu'explication, les éléments essentiels de ce
malaise qui aident à définir la fonction culturelle de l'Ecole aujourd'hui.

Il convient de distinguer là plusieurs éléments qui ne pèsent pas du
même poids dans l'explication d'ensemble et que nous pouvons classer en
ordre croissant d'importance:

En premier lieu viennent les difficultés de recrutement qui ont été

plaisait à rapporter les recommandations faites à un professeur débutant.à Nîmes, à propos
des guerres de religion et de la réforme en général.
[47] Il n'en est que plus cocasse de voir la définition dépassée dans la pratique depuis si
longtemps reprise récemment par l'actuel Ministre de l'Education, M. René Haby, dans son
factum *pour une modernisation du système éducatif, La Documentation française*, février 1975, pp.
51-52.
[48] Voir le témoignage de Marc Bloch: "Instituteurs, mes frères . . . qui, au prix d'une
immense bonne volonté, aviez su créer, dans notre pays, aux lycées somnolents, aux universi-
tés prisonnières des pires routines, le seul enseignement peut-être dont nous puissions être
fiers," *L'Etrange défaite* (Edition Franc Tireur de 1946), p. 160.
[49] De même que d'autres publications, comme *l'Ecole et la nation* (communiste), *Esprit*
(grande enquête de 1964 sur l'Enseignement supérieur et qui dépasse largement ce cadre),
etc.

créées dans une large mesure par la répression organisée par le gouvernement de Vichy:[50] la remise en état des Ecoles normales départementales après 1945 n'a jamais été complète; la suppression de la filière spécifique (E.P.S. et Ecoles Normales) a tari une partie du recrutement "populaire" du corps; enfin les gouvernements n'ont pas su faire face à la croissance démographique. Le résultat est qu'à l'heure actuelle, au moins la moitié des instituteurs n'ont pas reçu la formation pédagogique traditionnelle; recrutés sur titres (de bachelier), soumis à un stage sur le tas de plusieurs années, ils n'ont pas la rigueur de formation qui était donnée dans les "séminaires laïques," dont les produits s'évadent de plus en plus vers les Collèges d'Enseignement Général, c'est-à-dire vers le secondaire. Le fait est d'autant plus dommageable à l'enseignement donné que celui-ci devrait être refondu en totalité en fonction de l'allongement de la scolarité.[51]

En second lieu, il convient de se représenter que, dans le cadre rural (et *a fortiori* urbain), l'instituteur d'après la seconde guerre mondiale a perdu la stature socio-culturelle qui était antérieurement la sienne: la progression de nouveaux cadres, qui possèdent soit une formation scientifique poussée (vétérinaires, médecins) soit une formation sociale importante (militants du syndicalisme paysan) fait ombre sur le prestige traditionnel de l'instituteur qui a si longtemps représenté le savoir et le progrès lié au savoir dans le monde contemporain. Dès lors l'instituteur ne se maintient que dans la mesure où il n'a pas perdu la foi du charbonnier et où il entretient la flamme par un effort d'information générale qui le maintient au courant du mouvement scientifique pour l'essentiel: ce qui n'est pas nécessairement la vocation de toute la corporation.

Mais le plus important réside sans doute dans le décalage qui s'est institué entre l'école et les moyens nouveaux d'information, habituellement qualifiés de *mass media*. Certes l'enseignement primaire n'a pas ignoré l'audio-visuel, d'autant moins que l'application de la loi Marie-Barangé[52] lui a permis de s'équiper massivement en ce domaine; mais il est difficile d'admettre que, pour autant, les méthodes de l'audio-visuel aient été intégrées, au sens plein du terme, à la pédagogie (le fait est non moins vrai dans les enseignements secondaire et supérieur). Mais le plus grave est sans doute que l'école dite parallèle a nourri les cerveaux plus

---

[50] Quelques difficultés corporatives sont venues à la Libération se greffer sur cette répression: quelques syndicalistes, pacifistes intégraux, se sont trouvés mêlés aux compromis médiocres de juillet 1940; mais l'énorme majorité des instituteurs, après avoir escamoté "Maréchal nous voilà," se sont retrouvés dans la Résistance et dans les Comités de Libération.
[51] Sur ce point, la carence tient plus au Ministère qu'aux enseignants et à leurs organisations professionelles.
[52] Loi votée en 1951 qui attribue aux écoles, publiques et privées, des fonds d'équipement au prorata de leurs effectifs.

rapidement que l'école ne pouvait faire. Ce que aurait dû induire le corps enseignant et ses tuteurs à mettre l'accent à la fois sur l'éducation de l'oeil et de l'ouïe et sur l'enseignement de méthodes. L'inflation des *media* a, pour ainsi dire, submergé l'école: des jeux radiophoniques et télévisés à l'information planétaire distribuée en fin de chaque journée dans chaque foyer, il s'est fait une débauche d'information directe qui a submergé pour ainsi dire le savoir lentement distillé dans les austères salles de classes, tant vantées naguère par Alain.[53] Il n'est pas jusqu'au tourisme culturel, à grands renforts de Guides Bleus et de "Nous partons pour"[54] qui en élargissant sa clientèle, a fait une concurrence indirecte à l'instituteur: ces voyages organisés, où la photographie et la carte postale tiennent une si grande place, ne négligent ni le pittoresque géohistorique ni la curiosité socio-économique; ils distillent, moyennant finances, un savoir-souvenirs imposant qui n'est pas venu de l'école, ne lui doit rien et bénéficie d'un prestige nécessairement supérieur.

Tous ces éléments entrent ainsi dans un jeu complexe qui a réduit la place sociale et culturelle de l'instituteur et de son école: dans une large mesure, l'école-phrase de Gaston Bonheur est moribonde; c'est-à-dire qu'elle n'oriente plus que très partiellement la définition d'une culture populaire nationale, telle que l'avaient rêvée les fondateurs de la IIIe République, dans les termes que nous avons plus haut définis.

Ces deux exemples, sans doute trop longuement exposés, ont été choisis comme illustrations particulièrement significatives de perspectives dans lesquelles peut s'inscrire la recherche historique sur les contacts complexes et les rapports dialectiques qui peuvent s'instituer à l'intérieur d'une société globale, en termes que nous pourrions dire d'acculturation interne. La circulation du haut vers le bas, des classes dominantes vers les dominées, est certainement un schéma incomplet, simpliste et peu défendable aux yeux de l'historien qui cherche à rassembler toutes les données intervenant dans ces questions. Sans doute les voies ainsi tracées sont-elles pour une large part hasardeuses dans l'état actuel de nos connaissances:

[53]   Alain, *Propos sur l'Education* (Paris, 1932): "l'école est un lieu admirable; j'aime que les bruits extérieurs n'y entrent point. J'aime les murs nus. Je n'approuve point qu'on y accroche des choses à regarder, même belles, car il faut que l'attention soit ramenée au travail. Que l'enfant lise, ou qu'il écrive ou qu'il calcule, cette action dénudée est son petit monde à lui qui doit lui suffire. Et tout cet ennui, là autour, et ce vide sans profondeur, sont comme une leçon bien parlante; car il n'y a qu'une chose qui importe pour toi, petit garçon, c'est ce que tu fais" (VIe propos).

[54]   Les *Guides bleus*, des éditions Hachette, sont bien connus: quoique moins prestigieux que naguère le Baedecker, ils sont répandus largement même hors de France. La collection *Nous partons pour* est une entreprise plus modeste des Presses Universitaires de France qui a connu également un grand succès, ces dernières années.

nous avons pensé pouvoir cependant les tracer, ne serait-ce que pour susciter, le cas échéant, les études monographiques — de communautés ou de corpus — qui font encore défaut à l'heure actuelle pour baliser ces voies encore trop peu fréquentées. Mais précisément notre ambition première était bien de montrer combien ce secteur socio-culturel représente un domaine à la fois méconnu et fécond de l'histoire qui reste à parfaire de nos sociétés modernes et contemporaines.

2

Le Ton Inimitable de La Fontaine

MARC SORIANO

I

Comment définir la culture, savante ou populaire? L'attitude la plus prudente me semble-t-il, c'est de ne pas partir d'une définition préalable, mais d'un cas concret, d'une oeuvre où ces cultures interfèrent. C'est la méthode que j'ai adoptée à propos de Perrault, puis, à partir de 1968, avec La Fontaine. Pour donner une idée de cette recherche récente, je vais choisir une des fables les plus connues de l'artiste, *Le Loup et l'Agneau* et l'examiner, en tout cas au départ, dans la perspective la plus traditionnelle, en posant un des problèmes qui reviennent le plus souvent dans les livres de critique ou d'histoire littéraire, celui de son "ton inimitable."*

Les exégètes de La Fontaine insistent volontiers sur sa vaste culture. C'est l'un des poètes les plus "savants" de son époque. Sa formation a été longue et minutieuse. Il a pratiqué avec soin les "anciens," s'est constitué à partir de ses lectures de véritables dossiers d'"ornements" où il n'hésite pas à puiser en cas de besoin. A quoi il faut ajouter une curiosité encyclopédique dont nous trouvons les preuves dans le second recueil des *Fables* et qui lui permit de prendre part aux principales controverses philosophiques, médicales ou politiques de son temps.

Mais les commentateurs du fabuliste, en parlant de sa "science," entendent tout autre chose. Il suffit de se référer à une édition courante des *Fables*, par exemple celle de Couton, ou aux études récentes, du reste fort remarquables, de R. Jasinski ou de J.-P. Collinet. Les uns et les autres, à propos de chaque texte étudié, énumèrent avec soin les sources probables (Esope dans la traduction de Nevelet ou de tel autre, Phèdre, les *Emblemata*, etc.). En somme, les *Fables* ou les *Contes* de La Fontaine seraient le résultat d'une élaboration très poussée de sources écrites, livresques. Il les aurait vivifiées en y ajoutant les "ornements" dont il a été question et qui sont en réalité les prestiges de son "génie": brièveté, lyrisme, "burlesque tempéré," images sobres et éclatantes, cette "suavitas" que décrit Leo Spitzer, en bref ce pouvoir étrange qu'après Paul Valéry et La Fontaine

* L'édition des *Fables* utilisée est celle de Georges Couton, collection des classiques Garnier 1962.

lui-même, il faut bien appeler le "charme." Cette manière de voir aboutit à une expression toute faite, courante dans les manuels. On parle du "ton inimitable" de La Fontaine.

Comme en ce dernier quart de siècle, personne ne songe sérieusement à l'imiter, l'expression semble vouloir signifier qu'il s'agit d'un ton impossible à analyser, à étudier scientifiquement.

La question paraît à première vue de pure forme, mais elle ne reste pas longtemps du domaine de l'esthétique pure. En effet, si l'on accepte de considérer le ton de La Fontaine comme "inimitable," si l'on admet que son entreprise relève du seul souci narratif, qu'il s'agit d'un conteur et de rien d'autre, d'un "fablier" qui produirait des fables comme un prunier donne des prunes, sa "philosophie," du même coup, devrait être prise à la lettre. Il deviendrait alors le "moraliste" du "parti-pris des choses," c'est-à-dire de la lâcheté politique: "La Raison du plus fort est toujours la meilleure" ou, comme dans "*La Chauve Souris et les Deux Belettes*," "Le Sage dit, selon les gens,/Vive le Roi, Vive la Ligue/." On comprend mieux dans ces conditions, les réserves de J.J. Rousseau sur sa valeur éducative et aussi celles de Paul Eluard qui voudrait qu'on l'exile "loin des rives de l'espérance humaine."

Cet arrêt est-il valable? Est-il compatible avec une approche scientifique de l'oeuvre de La Fontaine, avec une perspective qui s'efforcerait d'utiliser au moins quelques-unes des sciences de l'homme qui se développent tumultueusement à notre époque?

On s'efforcera d'aborder ici le problème du "ton inimitable" de La Fontaine dans l'exemple du *Loup et l'Agneau* et en mettant en oeuvre les ressources de plusieurs de ces sciences: et en particulier, la sémiologie, la sémiotique, le folklore, la philologie et l'histoire. Pour éviter des difficultés de vocabulaire, je vais utiliser librement et sans expliciter les notions de codes et de circuits (Jakobson, Barthes), celles de structures narratives et d'"actants" (Propp, Greimas, Bremond, etc.), d'isotopies (Rastier), et m'intéresser plus spécialement au "rapport interlocutif" qui unit la personne du locuteur et celle du destinataire. Par ce biais, se trouve posé le problème — essentiel pour notre propos — de la "troisième personne," celle du héros. S'agit-il d'une "non-personne," comme l'assure E. Benveniste, ou comme l'explique A. Joly, d'une personne "délocutée" et qui peut à chaque instant entrer à nouveau dans le rapport interlocutif? Ces termes techniques qui se justifient dans une controverse ou dans un exposé théorique, ne sont pas absolument indispensables ici puisque mon analyse se borne à dégager les structures narratives du texte. Je ne m'y référerai donc pas explicitement et me limiterai à traquer la présence du narrateur (locuteur) à travers ses personnages (les "actants"), objectif restreint qu'on se gardera de confondre avec celui, plus ambitieux, d'une "explication de texte."

II

Pour la commodité de mon analyse, je diviserai cette célèbre fable en quatre unités de lecture (ce que Barthes appelle des "lexies").

La première se compose d'une morale paradoxale qui se présente comme un théorème à démontrer:

> La Raison du plus fort est toujours la meilleure
> Nous l'allons montrer tout à l'heure.

Cette assertion cynique est assenée ex abrupto à la troisième personne. Remarquons aussi le *nous* du second vers. S'agit-il du *nous de majesté?* (Nous, roi de France et de Navarre, etc.) On admettra sans peine que La Fontaine ne nous a guère habitué à ce ton. Autre éventualité: par ce *nous*, La Fontaine s'intègrerait à la longue tradition des fabulistes, Esope, Phèdre, Faerne, etc. Autre hypothèse qui me semble plus probable. Ce *nous* serait semblable à celui qu'utilise par exemple un professeur qui commence son cours par la formule: *nous allons démontrer*. En tant que professeur c'est évidemment *lui* qui va démontrer; mais le *nous* garde un sens; il sollicite la participation des élèves; aussi bien si le cours reste "magistral," s'il n'entraîne pas un effort de participation et de compréhension de la part de l'auditoire, la "démonstration" restera lettre morte. Dans le même esprit, le *nous* du second vers de cette fable sollicite, me semble-t-il, la connivence du lecteur. Il pourrait alors signifier: *vous qui me lisez et moi qui vous écris*; autrement dit, nous nous trouverions devant le "rapport interlocutif" lui-même, sollicitant sur un ton imperturbable, après une affirmation paradoxale, la complicité du destinataire. Il ne s'agit bien entendu que d'une éventualité et je ne la présente ici que comme une hypothèse que des analyses ultérieures vérifieront ou ne vérifieront pas.

La seconde lexie correspond à la présentation des personnages et amorce l'"action":

> Un agneau se désaltérait
> Dans le courant d'une onde pure
> Un Loup survient à jeun qui cherchait aventure
> Et que la faim en ces lieux attirait.

Cette "mise en place" des héros et du décor parait objective, neutre, puisqu'elle ne comporte à première vue aucun adjectif qualifiant les personnages, aucun jugement de valeur.

Remarquons toutefois que l'Agneau vient au ruisseau *pour boire* et le Loup *pour manger*, objectif immédiat pour l'un et médiat pour l'autre et qui suffisent à caractériser le premier comme pacifique et de bonne foi, le second comme un animal de proie. Les connotations (ou les "isotopies") associées à l'Agneau vont dans le sens de la pureté (vocabulaire lyrique: *se désaltérer, courant, onde pure*); celles qui sont associées au Loup renvoient au contraire à la lutte pour la vie et au moins aux réalités de l'instinct (*à jeun, la faim, chercher aventure, attirer*).

La troisième lexie — qu'il faudrait évidemment étudier avec plus de détails et approfondir dans une "explication de texte" digne de ce nom — nous présente le dialogue entre le Loup et l'Agneau.

> Qui te rend si hardi de troubler mon breuvage?
>   Dit cet animal plein de rage;
>   Tu seras chatié de ta témérité.
> Sire, répond l'Agneau, que votre Majesté
>   Ne se mette pas en colère;
>   Mais plutôt qu'elle considère
>   Que je me vas désaltérant
>   Dans le courant
>   Plus de vingt pas au-dessous d'Elle,
> Et que par conséquent, en aucune façon,
>   Je ne puis troubler sa boisson.
>   Tu la troubles, reprit cette bête cruelle
>   Et je sais que de moi tu médis l'an passé
>   Comment l'aurais-je fait si je n'étais pas né?
>   Reprit l'Agneau. Je tette encor ma mère
>   Si ce n'est toi, c'est donc ton frère.
>   Je n'en ai point. —C'est donc quelqu'un des tiens,
>   Car vous ne m'épargnez guère,
>   Vous, vos bergers et vos chiens.
> On me l'a dit, il faut que je me venge.

Me limitant ici à l'étude du "rapport interlocutif," je me bornerai ici à deux remarques.

Les arguments du Loup et ceux de l'Agneau ne relèvent pas de la même logique.

Le Loup se place dans une perspective résolument irrationnelle, celle du prestige, et ses griefs renvoient sans cesse au droit divin, au crime de lèse majesté (*si hardi, troubler mon breuvage, témérité, médire, vengeance*); l'Agneau est au contraire cartésien; il argumente pied à pied, avec respect certes (il parle de son interlocuteur à la troisième personne, lui donne du "Sire" et de "Votre Majesté") mais courage, en se référant à la raison et aux faits. Il pousse l'audace jusqu'à signaler l'aspect *passionnel* du réquisitoire du Loup (Que votre Majesté/ne se mette pas en colère/). Ces deux "univers du discours" ont en conséquence des caractéristiques impossibles à confondre: l'Agneau ne craint pas d'être long, il insiste sur les articulations logiques des arguments qu'il invoque (*Mais plutôt . . . Et que, par consé- quent*), insistance qui lui permet de faire par exemple ressortir l'impossibilité matérielle du délit dont on l'accuse: Je ne *puis* troubler sa boisson (. . .) Comment *l'aurais-je* fait (. . .) Je *n'en ai point.*

Cette première remarque débouche sur ce qu'il faut bien appeler des jeux de scène et une technique de la récitation. On peut évidemment réciter cette fable sur un ton monocorde, en insistant sur le sens; mais l'artiste nous oriente vers une autre interprétation; des indications très précises invitent le récitant à prendre tour à tour le ton du Loup et celui de l'Agneau, autrement dit à s'identifier à chacun des personnages et à mimer la scène.

Seconde observation: à plusieurs reprises, le comportement du Loup est jugé sans la moindre ambiguité soit par l'Agneau (Que Votre Majesté/ne se mette pas en *colère/*), soit par le narrateur qui intervient directement dans l'action en y insérant des qualificatifs qui sont des jugements de valeur (Dit cet animal plein de rage/Reprit cette bête *cruelle*), soit d'une manière encore plus efficace par le Loup qui dévoile lui-même sa nature de fauve (mauvaise qualité de ses griefs successifs qui se détruisent l'un l'autre, manque de sérénité dans les réquisitoires et surtout référence au concept de *vengeance*, la vengeance étant par nature incompatible avec la notion de justice).

La fable s'achève par trois vers qui composent la quatrième lexie:

> Là-dessus, au fond des forêts
> Le Loup l'emporte et puis le mange
> Sans autre forme de procès.

Conclusion certes attendue, mais aussi fort surprenante et révélatrice du véritable sens du message, ce que confirme l'expression proverbiale *sans autre forme de procès* qui me semble être la clé de l'énigme. La formule est traditionnelle, mais placée comme elle est, elle nous découvre que le dialogue auquel nous venons d'assister était un *procès*. Procès jugé d'avance, parodie de justice puisque le Loup, de toute façon, est décidé à "se venger," à manger l'Agneau.

Mais nous sommes en 1668 et plus probablement encore en 1663, puisque nous savons par les recherches de R. Jasinski que cette fable fait partie de la douzaine de poèmes qui circulent sous le manteau, à la Cour et dans les allées du pouvoir, au moment où le Tout-Paris et le Tout-Versailles suivent avec anxiété les péripéties du procès Fouquet. Le surintendant des Finances, arrêté en 1661, se défend avec obstination et parvient à plusieurs reprises à mettre en évidence les partis-pris et les illégalités de ses accusateurs. Le mot *procès*, au cours de cette période, a une dénotation et une connotation du même type que le mot *affaire* à la fin du XIXe siècle, au moment où s'affrontent à propos du capitaine Dreyfus les partisans du progrès social et ceux de "l'ordre moral." Le mot *procès* est donc ici très vraisemblablement une allusion qui donne son sens exact au poème et qui confirme les jugements de valeur caractérisant le Loup que nous avons appris à lire "entre les lignes."

III

L'étude attentive du texte nous a obligés à prendre en considération le contexte. Que nous apprend cette analyse de structures narratives complétée d'un rappel historique?

Première conclusion: malgré les apparences, la troisième personne (ici les deux héros de la fable) n'est pas une vraie troisième personne; elle est simplement "délocutée," c'est-à-dire provisoirement "exclue du rapport interlocutif qui, comme le note André Joly, repose sur la présence, réelle ou fictive, du locuteur et de l'allocutaire au sein d'un même espace temporel — l'instant de parole du locuteur — espace d'où la troisième personne est absente." Mais cette exclusion est, comme on le voit nettement dans cette fable, purement virtuelle. Cette "non-personne" est tout au plus une "non-personne interlocutive"; elle fait partie intégrante du système interpersonnel "à la fois en tant que personne spatiale (comme *hors-moi*) et en tant que personne temporelle."

Cette analyse d'André Joly qui me parait valable en général, nous aide en tout cas à distinguer l'importance du rapport interlocutif dans les *Fables* de La Fontaine. Le narrateur "délocute" sans doute ses héros, mais il ne cesse pendant le même temps de reinforcer le "rapport interlocutif." Il sollicite et même exige la connivence du lecteur. Il intervient sans cesse soit pour caractériser ses personnages, soit pour les juger. Bien plus, il les mime. Et pour être encore plus certain que nous ne nous égarerons pas, il parsème notre chemin de cailloux blancs qui nous serviront de repères. On a vu ainsi les connotations du mot *procès* à l'époque; mais il est possible de dégager celles de plusieurs autres mots de cette fable, par exemple les mots *colère* ou *rage*, expressions qui reviennent souvent dans les pamphlets du temps pour désigner Colbert. (On pensera par exemple au *Colbert Enragé*.)

Le rapport interlocutif est présent dans toute littérature, mais il a un rôle prédominant dans la littérature orale, ce qui est inévitable. Le "conteur doué" doit adapter continuellement son récit aux réactions de ses auditeurs, ce qui l'oblige à intervenir sans cesse dans l'action.

V. Propp s'est efforcé de dégager le schéma général du conte: présentation des "actants" en situation, épreuves mettant le héros en danger de mort, victoire finale. Le schéma ne semble pas convenir à cette fable puisque le personnage sympathique (l'Agneau) y périt de male mort, mais il faut remarquer que cette structure tronquée caractérisée par la fin malheureuse existe aussi ailleurs et qu'elle se rencontre par exemple dans les contes pour les enfants (contes d'avertissement) dont la fonction est justement de mettre en garde les plus jeunes contre les dangers de la forêt, de la rivière, etc. Et il faut noter que le narrateur, ici, prend le relais du héros. Dénonçant la partialité de l'accusateur et ses illégalités, il cloue en somme le Loup au pilori, devient en quelque sorte "le Loup du Loup," en tout cas pour le public averti qui est en mesure de saisir les allusions.

Nous venons du même coup d'entrevoir le secret du "ton inimitable" de notre conteur. Il s'agit d'une interférence de l'art savant et de la culture populaire. Sans nier la référence à Esope et à Phèdre — dont les oeuvres peuvent aussi être considérées comme des collectes plus ou moins élaborées de contes d'animaux, notées à des époques différentes — nous sommes amenés à découvrir que La Fontaine utilise ici les techniques narratives et le ton des "conteurs doués," conteurs qui, nous le savons par ailleurs, ont une large audience au XVIIe siècle.

La Fontaine les connait et les apprécie. Comment en serait-il autrement? Sa charge de Maître des Eaux et Forêts le mêle souvent à la paysannerie et nous savons par de nombreux témoignages qu'il apprécie la vigueur, l'invention et la franchise de l'art populaire. Familier de la littérature orale, La Fontaine l'utilise ici librement par une recherche très élaborée d'équivalence et de connivences.

Ce recours de La Fontaine, artiste savant, à l'art populaire est, comme toutes les conduites humaines, "sur-déterminé." Parmi les nombreuses causes qui l'expliquent, retenons celles qui nous renvoient au contexte historique, c'est-à-dire aussi bien à la biographie de l'artiste qu'aux problèmes politiques et sociaux qu'il a eu à affronter. Le poète, à cause de sa fidélité personnelle à l'égard de Fouquet, se trouve peu à peu et comme malgré lui pris dans l'engrenage de la lutte contre l'absolutisme, politique de "ressaisissement" élaborée par le pouvoir central pour prévenir le retour de secousses révolutionnaires comme celle de la Fronde. Opposant occasionnel au régime, La Fontaine retrouve tout naturellement la "littérature" et les structures narratives, le "dire sans dire" de l'éternel opposant, le peuple.

Mais c'est là découvrir aussi que la morale de La Fontaine ne doit pas être prise à la lettre. Elle n'oriente pas vers la lâcheté politique, mais au contraire vers le courage.

Du même coup, nous comprenons pourquoi les Fables, poèmes de circonstance, parviennent à échapper au sort de tant d'oeuvres liées de trop près aux événements. Le poète, par le biais de sa fidélité à Fouquet, découvre une injustice d'une portée plus générale, et le répertoire de la paysannerie qui, depuis longtemps, lutte contre elle.

Cette rencontre a choisi pour thème la culture populaire et la culture savante en France. En conséquence, je limite mon analyse aux données qui permettent de dégager cette "source inconnue" des Fables qu'est le folklore. Ailleurs, dans le numéro spécial de la *Revue d'histoire littéraire de la France* de septembre-décembre 1970 consacré aux Méthodologies, sur l'exemple des fables XV et XVI du Livre IV, je vérifie mon hypothèse de travail concernant La Fontaine en recourant à d'autres sciences humaines comme la psychanalyse, recours qui, du reste, m'a permis de découvrir de nouveaux documents concernant le poète et aussi une nouvelle interprétation de certaines données biographiques connues depuis longtemps. D'une manière générale, on aura remarqué que ces résultats ont été acquis grâce à la méthode interdisciplinaire. Il me semble démontré qu'il est impossible d'"'expliquer" la moindre fable de La Fontaine dans une perspective purement "textuelle," que cette explication se fonde sur des données d'ordre sémiologique, littéraire ou biographique. De même, la référence au folklore n'est pas facultative, mais absolument nécessaire si l'on veut comprendre le ton de l'artiste qui reste bien entendu "inimitable," mais qu'il n'est nullement impossible d'analyser.

IV

Cette analyse concrète permet un passage à la limite. Elle nous donne l'occasion de risquer une définition évidemment approximative et provisoire de la "culture populaire" à l'époque de La Fontaine et, pourquoi pas? à la nôtre.

Notons d'abord le caractère peu scientifique des définitions habituellement données de cette culture. Elle serait, affirment certains à la suite de Patrice Coirault, "la culture des incultes." Mais où commencent et où finissent culture et inculture? Se caractérisent-elles vraiment par la possession ou la non-possession des mécanismes de la lecture? Or nous savons aujourd'hui qu'il existe différents niveaux de lecture, que certains individus que l'on considère habituellement comme cultivés sont caractérisés par une intelligence livresque qui ne leur permet aucune adaption au réel et aussi que d'autres, qui disposent théoriquement des mécanismes de la lecture ne les utilisent pratiquement jamais et pourraient être assimilés à des analphabètes. Définira-t-on la culture populaire par ses "variantes" ou par sa "pureté," comme le fait, après Gérard de Nerval, P. Bénichou? Ces critères essentiellement descriptifs témoignent de l'intuition et du goût réellement exceptionnel de l'auteur de *Chansons et Recherches du Valois*; mais on peut se demander si, après plus d'un siècle, ils gardent une valeur opératoire susceptible de nous orienter vers une recherche objective. Les traits de l'"anonymat" et de la "création collective" qui sont, eux aussi, souvent invoqués manquent de rigueur. Comment imaginer en effet que cette cohérence complexe qui caractérise une oeuvre d'art pourrait être obtenue par hasard, par simple frottement d'une version contre une autre, ou suivant l'image de la prière d'insérer des "contes de ma Mère l'Oye" publiée par *le Mercure Galant* de janvier 1697, par un effet de filtrage qui fait que "tout ce qui [est] mal pensé [tombe] dans l'oubli."

L'analyse qui précède nous met sur la voie d'un autre type de définition. *Le Loup et l'Agneau* est un thème, un schéma dynamique qui fait partie d'un répertoire de sagesse polémique, héritage dont dispose au départ le "conteur doué," cet artiste à part entière dont tous les grands collecteurs du siècle dernier et du nôtre, de Millien à Paul Delarue, de Patrice Coirault à M.-L. Tenèze, nous signalent l'existence.

Le "conteur doué," en fonction des circonstances, assume et actualise tel ou tel thème de ce répertoire, en l'animant et en développant, pour un public complice qui comprend les allusions et les sous-entendus et qui partage les options politiques, sociales ou idéologiques de l'artiste.

La "littérature populaire" n'est donc pas nécessairement caractérisée par ses structures esthétiques et sa forme, mais bien davantage par ses tensions et par son contenu. Ainsi se résout du même coup l'irritant problème de l'"origine sociale" de l'artiste populaire, mais cette origine qui facilite évidemment la communication et la communion qu'il cherche avec son public n'est nullement obligatoire.

Quand il est issu de souche populaire et que les circonstances limitent sa création artistique au circuit oral, le "conteur doué" n'est connu que par le public populaire dont il exprime les amertumes, les besoins et les aspirations. En conséquence, sa réputation ne dure qu'autant que dure la mémoire humaine. La Fontaine, artiste savant, en récupérant pour les raisons analysées plus haut le répertoire contestataire de la paysannerie de son temps, assume la fonction du "conteur doué" et, en même temps, il fait passer les contes d'animaux dans un autre circuit, celui de l'imprimé, où le nom de l'auteur passe, ou en tout cas peut passer à la postérité. La création n'est pas pour autant collective; elle est toujours la mise en oeuvre individuelle d'un matériau collectif, ce qui suppose toujours chez le public une réceptivité créatrice et une participation active au processus de communication.

A ce niveau, le problème de la culture populaire et de la culture savante recoupe un autre problème, encore plus fondamental, celui de la définition de l'artiste, et d'une manière plus générale de l'"intellectuel."

Nos habitudes d'esprit font que nous limitons notre effort de définition au plan socio-professionnel. Nous insistons sur le type d'intelligence mise en oeuvre dans cette variété de travail: compréhension abstraite ou symbolique.

Or c'est là oublier (mais s'agit-il vraiment d'un oubli lorsqu'il caractérise les structures mêmes de notre enseignement) que la "littérature" a d'abord une fonction de communication et que cette qualité esthétique qu'on privilégie n'est qu'un des traits qui facilitent la diffusion du message intellectuel ou affectif?

Il faut donc, si l'on s'intéresse réellement à la culture populaire ou savante, consentir à une étude critique du problème des intellectuels, c'est-à-dire à une analyse historique des rapports qu'ils entretiennent avec les structures économiques ou politiques de leur société. Or la pensée socialiste nous offre la tentative la plus cohérente et la plus rigoureuse pour aborder ces rapports. Qu'on partage ou non son optique, il est donc indispensable d'étudier de près les célèbres analyses de Marx et Engels sur les liens qui unissent les idéologies et les infra-structures, et plus encore celles d'Antonio Gramsci, l'un des plus grands philosophes marxistes, qui a justement centré sa réflexion sur la dialectique complexe qui unit chaque groupe social à ses "intellectuels."

Toute classe, explique-t-il dans *Les intellectuels et l'organisation de la culture*, ne parvient à la conscience de ses possibilités et de sa force qu'en élaborant pour ainsi dire ses propres intellectuels, c'est-à-dire des individus capables de défendre efficacement ses propres intérêts. A titre d'exemple, les "intellectuels organiques" de la bourgeoisie industrielle sont en fin de compte les industriels eux-mêmes, puisqu'ils sont responsables de l'organisation économique qui reflète les intérêts essentiels de leur classe. Toutefois, une classe sociale, lorsqu'elle prend le pouvoir, se trouve dans l'obligation d'assurer une foule de tâches certes subalternes, mais malgré tout non négligeables, qui concernent toute la société: ainsi l'administration, le "maintien de l'ordre," l'enseignement. Or, bien évidemment, elle ne produit pas un nombre d'"intellectuels organiques" qui pourrait suffire à de tels besoins. Elle est donc obligée d'annexer les enfants les mieux doués des autres classes sociales, ceux qui auraient pu devenir leurs "intellectuels organiques" et plus particulièrement à ceux du peuple, ce qui est tout gain pour elle, car tout en assurant son hégémonie, elle prive ainsi les couches qu'elle tient sous sa dépendance des cadres qui auraient pu lui donner une claire conscience de leurs besoins et de leurs possibilités. Aussi la bourgeoisie élabore-t-elle un système d'enseignement et de promotion destiné à annexer les enfants les plus doués des classes laborieuses, à les lier à elle par des liens multiples et puissants, en particulier ceux de l'intérêt et de la parenté.

Gramsci note aussi que certains intellectuels, parce qu'on leur confie habituellement les tâches éducatives ou celles qui concernent l'art et la littérature, finissent par s'imaginer qu'ils constituent une classe à part, indépendante de la lutte des classes; toutefois il s'agit d'une apparence car aux périodes de crises, cette prétendue catégorie "socio-professionnelle" des "intellectuels traditionnels" se trouve placée devant un dilemme: renoncer aux avantages acquis ou bien épouser sans ambiguité les intérêts de leurs maîtres.

L'analyse de Gramsci nous permet de comprendre historiquement l'élargissement de l'inspiration de La Fontaine que nous n'avons pu jusqu'à présent que décrire au niveau des thèmes ou de la biographie. Le poète bénéficie d'un "office" qui lie ses intérêts au maintien de l'ordre existant; son existence est aussi facilitée par les libéralités d'un "mécène," système qui suppose l'existence d'une certaine indépendance de l'art par rapport à la politique. L'arrestation de Fouquet et l'établissement de la "monarchie absolue" inaugurent une politique de ressaisissement destinée à éviter le retour de secousses populaires semblables à celles de la Fronde. Une fois la révolte vaincue, le pouvoir central fait expier à ses officiers le péché d'avoir réveillé "la bête immonde." Les intellectuels en particulier seront mis en demeure de se rallier et de travailler activement à l'"image de marque" de la monarchie absolue.

Obligé de remettre en question non seulement les privilèges de sa "catégorie socio-professionnelle," mais aussi ses amitiés et jusqu'à l'idée qu'il se fait de la culture, La Fontaine choisit de résister et se retrouve rapidement, lui écrivain raffiné et fort éloigné des "superstitions populaires," sur des positions politiques et idéologiques qui sont celles des artistes populaires. Autrement dit, il assume progressivement sa position de "conteur doué," met sa verve et son talent au service des deux genres les plus décriés de son époque, la fable et le conte.

V

On me pardonnera de terminer par quelques réflexions sur le thème même de ce symposium: culture populaire, culture savante.

La distinction de ces deux cultures qui peut se justifier historiquement, ne doit pas nous faire oublier que toute culture est fonctionnelle, qu'elle reste, comme le rappelle Hegel, liée au travail humain.

C'est peut-être une des lacunes de cette rencontre (critique que bien entendu j'oppose d'abord à ma propre communication) que de chercher la culture populaire dans le passé. En fait, les structures créatrices de l'art du passé se maintiennent en France sous d'autres formes, et plus particulièrement dans la chanson (Charles Trenet, Georges Brassens, Jacques Brel, Maxime le Forestier, etc.), type d'art qui correspond aux possibilités d'écoute et de participation des travailleurs et des jeunes de notre pays. Ce phénomène n'est d'ailleurs nullement particulier à la France. Dans chaque pays, aux Etats-Unis comme au Viet-Nam, se maintiennent et se développent des formes spécifiques de culture qui reflètent les préoccupations fondamentales des masses laborieuses de chaque peuple.

Les Curiosités Françaises de Oudin, en 1650, et une mazarinade burlesque nous ont conservé une plaisanterie caractéristique de l'art populaire de l'époque et qui porte sur les noms propres. *Aller à Versailles*, expression qui ne parait avoir rien de risible par elle-même, par un jeu de mot sur le verbe *verser*, finit par signifier *avoir un accident de voiture* (à cheval). Or cette plaisanterie sur les noms propres se retrouve dans plusieurs chansons récentes qui ont connu un large succès populaire, à titre d'exemple, l'une de Nino Ferrer (Gaston, y a le téléfon qui son) et une autre qui a fait fureur en 1974, de Jacques Dutronc (Je laisse Giscard à son d'Estaing).

En résumé, il ne faudrait pas trop oublier qu si, historiquement, nous nous trouvons en présence de deux cultures, la populaire et la savante, dans la pratique, tous les grands créateurs, qu'il s'agisse de Rabelais ou de Walt Whitman, de La Fontaine ou de Twain, ont largement puisé dans le répertoire populaire. En somme, tout se passe comme s'il n'y avait qu'une seule culture, celle qui est liée aux besoins des masses laborieuses et qui est élaborée par des créateurs authentiques qui ont (trait caractéristique qui permet de les identifier sans erreur) une conception universelle, et non aristocratique, de leur fonction d'intellectuels.

Bibliographie

Barthes, Roland, "Introduction à l'analyse structurale des récits." *Communications*, n. 8 (1966).

Benichou, Paul. *Gerard de Nerval et la chanson folklorique*. Paris: J. Corti, 1970.

Benveniste, Emile. *Problèmes de linguistique générale*. Paris: Gallimard, 1966.

Brémond, Claude. "Le message narratif." *Communications*, n. 4 (1964).

Brémond, Claude. *Logique du récit*. Paris: Editions du Seuil, 1973.

Coirault, Patrice. *Recherches sur notre ancienne chanson populaire*. Genève: Droz, 1933.

Coirault, Patrice. *Notre chanson folklorique*. Paris: Picard, 1936.

Collinet, Jean-Pierre. *Le monde littéraire de La Fontaine*. Paris: Presses universitaires de France, 1970.

Couton, Georges. *La poétique de La Fontaine*. Publications de la Faculté des lettres de l'Université de Lyon, ser. 2, fasc. 4 (1957).

Couton, Georges. *La politique de La Fontaine*. (Bibliothèque de la Faculté des lettres de l'Université de Lyon, fasc. 2) Paris: Les belles lettres, 1959.

Chabrol, Claude. "De quelques problèmes de grammaire narrative et textuelle," dans *Sémiotique narrative et textuelle*. Paris: Larousse, 1973.

Delarue, Paul, et M.-L. Tenèze. *Catalogue raisonné du conte populaire français* . T. I, Paris: Erasme, 1953; T. II, Paris: Maisonneuve et Larose, 1955.

Gerard de Nerval. *Chansons et recherches de Valois*, dans *Oeuvres complètes*. Paris: Editions de la Pléïade, 1952. (Ed. critique, voir Benichou, supra.)

Gramsci, Antonio. *Gli intellettuali e l'organizzazione della cultura*. Turin: Einaudi, 1959 et 1975.

Greimas, A.-J. *Sémantique structurale*. Paris: Larousse, 1966.

Guillaume, G. *Langage et science du langage*. Paris: Nizet, 1964.

Guillaume, G. *Leçons de linguistique* (194849). 2 vols. Paris: Klincksieck, 1971.

Jakobson, Roman. *Essais de linguistique générale*. Paris: Editions du Seuil, 1970.

Jasinski, René. *La Fontaine et le premier recueil des Fables*. 2 vols. Paris: Nizet, 1966.

Joly, André. "Sur le système de la personne." *Revue des langues romanes*, n. 1973, ler fasc.

Joly, André. "Personne et temps dans le récit romanesque." *Recherches Anglaises et Américaines* (Université de Strasbourg), n. 7 (1974).

Marx, Karl, et Friedrich Engels. *Textes choisis concernant l'art*. Paris: Editions sociales, 1959.

Oudin, Antoine. *Curiositez françoises pour supplément aux dictionnaires*. . . . Paris, 1640.

Propp, Vladimir. *Morphologie du Conte*. Paris: Editions du Seuil, 1970.

Rousseau, Jean-Jacques. *L'Emile*. Paris: Editions de la Pléïade, 1969. (Plus particulièrement le livre II.)

Soriano, Marc. *La Fontaine, des contes aux fables*. T. II de *Culture savante et traditions populaires*. (A paraître. Trois extraits publiés dans la *Revue d'histoire littéraire de la France*, 1970; *Europe*, 1972; et la *Revue de l'Université de Limoges*, 1973.)

Spitzer, Leo. *Etudes de style*. Paris: Gallimard, 1970.

Valéry, Paul. "Au sujet d'Adonis," dans *Variété*, T. I des *Oeuvres*. Paris: Bibliothèque de la Pléïade, 1960.

3

Witches and Cunning Folk
in the Old Régime

CLARKE GARRETT

Studies of African and English witchcraft have produced a picture of this phenomenon which has become standard among anthropologists, especially British and American ones. Much of the impressive research in the field published in the last ten or fifteen years has derived its approach and theoretical presuppositions from the pioneering works of E. Evans-Pritchard on the Azande of the Sudan.[1] Several important generalizations emerge from the findings of Evans-Pritchard and his successors.

First of all, witchcraft is endemic rather than epidemic. It comprises a complex of beliefs and practices which not only reflect the fears and tensions of a given society but also provide a convenient explanation for misfortunes and remedies for overcoming them. While Evans-Pritchard found that, among the Azande, witches were blamed for nearly everything that went wrong, more commonly in Africa only certain kinds of illnesses and disasters are ascribed to them.

Witchcraft is furthermore a phenomenon of what Monica Wilson has called "small-scale societies," in which personal relationships are dominant and people think "in personal terms and seek personal causes for their misfortunes."[2]

Africans make certain important distinctions among witches. They tend to distinguish those who exercise their malevolent powers without

[1] In this summary of contemporary anthropological interpretations of witchcraft, I have relied primarily on the following: Lucy Mair, *Witchcraft* (New York, 1969); Mary Douglas, *Purity and Danger: An Analysis of Concepts of Pollution and Taboos* (Harmondsworth, 1970); Mary Douglas, *Natural Symbols: Explorations in Cosmology* (London, 1970); Max Marwick, ed., *Witchcraft and Sorcery: Selected Readings* (Harmondsworth, 1970); Mary Douglas, ed., *Witchcraft Confessions and Accusations* (London, 1970); John Middleton and E. H. Winter, eds., *Witchcraft and Sorcery in East Africa* (London, 1963); Monica Wilson, *Religion and the Transformation of Society: A Study of Social Change* (Cambridge, 1971); and John Middleton, ed., *Magic, Witchcraft and Curing* (Garden City, 1967).

[2] Monica Wilson, "Witch Beliefs and Social Structure," *American Journal of Sociology*, 56 (1951), p. 313.

the use of spells or "medicines" from those who do use them. (Evans-Pritchard calls the former witches and the latter sorcerors). They also tend to distinguish between witches who work by day from night witches, who go out in spirit and attack their victims while they sleep. The day witches are real people, and there is some real quarrel or grievance, climaxing in some tangible affliction, which the victim, sometimes aided by oracles manipulated by a professional diviner-healer, then ascribes to witchcraft and to a specific witch. In many cases, the accused individual is a kinsman or familiar person who happens to be in a situation of tension and distrust with the victim; alternatively, the accused witch is a person in some way marginal — a newcomer to the village, someone conspicuously wealthier or poorer than his neighbors, someone whose personality or morals violate the village norms. Someone who claims for himself or herself the occult powers of healing and divining may be suspect, since these powers are conceived as capable of being used either for good or for evil.

The night witches, on the other hand, represent what Wilson calls "the standardized nightmare of a group."[3] They reverse the conventions and moral values of the society. They travel upside down on their heads, or fly; their skins are pale instead of dark. Many of their actions are identical with those European demonologists ascribed to the alleged witches of the sixteenth and seventeenth centuries. In Africa, too, witches are believed to gather in the forest to eat babies and to dance naked; they concoct ointments to enable them to travel magically to their assemblies. They commit disgusting acts of hostility like vomiting in doorways.[4]

While many of the witchcraft studies of the anthropologists are limited simply to describing the social structures and witch beliefs of a given tribal society, Evans-Pritchard and some of his successors, notably Mary Douglas, have attempted considerably more. They want to show how witch beliefs are a "social fact,"[5] not only arising from the complex web of social relationships, political structures, and mores of a given society but also themselves an enduring and perhaps necessary part of that web. Mary Douglas argues that villages are especially vulnerable to witchcraft beliefs because the boundaries of their world are so confined and interaction with their neighbors so unavoidable. All relationships are personal ones.

[3]   Ibid. See also J.D. Krige, "The Social Function of Witchcraft," in *Witchcraft and Sorcery*, pp. 237-251.

[4]   See, e.g., Mair, *Witchcraft*, pp. 40-43; Douglas, *Natural Symbols*, p. 113; John Middleton, *Lugbara Religion: Rituals and Authority among an East African People* (London, 1960), pp. 239-240; E.E. Evans-Pritchard, "Witchcraft (*mangu*) among the Azande," in *Witchcraft and Sorcery*, pp. 29-30; Philip Mayer, "Witches," in ibid., p. 48; and Krige, "Social Function of Witchcraft," pp. 238-240.

[5]   E.E. Evans-Pritchard, "Sorcery and Native Opinion," in *Witchcraft and Sorcery*, p. 21.

The political and social structures within the village are rudimentary and the roles of its members ambiguous, undefined, and therefore likely to produce conflict and tension.[6]

Witch beliefs, Douglas contends, give symbolic expression to the anxieties that village life produces. Precisely because structures are rudimentary and roles ambiguous, unconventional ideas and actions and marginal individuals may seem especially threatening. Another anthropologist, Jeanne Favret, has said that witch beliefs provide villagers with a symbolism for comprehending the sole preoccupations of their lives: the survival and health of themselves, their animals, and their crops.[7] I should add that Favret is writing not about Africans but about peasants in the Norman bocage in 1974.

One result of the work of Evans-Pritchard and his successors has been the narrowing of the gap between the mind or "collective mentality" of primitive peoples and the rest of us. By insisting that we must never lose sight of the social context of ideas such as witchcraft, they also remind us historians of popular culture that structures are always social as well as mental, that primitive beliefs, rather than being necessarily evasions of reality, may be instead attempts to comprehend and deal with reality. "If we remember that it is a practical interest in living and not an academic interest in metaphysics which has produced these beliefs," Douglas writes, "their whole significance alters."[8] Evans-Pritchard showed that the Azande knew perfectly well that there were natural forces in the world outside their own or the witches' control, but when disaster did strike, the villager asked: why now? why me? who is to blame? "Fire is hot," Evans-Pritchard writes, "but it is not hot owing to witchcraft, for that is its nature. It is a universal quality of fire to burn, but it is not a universal quality of fire to burn *you*."[9]

Witchcraft beliefs are more closely related to science than to religion, but it is a "pre-Copernican" science.[10] Just as the sun seems to revolve around the earth, so misfortune seems to come from the ill-will of enemies. Once those enemies are identified, however, it may be possible to deal with them, either by threats or counter-magic. As Jean Delumeau has pointed out, magic and religion are essentially opposed in their tendencies. Religion points toward the cosmic, the transcendent. Magic and

[6] Douglas, *Natural Symbols*, pp. 103-108.

[7] Gerard Bonnot, "La Sorcière du C.n.r.s.," *L'Express*, August 19-25, 1974, pp. 52-57. I am grateful to Evelyn Ackerman for this reference.

[8] Douglas, *Purity and Danger*, p. 108.

[9] E.E. Evans-Pritchard, "Witchcraft among the Azande," in John Middleton, ed., *Studies in Social and Cultural Anthropology* (New York, 1968), p. 209; see also Bonnot, "La Sorcière du C.n.r.s.," p. 54.

[10] Douglas, *Purity and Danger*, p. 98; and Douglas, *Witchcraft Confessions and Accusations*, Introduction, pp. xvii-xviii.

witchcraft, on the other hand, are concrete, practical, directed at acquiring or protecting the blessings of this world — wealth, health, power.[11]

Most of those who have developed this anthropological concept of witchcraft are English, yet its intellectual foundations are French. Evans-Pritchard derived the notion that there were social facts which found their collective expression in the mentality or belief-structure of a given society from Durkheim, Levy-Brühl, and Mauss. But where Levy-Brühl was in effect derailed into an overly schematic examination of the primitive mind — mystical rather than rational, religious rather than scientific — Evans-Pritchard's fieldwork convinced him that any such categorization was unnecessary if one remembered Durkheim's great insight that *all* aspects of a collective mentality derived from a social context.[12]

While the *Annales* historians have utilized anthropological theory in a number of fields of inquiry, they have not done so in the study of witchcraft. But it has been used, with considerable success in my judgment, by a number of historians of European and American witchcraft, notably William Monter, Carlo Ginzburg, John Demos, Alan Macfarlane, and Keith Thomas.[13] It was Macfarlane's and Thomas's work that directed my attention to the role of the healers and diviners, the "cunning folk" of the English villages, who like their African counterparts provided their neighbors with an explanation of and means for counteracting the hostile forces that assaulted them.

In the county of Essex, Macfarlane found, no village was more than ten miles from a known practitioner. Moreover, the cunning men and women came from all groups in society and included even clergymen and schoolmasters.[14] It is clear that cunning folk were just as numerous and functioned in much the same way in France. In the sixteenth century, a series of church councils warned the faithful against them, without yet

---

[11] Jean Delumeau, *Le catholicisme entre Luther et Voltaire* (Paris, 1971), p. 252.

[12] E.E. Evans-Pritchard, *Social Anthropology and Other Essays* (Glencoe, 1962), pp. 51-53; Douglas, *Witchcraft Confessions and Accusations*, Introduction, pp. xvi-xvii; Douglas, *Purity and Danger*, pp. 80-98; and Raymond Firth, "The Right Hand and the Wrong," *Times Literary Supplement*, February 21, 1975, p. 190.

[13] E. William Monter, "Patterns of Wirchcraft in the Jura," *Journal of Social History*, 5(1971), pp. 1-25; Monter, "Witchcraft in Geneva, 1537-1662," *Journal of Modern History*, 43 (1971), pp. 179-204; Carlo Ginzburg, *I Benandanti: ricerche sulla stregoneria e sui culti agrari tra cinquecento e seicento* (Turin, 1966); John Demos, "Underlying Themes in the Witchcraft of Seventeenth-Century New England," *American Historical Review*, 75 (1970), pp. 1311-1326; Alan Macfarlane, *Witchcraft in Tudor and Stuart England: A Regional and Comparative Study* (New York, 1970); and Keith Thomas, *Religion and the Decline of Magic* (New York, 1971).

[14] Macfarlane, *Witchcraft in Tudor and Stuart England*, ch. 8; Thomas, *Religion and the Decline of Magic*, pp. 548-550; and Keith Thomas, "The Relevance of Social Anthropology to the Historical Study of English Witchcraft," in Douglas, ed., *Witchcraft Confessions and Accusations*, pp. 60-61.

insisting that magicians and diviners were in league with the devil.[15] Beginning late in the century, however, with the onset of the great witch-persecutions, the real witches, the village cunning folk, were muddled together with the Continental counterpart of the African night witches — the hags who worshipped the devil, danced naked at nocturnal orgies, and brought death and destruction for no reason other than maliciousness. When the persecutions ran out of steam at the end of the seventeenth century, the cunning folk were still there, as they had always been. In rural areas like the Auvergne and Anjou they continued to function through the eighteenth century and into the nineteenth.[16] In the 1850's, the archbishop of Orléans inquiries revealed that in the countryside both belief in witchcraft and resort to cunning men and women was as widespread as ever.[17]

The cunning folk are perhaps the most complete embodiment of the conglomeration of Roman Catholic doctrine, magical practices, animism, paganism, and common sense that were all to be found in the villagers' mental world, and which, as Jean Delumeau, François Lebrun, Christiane Marcilhacy, and Marc Leproux[18] have all shown, was often only nominally Christian. One pathway into that world is through the witchcraft trials of the sixteenth and seventeenth centuries, when a combination of village animosities and Christian zeal led to accusations of diabolical sorcery against rural practitioners of the cunning arts of healing and divination.

What I propose to do in the rest of this paper is to pick through what Hugh Trevor-Roper dismissed as "the mental rubbish of peasant credulity."[19] I should emphasize that my research so far has been limited to printed materials, and that it has ranged over all of France. It may be that there are important regional differences, linked to the persistence of pagan or heretical traditions, but at this point I am inclined to think that village witchcraft in France was more like that of England or Africa than it

---

[15] Henry Charles Lea, *Materials toward a History of Witchcraft*, ed. by Arthur C. Howland (Philadelphia, 1939), III, pp. 1286-1287. See also Kurt Baschwitz, *Hexen und Hexenprozesse: die Geschichte eines Massenwahns und seiner Bekämpfung* (Munich, 1963), p. 208; and Pierre Goubert, *The Ancien Regime: French Society 1600-1750*, trans. by Steve Cox (New York, 1973), p. 265.

[16] Abel Poitrineau, *La vie rurale en Basse Auvergne au XVIIIe siècle (1726-1789)* (Paris, 1965), pp. 617-620; and François Lebrun, *Les hommes et la mort en Anjou aux 17e et 18e siècles* (Paris, 1971), pp. 404-406.

[17] Christiane Marcilhacy, *Le diocèse d'Orléans au milieu du XIXe siècle: Les hommes et leurs mentalités*, pref. by G. Le Bras (Paris, 1964), pp. 263, 313-315, 371-373.

[18] Marc Leproux, *Dévotions et saints guérisseurs: Contributions au folklore charentais* (Paris, 1965). See also Harvey Mitchell, "Resistance to the Revolution in Western France," *Past and Present*, no. 63 (1974), pp. 97-99.

[19] Hugh Trevor-Roper, "The European Witch-craze of the Sixteenth and Seventeenth Centuries," in *The Crisis of the Seventeenth Century: Religion, the Reformation and Social Change* (New York, 1968), p. 116.

was unlike it. I have found no gnostics, no fertility cults, and no wave of peasant rebellion finding its outlet in devil worship.[20]

In an important study of late medieval witch trials published by the University of California Press, Richard Kieckhefer argues that the kinds of magic performed by cunning folk on the continent in the fourteenth and fifteenth centuries were "in large part not possessed but improvised, not traditional but spontaneous."[21] There are some echoes of the rites and practices of classical paganism, but they mingle with invocation of the saints, pilgrimages, and the use of the Christian sacraments for magical purposes. There are some spells that call on devils and werewolves, but in none of the trial records that Kieckhefer considers reliable are there any indications of the diabolism that was the main concern of inquisitors and demonologists.[22] In their improvisations, the cunning folk were inventing a kind of science to deal with a magical universe, working within the framework of a mental world that persisted into the seventeenth century and beyond.

In 1687, in the province of Brie, five shepherds and the sister of one of the five were condemned to death for having "by poisoning, impieties, sacrileges, profanations, and other witchcraft [*maléfices*]" caused the deaths of 395 sheep, seven horses, and eleven cows.[23] They appealed their sentences, and the local authorities had therefore to summarize the case for the Parliament of Paris. The trial of the six had been preceded by the condemnation to the galleys of the father of two of the accused, a shepherd named Pierre Hocque, for poisoning animals in the neighborhood of Pacy. When their animals continued to die, the *laboureurs* of the area were convinced that witchcraft and not just poison was at work. They managed to contact one of Hocque's fellow prisoners, and he in turn persuaded Hocque to agree to lift the spell. Hocque dictated a letter, to be sent by means of his son to a cunning man from Burgundy called Bras-de-Fer, directing him "to come to Pacy to raise the said Spell." Bras-de-Fer, formerly a shepherd and now a *laboureur*, set to work.

He identified the real culprit as Hocque's wife, who he said had aroused "the resentment of her husband and her children against the *intimé*."[24] Bras-de-Fer's efforts brought the mortality of the horses and cows to an end, the authorities said, but the sheep continued to die. Bras-de-Fer then

---

[20] I allude primarily to Jeffrey Burton Russell, *Witchcraft in the Middle Ages* (Ithaca, 1972); Ginzburg's masterpiece, *I Benandanti*; and the "Michelet tradition," expressed especially seductively in Emmanuel Le Roy Ladurie, *Les paysans du Languedoc* (Paris, 1966), ch. 5.

[21] Richard Kieckhefer, "Late Medieval Witchcraft Trials," p. 128 (typescript). Professor Kieckhefer kindly loaned me a copy of his manuscript before publication.

[22] Ibid., p. 59.

[23] *Factums, et arrest du Parlement de Paris contre des bergiers sorciers, executez depuis peu dans la Province de Brie* (Paris, 1695), pp. 5-6.

[24] Ibid., p. 9.

declared that their deaths were caused by a different spell. He would return after Christmas, at which time he would make a novena in order to try to counteract it.

In all of his efforts, Bras-de-Fer claimed to be guided by revelations from what he called "the spirit," whom the local authorities subsequently decided was really the devil. He now proceeded to try to identify and lift the spell that was killing the sheep. By means of a concoction of sheep's blood and holy water plus prayers and invocation, he discovered that the source of the problem was a "charge" called the Beau-Ciel-Dieu, consisting of sacramental wafers, animal excrement, holy water, and arsenic, placed in a pot together with scriptural passages and curses written on bits of paper and buried in the ground. The charge was activated, he said, by pouring vinegar on it.[25]

It was certainly an original kind of spell, and the authorities found what they considered to be confirmation when they found books on magic and quantities of arsenic and other drugs in the home of one of the shepherds Bras-de-Fer had named.

The account is rather unclear at this point. Apparently whatever was killing the sheep continued to kill them, and the farmers of the locality decided that what they faced was a plot on the part of the shepherds to destroy their livelihood, meanwhile getting money by claiming to cure the sick animals.[26] Hocque's sons were banished from the neighborhood, and three men — one of them the cunning man Bras-de-Fer — were sent to the galleys. His was a dangerous craft, since the power to deal with occult forces could be used for harm as well as for good. The authorities reported that when Bras-de-Fer's neighbors in Burgundy heard that he had been arrested, they wrote letters declaring the "uneasiness" and "fear" that they had had of him.[27]

Although I have found no other trial records quite like those involving Bras-de-Fer and the shepherds of Brie, I am convinced that it tells us more about the actuality of seventeenth century witchcraft than any number of confessions of sabbaths, night-flying, and obscene kisses on the devil's backside. One point especially needs more study, and that is the indication that the spells presupposed a degree of literacy. It is known that the itinerant book peddlers included books and pamphlets on magic in their wares, and records of other trials mention the use of books and manuscripts for magical purposes.[28] This may indicate that the barrier

[25] Ibid., p. 25.

[26] Ibid., p. 46.

[27] Ibid., p. 18.

[28] Francis Bavoux, "Les caractères originaux de la sorcellerie dans le Pays de Montbéliard," *Mémoires de la société pour l'histoire du droit et des institutions des anciens pays bourguignons, comtais et romands*, fasc. 20 (1958-59), p. 90; Jean Mellot, "La sorcellerie en Berry," *Tour Saint Jacques*, 11-12 (1957), p. 44; Robert Mandrou, *De la culture populaire au XVIIe et XVIIIe siècle: La*

between the culture of the lettered and that of the unlettered is less absolute, and the latter more recoverable, than has seemed to be the case.[29]

The nature of their work and their marginality within the community probably made shepherds unusually vulnerable to accusations of witchcraft. It is also quite possible that their relative isolation from the rest of rural society had facilitated the preservation of a popular culture that was strongly flavored with magic.[30] Thus the nature of their *métier*, their social marginality, and their economic importance in pastoral regions may all have been factors in the high incidence of witchcraft accusations in regions like the Alps, the Pyrenees, and Normandy which were dependent on grazing for their livelihood.

This is certainly the explanation for one of the last of the witch burnings in Normandy, in 1694. Something was killing the cows, and since their region depended on the production of butter and milk, the farmers around Fossé believed they faced economic destruction. One landowner, the sieur de Belleville, first tried to persuade the village curé to pray for the lifting of the curse. When he was refused, he went instead to a cunning man, "un homme fort extraordinaire," Pierre Du Fossé writes in his memoirs, who claimed to be authorized by the Church "to discover all the witches and all those who used witchcraft to harm men."[31] He told de Belleville that the villains were one of the local cowherds and three of his friends.

The immediate outcome was the sort of vigilante justice that was not at all uncommon in dealing with suspected witches. Two men were seized, taken to de Belleville's house, and tortured until they confessed. Only then were they turned over to the local authorities for trial. They were condemned, not for worshipping the devil (although that was also brought in) but for harming cows — killing them, drying up their milk, causing them to swell up or to abort.[32] Since veterinary science was at least as backward as medicine, all of these afflictions, I submit, could plausibly and almost necessarily be ascribed to witchcraft. The French peasant, like the Sudanese, would ask: why are *my* animals dying? who is responsible?

bibliothèque bleu de Troyes (Paris, 1964), p. 73; Jean Delumeau, "Ignorance religieuse et mentalité magique sous l'ancien régime," paper presented at the SFHS in 1972, p. 12 (typescript); Peyron, "Procès pour faits de sorcellerie à la fin du XVIIe siècle," *Bulletin de la société archéologique du Finistère*, 22 (1895), p. 91. See also Gene Brucker, "Sorcery in Early Renaissance Florence," *Studies in the Renaissance*, 10 (1963), pp. 7-24.

[29] Cf. Robert Mandrou, *Magistrats et sorciers en France au XVIIe siècle* (Paris, 1968), pp. 83-84. Kieckhefer, *Late Medieval Witchcraft Trials*, ch. 3, develops these possibilities persuasively for the earlier period.

[30] Christian Pfister, *Histoire de Nancy* (Paris, 1902-09), II, p. 570; and Julio Caro Baroja, *Inquisición, brujería y criptojudaismo* (Barcelona, 1970), pp. 223-224.

[31] Pierre Du Fossé, *Mémoires* (Rouen, 1879), IV, p. 143.

[32] Ibid., p. 152.

One affliction that commonly took people to the local cunning man or woman was sexual impotence. Since not even Masters and Johnson have managed to separate the physical from the psychological causes, it is hardly surprising that a belief in the possibility of impotence by bewitchment could easily lead to the fact of impotence. There are numerous indications that the belief in impotence by bewitchment, the *aiguillette*, was extremely widespread in sixteenth- and seventeenth-century France.[33]

At Mâcon at the end of the seventeenth century, there was a cunning man who made a specialty of curing impotence.[34] It was rumored that for several years past, most of the men married in the parish church in the faubourg of Saint-Clement had been made impotent by witchcraft. Some of those who believed themselves so afflicted had visited a man named Nicolas Chambard, formerly a vine-grower and now the keeper of Mâcon's municipal gate on the road to Lyons. He was reputed to be an honest, churchgoing man, who charged nothing for the practice of his art. He was said to possess both books containing occult lore and a staff made of walnut that had magical powers.

In 1690, a young shoemaker, seventeen and newly married, visited Chambard. He had been awakened on the night after his marriage with terrible pains in his stomach and believed himself bewitched. After several days of suffering, his father-in-law suggested that he ask the aid of the Church, through prayers to the saints appointed for afflictions such as his. He found some relief, but then a neighbor told him of the cunning man Chambard.

Chambard's treatment, as described in the complaint made against him sometime later by a priest who was a rival practitioner in the curing of impotence, was certainly singular. He first took up his walnut staff, opened his magic book, and placed beneath the staff a berry of sweet-smelling verbena. Having removed his jerkin and placed it over his arm, he paced back and forth across the room, "muttering some unknown words between his teeth." Then, suddenly, "an invisible force" caused his hat to fly off his head. Chambard announced that "the fall of his hat told him that all was accomplished." He showed the couple that the berry had

[33] Thomas Platter, *Journal of a Younger Brother: The Life of Thomas Platter as a Medical Student in Montpellier at the Close of the Sixteenth Century* trans. and ed. with an intro. by Sean Jennett (London, 1963), pp. 171-172; Alain Lottin, *Vie et mentalité d'un lillois sous Louis XIV* (Lille, 1968), p. 268; Jean Marx, *L'Inquisition en Dauphiné: Etude sur le developpement et la répression de l'hérésie et de la sorcellerie du XIVe siècle au début du règne de François Ier* (Paris, 1914), p. 586; and Kieckhefer, *Late Medieval Witchcraft Trials*, p. 229. There are no references to causing impotence in the calendar of accusations against alleged witches compiled by Macfarlane for Essex 1560-1680 (*Witchcraft in Tudor and Stuart England*, pp. 225-303).

[34] Gabriel Jeanton, "Un procès de sorcellerie à Mâcon au XVIIe siècle," *Revue de folklore français*, 2 (1931), pp. 317-327.

disappeared, and in its place there were two splinters, "which represented (he said) the cause of the evil . . . that he would infallibly cure if they were both determined [and] if they would piss together for nine consecutive days through a blessed ring that he could give them for this purpose."[35]

In his complaint against Chambard, the priest shows us just how the harmless symbolism of the rituals of the cunning folk had been transformed, during the previous century, into a satanic plot. He demanded of the local prosecutor that people such as Chambard, "detested by the Church as declared enemies," should not be allowed "to profane the sacraments themselves" by the practice of "infamous superstitions that tend visibly toward the cult of demons."[36] Brought before the prosecutor, Chambard insisted that he had done no harm and said that several priests had seen his magical books and saw nothing wrong with them. There is no record of how Chambard's case came out.

The belief in the magical properties of bodily excretions is as nearly universal as any idea can be. In the Vivarais, a cunning man identified the cause of a bewitchment by examining the urine of a victim. In Lorraine, one cured an affliction by prescribing a soup that included blood exuded from the victim's nose.[37]

I have tried to avoid using words like "panic" and "fear," because I want to emphasize that the function of witch beliefs was to offer answers and courses of action when neither science nor orthodox religion could provide them. In the tight, face-to-face world of the village, however, tensions and anxieties could break out in orgies of accusations and even mob violence. In what is perhaps the best full-length study of witchcraft at the local level in France, Francis Bavoux describes the outbreak that nearly decimated the village of Anjeux, in the witch-ridden province of Franche-Comté, in 1628. The crisis was exacerbated by the presence of a zealous official named Jean Clerc, a sort of bush league Boguet, a student of all the demonological tracts, eager to extirpate witches in his baillage and in the process to make a name for himself within the bureaucracy.[38]

As a result of village animosities and Clerc's zeal, in the little village of perhaps 300 people, accusations were made against a fifth of the popula-

---

[35] Ibid., p. 322.

[36] Ibid., p. 323.

[37] Jean Régné, "La sorcellerie en Vivarais et la répression inquisitoriale ou séculière du XVe au XVIIe siècle," in *Mélanges . . . offerts à Charles Bemont* (Paris, 1913), p. 484; and Oudin, "Un procès de sorcellerie au dix-septième siècle," *Mémoires de l'Académie des sciences, des lettres et des arts d'Amiens*, 35 (1888), p. 81. On the prevalence of similar magic in the south of Italy today, see Ernesto de Martino, *Sud e magia*, 2nd ed. (Milan, 1960), pp. 21-22.

[38] Francis Bavoux, *Hantises et diableries dans la terre abbatiale de Luxeuil d'un procès de l'Inquisition (1529) à l'épidémie démoniaque de 1628-1630*, pref. by Lucien Febvre (Monaco, 1956), p. 70. For interesting parallels to the Anjeux crisis, see Paul Boyer and Stephen Nissenbaum, *Salem Possessed: The Social Origins of Witchcraft* (Cambridge 1974).

tion. Tensions had apparently been building for generations between two clans, the Colas and the Vissots. When they fell to accusing one another, the arts of the cunning folk merged into the conventions of diabolism. One of the accused was said to have had a grandmother who healed animals but was also regarded as a witch. Complaints against another, a midwife, said that she had aroused the distrust and even the hatred of some of her patients. Gradually, accusations of everyday magic turned into descriptions of sabbaths. In his eagerness, Clerc admitted the testimony of children against their parents. Accusations led to counter-accusations, until it seemed that people were less concerned with defending themselves than with accusing still others. After one confrontation, Evotte Colas cried out to the fourteen-year-old girl who had accused her: "You have lied, daughter of a whore, witch, you have never been worth anything, neither you nor all your race."[39]

In Anjeux and the adjoining village, Clerc pronounced forty-two death sentences. Twenty-seven appealed to the Parlement at Dôle, which dismissed three sentences and reduced six others to banishment. Always wary of witchcraft cases, the magistrates were experiencing the same *crise de conscience* that their compeers across the Rhine and in Paris would experience a couple of generations later.[40]

I would comment in conclusion that research on French witchcraft at the popular level has only begun. We need the kind of microscopic studies that Boyer and Nissenbaum have done for Salem, Ginzburg for Friuli, Macfarlane for Essex, and that Monter has done for Franche-Comté. If we accept the anthropologists' hypothesis concerning the intimate connection between witch beliefs and village life, that will help us to comprehend the genesis and survival of witchcraft, but it is not an explanation for the waves of witch-accusations that do seem to have erupted in France in the century after 1580. Were these generated by the propaganda of inquisitors and demonologists? Were they also a reflection of heightened social tensions within localities and within regions? We have a long way to go.

If we historians of popular culture are to be good social anthropologists as well, we will have to try to get as much information on what people *did* as on what they said. In the case of witchcraft, we cannot ignore the confessions, many of them preserved in the demonological tracts, but we must see how well the picture of witchcraft presented there conforms to the picture of witchcraft extrapolated from local gossip and suspicion, which

---

[39] 'Tu as menti, fille de couchot, genalche . . ." (Bavoux , *Hantises et diableries*, p. 111).
[40] Ibid., pp. 128-130; Mandrou, *Magistrats et sorciers*, pp. 14-16; and H.C. Erik Midelfort , *Witch Hunting in Southwestern Germany 1562-1684: The Social and Intellectual Foundations* (Stanford, 1972), pp. 191-192.

surfaced (sometimes) when an accusation was made. For what people *did* was to accuse one another, often after consulting with cunning folk.

The rituals employed by the cunning folk, and those ascribed to the witches, will tell us a great deal about the mental universe of the western European peasantry in the early modern era, but I doubt that we will find either the survival of the doctrines of antique paganism or evidence that the fertility rites Carlo Ginzburg so magnificently described in the Veneto had significant resonances elsewhere.[41] We need to focus on the local or, at most, the provincial level, since those were the limits of a peasant's mental — and physical — world.

In trying to comprehend the waves of prosecutions of the late sixteenth and seventeenth centuries, we need to move from abstractions like "craze," "panic," and "fear" to specifics of social experience. How, for example, were witchcraft prosecutions related to epidemics of disease, wars, or religious upheavals? There are many facets of legal history that need to be explored, including the training and powers of judges and inquisitors, the kinds of evidence they admitted, and the restraints on local and seigneurial prosecutions imposed by the appellate jurisdiction of the parlements.

Historians have made an impressive beginning in the last decade toward an understanding of European witchcraft. What some of us have learned from the social anthropologists is that witchcraft must be seen within its context, the face-to-face society of the village, and that its comprehension must be sought in that context, not in religious or folkloric traditions.

[41] For a contrary view, see Mircea Eliade, "Some Observations on European Witchcraft," *History of Religions*, 14 (February 1975), pp. 149-172. I owe the reference to my colleague Harry Krebs.

4

Beyond Port-Royal:
Popular Jansenism in Eighteenth-Century Paris*

B. ROBERT KREISER

Periodically throughout the history of Christianity individuals and groups have charged the established Church with abandoning its original sanctity and holy responsibilities and with thereby failing to satisfy the passionately felt spiritual needs of the pious faithful. Such criticisms have sometimes turned from isolated protests and quests for renewal into thoroughgoing millenarian movements, frequently under the guidance or inspiration of some charismatic religious figure. Often as not these attempts at spiritual regeneration have remained short-lived, local affairs, without important or far-reaching consequences. Occasionally, however, they have managed to survive for relatively long periods of time, to attract a diverse and widespread following, and to attain considerable historical significance in the process. One such religious movement emerged in France in the second quarter of the "enlightened" eighteenth century.

On May 1, 1727, in the midst of the fierce controversy raging over the papal bull *Unigenitus* (1713), a saintly and revered Jansenist deacon named François de Pâris died in Paris. Two days later, when he was interred in the tiny cemetery of Saint-Médard at the foot of Rue Mouffetard, crowds of people from every station in society, but most of them from among the pious *menu peuple* who craved new forms of spirituality, began to flock to his grave. Here they witnessed the seemingly miraculous healings of apparently incurable diseases posthumously performed by this virtuous, holy man. As the crowds increased in the years that followed, it became clear that his name would not sink into oblivion. Indeed, by September 1731, the number of visitors frequenting his tomb, whether

* Mr. Kreiser was awarded the American Catholic Historical Association's Peter Guilday Prize of 1974 for this article. Research for it was supported, in part, by a grant from the American Philosophical Society. It was published in *The Catholic Historical Review* 61 (July 1975), under the title, "Religious Enthusiasm in Early Eighteenth-Century Paris: The Convulsionaries of Saint Medard." We are grateful for the permission to include it here.

in search of miraculous cures and from a profound sense of piety, or merely out of curiosity, had grown to unmanageable proportions. From the relatively calm and simple scenes of the worship services and the occasional miracles, the situation at Saint-Médard had progressed — or degenerated — to the wilder, often frenzied spectacle of people in convulsions, people who claimed to be inspired by the Holy Spirit through the intercession of M. de Pâris.[1]

By themselves these religious enthusiasts could hardly have posed a very serious threat to the established order, nor did they have any particular desire to do so. In the meantime, however, the opponents of the bull *Unigenitus* (the *appellants* or *anticonstitutionnaires*) had taken a considerable interest in the nascent Pâris cult. Having seen their forces considerably reduced since the beginning of Cardinal Fleury's ministry, many of the *anticonstitutionnaires*, like their Jansenist predecessors in the days of the Holy Thorn miracles, were eager to claim divine support and legitimation for their cause from the *appellant* deacon's posthumous cures. While *appellant* theologians began publishing numerous tracts and treatises exploiting the Pâris miracles, their sympathizers among the parish clergy encouraged the faithful to participate in the devotions at M. Pâris' tomb.[2] By their actions they helped to draw the cult into the stormy arena

[1] For a detailed analysis of the origins and early development of the cult of François de Pâris, see B. Robert Kreiser, "Miracles and Convulsions in Paris, 1727-1737: An Episode in the Politics of Religion during the *Ancien Régime*" (Ph.D. dissertation, University of Chicago, 1971), chs. 2-3. Most of the previous work on this subject — what little there has been — has come from utterly unsympathetic, indeed hostile, authors, both lay and clerical, who have uncritically accepted and perpetuated the contempt and disdain of eighteenth-century critics of the Pâris cult. With very few exceptions they have viewed the convulsionary movement as proof of the degeneration and decadence of the so-called "Jansenist movement" and have tended to dismiss the convulsionaries as merely an odd sect of bizarre and fanatical Jansenists, whose "antics" were of little or no consequence. Their one-sided interpretations have resulted, in large part, from a failure to utilize fully, carefully, or systematically the extraordinarily rich mass and variety of contemporary documents — memoirs, police records, civil and ecclesiastical decrees, pamphlets and manifestoes, private and official correspondence, newspaper reports, trial minutes, accounts of miracles with supporting testimony, eyewitness descriptions of convulsionary *séances*, discourses and prophecies — which have survived in at least a dozen Parisian archives and libraries and in numerous other repositories throughout the rest of France and even abroad. The present study, and the larger monograph of which it will form a part (Princeton University Press), is based primarily on a thorough re-examination and re-appraisal of these sources.

[2] On the theological writings, see Kreiser, "Miracles," ch. 3, passim; Joseph Dedieu, "L'agonie du jansénisme," *Revue d'histoire de l'Eglise de France*, 14 (1928), pp. 161-214; and also J.-R. Armogathe, "A propos des miracles de Saint-Médard: Les preuves de Carré de Montgeron et le positivisme des Lumières," *Revue de l'histoire des religions*, 180 (1971), pp. 135-160. On the very active involvement of the parish clergy in support of the Pâris cult — whether demonstrated through sermons and harangues delivered from various church pulpits or by the example of their own frequent attendance in great numbers at Saint-Médard — see Kreiser, "Miracles," pp. 169-174, 177-180, and passim.

of contemporary religious politics and to transform the events at Saint-Médard into a national *cause célèbre*. In the eyes of the civil and ecclesiastical establishment, the unauthorized Pâris cult had thus become too great a public nuisance and too vexing a religious scandal to permit its adherents to continue their observances undisturbed.

Various official measures were taken to put a halt to these activities. The police, who had been keeping the cemetery under constant surveillance for months, subjected the faithful to frequent harassment and numerous arrests.[3] The *constitutionnaire* curé of Saint-Médard, the zealous and unpopular Father Coëffrel, attempted to stop, or at least to impede, their religious observances at his church, denouncing François de Pâris as a damned heretic, defacing or tearing down some of the placards, scrawled prayers, and devotional petitions which the faithful had posted on the walls, and knocking over or extinguishing candles burning in M. Pâris' honor.[4] On several occasions Archbishop Vintimille denounced their activities and threatened them with excommunication if they persisted; he also repeatedly and adamantly refused to undertake a full-scale canonical investigation into the dozens of miracles which had occurred throughout his diocese since 1727.[5] The royal government, with Vintimille's concurrence and frequently on his urging, issued scores of *lettres de cachet* ordering the dismissal, exile, or imprisonment of many outstanding parish priests and confessors for their *anticonstitutionnaire* beliefs and activities, including those on behalf of the Pâris cult.[6] Finally, the Holy See, which had long been pressuring Fleury and Vintimille to stop the popular "superstitions" and "sacrilegious observances" at M. Pâris' grave, ordered the public

---

[3] At least one police officer had been stationed near Saint-Médard since 1730 and made daily reports on the activities occurring in and around the parish church and cemetery. The reports for this period are in Bibliothèque de l'Arsenal (hereafter, B. Ars.), 10, 196 (Archives de la Bastille). A complete list of those imprisoned in the Bastille may be found in Frantz Funck-Brentano, ed., *Les lettres de cachet à Paris* (Paris, 1903).

[4] On Coëffrel's strained relations with his parishioners and especially with the *marguilliers*, or churchwardens, of the parish, see Marcel Brongniart, *La paroisse Saint-Médard au faubourg Saint-Marceau* (Paris, 1951), pp. 73-74 and passim, and Albert Mousset, *L'étrange histoire des convulsionnaires de Saint-Médard* (Paris, 1953), pp. 81-88.

[5] See Charles-Gaspard-Guillaume de Vintimille du Luc, *Mandement de Msgr. l'Archeveque de Paris, au sujet d'un écrit qui a pour titre: Dissertation sur les miracles, et en particulier sur ceux qui ont été opérés au tombeau de M. de Pâris en l'église de S.-Médard de Paris* (July 15, 1731), a decree which had little effect. Vintimille's great fears about the Pâris cult and about the insubordination and disobedience of his diocesans who persisted in their observances are revealed most clearly in the remarkable correspondence which the archbishop maintained throughout this period with Cardinal Fleury, his longtime friend and benefactor. See Bibliothèque Mazarine, 2357, especially the letters after May 1731.

[6] See Funck-Brentano, *Les lettres de cachet à Paris*, passim; and *Nouvelles ecclésiastiques, ou Mémoires pour servir à l'histoire de la Constitution "Unigenitus"* (hereafter, *NNEE*), 1730-1731, passim.

burning of a pious biography that had extolled the saintly virtues and *appellant* beliefs of the revered deacon.[7] Meanwhile, despite the combined opposition of Rome, Versailles, the Paris police, and the archdiocesan and parish authorities — virtually the entire temporal and spiritual establishment — the many hundreds of followers of M. Pâris managed, amid a mounting sense of frustration and anxiety, to pursue their religious services and devotions virtually uninterrupted. On January 27, 1732, however, after all other efforts at dealing with these people had proved unavailing, the royal government issued a decree ordering the cemetery closed — and thus contributed a major impetus to the subsequent development of the cult.[8]

The royal ordinance, executed by the Paris police on January 29, made an immediate and powerful impact upon the crowds that had been so assiduously attending the cemetery and worshiping at the tomb of François de Pâris. A report in the *Nouvelles ecclésiastiques*, the *appellants'* clandestine gazette, described the pathetic scene among the shocked and troubled people at Saint-Médard. They gathered around the little parish church, consternation and despair visible on nearly every face. Some were moaning or sobbing; others stood in stunned and disbelieving silence. This pitiful, moving spectable seems even to have touched the large contingent of police officers charged with watching over the area as a precaution against potential disturbances — although pity never deterred these guards from effectively carrying out their duty.[9] Indeed, the ominous and intimidating presence of the police no doubt served to deter large numbers, priests and worshipers alike, from publicly venting their true feelings of hostility and frustration.[10] According to the *Nouvellistes* and

[7] A French transcription of the Inquisition's decree is reprinted in *NNEE*, September 17, 1731, p. 179. The decree concluded by threatening with excommunication all who owned, read, or printed the book in question, *La vie de M. de Pâris, diacre* (Brussels, 1731), generally attributed to the Oratorian Father Pierre Boyer.

[8] The royal ordinance, the text of which is in François-André Isambert, et al., eds., *Recueil général des anciennes lois françaises* (Paris, 1830), XXI, 369, brought the memorable response: "De par le roi,'Défense à Dieu/De faire miracles,/En ce lieu." These immortal lines of graffiti, penned by some anonymous wit, constitute the most lasting commentary to have survived from the history of the Pâris cult.

[9] *NNEE*, February 17, 1732, pp. 31-32; René Hérault (lieutenant-general of police) to Fleury, January 19, 1732, Archives des Affaires Etrangères (hereafter, AAE), Mémoires et Documents: Ile de France 1599, fols. 285-286; (Hérault?) to (Germain-Louis de Chauvelin, Keeper of the Seals?), January 29, 1732, AAE, Mémoires et Documents: France, 1274, fols. 124-125; Journal of De Lisle, *greffier* in the Parlement of Paris, Archives nationales (hereafter, AN), U-377, January 29, 1732, no fol.; Edmond-Jean-François Barbier, *Chronique de la régence et du règne de Louis XV (1718-1763)* (Paris, 1857), II, pp. 242-243, January 1732; Mathieu Marais, *Journal et mémoires sur la Régence et le règne de Louis XV (1715-1737)* (Paris, 1863-1868), January 31, 1732, IV, pp. 335-336.

[10] Hérault to Fleury, January 29, 1732, AAE, Mémoires et Documents: Ile de France, 1599, fol. 285.

other eyewitness accounts, submission and patience rather than tumultuous uproar constituted the predominant reaction among the faithful.[11]

To the convulsionaries (as the devoted followers of M. Pâris were thereafter called), the closing of the cemetery merely capped a long series of unjust and repressive measures directed against them by the civil and ecclesiastical authorities. Even before the royal ordinance the adherents of the Pâris cult had endured much adversity. In denying them access to their sacred shrine, however, the government struck these pious souls an especially severe and direct personal blow that seemed to threaten their cult's very existence. For most of these people, therefore, the period after January 1732 was a time of profound psychological crisis and emotional strain, a period of major readjustment. Punished and reviled for their extraordinary love of and devotion to François de Pâris, regarded as criminals or worse by the State, effectively isolated within the Church, and forcibly deprived and dispossessed of a major source of spiritual sustenance and consolation, the adherents of the Pâris cult found themselves in a difficult and trying situation. Under these stressful circumstances a dramatic transformation took place in the fundamental emphasis, character, and purpose of their religious devotions. Longing for collective deliverance from their present misfortunes, for an effective outlet for their repressed, undischarged frustrations, and for a reassuring message of future hope and consolation, many of the followers of M. Pâris turned eagerly to the quasi-millenarian ideology that was introduced into convulsionary circles at this time by a group of *anticonstitutionnaire* priests and theologians.[12]

Over the centuries, in the wake of innumerable social and religious crises, apocalyptic lore had been analyzed, reinterpreted, and vulgarized, often by anonymous and wholly obscure individuals. The apocalyptic tradition, though long since ruled out of official doctrine, had persistently retained its place in what Norman Cohn has described as "the obscure underworld of popular religion."[13] Emotionally charged eschatological

---

[11] *NNEE*, February 17, 1732, p. 32.

[12] Although it is difficult to determine the precise makeup of this influential group of *appellants*, they would seem to have come from among the same circle of ecclesiastics who had already done so much to prepare the followers of François de Pâris to interpret the miracles as validation for the *anticonstitutionnaire* cause and had been responsible for overseeing the "organisation merveilleuse" at the church and in the cemetery of Saint-Médard. See *NNEE*, August 10, 1731, p. 159; *Histoire des miracles et du culte de M. Pâris. Avec les persécutions suscitées à sa mémoire et aux malades qui ont eu recours à lui. Pour servir de suite à la Vie de ce saint diacre* (1734), pp. iv-v; *Réflexions sur les miracles que Dieu opère au tombeau de M. Pâris* (n.d.), p. 33; and Jean-Baptiste-Raymond de Pavie de Fourquevaux, *Catéchisme historique et dogmatique sur les contestations qui divisent maintenant l'Eglise* (Nancy, 1750-1768), IV, p. 372.

[13] *The Pursuit of the Millennium* (New York, 1961), p. 14. In addition to the Cohn work, there is a large and growing body of literature on apocalyptic and millenarian movements, of which I have found the following particularly useful: Sylvia Thrupp, ed., *Millennial Dreams*

fantasies, derived in particular from the Book of Revelation, but also from the prophet Daniel and the other Old Testament prophets, had traditionally spoken directly to the oppressed and the unprivileged, the frustrated and the discontented. These mystifying apocalyptic visions, full of fantastic, sometimes savage, imagery, held out the hope of ultimate compensation for current adversity and collective deliverance in a new age, one in which God would display His mercy to the persecuted and His vengeful justice to their enemies, whom He would cast down. Indeed, it was primarily in and through elements of this apocalyptic tradition — in a new and modified eighteenth-century Jansenist[14] version — that the convulsionaries would find their greatest inspiration, justification, and consolation.

For over two decades a number of prominent *anticonstitutionnaires*, initially aroused by the arbitrary, wanton destruction of Port-Royal, had been employing the traditional method of "figurative" or "symbolic" exegesis of Scripture in use since the days of St. Paul. In developing these exegetical principles and applying them specifically to the controversy surrounding the bull *Unigenitus*, these theologians followed in particular the influential and prolific Jean-Baptiste Le Sesne des Ménilles, abbé d'Etemare, lecturer at the famous Oratorian seminary of Saint-Magloire in Paris, whose numerous disciples and supporters included theologians, bishops, and lower clergy, among them François de Pâris himself.[15] These "figurists," as they were called, were especially interested in the eschatological aspects of Scripture and in the application of various millenarian predictions to the contemporary state of the Church. Meeting in

in Action (The Hague, 1962); Peter Worsley, *The Trumpet Shall Sound*, 2nd. ed. (New York, 1968); Henri Desroche, *Dieux d'hommes: Dictionnaire des Messianismes et Millénarismes de l'ère chrétienne* (Paris-The Hague, 1969); Eric Hobsbawm, *Primitive Rebels* (Manchester, 1959); Bryan R. Wilson, "Millennialism in Comparative Perspective," *Comparative Studies in Society and History*, 6 (1963), pp. 93-114; Yonina Talmon, "Pursuit of the Millennium: The Relation between Religious and Social Change," *European Journal of Sociology*, 3 (1962), pp. 125-148; and her "Millenarian Movements," ibid., 7 (1966), pp. 159-200.

[14] One can begin to appreciate the changes in character and emphasis which the Jansenist movement had undergone by the eighteenth century if one recalls the basic hostility to chiliasm and millenarianism that had traditionally been associated with Port-Royal. For a brief analysis of this question, see Alfred-Félix Vaucher, *Une célébrité oubliée: le P. Manuel de Lacunza y Diaz (1731-1801)* (Collonges, sous-Salève, 1941), pp. 163-164, n. 350.

[15] There is a need for a careful and thorough study of *anticonstitutionnaire* "Figurism." The available secondary literature, inadequate and often rather superficial and misleading, includes E. Mangenot, "Figurisme," *Dictionnaire de théologie catholique*, V², cols. 2229-2304; Roger Mercier, *La réhabilitation de la nature humaine (1700-1750)* (Villemonble, 1960), p. 283; Dedieu, "L'agonie du jansénisme," pp. 199-200 and passim; and Edmond Préclin and Eugène Jarry, *Les luttes politiques et doctrinales aux XVIIe et XVIIIe siècles*, Vol. XIX of *Histoire de l'Eglise depuis les origines jusqu'à nos jours*, ed. by J.-B. Duroselle and Eugène Jarry (Paris, 1955-1956), I, pp. 250-251. More reliable, but still not very satisfactory: Desroche, *Dieux d'hommes*, pp. 14, 110, 115, 117-118, 134, 155, 168, 186; and Vaucher, *Une célébrité oubliée*, passim.

small study-groups at Saint-Magloire and elsewhere, they attempted, through careful examination of and meditation upon the sacred texts, to penetrate beyond the most obscure and enigmatic passages, to the actual Biblical prefigurations of religious events down to the present and into the future.[16] Their work revealed striking parallels between cataclysmic incidents and situations described or announced in Scripture and those currently convulsing the Church in early eighteenth-century France. They claimed, in particular, that the destruction of Port-Royal, the promulgation of the bull *Unigenitus*, and the series of royal and ecclesiastical pronouncements issued in support of it were evident portents of the universal apostasy at the end of time which had been proclaimed by the Old Testament prophets and predicted by St. Paul. They also became increasingly preoccupied with reviving the ancient theme of the return of the prophet Elijah, the eschatological precursor whose mysterious advent was traditionally interpreted as a prelude to the conversion of the Jews, a herald of the coming of Jesus Christ, and an announcement of the imminence of the "Last Days."[17]

Although these "figurist" ideas and theological musings had already been circulating in *anticonstitutionnaire* circles for some twenty years, they had until recently reached no more than a limited audience. Before the mid-1720's only a few of the major exegetical works had been published, the others remaining in manuscript form.[18] But even after the appearance in print of a large number of important treatises and weighty tomes, the "figurist" viewpoint had remained confined to a fairly narrow group of theologians and regular and secular clergy.[19] In the early 1730's, however, a handful of *anticonstitutionnaire* writers, with the ardent support of a substantial group of *appellant* priests who had long been active participants in the Pâris cult, began a concerted effort to adapt the

[16] Two other leading *appellants* who, along with d'Etemare, made a major contribution to the early development of "figurist" exegesis were the venerable Father Jacques-Joseph Duguet, an Oratorian and a friend and confidant of Arnauld and Nicole, and his disciple and colleague, Jacques-Vincent Bidal d'Asfeld. At the parish church of Saint-Roch between 1710 and 1721 Duguet and d'Asfeld conducted numerous "conférences ecclésiastiques" in which they offered doctrinal instruction on "l'intelligence des Ecritures saintes." They were later to split with d'Etemare and many of the other *anticonstitutionnaires* over the question of the convulsionaries.

[17] D'Etemare's chief works include the *Principes pour l'intelligence de l'Ecriture sainte* (1712) and the *Explication de quelques prophéties touchant la conversion future des Juifs* (1724). Among the numerous treatises published during this period on the coming of Elijah, perhaps the most important was that of Alexis Desessarts, *De l'avènement d'Elie*, 2 vols. (1734-1735).

[18] Most of Duguet's works, for example, were published posthumously (that is, after 1733), while d'Etemare's *Explication de l'Apocalypse*, written in collaboration with two fellow *appellants*, Nicolas Le Gros and Paul Mérault, was not even published until 1866.

[19] Joseph Dedieu, "Le désarroi janséniste pendant la période du quesnellisme," in Victor Carrière, ed., *Introduction aux études d'histoire ecclésiastique locale* (Paris, 1934-1940), III, p. 579.

"figurist" writings to a less learned public.[20] They hoped to make the chaotic sequences, esoteric prophecies, and cryptic symbolism contained in the apocalyptic writings more understandable and immediate to the faithful adherents of M. Pâris. By the spring of 1732 the convulsionaries afforded them a potentially receptive audience.

Eventually exploited in justification of the convulsionaries' own prophetic visions and bizarre activities, the controversial "figurist" exegesis also formed the basis of the movement's newly found conception of its extraordinarily vital mission to effect nothing less than a total religious renewal of the Church. In this time of patent injustice, moral corruption, and spiritual bankruptcy, the convulsionaries began to believe that they had been specifically chosen to combat the malevolent forces in the ecclesiastical establishment and entrusted with the responsibility of restoring the Church to the pure faith and simple virtue of the apostolic age. They came to feel that they had received a divine call to be the messengers of redemption and regeneration, and that their appointment to such an important, awesome task had clear antecedents and precedents which could be traced back to the very sources of Christianity. The holy document of the primitive Church itself seemed unambiguously to define their role, their redemptive mission.[21] Like the first Christians and the early martyrs, fellow heroes and defenders of the true faith with whom they increasingly identified themselves, the convulsionaries determined to remain steadfast in the face of persecution and to carry on the struggle — and to continue practicing their devotions — even if these efforts required their own ultimate martyrdom.[22] Although they never managed to produce any formal or well-coordinated program or plan of attack for achieving these goals, the convulsionaries' growing sense of common purpose and collective mission gave their movement a more positive focus and a more definite direction than it had ever had before January 1732. At the same time, such beliefs did much to shape the group identity and self-consciousness which developed within the movement in

[20] See, for example, *NNEE*, November 25, 1731, p. 227, and Jean-Baptiste-Raymond de Pavie de Fourquevaux, *Introduction abrégée à l'intelligence des prophéties de l'Ecriture* (1731). The first edition of Fourquevaux's *Catéchisme historique et dogmatique* (cited above, n. 12) also appeared at this time, published in 1729-1730.

[21] Though not cited by them specifically, I. Cor. 1:26-29 and 12:27-28, along with other similar Biblical passages, must have been very familiar to the convulsionaries and their ecclesiastical supporters and provided them with descriptions of early evangelical communities which closely resembled their own.

[22] A knowledge of the ordeals suffered by many of their brethren, past and present, was transmitted through pious biographies, necrologies, and pamphlets, as well as by oral tradition, and provided the convulsionaries with their own equivalent of a martyrology. See, for example, Pierre Barral, *Appellans célèbres* (1753); René Cerveau, *Nécrologe des plus célèbres défenseurs et confesseurs de la Vérité du 18e siècle*, 2 vols. (1760); and the numerous obituaries published in the *Nouvelles ecclésiastiques* throughout this period.

subsequent months and years.

Far from stifling the convulsionaries' tenacious dedication to the memory of François de Pâris or putting an end to their observances in his honor, the closing of the cemetery thus served only to strengthen and deepen their commitment. What is more, by forcing the convulsionaries to disperse, the royal ordinance had the unanticipated effect of further spreading the cult and rousing its adherents to even greater heights of religious enthusiasm. Beyond Saint-Médard, in the months which followed the interdiction of the cemetery, alternative holy sites proliferated; the presence of relics from M. Pâris, including dirt from his tomb and water from a well which had once belonged to him, inspired religious services and practices which were often far more spectacular, bizarre, and controversial than those that had been witnessed at the deacon's grave. Largely in an effort to escape police surveillance, the convulsionaries — like the first Christians, intense and insecure — formed themselves into small bands or "cells" and began to hold clandestine meetings at private homes and religious houses[23] throughout the city. Joining together for mutual comfort and support, they patterned these embattled conventicles after the model of the Apostolic Church, and, in quite conscious emulation of their sacred forebears, turned these places into "domestic churches, places of worshsip and prayer, and, so to speak, stations of the little cemetery of Saint-Médard."[24] Scattered about though they were, each of the convulsionary groups maintained some kind of contact, usually informal and irregular, with the others. The city of Paris, an anonymous writer declared, had been turned into one large temple.[25]

While the convulsionaries did not engage in any active campaign of evangelism to recruit converts to their cause, they quite openly welcomed new "members," fellow *amis* (and *amies*) *de la vérité*, to join in their observances and to share in the experience of spiritual renewal.[26] Despite a sectarian sense that they constituted a divinely chosen elect, a gathered

---

[23] The cult flourished in several monastic settings in Paris, particularly in female orders and congregations, including the convent of Sainte-Agathe, the Sisters of the Visitation, the Ursulines, and the Sisters of Sainte-Marthe.

[24] *Pensées sur les prodiges de nos jours* (1734), p. 9. Similar references to such "petites églises domestiques" are found in Frère Hilaire (Chevalier de Blaru, convulsionary) to Bishop Jean Soanen, November 29, 1733, Rijksarchief, Utrecht, Ancien Fonds d'Amersfoort, Port Royal 6439.

[25] *Entretiens sur les miracles* (1733), p. 12.

[26] Testimony of Femme La Coste, convulsionary, Archives nationales (hereafter, AN), Parlement Civil (Minutes), X-1b 9690 ("Procès des Convulsionnaires"). The four large cartons of documents, X-1b 9690-9693, which comprise the record of the *procès* conducted in the Paris Parlement beginning in January 1735, collectively constitute one of the most valuable sources available for penetrating directly into the convulsionary milieu. These cartons contain thousands of pages of parlementary interrogations as well as innumerable papers and other effects seized at various convulsionary conventicles.

remnant charged with special responsibilities, the convulsionaries do not seem to have believed that they were to remain limited in size by divine command. They never asserted an absolute exclusiveness and precluded no one from becoming a full-fledged participant in their religious devotions. Most new adherents were specifically "sponsored" or invited by someone already active in the group and were thus accepted without the imposition of any prerequisites of entry. However, as a precaution against the infiltration of police spies or of other unfriendly or undesirable intruders, anyone who sought to gain admittance on his own was frequently required to know a certain secret signal or code word.[27] Even so, there was no covenant or oath of membership to which the individual had to adhere in order to "join" the movement, no rites of initiation, no strict doctrinal or specific behavioral standards of admission to the fellowship, no long or intensive process of "socializing" newcomers. There were, moreover, no tests of good faith, no sanctions against those who contravened the movement's fundamental precepts, no specific grounds or means of expulsion. On the other hand, considering the risks incurred in belonging to such a proscribed group, continued membership and active participation presumably implied a fairly intense ideological, doctrinal, or spiritual commitment as well as a strong attachment to the fellowship itself.

A very mixed company — persons of every age, condition, and temperament — was attracted to the convulsionary meetings.[28] Although a substantial majority of the adherents came from among the *menu peuple*, the composition of the movement was far from homogeneous. At one time or another the convulsionaries could count among their number priests and bishops, regular and secular clergy, nobles of the robe and sword, merchants and financiers, cultivated men of letters and royal functionaries, lawyers and notaries, medical doctors and theologians, many of whom provided the constant support, protection, and guiding influence which helped to sustain the movement.[29] Social diversity notwithstanding, status within the various conventicles derived exclusively

[27] According to the testimony of Claude Chambon (AN, X-1b 9690), "il falloit avoir à la main un papier roullé"; cf. Barbier *Chronique de Louis XV*, II, p. 385, February 1733.

[28] *Recherche de la Vérité sur l'oeuvre des convulsions* (1733), p. 8; *Lettre d'un ecclésiastique de province à un de ses amis, où il donne une idée abrégée de l'oeuvre des convulsions* (1733), pp. 16-17. The available sources unfortunately do not permit the kind of precise sociological breakdown one would hope to be able to provide. There are similar problems involved in trying to determine the number of people actually involved in the movement: see below, n. 45.

[29] Some of these people offered their homes both as sanctuaries from the police and as places of worship. Others used their influence to intercede with the police on behalf of convulsionaries who had already been arrested. They also provided substantial material assistance to those in need.

from the individual's contribution to the group itself — without reference to the noble and honorific ranks, titles, and privileges which obtained in the society at large. On entering into the *oeuvre* everyone adopted or was given a pseudonym, Soeur "X" or Frère "Y," not only to preserve anonymity and thereby perhaps escape detection by the police — which was naturally essential for the continued survival of the movement — but also to sustain the sect's fraternal and egalitarian spirit.[30] Some of the names were borrowed from Scripture, others drawn from the hallowed tradition of Port-Royal. Still other names derived from distinctive physical traits of the individual or from important personal reminiscences or events in his life.[31] Whatever the source of their names, many of these people, previously complete strangers, continued to know and to address one another only by such appellations, even after long and close personal contact in convulsionary circles. Any distinctions among the brethren were founded on a differentiation of the "dons charismatiques" bestowed by God upon the individual convulsionary and of the particular services, whether material or spiritual, which each member provided to or performed for the collective body.[32] The convulsionaries even elevated the religious standing of women, welcoming them as full and active participants on a basis of complete equality.[33] In short, unlike either the Gallican Church or the French state, neither social nor legal status — not even gender — counted for very much. From the highest noble to the lowliest and most humble of

[30] It is not clear whether any religious ceremony — some kind of second or "rebaptism" — accompanied the adoption of these new names, but in any event this act apparently marked the individual's admission into the fellowship and served to symbolize the beginning of his personal renewal and "resurrection" and his dedication to the convulsionary mission.

[31] Some examples: Soeur La Croix (Marie Gault) was so named because she was born on Good Friday; Soeur Roch (Suzanne Cellier) received her name because she had her first convulsions on the day of St. Roch; "La Soeur au Petit Pain" (Dame Roger) was so called because "elle fait des petits pains, dans lesquels elle met des reliques de M. de Pâris et autres, et qu'elle distribue à toutes les convulsionnaires . . . pour guérir les malades" (Testimony of Soeur Virginie, AN, X-1b 9690). Of course, their use of pseudonyms could give rise to a great deal of confusion, especially for the historian, since some names were used by more than one person, while some people — mostly as an added precaution against identification or capture by the police — went by more than one appellation.

[32] Cf. Bibliothèque Nationale (hereafter, BN), Nouvelles Acquisitions Françaises, 4262, fol. 82, and passim. Held in especially high regard were the so-called "quatre grands frères": "Ce nom leur a été donné parce qu'ils ont prononcé les plus beaux discours et ont annoncé les plus grands événements et non parce qu'ils occupoient un rang [supérieur]" (ibid., fol. 83).

[33] The fact that women constituted a majority in convulsionary society may account in part for their spiritual elevation. However, R.A. Knox has made the observation — worth pursuing — that, "From the Montanist movement onwards, the history of enthusiasm is largely a history of female emancipation" (*Enthusiasm* [Oxford, 1951], p. 20). For similar developments in the English Civil War, see the article by Keith Thomas, "Women and the Civil War Sects," in Trevor Aston, ed., *Crisis in Europe, 1560-1660* (New York, 1965), pp. 317-340.

the laboring poor, all were equally members of the *justes*, the *élus*, and called one another *frère* and *soeur*.

In the absence of any formally institutionalized structure or organization, it was these immediate personal bonds and close emotional ties among the adherents within each group as well as their intimate sharing of religious experiences which seem to have been major sources of the movement's fundamental unity and cohesion. Typically,[34] the convulsionary meetings brought together anywhere from a handful to two dozen or so pious devotees,[35] some of whom, in preparation for these sessions and in imitation of François de Pâris, had already undergone long periods of austere penitence, intensive mortifications, and excessive fasting. These small bands of convulsionaries would ordinarily gather at the same place several times a week and at a fixed hour of the day, usually in the evenings, the sessions lasting from several hours to perhaps as long as one or two full days.[36] Since no one was required to pledge exclusive allegiance or attachment to any particular group, individual *frères* and *soeurs* could (and did) feel free to attend several different conventicles each week. In any event, the *séance* was not intended as an all-consuming activity. The communal solidarity of these people did not demand that the participants remain together when they were not holding worship services, nor was it built upon a total rejection of the world outside. The convulsionaries had no particular obsession about withdrawing or holding themselves aloof and segregated from an "unredeemed" society at large. With few exceptions,[37] most of them continued to pursue their normal, mundane activities, gathering together as a community only to participate in their

---

[34] What follows is a composite based on manuscript sources and on several published convulsionist tracts, nearly all of them anonymous. Among the most useful manuscript materials are the sworn depositions of the following: Michel Meignan (AN, X-1b 9692), Louis-Alexandre Doutreleau (ibid.), Claude Chambon (ibid.), Edme Pierre Le Plaideur Sigy (ibid.), and Femme la Coste (AN, X-1b 9690). In addition to the pamphlets cited above, the most useful include: *Réflexions sur l'Ordonnance du roi du 17 février 1733* (1733); [Julien-René-Benjamin de Gennes], *Coup d'oeil, en forme de lettre, sur les convulsions* (1733); [Poncet Desessarts], *Lettres de M.* à un de ses amis, sur l'oeuvre des convulsions* (1734); [abbé d'Etemare], *Lettre d'un ecclésiastique à un évêque* (n.d.); [Nicolas Le Gros], *Lettre . . . à un de ses amis, au sujet de l'oeuvre des convulsions* (1734); Louis-Basile Carré de Montgeron, *La vérité des miracles opérés à l'intercession de M. de Pâris et autres appelants . . .* (1737) and *Continuation des démonstrations des miracles. . .* (1741); and *Défense de l'autorité et des décisions des merveilles que Dieu ne cesse point de faire en France depuis un grand nombre d'années*, 2 vols. (1752).

[35] They tried to keep their numbers fairly small and to practice their ceremonies as quietly and as unobtrusively as possible in order to avoid arousing the suspicions of unfriendly neighbors or those of the police. M. Le Grand to Bishop Soanen, October 6, 1736, Rijksarchief, Utrecht, Port Royal 6685.

[36] See, for example, BN, Manuscrits Français 22, 326, pp. 457-489.

[37] While the majority saw nothing incompatible about remaining in their usual jobs, others believed that they had been called by God to devote themselves full time to the *oeuvre*. Some were simply unable to continue their normal way of life because of the persistent convulsions

nocturnal religious observances.

These private domestic services were intended and conceived of as a direct extension and continuation of the religious ceremonies conducted at François de Pâris' sacred tomb. The fact that each conventicle — and sometimes every member in the conventicle — possessed some relic or holy object associated with M. Pâris guaranteed the deacon's spiritual presence in their midst at all times.[38] The group "renewed itself" with each meeting, which took place in an atmosphere of intense devotion and collective exaltation. In order to preserve a constant sense of anticipation, immediacy, and spontaneity among the congregation and to allow the power of the Holy Spirit to work its full effect upon the assembly, an effort was made to avoid imposing any direct controls or formal code of behavior on the participants or requiring them to follow any carefully prescribed set of rites and practices in their observances. At the same time, however, though no one was actually delegated responsibility for directing, managing, or structuring the group's activities, priests and other ecclesiastics present frequently tended to assume various leadership functions, opening and sometimes overseeing or conducting the ceremonies, offering uplifting words of encouragement and exhortation to the faithful, and in general ensuring that the services did not proceed in a wholly random, chaotic, or haphazard manner.[39] It was largely as a result of such priestly supervision that certain patterns and orders of procedure seem to have developed at these worship meetings.

The session usually began with a period of common prayers and meditation and the invocation of the Holy Spirit through the intercession of François de Pâris. Someone would read a passage from Scripture, which another participant might explain and comment upon, whereupon the assembled company joined in a recitation of psalms. Other acts of worship were similarly performed in common and served to reaffirm the unity of the members and the communal existence and collective purpose of the group. Thus was built up the feeling of spiritual solidarity and pious fellowship.[40]

they continued to experience for months — and in certain cases for years — on end; these people were forced to rely on others for financial support. See the testimony of Frère Noël (J.-B. Lamain), AN, X-1b 9690, and that of Jacques Spayement, ibid.; see also the cases of Frère Didier (M. Fontaine), Frère Simon (M. Auffroi), and Frère Louis (Louis Sabinet), BN, Nouvelles Acquisitions Françaises 4262, fols. 90, 92, 99, and 122-123.

[38] Some especially prized relics were shared in common among the various conventicles. Father Pierre Boyer, who possessed the *ceinture* of M. Pâris, brought it around to the different *séances* he attended, and "il [la] mit à tous ceux qui étoient là" (Testimony of Femme La Coste, AN, X-1b 9690).

[39] The very presence of substantial numbers of priests in their midst no doubt served as an implicit legitimation of the movement for many of the *menu peuple*.

[40] *Lettre d'un ecclésiastique de province*, p. 17; Bibliothèque Historique de la Ville de Paris (hereafter, BHVP), Nouvelles Acquisitions 125, I, p. 369.

These people had not come together in secret, however, simply for the purpose of holding prayer meetings and pietistic devotions, no matter how inspirational and uplifting these may have been. Indeed, many other activities and forms of behavior, some of them quite remarkable and strange, went on at these sessions and help to account for the subsequent uproar which greeted the *oeuvre des convulsions*.[41] At some point during the *séance*, while the assembled company redoubled their prayers and collectively reached extreme heights of religious enthusiasm, at least one of their number, emotionally overwrought and overcome by the mounting fervor and group tension, would suddenly be seized with violent movements and astounding agitations of the body, often far more elaborate and extensive than the paroxysms which had previously been observed at Saint-Médard. They rolled about on the floor in a state of frenzy, screaming, roaring, trembling, and twitching. Some adopted strange postures and expressions, their bodies and features often bent or twisted into grotesquely contorted shapes, their movements at times unseemly and even blatantly sexually suggestive. The excitement, which might last for several hours, usually proved highly contagious, indeed overpowering, with certain convulsionaries serving as a catalyst for the onset of various bodily agitations in others gathered about the room.[42] As intense waves of emotion swept over the group, individuals of a hysterical character and those who were most suggestible were probably the first to begin emulating these seizures.[43] The ability to have convulsions became itself a status symbol, a sign of truly belonging as well as a manifestation of the divine presence, and no doubt earned for at least some of these previously obscure individuals, now the focus of the group's attention, an importance, a degree of esteem, and a measure of fame that few would otherwise have ever known.[44] Under such circumstances the *séances* presumably attracted a fair proportion of persons already suffering from a variety

[41] BN, Nouvelles Acquisitions Françaises 4262, fol. 82 and passim. The terms *oeuvre* and *oeuvre des convulsions* were both used by the brethren to describe the diverse activities in which they engaged after the closing of the Saint-Médard cemetery. The terms are discussed in several works, most notably the anonymous *Mémoire sur le terme d'Oeuvre des convulsions* (n.d.). On the tremendous variety of phenomena associated with the *oeuvre*, see the *Lettre d'un ecclésiastique de province*, p. 18.

[42] Testimony of Denise Regnier, AN, X-1b 9690.

[43] From among the large body of medical and psychological literature on the problem of "hysteria," I have found the following article particularly useful: George L. Engel, "Conversion Symptoms," in Cyril M. MacBryde and Robert S. Blacklow, eds., *Signs and Symptoms: Applied Pathologic Physiology and Clinical Interpretation*, 5th ed. (Philadelphia, 1970), pp. 650-668.

[44] At the same time, each assembly came to acquire a certain notoriety and reputation, depending on the different aspects of the *oeuvre* practiced there and the variety of *dons charismatiques* displayed by its "stars."

of psychomotor disturbances and chronic nervous disorders, especially epileptics — a situation which probably helped to swell the numbers of actual convulsionaries within the movement. In fact, after the first year or so following the closing of the cemetery, several hundred people, a large majority of them women, were reportedly overcome with these seizures.[45]

Many of the participants who were especially adept at this aspect of the *oeuvre* professed to be in excruciating pain during the experience and demanded relief. Their suffering, it was discovered, could be alleviated only by the application of what came to be called *secours*.[46] The term *secours*, which incorporated the meaning of both assistance and relief, referred to a series of diverse procedures administered to the convulsionaries by fellow participants in the cult known as *secouristes* (or *valets de chambre*), who assumed the responsibilities of surveillance and assistance once the adepts were seized by these convulsive movements.[47] The *secours* themselves were of two types. In the so-called *petits secours* some pressure was applied to, or moderate blows struck upon, various parts of the body. The very controversial *grands secours*, also known as *secours meurtriers*, involved much more violent and extreme forms of bodily punishment. An almost unimaginable variety of physical "tortures" was available on de-

---

[45] It is very difficult, if not impossible, to determine with any degree of assurance the number of people who actually experienced these convulsions, especially since both proponents and opponents of the movement — none of whom could possibly have attended all of the *séances* — had their reasons for exaggerating the numbers. In addition, the "membership" was far from stable, with frequent comings and goings occurring in the various conventicles all over Paris (*Recherche de la Vérité*, p. 8). Between August 1731 and late December 1732, according to one report, some 270 people had been overcome with convulsions in Paris, of whom about 200 were women (unsigned letter of December 27, 1732, B. Ars. 5784, fols. 16-17). As of 1733 the most reliable estimates for Paris place the figure as low as 400 (*Lettre d'un ecclésiastique de province*, p. 7) and as high as 600-700 (*Recherche de la vérité*, p. 8) and note that up to three-fourths of the adepts were women. See also AN, U-379, "Janvier 1733" and "Février 1733," in which the *greffier* De Lisle, an ardent convulsionist, reports two different figures, 600 and 800, respectively. Trustworthy calculations of the total number of participants in the *oeuvre* — whether actually subject to convulsions or simply witnesses — are even harder to come by. Estimates range from several thousand (*Lettre d'un ecclésiastique de province*, p. 16) up to 20,000 ([Poncet Dessarts], *XIIe Lettre de M.*** à un de ses amis, au sujet de la Consultation contre les convulsions* [1735], p. 32), the latter figure applying to a slightly later period.

[46] Cf. André Rétif, "Histoire étrange du mot 'Secouriste'," *Vie et langage*, no. 217 (April 1970), pp. 223-227.

[47] *Entretiens sur les miracles*, pp. 129, 131. The author of the *Lettre d'un ecclésiastique de province* claims that there were at least 3,000 or 4,000 such *valets de chambre* in Paris as of early 1733 (p. 16). In the case of women, their task included making sure that the convulsionaries did not become immodestly exposed when they were thrashing about — a task some of them had previously performed at M. Pâris' tomb. Despite the defamatory strictures of their critics, most of the brethren, it should be noted, were very much concerned with abiding by strict standards of decency and propriety. See letter of Jeanne-Marthe Le Grand to Bishop Soanen, October 6, 1736, Rijksarchief, Utrecht, Port Royal 6685.

mand, ranging from severe beatings that were dealt with very heavy objects, to knives, pins, and even sharply pointed swords that were forcibly pressed against the body.[48] Occasionally the convulsionary called for a board to be placed on top of his body and had as many as a dozen people stand or jump up and down on it for long periods of time. Others allowed themselves to be dragged and pushed along the floor, face down, for hours on end. Still others demanded to be choked or even crucified, all the while praying for the patience, the will, and the strength to endure.[49] Whatever the means employed, the results, according to most sympathetic observers, were generally the same. Those subjected to this treatment, many of whom had fallen into a trance-like, semiconscious state of intense ecstasy, seem to have felt little or no pain; some even found the experience highly pleasurable.[50] What is more, they reportedly showed no sign of injury, not the slightest trace of wounds or bruises. Even persons in a relatively weak or delicate physical condition allegedly came out unscathed, obtaining in the process the "relief" which they had been seeking.

This apparent invulnerability as well as the accompanying sense of relief depended in large measure on the proper management and regulation of the *secours*.[51] It was necessary that the type used and the exact location and duration of its application be in conformity with the particular requirements of the individual convulsionary. In addition, it was important that they be administered by degrees and with great care, not haphazardly, as many of their critics were to charge. The successful administration of the *secours* thus depended on the existence of a close,

---

[48] More nonsense has been written on this aspect of the *oeuvre des convulsions* than on any other. Much of it is traceable to hostile *constitutionnaire* writers who pointed to the *secours meurtriers* as symbolizing the fundamentally fanatical and degenerate character of the entire convulsionary movement. See, for example, Mme. Duguet-Mol, *Journal historique des convulsions du temps* (1733), and Louis-Bernard La Taste, *Lettres théologiques aux écrivains défenseurs des convulsions et autres prétendus miracles du temps* (1733-1740). The *secours* were also at the heart of the split which developed among the *anticonstitutionnaires* over the issue of the convulsionaries; hence a lot of distortion, exaggeration, and misstatement of facts came from *appellant* pens as well.

[49] Firsthand personal experiences of the *secours* are reported by Marguerite Turpin (AN, X-1b 9690) and Jeanne-Marthe Le Grand (ibid., and letter to Bishop Soanen, October 6, 1736, Rijksarchief, Utrecht, Port Royal 6685). See also the testimony of Claude Chambon (AN, X-1b 9692).

[50] See the somewhat dated, though still useful, medical discussion in Paul Richer, *Etudes cliniques sur l'hystéroepilepsie ou grande hystérie* (Paris, 1881), p. 694. Richer, along with his mentor and colleague, Charcot, and other leading French neurologists at the end of the nineteenth century, demonstrated an unusually keen interest in the various "hysterical" phenomena associated with the entire convulsionary episode. Cf. Charcot's own article, "La foi qui guérit," *Revue hebdomadaire*, 7 (1892), pp. 112-132, which deals in large part with this very subject. A more recent analysis of related phenomena may be found in the Engel article cited above, n. 43.

[51] *Lettre d'un ecclésiastique de province*, p. 24; testimony of Marguerite Turpin, AN, X-1b 9690.

trusting relationship between the convulsionary and his *valets de chambre*. At intervals all throughout the session, the convulsionary signalled his special needs with various gestures, body movements, and vaguely expressed instructions. The *secouristes*, for their part, were responsible for recognizing and interpreting these signals and adjusting the intensity, pressure, and extent of their "assistance" accordingly, so as to ensure that the *secours* would fulfil their purpose of providing relief. It was not uncommon for convulsionaries, on receiving these various blows, beatings, and thrashings to exclaim rapturously, "that is going well! that feels good!"[52] As a result, therefore, even in the face of the treatments ominously dubbed "*meurtriers*," the recipients submitted "with a confidence full of joy."[53] Indeed, despite their frightful external appearance, the *secours meurtriers* gave those who experienced them not only instant relief from the pains they had been feeling but also a tremendous sense of interior consolation. One adept reportedly found the spiritual consolation so rewarding that she confessed a willingness to endure the *secours* for the rest of her life in exchange for "the small moment of joy which God pour[ed] into her heart at the end of each torture."[54] Equally striking, when the administration of the *secours* was all over — sometimes after several hours — the convulsionary was usually quite calm and refreshed.[55]

These mysterious goings-on, enveloped in an aura of secrecy and obscurity, aroused widespread curiosity and alarm about possibly immoral practices and promiscuous behavior. Indeed, sensationalist critics of the convulsionaries, scandalized by rumors of licentiousness and debauchery, denounced the assemblies as little more than unrestrained, uninhibited orgies, an allegation for which there is no proof.[56] At the same time, however, there is no doubt that the *secours* did have sexual and masochistic overtones. When, for example, women occasionally called on their male *secouristes* to press and to pull their breasts or to pierce their bodies with swords and pins, the sexual symbolism is unmistakable. It seems likely, too, that these convulsionaries allowed themselves to be subjected to various tortures as a substitute for actual sexual experience, achieving excitement, arousal, and tremendous gratification — if only at

---

[52] *Lettre d'un ecclésiastique de province*, p. 16. See also the testimony of Marguerite Turpin (AN, X-1b 9690) and that of Claude Chambon (ibid., X-1b 9692).

[53] *Recherche de la Vérité*, p. 8.

[54] *Lettre d'un ecclésiastique de province*, p. 16.

[55] Ibid., p. 9. On this point, see also the testimony of Jeanne-Marthe Le Grand, Marguerite Turpin, and Denise Regnier (AN, X-1b 9690). Unlike the convulsionaries, their *secouristes* were often thoroughly exhausted, a few reportedly collapsing from fatigue when the sessions were over.

[56] Cf. Jeffry Kaplow, *The Names of Kings: The Parisian Laboring Poor in the Eighteenth Century* (New York, 1972), pp. 124-125.

the level of unconscious fantasies.[57]

Whatever their clinical nature and their latent or unconscious sexual content, these physical expressions and manifestations served to evoke the movement's aspirations and achievements as well as to reaffirm its collective existence and emotional power. According to the "figurist" exegetes, the wildly convulsive agitations and the so-called *secours meurtriers* were all forms of religious witness, fraught with symbolism related to the convulsionaries' mission of redemption and designed to instruct and to warn both the participants in the *oeuvre* and their "malevolent" enemies. These manifestations were said to be, in part, a living representation of the current spiritual turmoil within the Church that began with the promulgation of the bull *Unigenitus* and culminated in the closing of the cemetery at Saint-Médard: the convulsionaries represented the righteous defenders of the Truth, whereas the *secouristes* were their evil tormenters and oppressors.[58] In addition, while holding up a "mirror" to the sins and crimes committed against God and the faithful in the present, the *secours* were supposedly symbolic of the long and painful persecutions that had preceded God's deliverance of His people in the days of the first Christians. Finally, and perhaps most importantly, the *secours* purportedly gave the convulsionaries the feeling that they were figuratively sacrificing themselves to assuage God's anger. Before God would renew the Church, it was maintained, His wrath had first to be appeased.[59] He would accomplish His promises of assistance and consolation only "to the extent that He is moved by the laments of the dove."[60] Arousing and physically embodying such laments was thus a primary task of the convulsionaries, who offered themselves as Christ-like "victims" by and through whom the Church was to be renewed.[61] From their role as figurative victims of propitiation and the chosen instruments of divine justice and renewal, they derived "the force and the courage necessary to sustain all the trials to which they [might] be exposed."[62] Like their immediate inspiration, François de Pâris, and like many of the early Christian martyrs as well, the convulsionaries believed that they would "triumph with Jesus Christ only through suffering."[63]

[57] For a brief discussion of this concern to satisfy "des instincts lubriques," see Richer, *Etudes*, p. 694. More useful, though not directly related, is George L. Engel, "'Psychogenic' Pain and the Pain-Prone Patient," *American Journal of Medicine*, 26 (1959), pp. 899-918.
[58] Unattributed *appellant* letter of November 4, 1732, B. Ars. 5784, fols. 298-299.
[59] *Entretiens sur les miracles*, pp. 144-145.
[60] Ibid., p. 145. [61] "C'est par l'oeuvre des Convulsions qu'il [Dieu] se prépare des victimes, qu'il les annonce, et qu'il commence à les former . . . et ils le prient avec instance de hâter le temps de la persésecution, afin de voir ensuite celui de sa miséricorde" (ibid.).
[62] Ibid., p. 158.
[63] *Réflexions sur l'ordonnance du roi, en date du 27 Janvier 1732* (1732), p. 88.

The apocalyptic tradition provided an additional sanction and further "explanation" for the convulsionaries' extravagant behavior. According to several "figurist" theologians associated with the *oeuvre*, the convulsionaries were the spiritual precursors and forerunners of the prophet Elijah, who, at some unspecified time, was to return mysteriously to earth as one of the witnesses against Antichrist and as a herald of the Messiah.[64] As a minister of divine justice and an agent of religious renewal and regeneration, Elijah was expected to place himself at the head of the convulsionary brethren, to liberate the persecuted, to ensure the triumph of the true faith, and eventually to re-establish peace and well-being throughout the Christian community.[65] In the course of his dramatic earthly career, this formidable prophet and preacher of repentance would also accomplish the reprobation of the Gentiles and the conversion of the Jews as signs of the coming new epoch.[66] But before his arrival "to restore all things," it was necessary that all crimes first be honorably expiated and that there be a flowing of blood, symbolic or real, representing the blood of Jesus Christ, to mark the beginning of the "Last Days." From this point of view the convulsionaries' ritual measures of symbolic self-sacrifice were a means of preparing the way for Elijah's awaited return and of thereby hastening the moment of decision and change. In this sense, too, the *secours*, while symbolizing the evils and corruption that had already befallen and overtaken the Church, were also supposed to represent the additional trials and ordeals (*épreuves*) which the Church would endure in the future — a period of terrible catastrophe and confusion which must precede, accompany, and follow the advent of Elijah, who would himself be subjected to suffering and persecution for assisting the convulsionaries to resist the "tortures" of the established authorities.[67]

These elaborate "figurist" interpretations of the *secours*, developed in

[64] The principal Old Testament references to the prophet Elijah are I Kings 17 through II Kings 2, passim, and Malachi 4:5-6; passages in the New Testament include Matthew 11:14, 17:10-12; Mark 9:11-13; and Luke 1:17.

[65] "Prière à Dieu le Fils par le Saint Diacre," in *Supplément des Nouvelles ecclésiastiques*, April 8, 1735, p. 51; *Entretiens sur les miracles*, p. 149. According to one prominent writer, God had exclusively designated the convulsionaries "à le reconnoître et de les engager à se préparer à ce grand événement par la pénitence et la prière" (Montgeron, II: "Idée de l'état des convulsions," p. 5).

[66] *NNEE*, November 25, 1731, p. 227. According to Arthur Hertzberg, the conversion of the Jews was seen as "a central task of Christianity" and "the indispensable tool for the Church's restoration and regeneration . . . , a necessary preamble to Christian eschatology" (*The French Enlightenment and the Jews* [New York, 1968], p. 259).

[67] BHVP, Nouvelles Acquisitions 125, I, 26; Frère Hilaire to Bishop Soanen, November 29, 1733, Rijksarchief, Utrecht, Port Royal 6439; *Entretiens sur les miracles*, pp. 150-151; Montgeron, II: "Dissertation sur l'autorité des miracles," p. 50.

numerous tracts and treatises by various convulsionist spokesmen, provided the convulsionaries with a convenient theological justification or rationalization for their strange actions and rituals. The *secours*, like the other convulsive movements, were simply the physical manifestations God had chosen to prepare the followers of M. Pâris both to receive and to announce the most sacred truth̃s. God had rendered some of the convulsionaries invulnerable — just as He had cured others — in order to demonstrate their conspicuous worthiness and to show that He favored their cause. As far as they were concerned, divine intervention enabled them to endure what would otherwise have been quite impossible and thus furnished them with clear, irrefutable proof of their divine election and convincing evidence that God's influence and protection graced the entire *oeuvre*.[68] In practicing their religious observances (the *oeuvre*), therefore, they were fulfilling a holy responsibility and, in a very real sense, performing the work of God, the *"ouvrage de Dieu"* or *"opus Dei."* Such an interpretation, moreover, allowed the convulsionaries to "prove" that they were neither fanatical nor insane. Their various activities, they could argue, were simply the outpourings of the Holy Spirit, demonstrably orthodox and rooted in traditional religious conviction.[69]

The convulsionaries had other methods or forms of bearing witness to the divine presence and of representing the divine message, though none of these was quite so spectacular as the *secours meurtriers*. Large numbers of miraculous cures, for example, continued to occur at these *séances*, most of them attributed to the intercession of François de Pâris, and many of them accompanied by convulsions. There were also diverse types of "figurative representations" in which the adepts, allegedly under divine inspiration, were said to be acting out important episodes in the history of the Church. Some convulsionaries made various involuntary gestures and movements which were supposed to represent important events in the life of Jesus Christ, particularly His sufferings, crucifixion, and final Ascension. Others "recreated" the conversion of St. Paul or "depicted" some act of François de Pâris.[70] These so-called *"tableaux vivants"* were among the most innocuous and least controversial aspects of the entire *oeuvre*.[71]

---

[68] Testimony of Denise Regnier, AN, X-1b 9690; cf. *Entretiens sur les miracles*, p. 158.

[69] Their enemies, ironically, including numerous Jesuits, would denounce this argument as pure casuistry, an attempt to cover up obviously degrading and insane practices.

[70] *Lettre d'un ecclésiastique de province*, p. 11. For a more elaborate and detailed description of the various kinds of figurative representations, see ibid., pp. 10-11. See also, *Recherche de la Vérité*, p. 9.

[71] Nevertheless, some of these "figurative representations" actually did arouse a great deal of criticism. Certain female convulsionaries, for example, were charged with saying Mass and performing other priestly functions during the *séances*. In fact, however, as one convulsionist defender pointed out, "il s'agit d'une simple imitation des gestes d'un Prêtre qui

Far more controversial and in greater need of interpretation or rationalization were the blasphemous utterances and the acts of (apparent) profanation committed by a number of convulsionaries. One semiconscious woman, for example, reportedly threw a Bible on the ground and stamped upon it; when she came out of her "convulsive state," she begged God for forgiveness. Such strange behavior was easily explained as yet another divinely inspired "figurative representation." God had chosen this symbolic act as a means of dramatizing the "horrible profanations" to which the wicked *constitutionnaires*, through the bull *Unigenitus*, had subjected Holy Scripture.[72]

However controversial, edifying, or instructive their diverse "performances" sometimes were, these primarily physical manifestations of the *oeuvre* were by no means the only way in which God made His presence felt among the brethren. Indeed, perhaps the most noteworthy feature of their sessions — and, with the *secours*, the most widely debated — was the different forms of speech pronounced by many of the convulsionaries at some point in the *séance*. Suddenly "overcome by the spirit," often in the very midst of a convulsive seizure or even during the administration of the *secours*,[73] the inspired one gave out with various kinds of vocal utterances. Some of this "speech" consisted of little more than unintelligible mutterings, incomprehensible exclamations, and childlike babbling. In other cases, it involved equally incoherent screaming and roaring, howling and yelling.[74] Still other convulsionaries were limited in these periods of "inspiration" to the mere repetition of religious phrases and well-known Biblical expressions, often pronounced without any particular logic, sequence, or theme. The phenomenon of glossolalia, or speaking in tongues, in a strange, new "language" of words, syllables, and sounds they had never learned and did not comprehend, was also quite common and gave many convulsionaries a sense of direct communication and contact with God.

Along with these relatively inarticulate and virtually impenetrable outpourings, there was a large number of far more elaborate and more fully developed speeches and discourses pronounced during the *séances*. These discourses, some of which went on almost uninterrupted for several hours, were supposedly delivered spontaneously, without any premedita-

célèbre, sans pain ni vin, sans vases sacrés, sans ornemens sacerdotaux, sans même aucune représentation d'autel. . . . Dire la messe lorsqu'on n'est pas prêtre est un attentat que les lois punissent par le feu. Pourquoi donc affecter d'exprimer par le nom d'une profanation horrible, une action qui en est si prodigieusement différente?" (*Exposé de la manière de penser de M. l'abbé [d'Etemare] touchant l'événement des convulsions* [1753], p. 8.)

[72] *Entretiens sur les miracles*, p. 156.

[73] Frère Hilaire, January 31, 1733, BN, Nouvelles Acquisitions Françaises 4262, fols. 79-80.

[74] One female convulsionary, known for her "barking," was dubbed "l'Aboyeuse."

tion or preparation, and usually unwittingly and involuntarily, as "in a kind of ecstasy, stupor, or dream."[75] In the highly charged atmosphere which characterized the assemblies held all over Paris, some 300 persons were said to have been blessed with this particular divine gift (*don*) within the first year and a half after the closing of the cemetery at Saint-Médard.[76] The presence in each conventicle of a scribe or copyist charged with the responsibility of keeping a journal of whatever activities went on at the session, and particularly of recording the discourses, has meant that many hundreds, perhaps thousands, of these documents have survived.[77] Although certain *frères* and *soeurs* at times spoke too quickly for the scribe to keep pace with them and occasionally allowed their voices to trail off in a barely audible whisper or to be drowned out by their own convulsive movements, the "secretary," using a barely legible scrawl and various shorthand notations, apparently managed to take down most of the speeches substantially "as dictated," and often was even able to provide surprisingly rich and detailed accounts of the accompanying changes occurring in the speaker's bodily movements, gestures, facial expressions, or general mood and demeanor.[78] Once the session was over, the copyist would usually transcribe the discourse in a fine secretarial hand and make a few interpolations and editorial additions, occasionally providing brief theological explanations or supplying appropriate Biblical references.[79] Discourses of exceptional quality[80] were subsequently copied and re-copied, exchanged among the different conventicles, passed on from one *frère* or *soeur* to another, and eventually circulated — separately or in bound collections and "anthologies" — within convulsionary circles all

[75] *Recherche de la Vérité*, p. 7.

[76] D'Etemare to Pierre Sartre, July 18, 1733, B. Ars. 5784, fol. 26.

[77] Major collections in Paris may be found at the Bibliothèque Port-Royal, the Bibliothèque Nationale, the Bibliothèque de la Société de l'Histoire du Protestantisme Français, the Bibliothèque Historique de la Ville de Paris, the Archives Nationales, and the Archives Historiques de l'Archevêché de Paris.

[78] On the importance of scribes, see the testimony of Claude Chambon (AN, X-1b 9692) and that of M. Prévost, Soeur de la Confession (ibid., X-1b 9691). On the problems confronting the scribes, see the testimony of Femme La Coste (ibid., X-1b 9690) and the comments of one of these copyists at a *séance* in June 1733 (B. Ars. 10204, no fol.).

[79] One of the principal convulsionist scribes for many years was the noted Jansenist *avocat*, Louis-Adrien Le Paige. Surprisingly neglected by most historians, this curious and important individual, whose life spanned the entire eighteenth century, and who was active in the affairs of the Paris Parlement, especially during the campaign against the Jesuits, definitely merits a full-length study. The extraordinary "Collection Le Paige" at the Bibliogthèque Port-Royal would be the natural starting point for such an investigation.

[80] Included in this category were the discourses of the so-called "Quatre grands frères" — Hilaire, Noël, Etienne, and Pierre — and those of a handful of women, Soeur Colombe and Soeur La Croix Got among them. According to a fellow convulsionary, Soeur La Croix was regarded "comme une sainte, comme un oracle, qu'elle savoit tout. . . ." (Testimony of La Virginie, AN, X-1b 9690).

over France.[81] They were carefully preserved, both by individual brethren and by the various conventicles, and treated as highly treasured
possessions. Indeed, they became major sources of edification and inspiration for all those in the *oeuvre* and were frequently read, discussed, or
commented upon during the *séances*.[82]

Reflecting the diversity of backgrounds, abilities, and preoccupations
which characterized the membership in the *oeuvre*, these discourses were
tremendously varied in quality, style, and major themes. Though little is
known about the specific attributes of mind or personality of the individual convulsionary speakers, it would appear that a majority were
persons of limited or mediocre intelligence, with little or no formal education or religious training, and some were even quite young children. Not
surprisingly, many of these people were limited to repeatedly and
monotonously evoking rather simplistic or banal Biblical images and
symbols, their discourses consisting of little more than the recitation or
paraphrase of certain psalms and Scriptural passages that had frequently
been read or discussed among the brethren.[83] At the same time, there
were other convulsionaries from reportedly the same milieux who somehow demonstrated in their discourses a level of knowledge and a degree
of sophistication and understanding which seemed to go far beyond their
ordinary capacity and to surpass anything they had displayed in their
"natural state." Admiring observers frequently marvelled at their command of the language, the richness of expression and imagery, the great
eloquence and forcefulness of tone. Many of these *frères* and *soeurs* also
displayed a remarkably intimate and penetrating familiarity with Scripture, often providing extended explications of or commentaries upon
particular Biblical texts. Others even demonstrated an ability to expound
at great length and with considerable clarity and apparent erudition on
some of the most abstruse questions of theology and mysteries of the
faith.[84]

Though they have until recently remained virtually unexplored,[85] the
discourses are among the most revealing and instructive sources available

[81] BHVP, Côte Provisoire 3509, p. 36; cf. B. Ars. 11439, fols. 154-155. I have located
substantial collections of discourses in more than a dozen libraries outside of Paris. Some
discourses were even published: *Recueil de discours de plusieurs convulsionnaires* (1734).
[82] Testimony of La Virginie, AN, X-1b 9690.
[83] Testimony of Frère Paul le Petit (Paul-François Langlade), ibid., X-1b 9691.
[84] BHVP, Nouvelles Acquisitions 125, I, 24; Montgeron, II: "Idée de l'état des convulsions," pp. 17-18; BN Nouvelles Acquisitions Françaises 4262, fols. 123-124, 130-131 (observations of Le Paige).
[85] Aside from the work of the present author, the only other attempt to deal with the
discourses is a *mémoire de maîtrise* by a student of Jean Delumeau, Roxanne Kural, who has
analyzed two large volumes of discourses (MSS 196 and 197) in the collection of the
Bibliothèque de l'Histoire du Protestantisme Français. Notwithstanding these preliminary

for entering into the convulsionaries' mental universe.[86] These discourses gave spoken form to, or were a verbal analogue and oral confirmation of, the physical exhibitions of convulsions and *secours*, with many of the same themes of official persecution and spiritual renewal recurring in both. But whereas the various physical manifestations of the *oeuvre* supposedly gave bodily expression to certain of the movement's fundamental principles and may have provided the convulsionaries with a means of symbolically venting and articulating their pent-up frustrations, the discourses, pronounced aloud in the very midst of the *séances*, served as a more direct vehicle for enunciating convulsionary attitudes and for defining the hopes and aspirations, the fears and apprehensions of the brethren themselves. Without necessarily regarding themselves as actual prophets, the convulsionaries did believe that God was speaking directly through them, and that they were acting as His intermediaries and "instruments," conveying the divine will and message to the assembled faithful.[87] Although some speakers were primarily preoccupied with the announcement and defense of "true" doctrine and piety and the condemnation or refutation of the false,[88] for the most part their discourses fulfilled a much more dramatic and immediate purpose. In particular, they served to provide the brethren with signs and warnings of the impending calamities that were to be visited upon Christendom and to offer vital instructions to enable them to prepare for the events to come.[89] At the same time, by holding out the promise of ultimate deliverance, these discourses were also a means of exhorting all those present to place their trust and confidence "in God and in the force of His grace."[90]

efforts, this vast body of source materials, which extend throughout the century and even beyond the Revolution, definitely merits further serious study and close textual analysis. Cf. the comments of Delumeau, offered in a somewhat broader context, on the need for such an analysis of popular spiritual literature of the *ancien régime* (*Le Catholicisme entre Luther et Voltaire* [Paris, 1971], p. 226).

[86] Such a view of the significance of the discourses was also shared by the convulsionaries. According to Soeur Colombe (AN, X-1b 9690), "ils contiennent l'explication de l'oeuvre"; while the editor of a published collection of these discourses (*Recueil de discours*, "Avertissement") noted that, "On y trouvera de quoi d'instruire d'une manière très solide et très juste sur l'oeuvre des Convulsions, ce qui est bien plus capable de donner une juste idée des convulsions que tous les Ouvrages qu'on a tant multipliés inutilement sur cette matière."

[87] BN, Nouvelles Acquisitions Françaises 4262, fol. 96; Testimony of Soeur Colombe, AN, X-1b 9690.

[88] The locksmith Louis Sabinet, for example, explored at some length various questions of dogma and Christian morality (BN, Nouvelles Acquisitions Françaises 4262, fol. 131). Many of these speakers delivered long harangues against the Jesuits and their Molinist theology, whether they understood its doctrines or not.

[89] *Entretiens sur les miracles*, p. 158; cf. letter of M. Simart to Bishop Soanen, July 19, 1733, Rijksarchief, Utrecht, Port Royal 6863.

[90] Although the two-sided, "paradoxical" nature of God appears throughout these discourses with striking force and frequency, it is the menacing vision of the wrathful, vengeful

A powerful consciousness of their persecution and an exaggerated sense of putative martyrdom called forth feelings of pride and terror, both of which found expression in these speeches. Speaking in millenarian strains and with great force and conviction, they announced, sometimes with the most violent and frightening imagery, the imminent doom that awaited all who rejected or oppressed the "Truth." Certain convulsionaries reported a variety of weird dreams and baffling visions, some of which seemed to draw heavily (if perhaps unconsciously) upon the prophets of the Old Testament, particularly Daniel, and also to evoke certain apocalyptic symbols and eschatological themes of Revelation.[91] Frequent and impassioned invocations addressed to Elijah were accompanied by equally fervent apostrophes to God and to François de Pâris, many of them appealing for divine protection for the righteous brethren and simultaneous punishment for their corrupt and perfidious persecutors.[92] Alternately prayerful and hortatory, consoling and accusatory, these sermon-like speeches, accompanied much of the time by convulsions and *secours*, no doubt made a great impression not only upon those *frères* and *soeurs* present during their delivery, but also upon those fortunate enough to possess copies of their own.

Except for a final brief period of common prayers, the termination of the discourses, along with the cessation of the *secours*, generally marked the conclusion of the *séance*. Once tentative plans were made for the next communal assembly, the brethren left, having experienced a profound emotional catharsis. Assured of divine acceptance and consolation, they felt a highly satisfying release from tension and a sense of spiritual liberation and personal exaltation. Many participants reported a feeling of deep interior peace and well-being, of intense warmth and joy, as a result of their direct, immediate encounter with God during these devo-

God of justice which prevails over the more directly consoling image of the loving, compassionate God of mercy. See *Entretiens sur les miracles*, p. 163; Frère Simart's letter to Bishop Soanen, cited above, n. 89; and letter of Frère Hilaire to Bishop Soanen, November 29, 1733, Rijksarchief, Utrecht, Port Royal 6439.

[91] Claude Yvon, *maître perruquier*, reported having "des visions pendant lesquelles [son père] voit des soleils, des étoiles, des diamants, des tabernacles, des suspensions et autres choses" (AN, X-1b 9690). Perhaps the most famous "dream" was the one attributed to Jérôme-Nicolas de Pâris, the deacon's *parlementaire* brother, which consisted of an elaborate figurative representation of all the major individuals involved in the convulsionary controversy, both for and against. While a number of manuscript editions of this dream have survived, it has also been published — with commentary — by Prince de Cardé and J. Roubinovitch, *Contribution à l'étude de l'état mental des Jansénistes convulsionnaires* (Poitiers, 1902).

[92] In one of the most celebrated and widely circulated discourses ever delivered during this period, Frère Hilaire (Chevalier de Blaru) related an extended "parable," in which he likened the convulsionaries and their *oeuvre* to Noah's ark and compared their oppressors to the faithless hordes who succumbed in the flood. For a brief excerpt and discussion, see BN, Nouvelles Acquisitions Françaises 4262, fols. 80-81.

tional services.[93] Although a mere collection of words can hardly begin to capture or convey the full impact and magnitude of these fantastic psychodramas which were daily being re-enacted all over Paris, it is clear that the convulsionaries were able to attain, through the *oeuvre*, a degree of emotional uplift and a kind of spiritual energy and vitality that had been previously available nowhere else — not even at Saint-Médard. Feelings of religious solidarity and bonds of pious fellowship, born out of their active collaboration in a joint enterprise and out of an enthusiastic commitment to a common purpose, were a source of great strength and cohesion and gave their lives a new meaning and significance, while affording them a means of establishing their identities and a way of maintaining their self-respect and sense of personal worth and dignity. But in the process they had also achieved something more.

Implicitly, if sometimes unwittingly, the convulsionary movement raised a number of significant and disturbing questions regarding the nature of both State and Church in eighteenth-century France. To be sure, the convulsionaries never thought of themselves as anything other than the faithful subjects of their king. Their political criticisms, for example, rarely encompassed a direct or very harsh attack on the king or on monarchical authority. And yet, though they were basically attached to the maintenance of royal authority and were not prepared to challenge the nature of existing political relationships or to favor any fundamental institutional redistribution of political power, their spiritual revolt did represent a growing mood of popular criticism and anti-establishmentarian independence, especially where the ecclesiastical authority was concerned. Some of the ideas of the convulsionaries seemed incompatible with — indeed, subversive of — many of the religious, political, and social conceptions so sacred to the *ancien régime*. The Bourbon monarchy, like the Gallican Church, was based on time-honored principles of order and hierarchy, authority and corporate privilege — principles which the convulsionary world view and liturgical and devotional innovations tended to undermine. While promoting the concept of spiritual liberation and endeavoring to create a new fraternal and egalitarian society of *frères* and *soeurs* in the midst of the Church, the followers of M. Pâris were implicitly calling into question the very nature of that institution. Largely under the influence of *anticonstitutionnaire* parish priests, the convulsionaries were increasingly coming to regard the Gallican episcopate as an entrenched "corporate elite" possessed of an arbitrary and despotic power and to mistrust the intrusive influence of papacy and Jesuits on royal ecclesiastical policy. At the same time, in opposition to

[93] Ibid., fol. 120.

the episcopal hierarchy they began to exalt the role of the laity and of the second order of clergy, advocating a kind of popular republic, a more democratic, congregational polity, within the Church. More than a year before Voltaire published his *Lettres philosophiques*, the supposed "first bomb" hurled at the *ancien régime*, the convulsionaries were thus already vigorously challenging the repressive, reactionary religious — and, in effect, the political — status quo. Indeed, next to Voltaire's Quakers, who represented a fairly mild and indirect critique of conditions in France, the convulsionaries represented a much more serious indictment of the established order and seemed to have been calling for a potentially more fundamental re-evaluation of French society.

But this first generation of convulsionaries had no opportunity to realize any of their broader aspirations at this time. Driven by persecution and intimidation to ever more bizarre and antisocial behavior, disgraced and discredited by the appearance in their very midst of the more activist, literal-minded, and fanatical sects of Vaillantistes and Augustinistes,[94] the followers of M. Pâris fell out of favor with many of their erstwhile *anticonstitutionnaire* partisans and supporters, lay and clerical alike. A majority of the *appellant* clergy and theologians ultimately joined with the *constitutionnaire* bishops and the royal government to repudiate and to denounce the convulsionary movement. To be sure, even with a virtual monopoly of force as its disposal, Fleury's administration never managed to bring the sect completely to its knees. Through political vicissitudes and despite the torments of official persecution and repression, many convulsionaries clung tenaciously to their beliefs and practices. Hence, although by the late 1730's they were no longer a *cause célèbre* in contemporary ecclesiastical controversy, their movement persisted throughout the century[95] as an expression of popular disaffection with and alienation from the established authorities and as a sign of a nascent, albeit vague, political consciousness developing among certain segments of the *menu peuple*.

[94] Most of the historical literature on the convulsionaries tends to obscure the distinctions between the so-called "orthodox" brethren — the original adherents of François de Pâris, who remained faithful to his message and spirit, emphasizing in their observances of the *oeuvre* the virtuous purity and innocent simplicity of the apostolic religious life — and a number of fanatical sects — some of them antinomians, like the Augustinistes, others radical millenarians, with an exceptionally intense and urgent expectation of the "Last Days," like the Vaillantistes — that were offshoots of, and quickly repudiated by, the "parent" movement. For a description and assessment of the beliefs and practices of these sects, see Kreiser, "Miracles," chs. 5-6, passim.

[95] Collateral branches of the original Pâris cult, some of Augustiniste inspiration, continued to survive in Paris, Lyons, and elsewhere well into the nineteenth century.

5

Savoir et Art de Vivre Campagnard

LUCIENNE A. ROUBIN

Les remarques qui vont suivre relèveront d'une perspective conjugant méthodes ethnologique et historique, appliquées conjointement à l'examen du patrimoine culturel des campagnes françaises. Cette double option méthodologique sous-entend la part considérable faite, aux côtés des sources écrites, à l'analyse d'exemples concrets de terrain, exploitant à la fois matériaux dialectologiques et documents iconographiques. Très vite, il apparaîtra que les observations présentées ici, par leur caractère succint, méritent seulement d'être considérées comme "schéma de travail" à partir duquel pourront s'ouvrir échanges et confrontations — tout comme, dans l'Ancienne France, "s'agrégeaient au son de cloche" ces assemblées de Communautés, où se débattaient en plein vent, sur la place publique, les affaires importantes pour la vie du village.

Et tout d'abord en France — puisque nous concentrons notre attention sur elle, alors que ce qui va être dit est vrai de tout un ensemble des campagnes européennes — en France, donc, ces campagnards, objet de notre réflexion, que représentent-ils? Ce flux humain considérable, en place dans sa diversité ethnique depuis plus d'un millénaire, a constitué jusqu'à la première guerre mondiale le noyau essentiel, le réservoir biologique du pays. Dans cette famille féconde, à la descendance active et variée, ce duel sans merci transformant pendant plus de quatre ans les laboureurs en fantassins a opéré parmi eux une saignée si meurtrière que la campagne française en a été laissée exangue pour un quart de siècle et qu'elle doit aujourd'hui encore en soigner les séquelles.

Dès le VIe siècle de notre ère, ces habitants des campagnes sont désignés par Isidore de Séville comme les "Rustici." Le terme est employé par lui sans nuance péjorative, à l'encontre du terme *Plebs* qui en est chargé. Les rustici sont simplement la foule innombrable de tous ceux qui ne sont pas des "clercs," qui ne sont pas des "lettrés." Jusqu'à la fin de l'âge classique, pour les cercles diffusant la culture savante, la vie profonde de ces millions d'hommes est demeurée, selon l'expression de H. Focillon "un monde étrange, obscur et dédaigné."[1]

"L'on voit certains animaux, farouches, des mâles et des femelles, répandus par la campagne, attachés à la terre qu'ils fouillent et qu'ils remuent avec une opiniatreté invincible, ils ont comme une voix articulée, et quand ils se lèvent sur leurs pieds ils montrent une face humaine et, en effet, ils sont des hommes. Ils se retirent la nuit dans des tannières où ils vivent de pain noir, d'eau et de racines."[2] Ce portrait que La Bruyère a voulu lapidaire, souligne la distance maintenue, sous le siècle de Louis XIV, par les classes éclairées, à l'endroit de ce monde étrange: les hommes de la terre et de la vie des champs. Ce sont précisément les éléments d'une armature stable et sous-jacente à la variété des physionomies provinciales, qu'on tentera de dégager ici comme assises génératrices d'une façon de vivre et de penser caractéristiques du monde campagnard.

De la confrontation d'observations menées en groupes ethniques aussi différenciés que Bretons, Basques, Alsaciens ou Provençaux ressortent deux séries de constatations. En premier lieu: partout discernable, un ensemble d'éléments constants qui, par delà les colorations ethniques, exprime un dénominateur commun, sorte de faciès spécifique, où l'ethnologue retrouve des données familières à toute l'aire eurasiatique. Parmi eux — et peut-être, l'élément fondamental — l'omniprésence de cette institution vénérable, la Communauté villageoise, sur laquelle il nous faudra revenir plusieurs fois. Par elle, ces groupes ont élaboré une remarquable appropriation, simultanément concrète et symbolique de leur espace nourricier qui répond à la triple nécessité soulignée par A. Leroi-Gourhan: "Créer un milieu techniquement efficace; assurer un cadre au système social; mettre de l'ordre à partir du périmètre habité, dans l'univers environnant."[3]

En second lieu, il apparaît à l'évidence que ce faciès campagnard était partout saisissable sous une forme cohérente jusqu'aux abords de 1914, et qu'il reste lisible dans ses grandes lignes à peu près partout. Cependant, il est à préciser que ce déchiffrage ethnologique passe inévitablement par la pratique du dialecte dans lequel sont inscrites les correspondances latentes en chacun de ses profils culturels.

Ces préliminaires posés, quels sont les traits qui peuvent être retenus comme particulièrement significatifs de cette physionomie aux cent visages? Tout d'abord la constance d'un calendrier d'activités économiques et

---

[1] Henri Focillon, *Art populaire, travaux artistiques et scientifiques du ler Congrès International des Arts Populaires, Prague, 1928* (Paris, 1931), T. I, Introduction.

[2] La Bruyère, *Les caractères*, xi, 128.

[3] André Leroi-Gourhan, *La mémoire et les rythmes*, T. II de *Le geste et la parole* (Paris, 1965), p. 150.

cérémonielles partout étroitement dépendant des rythmes saisonniers et par là étroitement intégré dans un temps cyclique, répétitif, à oscillations lentes, comme on peut encore le percevoir d'expérience par un séjour dans ces Communautés. Ce temps ralenti en quelque sorte, apparaît bien comme antithétique de celui qui régit notre propre existence, c'est-à-dire le temps de l'occident urbain, temps ouvert et accéléré, morcelé en périodes courtes et pleines.

Egalement l'omniprésence d'un réseau d'instructions coutumières qui se perpétuent aux côtés des structures administratives officielles, issues de la lègislation napoléonienne est assurée par la règle toute-puissante de l'usage, c'est-à-dire par le droit coutumier. Comme M. Mauss l'a souligné, dès longtemps, ce dernier régit encore une part importante du droit français, il était partout en honneur dans la France d'Ancien Régime où la législation royale a dû le prendre en compte dans tous les domaines. En ce sens, la perspective juridique qui préside aux actes de la vie campagnarde présente maintes analogies avec celle qui baigne les sociétés archaïques longtemps seules dévolues à l'étude ethnologique. Ce réseau d'institutions coutumières maintient la cohésion villageoise, à partir de processus complexes qui ordonnent et intègrent progressivement les différentes classes d'âge dans le pacte villageois d'entr'aide et d'assistance mutuelle. Ce que j'ai appelé ailleurs "la solidarité des hommes du lieu," permet à ceux-ci, par delà les inévitables tensions individuelles, de se reconnaître comme une unité agissante en face des groupes voisins.

Enfin, un commun mode de penser, procédant de l'observation constante du microcosme local, et de l'expérience. Car la condition d'homme, à affronter en ce point précis de l'espace en tant que milieu d'action et de création, engendre, ici, selon l'expression de Roger Bastide, "une connaissance-acte, participant à la réalité vécue." Celle-ci a conduit à l'accumulation d'un stock de procédés technologiques étroitement intégrés à un complexe de pratiques magico-religieuses dont certaines, héritières d'un passé immémorial ont préservé et véhiculé jusqu'à nous des survivances préhistoriques. La maîtrise de cette somme, en apparence disparate, qui allie les techniques de survie dans un biotope donné, à une vision du monde cohérente chez les hommes qui l'habitent constitue le *savoir* dans ces Communautés. Constamment contrôlé par une véritable éthique villageoise, progressivement enraciné dans la conscience collective, ce savoir est thésaurisé par l'ensemble des mémoires individuelles et directement transmis d'une génération à l'autre de bouche à oreille, de la main à la main et de l'oeil à l'oeil.

La transmission de ce savoir qui conditionne les principes de l'éducation enfantine et la forme prise par le jeu en milieu campagnard est importante à préciser pour notre propos, car elle est fondamentalement différente des voies de transmission propres à la culture savante. Deux relais complémentaires en assurent l'accomplissement.

Le premier, un lent apprentissage corporel, doit aboutir au savoir-faire, au *know-how*; l'entraînement de la *main* et du *regard* en sont les pôles fondamentaux qui vont développer l'aptitude à fabriquer l'outil. Celui-ci a pu être récemment considéré par A. Leroi-Gourhan "comme une sorte de sécretion du corps et du cerveau, véritable organe artificiel intégré dans la matière et dans la fonction."[4] Il répond pour un type donné d'outil à des formes constantes à travers les âges.

J'en ai éprouvé un exemple, au cours de mes recherches sur le complexe de la vigne et du vin. La serpette taille-vigne de l'Aquitaine française, autour de laquelle les vignerons de Gaillac élisaient publiquement au XVIe siècle leur "Rei de la Pondo," "le roi de la serpette" reste identique au XIXe siècle au Kocer bulgare qui intronise actuellement le roi des vignerons pendant la danse de la Saint-Tryphon, comme à celui qui figure parmi les offrandes votives offertes à Dionysos, plusieurs siècles avant notre ère, dans la grotte de Madara en Bulgarie orientale. Et, une série de jalons s'échelonnant entre ces deux maillons, Bulgarie-Provence, soulignent à travers l'Europe la similitude de formes de cet outil. On comprend mieux dès lors le sens du jeu enfantin en société campagnarde. Ce dernier n'est pas activité exclusivement gratuite comme dans nos modernes sociétés urbaines, mais imitation de l'activité parentale quotidienne — déjà une occasion de développer l'adresse corporelle et une manière de se familiariser avec les techniques de l'âge adulte que l'enfant voit se développer sous ses yeux, pour le garçonnet en accompagnant son père aux champs, pour la fillette en compagnie de sa mère à la maison.

Le second relai développe une formation *orale* dont le pôle fondamental est la *mémoire*; car l'essentiel de ce savoir paysan est entreposé en elle, nous l'avons vu, et dès la petite enfance un entraînement intensif lui est imposé. Celui-ci va doter l'enfant de points de repère destinés à le familiariser avec son terroir et tout d'abord avec le réseau serré et fonctionnel des toponymes qui l'enserre, mais aussi va l'introduire à la connaissance de la tradition orale en ce qui concerne en particulier les nuances dialectales du parler quotidien, les usages sociaux, les symboles préférentiels du comportement esthétique.

Cet enseignement relèvera simultanément de sources différentes. Il peut être dispensé dans le cadre familial, par exemple l'apprentissage d'une "trempe de l'acier," secret de famille jalousement gardé chez certains forgerons de village en Vendée, en Alsace; ou encore l'initiation à la reconnaissance puis à la récolte des plantes médicinales; il peut être

---

[4] Ibid., p. 132.

également corporatif, par exemple la familiarisation avec certaines techniques de pêche collective, telle la seinche aux thons pratiquée par les cercles de pêcheurs en Provence littorale. Enfin, c'est d'une véritable initiation confrérique que relève l'assimilation de la mentalité locale dans ses aspects les plus irréductibles. Ainsi, pour la Provence, les grands rassemblements hivernaux des Chambrettes-Cercles ont-ils représenté dans leurs villages toutes classes d'âge réunies et dans la liesse collective, des moments privilégiés pour la perpétuation de la tradition locale.

Simultanément s'affirme ici la dimension collective donnée par cet art de vivre campagnard à l'éducation du corps de jeunesse. Car la charge de façonner les jeunes générations aux valeurs privilégiées par le consensus villageois, reconnaissait à chacun, et non pas seulement à la parenté proche, un droit de regard permanent et de réprimande, sur les agissements des enfants villageois, aussitôt franchi le seuil de la maison familiale; ainsi se trouvait allégée la tâche parentale et simultanément instauré autour des enfants, un véritable climat de formation permanente diffusée par la mentalité locale et la perpétuant.

Par ces voies originales les Communautés villageoises assuraient la pérennité de leur manière de penser et l'échelle des valeurs reconnues par tous les membres. Cependant, la culture savante qui fleurissait parallèlement à elles n'a su reconnaître ni la richesse, ni la cohérence de ce patrimoine culturel campagnard, faisant montre à son endroit de la même éclatante myopie que Ruth Benedict stigmatise chez les Occidentaux "ne prenant pas au sérieux"[5] les cultures des autres peuples.

Mais certains d'entre mes lecteurs, engagés jusqu'ici sur d'autres perspectives de recherche ont probablement à l'esprit une question immédiate: celle des rapports entre ces modes de connaissance et les exigences d'une étude historique intéressée à les appréhender. En fait, ceux qui travaillent sur ces faits traditionnels savent d'expérience que les documents écrits, fondements de la démarche historique, livrent sur eux des informations qui, pour être souvent incidentes ou allusives, n'en demeurent pas moins très précieuses. J'illustrerai la fécondité d'une coopération entre les deux disciplines que m'a constamment prouvée ma propre recherche à travers deux exemples succints.

Dans ce genre d'entreprise qui appréhende deux institutions coutumières liées aux classes d'âge, l'Ethnologie apportant son expérience des différents types de société permet de situer l'usage dans l'aire culturelle large dont il procède par son agencement. Simultanément par son attention au vécu — symboles diffusés dans les objets de fabrication locale, coloration des faits communautaires entre autres — elle est en mesure de cerner les lignes de force à travers lesquelles se perpétue le génie autoch-

[5] Ruth Benedict, *Echantillons de civilisations*, trad. de l'Angl. par W. Raphaël (Paris, 1972), p. 14.

tone intéressé, tout en informant sur les aspects les plus actuels de ce dernier. De son côté l'Histoire puise dans sa familiarité avec les matériaux d'archives l'irremplaçable aptitude à mettre en parallèle des strates chronologiques étagées, démarquant ainsi le constant de l'occasionnel et dessinant fermement la ligne évolutive des collectivités.

C'est la France de l'Est qui a clairement perpétué le premier usage. En Champagne et en Lorraine le mois de mai ramenait, naguère, dans tous les villages le cortège de la Reine de Mai ou "trimouzette," adolescente accompagnée de sa suite juvénile, qui venait exécuter une danse chantée devant chaque maison. De même à Thann, en Alsace, la Rose de Mai, petite fille couverte de fleurs et de rubans, parcourt les rues de la ville avec une amie chargée de recueillir les dons dans une corbeille pour une fête de printemps:

> Rose de Mai, viens dans la verte forêt,
> Réjouis-nous, Mai, qui nous amène au milieu des roses.[6]

Voilà le fait ethnographique local. Il s'insère dans les Coutumes de Mai, complexe folklorique célèbre mais encore imparfaitement élucidé. Une enquête comparative m'a permis de montrer que ces troupes d'adolescentes étaient desservantes d'un culte funéraire de printemps, dévolu d'un bout à l'autre de l'Europe aux jouvencelles, alors que celui d'automne, encore parfaitement lisible, semble avoir été, à l'origine, apanage des jeunes gens.

Les jeunes filles couronnées de fleurs des champs et de verdure remplissent alors un véritable service public, en exécutant pour leur Communauté villageoise la danse chantée en l'honneur des esprits ancestraux, garants de la fertilité du terroir. Et l'ascendant prestigieux qui, partout, les entoure, souligne cette royauté saisonnière, reconnue en quelque sorte à cette catégorie d'âge à des fins de propitiation magique. Cette recherche en cours a été retenue pour souligner la contribution déterminante que l'historien des coutumes peut apporter à l'analyse des implications sociologiques d'un pareil usage, car son intégration communautaire peut se trouver singulièrement enrichie si des textes passés éclairent par exemples les critères retenus pour le choix des desservantes: beauté ou prestige familial? Sur l'ordre de préséance des maisonnées ordonnant l'hommage dansé: cet ordre coincide-t-il avec la hiérarchie administrative officielle ou bien relève-t-il d'une hiérarchie parallèle plus complexe? Quels sont les acteurs, les organisateurs, les temps forts de la fête de Thann? Bref, le témoignage des textes venant préciser le schéma de la mémoire orale permettront peut-être de détecter quelques-uns des processus de perpé-

---

[6] André Varagnac, *Civilisation traditionnelle et genres de vie* (Paris, 1948), p. 122.

tuation de l'équilibre villageois accroché à la reconduction périodique de cet usage; car ce dernier concrétise une des étapes du calendrier cérémoniel où nous avons reconnu une constante fondamentale de l'horizon campagnard.

Le second exemple nous ramène à l'aire méditerranéenne dont relève la Provence où a prospéré l'Abbaye de Jeunesse. De cette étude j'essaierai seulement de dégager les apports respectifs des deux disciplines, renvoyant pour sa présentation d'ensemble à celle qui figure dans mes *Chambrettes des Provençaux*.[7] L'Abbaye de Jeunesse est donc un usage provençal très ancien qui a su, sous une forme renouvelée, s'adapter au mode de vie contemporain. Dans une perspective large saisissant les faits européens elle relève de la famille de ces bachelleries juvéniles, rassemblant l'élément masculin de la puberté à la naissance du premier enfant en mariage, que les travaux du Professeur Natalie Zemon Davis ont magistralement éclairées pour la France du début des Temps Modernes.[8]

Un texte du XIIe siècle, charte de l'Albigeois de 1136, faisant référence à de très anciens usages, nous restitue l'appellation officielle de son titulaire comme "Roi des Jouvençaux." Des documents plus récents, délibérations des Conseils de Communautés des XVIIe et XVIIIe siècles, y précisent son organisation. Magistrature élective qui dote d'un chef annuel, choisi par libre acclamation au cabaret, la partie masculine du Corps de Jeunesse, celle-ci est soumis à l'approbation des pères de famille puisque ce n'est qu'après ratification de l'élection juvénile par le Conseil de la Communauté que "l'Abbé et son train," c'est-à-dire ses lieutenants ou "enseignes," sont officiellement investis.

De même attributs et prérogatives des élus se dégagent des documents judiciaires des mêmes périodes — procès en cours seigneuriales, arrêts de procédure civile ou criminelle. Ceux-ci nous transmettent les récriminations des villageois lorsque les Abbés en charge outrepassent les droits que leur reconnaît le consensus populaire. Quels sont ces derniers et quels sont en définitive les fonctions inhérentes à l'Abbaye de Jeunesse? Ici encore la complémentarité ethno-historique est parlante. L'observation ethnographique décèle un substrat très archaïque maintenu comme une survivance vénérable mais obscure apparentée à certains rites hivernaux du palais royal en Chine ancienne.[9] C'est la visite de l'Abbé et de ses lieutenants, à des fins prophylactiques, dans les rues du village provençal dans la nuit du passage d'une année à l'autre, c'est-à-dire la nuit du 31 Décembre au 1er Janvier. Les textes, de leur côté, mettent l'accent sur des activités prestigieuses et perçues comme les plus importantes pour la

---

[7] Lucienne A. Roubin, *Chambrettes des Provençaux* (Paris, 1970).
[8] Natalie Zemon Davis, "The Reasons of Misrule: Youth Groups and Charivaris in Sixteenth-Century France," *Past and Present*, 50 (February 1971), pp. 41-75.
[9] Marcel Granet, *Danses et légendes de la Chine ancienne*, nlle. ed., 2 vol. (Paris, 1959).

collectivité: au premier chef, l'organisation par l'abbé des réjouissances en temps de fête — Carnaval et fête annuelle du Saint Patron local. Car, dans cet univers méditerranéen, la fête représente le temps de conjonction périodique et faste, gage de couples neufs qui tempère l'habituelle ségrégation des deux moitiés masculine et féminine de la société villageoise. Aux termes de l'analyse fonctionnelle c'est l'enquête directe qui prend à nouveau le relai, et permet de percevoir comment s'est opéré le passage de l'antique Abbaye de Jeunesse au dynamique Comité des Fêtes mixte qui, en Provence, continue à animer, cocarde à la boutonnière, les festins villageois de l'été.

Malgré la brièveté de cette esquisse la référence aux pratiques de la Chine ancienne met en évidence la nécessité, pour éclairer dans leurs significations "premières" ces institutions coutumières auxquelles se rattache l'usage provençal, de faire converger documents ethnographiques contemporains et textes historiques de toutes les époques et parfois des plus archaïques. En effet, par delà ses variations régionales l'armature des groupes français témoigne d'un dualisme culturel[10] qu'ils partagent avec le reste de l'Europe. Celui-ci voit se cotoyer: d'une part, une culture savante, se transmettant au moins depuis le monde gréco-latin par voie écrite et officielle; et d'autre part, un savoir populaire, dans lequel s'intègre le savoir campagnard, plus vénérable encore puisqu'il a véhiculé jusqu'à nous les survivances de la Préhistoire. La voie de transmission de ce dernier, rappelons-le encore, est orale et manuelle. C'est la tâche conjointe des historiens et des ethnologues de définir, dans leurs différentes manifestations, la nature de leurs échanges et les canaux constamment renouvelés par lesquels transitent ces données.

[10]   André Varagnac, *La conquête des énergies* (Paris, 1972).

6

Chambrettes de Provence: Un Exemple de Club Villageois Méditerranéen

LUCIENNE A. ROUBIN

Des différentes communications présentées ici s'impose, à l'évidence, la notion de *multiplicité* des cultures populaires. Le dualisme culturel qui se perpétue en Europe au moins depuis le monde romain les a vu coexister sans discontinuité avec la culture savante mais se développer, par rapport à cette dernière, sur un registre différent.

Dans la perspective d'Ethnologie et d'Histoire conjuguées qui est la mienne, il m'a paru intéressant de présenter une institution de l'univers villageois qui fut, de longue date, un des grands pôles d'impulsion et de perpétuation de la manière de vivre et de penser chez les hommes de la Provence.

Ce faisant sera mis en évidence un des caractères fondamentaux qui différentie la culture des "non lettrés" de la culture des "lettrés," c'est-à-dire sa *spécifité locale*. En effet, l'institution analysée tire précisément son originalité de ce localisme en soulignant dès l'abord, l'intégration de la Provence — où elle s'est développée — au monde méditerranéen septentrional.

En corollaire à ce caractère fondamental de localisme apparaît la première exigence requise par ce genre d'étude: la maîtrise du dialecte. Et cette nécessité fait écho aux précisions apportées par le Professeur Eugen Weber[1] touchant à l'importance maintenue des parlers locaux dans la France de la fin du XVIIIe siècle. Seul, en effet, le dialecte permet d'accéder à la mentalité de ces hommes dans ce qu'elle a de plus irréductible, puisqu'il détient les clés des représentations collectives les plus inconscientes.

---

[1] Eugen Weber, "Who Sang the Marseillaise? Speech and Mentalities in the French Country-side during the Nineteenth Century," communication présentée au colloque "Popular Culture and Learned Culture in France," Stanford University, 1975, et reprise dans ce volume.

Dans la culture provençale cette institution des Chambrettes ne représente pas un élément isolé; bien au contraire, elle est partie intégrante d'un ensemble d'institutions coutumières omniprésent dans l'horizon campagnard.

Ce dernier, que l'on relève aisément un peu partout dans les campagnes européennes, se perpétue en France aux côtés des structures administratives officielles, issues de la législation napoléonienne — qui procèdent du droit écrit. Ce réseau de permanences institutionnelles est perpétué par l'*usage* c'est-à-dire par le droit *coutumier*.[2] Il maintient la cohésion villageoise et la sous-tend d'un véritable pacte d'entr'aide et d'assistance mutuelle entre les individus du groupe qui assument ensemble la condition humaine en un point précis de l'espace où se trouve implanté leur équilibre nourricier et où ils oeuvrent comme unité agissante en face des groupes voisins.

*   *   *

Chambrette: Maison des Hommes provençale

Pour désigner l'usage qui les rassemble et qu'ils désignent aujourd'hui sous le nom de *Cercle*, les Provençaux ont naguère employé le terme de "Chambrette," "petite chambre," diminutif du mot Tchambro. Le terme fait ici référence au sens que lui donne Olivier de Serres de refuge naturel, discret et sûr.[3] Présentes dans toute la Provence et jusque dans le moindre hameau, prospères jusqu'à la première guerre mondiale, la Chambrette représente:[4]

a) une *association* sélective entre les villageois, c'est-à-dire le pacte entre un groupe d'hommes qui institutionalise le rassemblement électif, face à la parenté biologique subie.

b) *le local* qui est le lieu de réunion de l'Association. L'Association est soumise à la contrainte du secret. Il était interdit naguère sous peine d'amende — et actuellement par entente tacite — de raconter à l'extérieur ce qui se passe à la Chambrette-Cercle. Le local est encore aujourd'hui, en certains bourgs, frappé d'interdit féminin absolu. En bref, la Chambrette est proprement en Provence, la réplique de cette institution que connaissent les ethnologues familiers de l'Océanie, de l'Afrique, de certains groupes de montagnards asiatiques: une Maison des Hommes.

[2] Marcel Mauss, *Manuel d'Ethnographie* (Paris, 1967), p. 140.
[3] Olivier de Serres: "Il observera les bestes, leurs repères et gestes, liets, *chambres*, reposées et bauges."
[4] Lucienne A. Roubin, *Chambrettes des Provençaux* (Paris, 1970).

Deux formes de l'institution ont pu être saisies: une forme ancienne, la Chambrette, en Provence intérieure, éteinte vers 1914; une forme contemporaine, le Cercle, dans les bourgs prospères de la région du Rhône, et du littoral. Entre les deux formes, l'organisation, le recrutement, les fonctions sont similaires et les deux formes sont deux aspects successifs du même usage, une adaptation aux exigences d'horizons historiques différents. En fait, plus que d'un Club villageois, la densité de l'institution permettrait de parler d'une confraternité villageoise.

Partout, en effet, l'usage comporte un rituel d'admission dont les phases et les éléments demeurent constants d'un village à l'autre. Cette intégration à l'association, officialise pour l'adolescent le passage du groupe étroit de la famille dans le groupe des citoyens villageois, base et pôle de contrôle de la vie communautaire. Les Chambrettes, non pas sociétés secrètes, mais "sociétés à secret," inculquaient à leurs membres une manière d'être, sorte d'empreinte dont l'association marque ses adhérents. Cet usage provençal qui constitue une originalité par rapport aux autres groupes français, apparaît comme un critère d'appartenance de cette province à l'aire méditerranéenne. Toute une série d'associations aménage dans cette aire la confraternité masculine soigneusement gardée, ici, de la Société des Femmes. Celles-ci donnent lieu un peu partout à des groupements sélectifs, tantôt professionnels, tantôt de voisinage, liées au quartier et les formes engendrées sur le versant septentrional méditerranéen connaissent maintes répliques sur le versant méridional maghrébin. Pour s'en tenir à quelques exemples: à côté des Chambrettes-Cercles, et relevant du même ensemble institutionnel l'Oda turc, les casinos andalous, et de la Provence à la Macédoine, les Caves où les villageois méditerranéens ont longtemps perpétué, sous le signe de la libation, certains rites propitiatoires pour leurs Communautés, en même temps que leurs veillées oisives et délibérantes.[5]

Cet univers méditerranéen départageant soigneusement les champs respectifs de l'espace masculin et de l'espace féminin constitue la toile de fond qu'il importe de garder sans cesse à l'esprit pour comprendre la place et le rôle de la Chambrette-Cercle dans le village provençal. Car les habitudes mentales et affectives qui présentent une tonalité spécifique dans chaque groupe, suscitent les actes par lesquels se concrétise le style ethnique. Et ces actes sont également porteurs du *Savoir* qui exprime et perpétue ces différentes cultures.

J'ai essayé de montrer ailleurs la richesse et la cohérence de la pensée villageoise, caractérisée par son étroite dépendance vis-à-vis du biotope

---

[5] Lucienne A. Roubin, "Libations et Communion villageoise de viticulteurs traditionnels," *Archéocivilisation*, Décembre 1972, pp. 110-117.

local.[6] Car c'est la maîtrise empirique de ce biotope — à tous les nivaux: pédologique, climatique, floristique et animalier — qui constituent précisément ici la culture.

Pour la "geuse parfumée," puisque c'est l'expression qui désigne la Provence dans les vieux textes, l'attrayante luminosité s'allie à un sol fragile, sans cesse menacé par la sécheresse et par l'érosion. C'est à partir de cette donnée cependant, que les Provençaux, propriétaires en faire valoir direct, ont élaboré un équilibre nourricier durable qui s'appuie sur un terroir découpé en parcelles exiguës, accrochées au versant rocailleux où chacun doit travailler seul, et le plus souvent à la main. Aussi, toute domestication florale nouvelle, toute innovation devait pouvoir être commentée et rapidement diffusée à l'ensemble des villageois, car c'est cette patiente prospection empirique qui a progressivement abouti à la maîtrise de cultures nouvelles. Ainsi, pour le pays de Grasse, la diffusion — dans le domaine des espèces odoriférantes et des vignes à raisin de table — de variétés récentes s'est réalisée dans une aire très dense de Chambrettes prospères. Ce lieu de rassemblement masculin permanent tempère, en effet, l'état d'isolement dans lequel l'éparpillement parcellaire maintient les hommes pendant le travail aux champs.

Mais ce rôle de club agronomique qu'assure la Chambrette dans toute la montagne provençale n'est qu'une des plus apparentes parmi les fonctions que l'examen des activités en honneur dans l'institution vont nous permettre de recenser et d'analyser.

Chambrette, pôle de savoir autochtone

Et, tout d'abord, comment l'association se définit-elle pour ses propres membres? Dans les statuts que les archives nous ont conservés, elle se désigne souvent comme "société d'agrément" — société dont les membres s'agréent, dont les membres se cooptent. La Chambrette-Cercle, en ce sens, est le contraire même d'une simple société de divertissement. La constance des critères de recrutement, la minutie du rituel d'admission, et surtout la rigueur de la fonction de censure qu'elle assume vis-à-vis de ses membres en délivre autant de preuves irréfutables.

C'est précisément cette richesse fonctionnelle qui m'a permis de distinguer de prime abord, pour le XIXe siècle, les *Chambrettes Villageoises* — regroupant paysans, viticulteurs, artisans, pêcheurs ou charretiers — des "Sociétes d'agrément" prospérant parfois dans les mêmes bourgades qui sont des *Cercles de notables* et fonctionnaires liés à la bourgeoisie.[7] Le même

[6] "Savoir et art de vivre campagnard," communication présentée à la réunion de la Society for French Historical Studies, 1975, et reprise dans ce volume.

[7] Dés 1967, j'ai précisé mon interprétation fondamentalement différente de celle de Monsieur M. Agulhon, quant à l'insertion de la Chambrette dans la collectivité villageoise par

terme de cercle sert à désigner les deux séries d'associations qui présentent entre elles une véritable *différence organique*, en dépit de règlements administratifs en apparence parfois très proches. Les seconds, cercles de bourgeoisie, sont des associations à fonction proprement et exclusivement récréative. Leurs réunions rassemblent, à côté des notables locaux, des fonctionnaires en service dans la région où ils sont en résidence passagère. La bourgade de Castellane, en Provence orientale, par ses fonds d'Archives[8] livre un panorama significatif des deux ensembles de cercles qui l'animent pour la seconde moitié du XIXe siècle.

Il y avait deux cercles de notables:

a) *Le Cercle de la Paix*, qui se forme en 1858, regroupe propriétaires terriens aisés faisant exploiter leurs terres; médecin, pharmacien, fabricant de draps, notaire, garde général des eaux et forêts.

b) *Le Cercle National*, qui se crée en 1899; là se rencontrent magistrats, banquier, ingénieur, procureur, médecin.

La série des Chambrettes est représentée par:

a) *La Société de Saint-Antoine*, Chambrette qui dépose ses statuts en 1866. Elle regroupe deux maçons, un cordier, cinq agriculteurs, deux boulangers, un cordonnier et un menuisier.

b) *Le Cercle Saint-Vincent de 1870*, qui compte un bourrelier, deux chapeliers, un boulanger, un charron, un tailleur de pierre, un boucher, un coiffeur, un entrepreneur de voiture, un menuisier, un ferblantier. On pourrait aisément multiplier les exemples à partir d'autres bourgades.

Entre les deux séries de groupements, nous le soulignons, la différence n'est pas seulement sociologique; elle est beaucoup plus fondamentale et proprement fonctionnelle. En face des Cercles de Bourgeoisie, simples sociétés de divertissement, les Chambrettes-Cercles représentent d'abord et avant tout une institution de solidarité qui lient dans un pacte permanent de solidarité socio-économique les pères de famille de chacune des communautés rurales où elles fleurissent. La fonction de divertissement ne représente ici qu'une entre plusieurs autres de leurs fonctions constantes. Il est malaisé de suggérer en quelques mots la cohérence et la richesse des activités se déroulant dans l'association. Le rassemblement communiel de la communauté masculine, la diffusion du *savoir*, et la perpétuation du *style ethnique* en sont les pôles constants.

rapport aux Cercles de notables. Face à ceux-ci, simples clubs de divertissement, la Chambrette, par sa densité fonctionnelle, s'affirme comme la forme provençale d'un très ancien mode d'*alliance* villageois, en perpétuel ajustement avec son temps et simultanément attentif à la démarcation maintenue, par la mentalité méditerranéenne, entre champ d'action masculin et féminin. Cf. *Arts et Traditions populaires* (1967), pp. 326-327.

[8] Archives Départementales-Digne-Série M. 6.

Le rassemblement de la Communauté masculine

Contrastant avec la vie journalière et laborieuse qui disperse les villageois aux champs le temps du malheur et le temps de la fête rassemblent les hommes et renforcent la cohésion communautaire. C'est précisément dans la cadre des Chambrettes que s'ordonnaient en Provence les manifestation qui concrétisent cette dernière.

En face de la maladie et de la mort, les usages perpétués et les statuts que nous ont conservés les Archives tissent les solidarités les plus affirmées. Les modalités de cette assistance étaient multiples: secours à un sociétaire accidenté, soutien en cas de maladie ou de veuvage, et, selon une règle qui ne connaît pas de dérogation, escorte en corps constitué et jusqu'au cimetière, d'un sociétaire défunt. Tout manquement à ce devoir d'accompagnement funéraire était pénalisé d'amendes et de sanctions diverses renouvelées à l'envie dans tous les statuts qui nous sont parvenus.

Cette même participation collective de l'association atteint à la même unanimité dans la fête qui trouve les sociétaires tout à la fois acteurs et organisateurs. Les deux pôles en sont le Carnaval et la Fête Patronale d'hiver. Le premier, le temps de Carnaval, a donné lieu à des réjouissances dans toutes les Chambrettes; mais les sorties régulières de sociétaires regroupés en troupe autonome de masques ont été particulièrement brillantes en Chambrettes de la Provence centrale et orientale. Cependant, c'est la seconde, la fête d'hiver, au cours de laquelle se fait la passation des pouvoirs entre gestionnaires et l'intégration officielle des nouveaux membres, qui souligne le plus clairement la fonction d'intégration et la fusion sociale assurées par les Chambrettes dans la Communauté villageoise. On reviendra dans un instant sur le rôle de ces grands rassemblements hivernaux dans la transmission des modèles culturels, mais il faut souligner leur importance comme lieu privilégié pour le renouvellement du pacte d'entr'aide, resserrant par l'intermédiaire du vieux rituel païen de la Libation au vin les liens qui cimentent la collectivité villageoise.

La diffusion du savoir et la perpétuation du style ethnique

Dans l'univers de savoir oral qui baigne la Provence rurale jusqu'au premier quart du XXe siècle, les Chambrettes fonctionnaient tout à la fois comme *pôle de concertation agronomique*, remodelant sans cesse la connaissance du terroir, comme nous l'avons précédemment souligné, et bourse agricole locale, ouvrant sur l'extérieur le périmètre villageois en transmettant l'information venue d'ailleurs. C'est d'elles que partaient les opérations collectives du calendrier annuel: bans des moissons, des vendanges, modalités d'irrigation, mise en service ou en défends des pâturages, organisation des expéditions de chasse ou de pêche collective. Mais leur rôle de diffusion ne se limita pas au secteur techno-économique; responsables de la subsistance de la communauté, ces sociétés de pères de famille apparaissent en outre comme garantes de la transmission *des usages régissant les échanges sociaux* et au niveau des rencontres juvéniles (sanctionnant les unions étrangères au Corps de Jeunesse), et au niveau de la famille (privilège attaché à la naissance d'un enfant mâle par exemple). Enfin, centre de propagation des courants idéologiques qui traversent le territoire national, les Chambrettes ont peu on prou fonctionné pour la période de 1840 à 1900 comme des centres de diffusion des idéaux républicains pour lesquels les artisans-compagnons ayant accompli leur Tour de France, semblent avoir joué un rôle important.

A ce point se trouve donc étroitement imbriquée leur action au plan local et au plan national, puisque ces sociétés ont oeuvré dans le sens d'une implantation des modèles nationaux dans l'aire provençale. Cependant, tout se passe comme si la substitution radicale d'une fonction d'information privilégiant les modèles nationaux au détriment du rôle de pôle local d'intégration leur avait été fatale; on constate, en effet, que celles qui l'ont pratiqué exclusivement sont tombées en sommeil puis ont disparu, tandis que se sont maintenues prospères celles d'entre ces sociétés qui ont su demeurer un centre d'attraction pour l'ensemble de la collectivité. Et c'est au cours de ces rencontres répétées des jours ordinaires et des grands rassemblements festifs annuels que se diffusaient le plus sûrement les choix esthétiques retenus par le consensus du groupe, ceux dans lesquels il se connaît et qui cimentent son identité en face d'autres groupes proches.

L'adaptabilité à l'horizon contemporain

Cependant il est important de noter que l'observation des Cercles actuellement prospères sur le littoral et dans la région rhodanienne permet de ne pas s'arrêter à ce qui pourrait être considéré comme une vision idyllique et passéiste des choses, dont, à juste titre, Professeur Soriano souligne le danger.[9] Certaines activités liées à des secteurs autonomes de la société contemporaine, par exemple l'assistance économique, perdant ici leur raison d'être, sont progressivement relayées par des fonctions nouvelles.

La situation ethnique de la Provence en donne une bonne illustration. Depuis le début du XXe siècle, cette province a fonctionné comme un pôle important d'attraction pour l'émigration étrangère: italienne, plus récemment espagnole, puis portugaise et nord-africaine. Dans ce contexte, les

[9] Marc Soriano, "Le 'ton inimitable' de La Fontaine," communication présentée au colloque "Popular Culture and Learned Culture in France," Stanford University, 1975, et reprise dans ce volume.

Cercles actuels développent sous nos yeux une récente fonction d'intégration en s'ouvrant à des catégories de sociétaires non villageois: essentiellement les Français en résidence secondaire et les étrangers anciennement implantés dans le bourg. En cercle de gros bourg prévaut l'assimilation des tenants de résidences secondaires; en cercle terrien ou de pêcheurs prévaut l'assimilation de tous les Méditerranéens — Français rapatriés d'Afrique du Nord, Italiens, Espagnols — tandis que la communauté locale reste plus distante vis-à-vis des "Parisiens."

En ce sens le Cercle continue à regrouper, comme la Chambrette dont il a pris le relai, la collectivité des hommes qui habitent de façon permanente dans le bourg où il prospère. Et l'admission au Cercle, des étrangers, offre, selon les remarques de Roger Bastide, à la personnalité destructurée de l'étranger-résident une voie accélérée de restructuration selon les normes d'une culture à la fois majoritaire et locale.[10]

De même le Cercle perpétue cette fonction de *détection des élites locales* qu'assumait déjà la Chambrette, c'est-à-dire qu'il aide la collectivité à repérer, parmi ses sociétaires, les plus attentifs aux problèmes contemporains; par là il influence les options des municipalités et débouche de proche en proche sur le groupe national. Centres de contestation et d'arbitrage constamment ouverts, les Cercles sont le lieu où peuvent s'expliciter dans une atmosphère de conciliation toutes les tendances et par échange de vues, se préciser, se nuancer, le jugement de chacun sur chacun et sur tout.

Ainsi, à l'observation, cette institution provençale que je suppose très ancienne, à travers des formes constamment renouvelées, témoigne de son haut degré de plasticité, et oeuvre comme un véritable centre de formation locale, axé sur une conscience communautaire très profonde, alimenté de jour en jour par les préoccupations quotidiennes des hommes concernés. C'est proprement, de situation en situation historiques différentes, ces mêmes hommes affirmant et aménageant la façon de vivre qu'ils ont choisie. C'est-à-dire un art d'agir et de penser harmonieusement lié — proprement une culture populaire au sens total où l'entend Robert Mandrou — et c'est pourquoi il m'a paru intéressant de la présenter sommairement ici.

[10] Roger Bastide, "Les études et les recherches interethniques en France de 1945 à 1968," Publications de la faculté de Nice (C.E.R.I.N.), n. 1 (Octobre 1968).

7

Folklore as an Ethnographic Source: A "Mise au Point"

MICHAEL R. MARRUS

I

At the beginning of the twentieth century, folklore died quickly in the little Breton village of Saint Pierre de Quiberon once 18,000 tourists began to flood in each summer. The memorialist who describes this for us, a former school teacher, was perhaps more sensitive than most to the end of folklore, having benefited little from the influx of tourism. According to him, what the village lost in this process was nothing less than "the poetry of life."[1] Saint Pierre, with its hordes of sun worshipers, was of course exceptional. Yet this lament was especially familiar as the nineteenth century turned into the twentieth, and as community after community saw the old poetry lose its meaning and significance. To be sure, much of the loss happened only in the imagination. People have always mourned the passing of the good old days, just as others have always, secretly or otherwise, found reason to rejoice. But those who joined this sad chorus at the end of the nineteenth century often had something rather specific in mind when reflecting upon the past, and essentially the argument of this paper is their own.

My contention is twofold. First, the local *érudits* and antiquarians of this time were talking about something *real*; they were looking sympathetically at bits and pieces of a cultural system centuries old, about which ethnologists and historians would now like to know more. I propose to discuss this system as it applies to France, and the evidence provided by folklore. Second, the change which was apparently so swift and decisive in Saint Pierre de Quiberon was occurring at a much more gradual pace throughout most of France during this period. I would like to say something about this process, which is a turning point of enormous significance.

For the immediate forerunners of the folklorist school, folklore was one

[1] A. Carlier, *Un village breton en 1895: Saint-Pierre de Quiberon* (Cannes, 1949), p. 30.

way of describing "the poetry of life." Their picture of the rural world in the middle decades of the nineteenth century was heavily coloured by Romanticism. This tradition was primarily literary, and strove to transmit the beauty of peasant stories, legends and songs from their original rustic environment of the world of Parisian salons.[2] But by the mid-1880's this original orientation had an old-fashioned ring. By then Paul Sébillot had introduced to folklore a much wider scope. The discipline was, he explained in the imposing new *Revue des traditions populaires*, "a part of anthropology, at least the non-medical portion of that science."[3] He recommended the mode of "popular ethnography," as opposed to the earlier concern with literary themes. Folklorists took this advice to heart. They set out busily to collect and classify rural customs, traditions and practices of all sorts. They aspired to be *sérieux*. Pausing seldom to analyze or to explain, impressed more perhaps with the need to record as much as possible of a rapidly expiring culture, they assembled a staggering volume of information. Most of this material found its way into Arnold Van Gennep's monumental *Manuel de folklore français*, published in nine large volumes between 1937 and 1958. As this work of France's master folklorist began to appear, the French government founded the *Musée des arts et traditions populaires*, directed by Georges-Henri Rivière and his assistant André Varagnac. With a sure institutional footing, and with a mass of assembled data to which it could refer, folklore won intellectual respectability by the time of the Second World War.[4]

"Folklore" has, in fact, many sides. Some continue to consider it "oral literature" — stories, legends and songs, "a kind of recreative culture for

---

[2] For a good discussion of the work of the early folklorists, see Pierre Saintyves [Emile Nourry], *Manuel de folklore* (Paris, 1936), ch. 5. See also Charles Rearick, *Beyond the Enlightenment: Historians and Folklore in Nineteenth-Century France* (Bloomington, 1974); and Richard M. Dorson, "Foreword" to Genevieve Massignon, ed., *Folktales of France* (Chicago, 1968).

[3] Paul Sébillot, "Le folk-lore: les traditions populaires et l'ethnographie légendaire," *Revue d'anthropologie*, 15 (1886), p. 293; "Programme et but de la Société des traditions populaires," *Revue des traditions populaires*, 1 (1886), i-iv; Rearick *Beyond the Enlightenment*, pp. 163-164. Sébillot was a Breton folklorist who founded and edited the *Revue des traditions populaires* and conducted research widely in France. His numerous published works helped to popularize the field of study and stimulated other research. See his *Coutumes populaires de la Haute-Bretagne* (1886; new ed., Paris, 1967); *Le folk-lore: littérature orale et ethnographie traditionnelle* (Paris, 1913); *Le folklore de la Bretagne*, (new ed., Paris, 1968); *Le folk-lore de la France*, 4 vols. (Paris, 1904-1907); and *Le paganisme contemporain chez les peuples Celto-Latins* (Paris, 1908).

[4] See the imprimatur given by Lucien Febvre, "Folklore et folkloristes," *Annales d'histoire sociale*, 1 (1939), pp. 152-160. Cf. André Varagnac, "Folklore et histoire des civilisations: cultures dissociées et cultures homogènes," *Annales d'histoire sociale*, 8 (1945), pp. 95-102; Nicole Belmont, *Arnold Van Gennep: le créateur de l'ethnologie française* (Paris, 1974); and H. A. Senn, "Arnold van Gennep: Structuralist and Apologist for the Study of Folklore in France," *Folklore*, 85 (1974), pp. 229-243.

those who could not, through ignorance or lack of time, use books."[5] In this vision folklore appeared as accessory, and to some extent this definition is popular today. French, on the other hand, has given the term a mildly pejorative ring, usually signifying a colourful but inconsequential aspect of something. But when the search for traditional artifacts broadened to include customs, rituals, and traditional practices of all sorts it became clear, among practitioners at least, that more was involved than colour or recreation. Aspiring to be more than mere collectors, professional folklorists considered their specific findings to be accent points of a cultural system. To them, folklore stood for the system itself, very broadly speaking, the way of life in a traditional, European, rural society.

And this is my position too. For these various catalogued items relate to one another in a coherent way. Together they convey what is the essence of culture, "a people's ethos," as the anthropologist Clifford Geertz puts it, "the tone, character and quality of their life, its moral and aesthetic style and mood."[6] In this case, the specific culture is village culture, the social foundation of peasant life in traditional France. Folklore was at once an expression of village solidarity and a means to preserve it; it was a reflection of the world-view which was rooted in the village, and a mechanism by which the work of the village could be done. Or, better put, folklore *was* village culture. Of course, the centre of folkloric observance was sometimes other than the village; the individual, the family, the town, or the region could appear as the generators of practice. But sooner or later the whole system depended upon the cohesion of the village structure.[7] And when that cohesion declined precipitously during the last quarter of the nineteenth century, folklore collapsed. It was significantly during that time that folklore became an object of serious, intensive study. As so

[5] Sébillot, "Folk-lore," p. 292. For a comprehensive discussion of concepts of folklore in a much wider context than that offered in this paper, see Richard M. Dorson's introduction to idem, ed., *Folklore and Folklife: An Introduction* (Chicago, 1972).

[6] *The Interpretation of Cultures: Selected Essays* (New York, 1973), p. 89. For an extremely useful discussion of "culture" in France, which explores many of the themes raised in this paper, see Maurice Crubellier, *Histoire culturelle de la France, XIXe-XXe siècle* (Paris, 1974). Much stimulating discussion is to be found in Natalie Z. Davis, *Society and Culture in Early Modern France: Eight Essays* (Stanford, 1975). Cf. the fascinating discussion by E.P. Thompson, "Patrician Society, Plebian Culture," *Journal of Social History*, 7 (1974), pp. 382-405.

[7] Left out of this paper is any discussion of whether a specifically "urban" folklore exists. This is a complex question, and one which troubled French folklorists attempting to define their field of study. It is here assumed, however, that folkloric culture was essentially rural, and that such urban manifestations as did exist were largely derivative. "Folklore" is not meant to include all aspects of popular culture in traditional France, but rather those which made up a coherent package of practices and beliefs common to a vast majority of the population over a very considerable period of time.

frequently happens, scholarship came in the train of social change, bringing into intellectual reality what social forces had already destroyed. "The poetry of life" was only poetry when it existed in reality no more; before then it was either "life," for those who lived it, or a poetic projection of what people wished life to be.

All sources have their biases, and it is well to consider what historians are likely to encounter in using this material. The scattered descriptions of practices and customs, strewn about folkloric manuals with little care for systematic organization or theory, represent a different approach to rural folk than one finds in most historical accounts. Mainly the product of painstaking, antiquarian interest, folklore looks at the life of common folk with the bureaucrats left out. Neither the police, nor the hospital authorities, nor the bishop, nor the mayor, nor the government official intrudes. By temperament and conviction, folklorists preferred to avoid such obvious contact points in favour of the most direct approach — interview and observation. Thus their sources tend perhaps to accentuate the degree to which peasants lived apart from the rest of the population. In addition, they direct attention away from those villagers who had such contact, and towards the most "authentic" expressions of folkloric culture. And the folklorists had their axes to grind, too — their perspective was most often a particular blend of bourgeois nostalgia and a delight with quaintness. At the same time, however, they elevated accurate observation to a virtual cult. Historians must decide for themselves whether there is serious distortion here, and whether the folklorists uncovered a somewhat different rustic than those who examined various official sources. My own feeling is that folklore provides a useful corrective to a view based upon the small minority of peasants caught up in the official net.[8]

II

Folklorists who tramped through the French countryside collecting material from the 1880's had great difficulties describing patterns. When it came to details their observations were clear and precise; when it came to the broad picture they were generally helpless. To be sure, the second generation of *savants*, in particular Van Gennep, had a sufficiently firm grasp of the folkloric map of France to denote major divisions of common culture — there were at least seven traditional languages which helped originally to transmit folklore: Flemish, dialects of Oïl and of Oc, Breton,

[8] For a different point of view, which I think overstresses the "political" intentions of the folklorists, see Michel de Certeau, Dominique Julia, and Jacques Revel, "La beauté du mort: le concept du 'culture populaire,'" *Politique aujourd'hui*, (December 1970), pp. 2-23, and the same authors' "Une ethnographie de la langue: l'enquête de Grégoire sur les patois," *Annales: économies, sociétés, civilisations*, 30 (1975), pp. 3-41.

Basque, Franco-Provençal, Catalan, and Germanic dialects from Alsace-Lorraine; and there were also major climactic and geographic distinctions which put a stamp upon cultural patterns.[9] But even when "cultural zones" could be broadly identified, a bewildering variety within them was the rule. This is one factor which contributed to the catalogue character of early folkloric articles, some of which read like mere lists of practices peculiar to specific villages. On the ground, more often than not, was a chaos of diversity. Whether it was the local harvest feast, the activities of Carnaval, or the gamut of popular superstition which folklorists reported, one thing was clear — no two villages were exactly alike. In one commune there were annual *feux de Saint Jean*, the ceremonial bonfires lit in celebration of the day of that saint; close by the custom appeared to have been either neglected for many generations, or never practised at all. There were some areas, devoted to the patronage of Saint Jean, where the fires had never been heard of; and similarly elsewhere, such as in Flanders, Maine, Anjou, and a few places in the Alps, there were no seasonal fires of any sort.[10] Certain regions had a rough consistency when it came to certain practices: but knowing, for example, that a certain kind of popular pageant was common in Alsace on Sunday or Monday of Pentecost would not guarantee that it was done in specific Alsatian villages. Van Gennep's investigative response to this problem was the "cartographical method," in which maps were constructed denoting positive and negative "zones" for the presence of certain phenomena. However, it was frequently impossible to make sense out of the findings, and the pointillist visions which emerged from so much painstaking effort often did not say more than what every local knew: no two villages were alike.[11] Villages, in a certain sense, were sovereign.

This points, I think, to the fundamental aspect of folklore I have mentioned, the fact that it was village culture, shaped and controlled by small rural communities. Folkloric culture proved so durable in France because its organizing points, the village communities, were sunk so deeply in the soil of the French countryside. At the close of the eighteenth century, according to one authority, there were well over 40,000 such rural communities in France.[12] These were the nuclei of France's rural

[9] See Arnold Van Gennep, *Manuel de folklore français*, 9 vols. (Paris, 1937-1958), I[1], pp. 1-3.

[10] Ibid., I[4], pp. 1743, 1776; André Varagnac, *Civilisation traditionnelle et genres de vie* (Paris, 1948), p. 21.

[11] Arnold Van Gennep, "Contribution à la méthodologie du folklore," *Lares: organo del Comitato nazionale italiano per le arti popolari*, 5 (1934), p. 27 ff. Cf. Belmont, *Arnold Van Gennep*, p. 144.

[12] A. Babeau, *Le village sous l'ancien régime* (Paris, 1878), p. 46 n. On the subject of villages and their importance, see the useful articles by Jerome Blum, "The European Village as Community: Origins and Functions," *Agricultural History*, 45 (1971), pp. 157-178, and "The Internal Structure and Polity of the European Village Community from the Fifteenth to the

population, so important for so long in terms of both culture and demography. In roughly two-thirds of the country these communities tended to be small hamlets, with never more than a cluster of families — the *habitat dispersé* of the geographers. It was somewhat different in the North and East (in the old provinces of Artois, Picardy, Flanders, Champagne, Lorraine, Franche-Comté, Alsace, Orléanais, and the Ile-de-France), and also in the Midi. There the dominant form was the *habitat groupé*, more sizeable villages of less than 2,000 people which were still beneath the level of small towns.[13] Statistics on the numbers of people involved illustrate the continued importance of dispersed settlement at the end of the nineteenth century. Taking the entire population, official censuses made a crude distinction between *population agglomérée*, which usually referred to people living in the *chef-lieu* of the commune, in contiguous dwellings, whether rural or urban, and the *population éparse*, referring to hamlets or isolated homesteads. From 1872, when these statistics were first collected, over half of rural France lived in these generally small and relatively isolated settlements. In 1901 over 13.5 million people were classified as *population éparse*, more than a third of the total population.[14]

If we may go by a variety of ethnographic materials, the village community of the *ancien régime* was a universe unto itself, with very few openings to the worlds of city, province or state. Communal roots were sunk deep in the medieval past. During the twelfth, thirteenth and fourteenth centuries the great revolution in European agriculture made necessary some form of common decision-making; in the new system of biennial or triennial crop rotation, villagers whose individual holdings were scattered about the fields in strips engaged to some varying degree in a collective agricultural enterprise. Common resources of land for pasture and forest, common capital such as ovens, mills or presses, and common obligations such as seigneurial dues required village organization and some basic rules for cooperation. Despite wide variations in agrarian and seigneurial regimes, communal organization of some sort maintained a fixed presence in the French countryside. Moreover, the

Nineteenth Century," *Journal of Modern History*, 43 (1971), pp. 541-576. See also Albert Dauzat, *Le village et le paysan de France* (Paris, 1941), Roger Dion, *Essai sur la formation du paysage rural français* (Tours, 1934), and Charles Parain, "Une vieille tradition démocratique: les assemblées de communauté," *La Pensée*, no. 4 (1945), pp. 43-48. The classic treatment of the subject is by Marc Bloch, *French Rural History: An Essay on Its Basic Characteristics*, trans. by Janet Sondheimer (Berkeley and Los Angeles, 1966), ch. 5.
[13] Albert Demangeon, *Problèmes de géographie humaine*, 4th ed. (Paris, 1952), p. 159 ff.; Alfred de Foville, introduction to Ministère de l'Instruction publique, des Beaux-Arts et des Cultes, *Enquête sur les conditions de l'habitation en France*, 2 vols. (Paris, 1894), I.
[14] *Statistique générale de la France. Résultats statistiques du dénombrement de 1891* (Paris, 1894), pp. 61-64.

communal units thus formed by work and political life were reinforced by the parish structure, which was normally superimposed upon villages or sometimes a small cluster of hamlets. Consequently, the religious community and the agrarian community were one and the same. The village community was thus not merely a working unit, it was a living unit, in which the fundamental activities of working life intermixed with those of religion and sociability. Throughout time, the great moments in the lives of villagers were invariably communal events: birth, marriage and death, plague or famine, drought or an unusually prosperous year, celebration or bereavement, all brought the villagers together in some collective manifestation.

To be sure, villages were not hermetically sealed. In some areas, especially the North or Northeast, the textile industry reached out to the villages; elsewhere, particularly from the mid-eighteenth century, stocking knitters, glovemakers, lacemakers and many others maintained occasional contact with the outside. Wet nurses, apprentices, servant girls, agricultural labourers, beggars and soldiers, all moved about, and at times roamed far beyond their own regions. But Pierre Goubert is probably right to suggest that these migrants (who naturally figure more heavily in administrative records than do their less mobile counterparts) were relatively few in number for most of the *ancien régime*. "Nineteen and a half out of twenty million people remained bound to the land, plot, hut or *quartier* where they grew up. Old France is characterized not by unrest, social mobility and popular migration, but by sedantariness. Except for the perennial adventurers, people only became mobile when driven by necessity, which usually meant destitution."[15] Villages remained the most visible mark of this traditional stability, and the fundamental social grouping for the overwhelming majority of Frenchmen.

These village communities preserved and nourished a cultural life of their own. Because they were relatively cut off from one another the details of this culture, upon which the folklorists reported, frequently differed; because the patterns of life within them were so basically similar, the fundamental characteristics were the same.

Foremost among these is an almost compulsive ordering of ceremonies and practices, to the point where modern observers frequently did little else but construct inventories of local beliefs on the most banal of activities. In Bas-Languedoc, the master folklorist Paul Sébillot took the trouble to tell us, hair cannot be cut on Fridays, for fear of catching a cold;

---

[15] Pierre Goubert, *The Ancien Régime: French Society, 1600-1750*, trans. by Steve Cox (London, 1973), p. 43. On migrations, see the excellent discussion in Olwen H. Hufton, *The Poor of Eighteenth-Century France, 1750-1789* (Oxford, 1974), ch. 3.

the foot of the bed must not face the door, for that hastens death.[16] Breton villagers who lined up in the barn to thresh grain during the winter did not place themselves randomly, but in a strict hierarchical order, fixed by local custom.[17] And so on.

Traditions such as these, once multiplied a hundred-fold, regulated rigidly daily life. Of course, all cultures involve rules for the governing of behaviour to a certain degree. But folkloric culture is impressive for the wide range of such beliefs, and hence the all-inclusive character of regulation. From the writings of the folklorists it is evident that there was virtually no facet of existence not covered by some prescript or superstition: the preparation of food, the use of agricultural tools, the treatment of animals, the care of the sick, the ordinary forms of discourse, were all closely integrated into a system of custom. Whether inspired by habit or "superstition" the result was the same: the ordering of conduct in a highly visible and comprehensive way.

Consider for a moment the *fêtes patronales* (the commemoration of the day of the local patron saint), seasonal or calendrical festivals, pilgrimages, and other village celebrations. In a classic study of festivity, Roger Caillois once stressed the crucial function of release from the rules of daily life, the orgiastic reversal of everyday controls.[18] My own reading of the significance of *fêtes* in French rural society is quite the opposite: while it is true that there was plenty of drinking and blowing off steam during the *fêtes*, there was also an even greater degree of regulated behaviour than in the course of *la vie quotidienne*. Villagers marched about, danced, prayed, drank and feasted according to a regimen whose rigor impressed many observers. One example is the *quête* or collection which often preceded the *fête*. Village festivity was often made possible by a systematic gathering of food to be offered to a saint or the *curé*, of wood to be burned in a bonfire, of special cakes to be distributed to the poor, and so on. These collections, usually undertaken by the organized unmarried men of the village, were pointedly coercive: those who failed to contribute were held up to severe public ridicule, or even worse. Village culture contained an entire arsenal of formulae predicting grave misfortune to fall upon the recalcitrant.[19]

[16] P.S., "Traditions et superstitions du Bas-Languedoc," *Revue des traditions populaires*, 6 (1891), pp. 548-550.

[17] Olivier Perrin and Alexendre Bouet, *Breiz izel, ou la vie des Bretons dans l'Armorique*, new ed. (Quimper, 1918), p. 150.

[18] Roger Caillois, *L'homme et le sacré*, 3rd ed. (Paris, 1950), ch. 4. For an interesting recent view see Agnes Villadary, *Fête et vie quotidienne* (Paris, 1968).

[19] There are numerous descriptions of *quêtes* in Van Gennep, *Manuel*, passim. On the highly regulated character of *fêtes* see, for example, Varagnac, *Civilisation*, pp. 71-73; Roger Lecotte, *Recherches sur les cultes populaires dans l'actuel diocèse de Meaux* (Paris, 1953), p. 285;

These maledictions made participation in the *fête*, and participation in a closely prescribed fashion, compulsory. Folkloric descriptions were studded with other references to universal involvement according to the rules. And the rules covered everything, from what was to be worn, to the order of march in village processions, to virtually every form of public activity.

One cannot conclude from these descriptions of the detailed ordering of events that in every village every one of the precepts was followed, or that every hamlet had a complete inventory of do's and don't's. Indeed, it would be useful to know more about how villages or regions differed in this respect, and what the significance of this was. But from the descriptions we have one can get a sense of the general mood of folkloric belief and practice, a mood of calm submission akin to that of ritualistic observance. Villagers did not feel particularly coerced, for the world of folklore was the only world they knew. Yet a truly formidable network of regulation attended their daily existence — to a point which we would find staggering in its intensity. For the presence of so many grave sanctions for rule breakers, and the obvious dread which such a status inspired in the minds of ordinary villagers, indicate that these precepts were more important to traditional peasants than are mere social conventions to us. These were vital matters which were constituent elements of a world-view. At the same time they were normal and familiar matters, in the sense that they were fully integrated into the rhythms of life.

How did this system maintain itself over the course of centuries? Traditional culture on the local level was a response of communities to an agricultural world in which dearth was a fundamental condition of existence. In practical terms this meant that there was barely enough to eat. From the thirteenth to the eighteenth centuries, Henri Mendras tells us, the yields of barley, rye, wheat and vegetables remained more or less constant. Periodic payments to lords, church and state, while varying widely, usually absorbed whatever surpluses a primitive technology could provide. Throughout this period the material basis of life in the village community remained at the often precarious levels which he describes. Given this situation, in which men fought a constant battle against hunger, novelty or innovation would represent a desperate gamble, always threatening to cast a community over the brink of starvation; unchanging peasant routines therefore constituted a storehouse of accumulated wis-

Prugne Antoine, *Paysan sans terre: récit* (Clermont-Ferrand, 1971), pp. 122-123; Georges H. Rivière and Marcel Maget, "Fêtes et cérémonies de la communauté villageoise," in Jean Charbonnier et al., *Agriculture et communauté* (Paris, 1943), pp. 75-95; and Jean Fourastié, *Les loisirs: pour quoi faire?* (Paris, 1970), p. 21. For a fascinating treatment of a related matter, the concept of "honor" in traditional society, see Peter Berger, Brigitt Berger and Hansfried Kellner, *The Homeless Mind: Modernization and Consciousness* (New York, 1974), pp. 83-96.

dom which could, with luck and the favour of the gods, be exchanged for survival.[20]

Communal life bore the imprint of these conditions, in which life remained a constant peril, and in which people went over the brink despite a faithful adherence to the lessons of the past. An awful dread was a part of the village mood, as Gérard Bouchard points out in his excellent study of Sennely-en-Sologne.[21] Continually menaced, in the most direct, vital and immediate way, peasants could not help but view the universe with a sense of powerlessness and fear. The popular imagination, described by Robert Mandrou, abounds with phantoms, monstrous animals, evil spirits, and other menacing creatures.[22] Much of village culture was devoted to the task of appeasing these mysterious forces, warding them off, or appealing to countervailing agencies such as the saints in heaven, sacred fountains, wise women, menhirs or other shrines. Here too, through a process of transposition, the logic of traditional work routines applied: in repetition there was security, or at least the greatest measure of security or at least the greatest measure of security which life could ever be expected to afford. A break with the past could easily mean disaster. At the same time, a faithful execution of traditional ways in this sphere helped to create a moral atmosphere within which the more practical dimensions of tradition could maintain their force.

Folk traditions meshed easily with Christian practice once these nominally divergent world-views found themselves alone in the village together. This is an extremely interesting question, which deserves further study; it can only be touched upon here. The emissary of the church at the local level, the *curé* who was usually far closer to peasant life than he was to

[20] Henri Mendras, *The Vanishing Peasant: Innovation and Change in French Agriculture*, trans. by Jean Lerner (Cambridge, Mass., 1970), ch. 1; Jerome Blum, "The Condition of the European Peasantry on the Eve of Emancipation," *Journal of Modern History*, 46 (1974), pp. 395-424. Cf. Placide Rambaud and Monique Vincienne, *Les transformations d'une société rurale: La Maurienne (1561-1962)* (Paris, 1964), p. 18; Robert Mandrou, *Introduction à la France moderne, 1500-1640: essai de psychologie historique*, 2nd ed. (Paris, 1974), pp. 44-47. See also the interesting comments of R.W. Southern, *The Making of the Middle Ages* (New Haven, 1953), pp. 74-76. The course of agricultural production in the past two hundred and fifty years is charted in J.-C. Toutain, *Le produit de l'agriculture française de 1700 à 1958*, Vol. II, *La croissance*, in *Cahiers de l'institut de science économique appliquée*, no. 115 (July 1961), p. 143. Cf. William H. Newell, "The Agricultural Revolution in Nineteenth-Century France," *Journal of Economic History*, 33 (1973), pp. 697-731.

[21] *Le village immobile: Sennely-en-Sologne au XVIIIe siècle* (Paris, 1972), pp. 317, 340, passim.

[22] *Introduction à la France moderne*, pp. 83-84. For Mandrou this "daily anguish for tomorrow" is basic to the *mentalité* of traditional society in Europe: "Cette hantise de mourir de faim, inégale suivant les lieux et les classes, plus forte à la campagne qu'à la ville, rare chez les gens d'armes bien entretenus et chez les grands, permanente chez les petites gens, est le premier trait, le plus frappant, de la civilisation moderne. En quoi elle ne fait d'ailleurs que prolonger le moyen âge." Ibid., p. 47.

the universe of Catholic theology, often helped to bring these beliefs and formulae under the mantle of the Church. But the fit was almost always poor, and suffered much from the scrutiny of clerical superiors whenever this could be brought to bear. Elements of folklore remained completely outside this Catholic cover, and a good deal more appeared to outsiders only lightly cloaked by formal Christianity.[23]

What we know as folklore, the cultural equipment of village life, was thus one of the means by which communities or individuals could attempt to ease the cruel burdens which life imposed upon them.[24] Folklore helped to bind villages together by its network of regulations which applied to all, and also by making individual actions of common concern. Rural communities were so frequently involved as corporate bodies in folkloric practice because these communities engaged corporatively in this struggle for survival. This was why everyone had to participate and why the community as a whole had such a deep interest in seeing that everything was done properly, according to the rules.

On a somewhat less crucial level, moreover, the community had other, regular business to do, much of which was discharged in the same ritualistic manner within the framework of the collectivity. Village festivals, for instance, provided a regular forum for the local marriage market. Festivity almost always included circumstances, such as dances or special games, which afforded closely supervised contact between marriageable young people. The annual or semi-annual servants' hiring fair, the *louée*, was built into the framework of a village festival, as were agricultural fairs or cattle markets. The *fête* was an occasion for more casual sociability, of course, and one of the few opportunities (limited mainly to the men) to visit neighbouring villages. Central to the experience, however, was the mixture of communal fun and frolic with some serious business conducted in a closely prescribed manner. When it came time to beat down the village threshing floor, to take one striking case, entire Breton villages assembled to pound the earth with their *sabots*, in the great circle dances

[23] On the relationship between the Church and folk traditions in France, see, for example, Crubellier, *Histoire culturelle*, pp. 82-83; Jean-Baptiste Thiers, *Traité des jeux et des divertissemens* (Paris, 1686), pp. 454-455; Charles Dard, "La fête des brandons," *Mémoires de la société d'histoire et d'archéologie de Chalon-sur-Saône*, 18 (1934-1935), p. 142; T.J.A. Le Goff and D.M.G. Sutherland, "The Revolution and the Rural Community in Eighteenth-Century Brittany," *Past and Present*, no. 62 (February 1974), p. 99; J. Canard, *Folklore chrétien: coutumes d'origines religieuses, disparues ou en voie de disparition, en Forez et en Lyonnais* (Lyon, 1952); Paul Schmitt-Eglin, *Le mécanisme de la déchristianisation: recherche pastorale sur le peuple des campagnes* (Paris, 1952), pp. 182-183; and Ulysse Rouchon, *La vie paysanne dans la Haute-Loire*, 3 vols. (Le-Puy-en-Velay, 1933-1938), II, p. 145.

[24] For a brilliant discussion of the workings of shrines and generalized devotions in another village context, see William A. Christian, Jr., *Person and God in a Spanish Valley* (New York, 1972).

for which they were famous.[25] In part the dance was fun, as all dances were; in part it was also necessary work, done in a similar way for generations. It is only in modern times that we are accustomed to individualize our pleasure, and to separate our work from "leisure."

III

Because tradition was the essence of village culture, the folklorists were almost obsessed with its persistence; curiously, at the very moment when folklore studies were becoming popular, the chains of continuing practice were breaking apart. In the 1880's it was still possible to conduct extensive field research; a few decades later investigators had only the memories of villages to explore. For example, when the ethnologist Louis Marin examined the functioning of traditional institutions in Lorraine for the two decades before the First World War, he reported on a system which was basically intact at the turn of the century. By the end of the War, the institutions had almost entirely vanished.[26] Marin's observations, with a fair allowance of a few decades either way, hold true for most observers who point to *la fin du folklore*. The *veillée* (a sort of winter work bee in which people assembled in barns once or twice a week to do spinning or repair tools), rural blood sports, folk dances, local pilgrimages, the elaborate schedule of *fêtes*, folk medicine — all of these artifacts of traditional culture virtually disappeared during the half century after 1870. Before then they were alive and well, a functioning part of rural life in many parts of the country; after they existed no more, except in staged and awkwardly costumed versions put on for tourists, or those with an ideological penchant for regionalism.

Of course, village culture in 1870 was not as robust as it had been, say, two hundred years earlier. Reports at the end of the eighteenth century also tell of *la fin du folklore*, and it is probably fair to say that there was a long secular decline of folkloric institutions, stretching back at least as far as the middle of the eighteenth century.[27] If, as we have argued, the principal basis of folkloric culture was an agricultural environment ruled by necessity, one can link the decline of this culture to eighteenth-century developments: the spread of the market system, the ending of village

---

[25] Perrin and Bouet, *Breiz izel*, pp. 241-242; and Jean-Marie Guilcher, *La tradition populaire de la danse en Basse-Bretagne* (Paris, 1963), pp. 20-21. Cf. Fernand Butel, *Une vallée pyrénéenne: La vallée d'Ossau* (Pau, 1894), pp. 101-102.
[26] Louis Marin, *Les contes traditionnels en Lorraine: institutions de transfert des valeurs morales et spirituelles* (Paris, 1964).
[27] See, for example, *Dissertation sur les amusemens des Français depuis le commencement de la monarchie jusqu'à nos jours* (Strasbourg, 1789).

autarchy, the rise of agricultural productivity and the spread of manufactured goods. Fruitful research can establish this linkage, especially by contrasting areas with different experiences. I would guess, however, that the forces we have mentioned operated similarly. All of them turned the village outward, and reduced the need for its coherence as a social unit. Yet cultural forms, especially when they relate to values, have a way of outlasting the social or economic conditions upon which they are based; folk culture had a certain momentum of its own, and even an adaptability to change within certain limits.[28] Moreover, it is easy to exaggerate the extent and thoroughness of these changes in rural France, where the pace of modernization was often extremely slow, and where differences within and between regions were extraordinary. In 1894, when a government survey of rural housing was made, peasants were still found living in one-room hovels, often alongside their animals, in a style not much different from peasants at the time of Louis XVI.[29] In a classic work on French agriculture published in 1912, Michel Augé-Laribé stated that French peasants had still not, by and large, broken definitively with primitive methods of cultivation.[30] And up to 1925, according to André Varagnac, peasants still made most of their equipment themselves.[31] It is not surprising, then, given this slow pace of material change, that the decline of folklore took time, and was by no means the sharp and brutal development which folklorists sometimes imagined.

Nevertheless, there are two signs that the period to which we have been referring was decisive. First, there is a question of degree. Those who described the end of folkloric practices in rural communities after 1870 noted that the various impulses of modernization operated in a more conclusive way by the end of the nineteenth century than ever before. Practices and customs had already been shorn away from the core of rural tradition, but it is particularly in the latter period that modernity struck at the core itself.[32] The arrival of the folklorists, as we noted earlier in this paper, coincided with the disappearance not only of specific folkloric practices, but of the entire *genre* of traditional village culture. Consequently, the folkloric vogue fed upon a sense of nostalgia for an entire

[28] On this point, see R[obert] M[androu], "L'histoire des mentalités," article in *Encyclopaedie universalis*, 15- vols. (Paris, 1968-), VIII, p. 438. Cf. Jacques Le Goff, "Les mentalités: une histoire ambiguë," in Jacques Le Goff and Pierre Nora, eds., *Faire de l'histoire*, III, *Nouveaux objets* (Paris, 1974), pp. 76-94.

[29] Ministère de l'Instruction publique, *Enquête*, cited in note 12, above.

[30] *L'évolution de la France agricole* (Paris, 1912), p. 7.

[31] "Les gestes de travail traditionnels," *Folklore de France*, no. 131 (September-October 1973), p. 149.

[32] For an excellent discussion of this process see Eugen Weber, "Fin-de-siècle: The Third Republic Makes a Modern Nation," in Mathé Allain and Glenn Conrad, eds., *France and North America: Over Three Hundred Years of Dialogue* (Lafayette, La., 1973), pp. 87-101.

moral order which had gone, and satisfied a curiosity that is normally reserved for a world completely apart.

Second, a related point made by Varagnac, the most disquieting symptom of the disease affecting village culture showed up particularly at this time: after 1870 folklore was no longer renewing itself, was proving incapable of generating new traditions to replace the old.[33] The best of the folklorists had observed that village culture was never fixed or unchanging, but was constantly in a state of evolution and modification.[34] More often than not, customs once assumed to be of great antiquity turned out to date from some fairly recent past. Perhaps the last series of "new" traditions sprang up in the first half of the nineteenth century in response to conscription, and the drawing of lots by young men in a village. What made such creations "folklore," rather than something else, was their conformity with the basic characteristics we have described: they were village-centered, highly-structured, and tradition-bound. But as Varagnac observed, this vital element of folkloric creativity and renewal can no longer be found anywhere in the French countryside during the last quarter of the nineteenth century. Instead, specific traditions were allowed to die *tout court*; their replacements, if any, were from another cultural universe, and shared few if any of these characteristics.

The reasons for this transformation are to be found in the histories of thousands of villages. Although these histories vary widely, it is probably true to say that a crucial change occurred in most of them during the generation or so before the First World War. Villages at this time lost the cohesion which derived from their role in sustaining and maintaining life. Not until late in the nineteenth century were doctors more sure than ashes from the *feux de Saint Jean*, French history more potent than old village tales, and chemical fertilizer more resorted to than holy water. It took until then for the impact of such novelty to be massive, and almost universal. Once this happened, village structures and the culture which they supported were no longer of such vital importance. Once the villagers no longer lived regularly on the brink of famine — which was finally the case after mid-century — and once they could rely practically upon something other than the lessons of the past, folklore could give way to a national culture. The railway, the schools, the newspapers, and other such factors, usually regarded as the cause of this cultural change, could only do their work upon a population prepared to receive them.

[33] *Civilisation traditionnelle*, pp. 57-59.
[34] For example, Van Gennep, *Contribution*, p. 25; idem, *Le folklore des Hautes-Alpes: étude descriptive et comparée de psychologie populaire*, 2 vols. (Paris, 1946-1948), I, p. 31; Paul Sébillot, *Le folklore de la Bretagne*, new ed., 2 vols. (Paris, 1968), I, p. 389; and Varagnac, *Civilisation traditionnelle*, pp. 302-303.

Some communities withstood change longer than others, and there were wide variations in the tempo of folklore's collapse.[35] In the Auvergne, a whole array of folkloric practices associated with Saint Verny, the patron of the vineyard workers, eroded during the phylloxera epidemic of the 1870's and 1880's, which eventually ended the large-scale cultivation of grapes in the region.[36] And there was no patron saint of any sort for new professions which the former *vignerons* turned to: railway workers, *garçons de café*, factory workers, postmen. Here folklore wore away; but elsewhere, as we have seen with Saint Pierre de Quiberon, the end was sudden and complete, but for reasons not normally associated with the *grandes lignes* of modernization. Different again were mountainous areas of the Pyrenées-Orientales, in the far south of France where the high country had normally been an important bastion of folklore. Here modernization brought a great population shift: French peasants descended the mountains, and their places were taken by Spanish immigrants who knew little of local traditions. Both groups took advantage of a vastly expanded railway network at the end of the nineteenth century. A student of the area's folklore has linked its decline to the steady ascent of the rails — putting Perpignan on the coastal plain under the influence of Toulouse and Montpellier, then the mountainous regions under the influence of Perpignan. Ideas, like migrants, moved up from the valleys, and folklore suffered heavily from this kind of mobility.[37] Here as elsewhere, the most important contingents of migrants were made up of young people, who had been the mainstay of village culture. Their departure — in search of greener pastures or conscripted into the army — frequently meant the discontinuance of folkloric traditions.[38]

Such changes undercut local culture by removing old social contexts. At the same time new, specialized agencies were creeping into rural life, assuming tasks which were once consolidated by folklore. Folklore had

---

[35] See M. Jollivet and Henri Mendras, *Les collectivités rurales françaises* (Paris, 1971). Some other studies which make this point are: Antoine Borrel, *Les villages qui meurent* (Paris, 1932); Henriette Dussourd, *Au même pot et au même feu . . . Etude sur les communautés familiales agricoles au centre de la France* (Moulins, 1962); Pierre Bozon, *La vie rurale en Vivarais: étude géographique* (Valenge-sur-Rhône, 1961); Rambaud and Vincienne, *Transformations d'une société*; Roger Thabault, *Education and Change in a Village Community: Mazières-en-Gâtine, 1848-1914*, trans by Peter Tregear (London, 1971); and Edgar Morin, *Commune en France: la métamorphose de Plodémet* (Paris, 1967). The end of folklore is discussed in a general way in Crubellier, *Histoire culturelle*, chs. 6, 7.

[36] Arnold Van Gennep, *Le folklore de l'Auvergne et du Velay* (Paris, 1942), p. 217.

[37] Horace Chauvet, *Traditions populaires de Roussillon* (Perpignan, 1947), pp. 237-238.

[38] Emile Maussenet, *Recherches statistiques et historiques sur le village de Châlons-sur-Vesle* (Reims, 1898), p. 99; Varagnac, *Civilisation traditionnelle*, pp. 62-63; and Marcel Maget, "Les Ruraux," *Esprit*, 27 (June 1959), p. 928.

satisfied village needs by a blending of many functions into single folkloric institutions; modern cultural forms broke these institutions apart, at the same time as the village itself was being rent asunder. Where once, for example, the *fête de Saint Jean* was an occasion for sociability (the annual visit to neighbouring communes), hiring of servants (the *louée*), miscellaneous healing and preventative medicine (using the ashes from the *feux*), courtship (dancing around the bonfires), and wild drinking (in contrast to the long dry periods between *fêtes*), there were, by the end of the nineteenth century, distinctly different and generally more efficient means to do each of these: railways to facilitate communication throughout the year, a modern job market, a reasonably efficacious medical practice, individualized styles of mating and dating, sometimes with Saturday-night dances at dance halls, and widely available cabarets in rural areas which encouraged regular consumption of alcohol. In the face of these new agencies, all of which related to a new, urban-based culture, the old *fêtes de Saint Jean* were bound to fare badly. Inevitably, the prestige which had clung for centuries to the faithful execution of these and other folkways now attached itself to the products of modernization.

For the most part, folklore left quietly. But in some cases the departure was noisy, filled with the jeering attacks of *maires*, *instituteurs*, or others, whose mockery helped to speed what was already under way. The early decades of the Third Republic saw a number of attempts to eradicate folkloric culture as backward, immoral, un-Christian, or all of these at once. It may seem curious now that such assaults on folklore could be launched from both sides of the great divide which is supposed to have cut through all major issues in French life. But the two parties to the great national debate had often a good deal in common. Just as one can find prefects and municipal officials sniping away at Catholic processions from the 1880's, so one can find clerical authorities, like the Bishop of Blois, who tried to ban a cult of Saint Loup in a small village of the Sologne, because the local peasants' veneration of a wolf's statue appeared to his enlightened sense to be on the verge of idolatry.[39] Peasants frequently resisted, of course, often successfully. (The bishop, in this case, was run out of the village.) In the long run, however, these conflicts were inconsequential, for struggles on the local level could not have much effect in the face of major social change. Without much fuss, therefore, the *fête patronale* frequently gave way to a village celebration on the *quatorze juillet*. Similarly, the schoolteacher's annual award of prizes to the graduating class, in effect the Republican *fête* of the *école laïque*, became a more

---

[39] Abbé Lucien Crouzil, *La publicité du culte catholique* (Paris, 1904), p. 6; and Paul Guieysse, "La statue à tête de loup," *Revue des traditions populaires*, 17 (1902), p. 287.

significant event in local life than the harvest festival. And peasants whose principal amusements on Sundays had involved decapitating geese eventually gave up the practice, in favour of drinking, *boules* and, later, football matches. In all these instances, and in countless others, missionaries of modern urban culture carried their message of respectable behaviour directly to the peasants; by the beginning of the twentieth century, their conversion was practically complete.[40]

For those who had encouraged these changes, the turning away from folklore was a triumph for civilization. It is hard to blame them now, even though we are disposed to mock their moralizing self-assurance. Most of us, after all, go to doctors rather than statues, live in warm houses, and refrain from torturing animals. Looking back, I would suggest that folkloric culture was a human adjustment to an agricultural economy living close to the level of subsistence. When the end finally came, toward the close of the nineteenth and the beginning of the twentieth centuries, there were few indeed who had regrets, and few among the civilized who even noticed. Among the latter, however, were the folklorists, and for this historians are in their debt.

[40] See Weber, "Fin-de-siècle"; Jean-Marie Mayeur, *Les débuts de la IIIe République, 1871-1898* (Paris, 1973), pp. 48-54, 134; René Nelli, *Le Languedoc et le Comté de Foix, le Roussillon* (Paris, 1958), pp. 347-353; and Marie-Madeleine Rabecq-Maillard, "Jeux, fêtes, spectacles," in *La vie populaire en France du Moyen Age à nos jours*, Vol. II, *Les Loisirs* (Paris, 1965), p. 99.

8

The "Veillée"
and the Great Transformation

EDWARD SHORTER

If social life in traditional France differed from that of today, it was partly because villagers customarily spent their evenings together during the winter. They called these gatherings *veillées*. Two or three times a week, or even more often, farm families would congregate to work and chatter and tell tales of werewolves and ghosts. In the context of modern times the custom is bizarre: regularly spending your evenings with non-relatives, with people toward whom moveover you weren't even especially friendly, with people you saw simply because custom required it.

But if we look at traditional village life as a whole, the veillée immediately becomes understandable. It was an essential force for breaking down family privacy by giving individuals systematic contact with a larger community, and by reminding them of the ways of the collectivity. The veillée was among the central village mechanisms for weaning individuals from what contemporaries liked to call "egoism," and for reinforcing the principle that the purpose of existence was doing what other people expected you to do. Sitting about these drafty cowbarns or big farm kitchens late in the evening, busy at handwork or playing cards, telling tales and watching the children "draw circles in the air with brands from the fire," these peasants and agricultural laborers found themselves laced into a larger pattern of sociability that is as different from modern sociability as night is from day.

This essay makes two points: (1) that these evening gatherings helped cement together — perhaps more than any other single custom — a "traditional" way of life; (2) that as this way of life was shattered under the hammer blows of modernization, heaviest of which was a new attitude towards the family, the veillée disappeared.

I hasten to remind the reader that the base of evidence on which this interpretation of the veillée rests is fairly thin. Three kinds of sources came into being towards the end of the eighteenth century which permit us to look at the last days of the traditional order, a way of life that in West European villages was definitively locked into place some time during the sixteenth century and that has disappeared in the course of the last hundred years. First, we have the "medical topographies" of the new-style local doctors who followed in their own communities the exhortations to observe and experiment which radiated from the Royal Society of Medicine in Paris.[1] They commented occasionally on how villagers spent their time, and because these doctors were cool-headed, literate observers who dwelt in the midst of village and small-town society, their ethnographic jottings are of some value. Second, the Napoleonic bureaucrats devoted themselves to describing the economic and social patterns of their various administrative districts in a series of "statistiques départementales et locales."[2] Because they often touched on the veillée, these documents make tentative regional comparisons possible. Third, we have the antiquarians who, in a torrent of little "mémoires" and "notes" during the nineteenth century, have made available an extensive though dangerously nostalgic catalogue of village customs. These three kinds of sources give us a quick, haphazard glimpse of the evening work bee from late in the eighteenth century, when it was still commonplace in popular life, to the beginning of the twentieth century, when the *veillée en commun* was replaced by the *veillée en famille*.[3]

First let us describe the elephant. Here we are like the proverbial blind men, running their hands over different parts of the beast's body, for a veillée which one scholar grasps in one village might turn out quite unlike the veillée another might see elsewhere. Still, there are some prominent common features. According to one antiquarian:

> Peasants have simple habits. They rise at daybreak, and in winter go to sleep only late when they give their veillées, at which are present a number of households from the nearby farms and hamlets. They work together in the feeble glow of a resin candle, fastened at a corner of the fireplace to a little piece of iron or charred wood. The men busy themselves with harness repairing, the boys with building little bird traps. For the women it's spinning, or darning theirs and their husbands' clothes. . . . Should a good *conteur*, frightened even himself by his own tale, turn up with some shuddery story of dead spirits, ghosts [*esprit-follet*] or werewolves, the whole group falls

---

[1] A number of manuscript medical topographies are in the archives of the Académie de Médecine, series "SRM." Others were published, and have been conveniently gathered by the Bibliothèque Nationale under the shelf listing Tc⁶.

[2] For an overview see A. de Saint-Léger, "Les mémoires statistiques des départements pendant le directoire . . .," *Le Bibliographe moderne*, 19 (1918-19), pp. 6-43.

[3] The best systematic bibliography of French folklore is vols. III and IV (1937-38) of Arnold van Gennep's massive *Manuel de folklore français contemporain* (Paris, 1937-1958).

mute, attentive. The work and the games are suspended, the circle draws together and closes up, and fear establishes its sovereignty in the midst of the terrified band.[4]

All this recalls boyscouts around the campfire. But these are not scouts. They are staid peasants who assemble just after the evening meal, let us say towards six p.m., but perhaps as early as four, in someone's barn. In our standard model, the whole family turns up so that by the time a number of households have convened, each bringing its servants and hired hands, twenty or thirty people may be crowded together amongst the cows and their steaming piles of dung, as in the Mâconnais, or before the great kitchen hearths of farmhouses in Lorraine. Then the women gather closely about the light of the nut-oil lamp (later it would be a gasoline lantern) to stitch gloves and make baskets. To earn spare change, some take in work from urban entrepreneurs. Others might just spin, knit or darn to keep their own family's clothes in shape. In the background the men might husk corn or crack nuts, or perhaps merely smoke pipes and play cards. As these people work they talk: and here is the most interesting part from the viewpoint of the cultural historian. The participants tell stories and recite the old tales. Or maybe, as one disgusted observer reported of the late-nineteenth century, they just "gossip."[5] Perhaps then towards nine or ten, or as late as midnight in some accounts, there'll be a bit of dancing or singing. Finally the families from outside trudge home "over the snow."

Remember that these gatherings are not just occasional evening "parties," on the modern model. These peasant families get together several times a week, rotating from barn to barn. Little hospitality is involved, for although some writers state that the evening might end with a small libation, others note that there is no drinking at all, not even coffee, and that those attending in no way consider themselves the "guests" of the family whose barn they happen to be in.[6] Nor is there the kind of selectivity one associates with modern sociability. Everyone who is so inclined comes to the single veillée of a small hamlet, and only in large peasant villages would several veillées go on at the same time, because no one barn or kitchen could accommodate everyone. (What proportion of the village's total population actively attended the veillées, and what distinguished the active from the inactive? These are still unanswered questions.) We are

[4] M. de Beauvais de St-Paul, *Essai historique et statistique sur le canton . . . de Mondoubleau* (Le Mans, 1837), p. 46.

[5] A. Carlier, *Un village breton en 1895*, Bibliothèque de travail (Cannes, 1949), p. 13.

[6] Louis Marin, *Les contes traditionnels en Lorraine* (Paris, 1964), p. 93. Although relying heavily upon childhood memories, the author had done some systematic investigation of customs in Lorraine. I am indebted to Michael Marrus for this and several other references.

dealing here with an entirely different attitude towards individual privacy and family intimacy: if you spend all your evenings with other people, you will have relatively little solitude; and if you spend those evenings with people to whom you aren't related, you will have little opportunity to relish domestic togetherness.

So these evening work bees direct us to some of the central questions of modern social history: family patterns of emotion, individual obligations towards the community, the deference of young to old, of women to men, of innovation to tradition. The veillée could be a key to rediscovering the world we have lost. But to understand it, in France at least, we have to grasp the great variations in form. For only by seeing how the ideal-type veillée varied in reality from place to place can we see what functions it usually filled for the larger society.

Significant regional differences existed in the veillée's form and implantation. The type which brought together a number of families, for example, was seldom known in the Midi. There, it was mainly the men who would congregate in the stables to smoke and play cards.[7] The regular work veillée was much more a product of the *contrées septentrionales*, i.e., the north of France.[8]

Who attended? In Provence, custom dispensed with the mixed veillée because "la sociabilité méridionale," with its strong emphasis on male bonding, disapproved of exposing men to the company of women. But elsewhere as well in Southern France the veillée was often segregated along sexual lines. Indeed in many descriptions it was not an assembly of families at all, but a gathering of women accompanied by their marriageable daughters. While the men of Vigan canton (Gard), for example, were off together in the evening drinking in a bar or clubroom, the women would get together in some neighbor's house. "They bring their work and a little heating pot; they munch on *bresucada* and sometimes drink a bit of white wine, going home towards 9 or 10."[9] The same process took place in the nearby Cantal department, as Abel Hugo reports:

> After lunch in winter the men convene, seated about on benches in the largest and warmest stable; they chatter and shout; they curse the taxes and the taxcollectors; they recount the latest rumors about the boys and girls;

[7] On Provence see Lucienne A. Roubin, *Chambrettes des provençaux: Une maison des hommes* (Paris, 1970). "La forme prise chez eux par les réunions masculines se démarque de la Chambrette. Elles se tenaient naguère dans une série d'étables entre lesquelles se répartissait le groupe des hommes par dix ou quinze individus" (p. 31). On women's veillées see p. 163.

[8] E.-G. Léonard, for example, writes, "L'on n'y connaissait guère ces veillées, propres aux contrées septentrionales. . . ." *Mon village sous Louis XV, d'après les Mémoires d'un paysan* (Paris, 1941), p. 147.

[9] François-Alexandre Rouger, *Topographie statistique et médicale de la ville et canton du Vigan* (Montpellier, 1819), p. 103; the doctor came to Vigan in 1762.

there's lots of slander. At five o'clock they break up and go eat, and then return to talk a bit longer, finally going home to bed. Here it's a question *only of the men* [my italics]. The women, because of the inferiority of their sex, are not admitted at all to conversation with their lords and masters. But after the men have retired, the women's reign begins and the veillée, which ends for the men at eight in the evening, finishes for the women only at midnight or one in the morning.[10]

But this separation of the sexes was not merely a Mediterranean phenomenon. We're told that in Savoy the women got together in the cowbarns, "which are ordinarily large and comfortable, to spin, sew or knit in the glow of a lamp, fuel for which they purchase jointly. These meetings are enlivened by the tales of the oldsters and by the young girls' song, as well as by the presence of the young lads." The men, on the other hand, stay resolutely away from these veillées, and "go to bed early because they have to rise at daybreak to thresh the wheat in the barns."[11] In parts of the North, too, it was only the women who met at night. They would bring their own chairs to a rented room in Anseauvilliers (Oise), and supervise the young girls who were sitting side-by-side with their boyfriends.[12] Thus quite often the veillée would bring two sexual solidarity groups into opposition: the women and young girls inside the barn versus the men and young boys. The boys would assemble elsewhere before invading to court the girls, and would always be considered outsiders.[13]

This separation of the sexes was not limited to the peasants. Doctor Lépecq de la Cloture tells us, for example, that among the cottage-industrial population of the Evreux district (Eure), "The women, all occupied with spinning, assemble in dozens to spend the evening together, working until midnight; each has her footwarmer or cinder pot filled with brands or coals."[14] Nor would the fishermen's wives of Saint-Pierre de Quiberon (Morbihan) spend the winter evenings with their husbands either. "While the men assemble in the cabarets of the port, the women get together for the veillée in the stables, where the animals and the manure pile give off heat. A big lantern hung from the ceiling joists lights the walls where the nets are hanging, but there's so much shadow that sewing is impossible. At most the women are able to knit."[15] Thus the

---

[10] *La France pittoresque*, 3 vols. (Paris, 1835), I, p. 238.
[11] Verneilh, *Statistique générale de la France . . . département du Mont-Blanc* (Paris, 1807), p. 301. The author was departmental prefect.
[12] Cambry, *Description du département de l'Oise*, 2 vols. (Paris, 1803), I, p. 260.
[13] The image of the two opposed sexual groups appears in André Varagnac's *Civilisation traditionnelle et genres de vie* (Paris, 1948), pp. 96-97.
[14] *Collection d'observations sur les maladies et constitutions épidémiques . . . de la Normandie* (Rouen, 1778), p. 126.
[15] Carlier, *Village breton*, p. 13.

veillée highlights a sexual division of sociability that runs through not just peasant life but all traditional French society.

Like attendance, the forms of recreation at the veillée varied from place to place. If the Mâconnais saw little dancing, it was possibly because the peasants didn't want to frighten the barn animals — that is one scholar's opinion, at least.[16] Yet in Lorraine, where singing, dancing and even loud talking were declared out of order in the regular veillées, more complex cultural factors seem to have been at work. "There's never dancing at the veillées. . . . The men of Lorraine [all these accounts are highly male-centered] don't like to make themselves conspicuous. They learn methodically how to dance because a thing worth doing is worth doing well, and still more because they don't want to make themselves look ridiculous, especially in the eyes of women. So if they take up dancing, it's to have the pleasure of [some female] company."[17] But married Lorrainers felt, evidently, that they could dispense with this pleasure, and so there was no dancing at the veillées.

Yet it is difficult to decide what is typical: we line up all the quotes that mention dancing against all those they deny it specifically and try to assess which is more representative.[18] But some work veillées did involve dancing, a circle of handclapping women or a fiddler's jig providing standard punctuation marks for the end of an evening. When men and women in the Cantal had joint veillées, dancing might follow. "The man who's supposed to be the best musician stands up and sings; the women who don't dance accompany him with their harsh voices, and everyone else hops and skips about while the oxen ruminate to the cadence of the wooden clogs. . . . The man who sings marks the time, striking the ground with a stick. . . . This is the triumph of our traditional dances [*danses nationales*], the bourrées, plain and fancy alike."[19]

The dances at the end of these veillées fitted into a larger sequence of events: first, the assembled women (or families) would apply themselves to work; then the suitors would show up and begin the courtship rituals about which we shall hear more in a moment; finally the dancing would begin, taking over from the harrow-repairing and wool-carding that until then had been the center of the evening's activities.[20] In the Gâtine district, for example, the women and young girls would gather every

---

[16] Suzanne Tardieu, *La vie domestique dans le Mâconnais rural préindustriel* (Paris, 1964), p. 160.

[17] Marin, *Contes traditionnels*, p. 99.

[18] A number of sources which list specific occasions for dancing say nothing about veillées.

[19] Hugo, *France pittoresque*, I, p. 238.

[20] For typical descriptions see Edward Gazin, "Usages locaux," in Léon Louis, ed., *Le Département des Vosges: Description, histoire, statistique* (Epinal, 1887), IV, p. 564; and H. Gelin, *Les farfadets* (Ligugé, 1900), p. 9.

evening in the caverns of the rock quarries, "the most shadowy being most preferred. . . . The girls have a passion for dancing; they leap about to the point of exhaustion, and some have been seen to expire of fatigue. The dances are very gay and animated with gestures and cries: it's the Saintonge, the gavotte, the minuet, the *branle* of Poitou. . . . The fellows also show up to visit their girlfriends [*maîtresses*]. The young shepherdess lets her spindle fall to the ground in order to see who's interested. The boys all leap to pick it up, and the bagful of plums she carries with her will be their sweet reward. The evening ends with dancing."[21]

Why is it important to know whether these veillées involved dancing? Michael Marrus has shown the extent to which dancing symbolized a larger realm of community interaction for these people, how they reminded themselves of their common pasts and their present ties as they clomped ponderously through these old-fashioned farandoles and bourrées.[22] The presence of dancing would thus suggest that these regular evening gatherings reinforced people's sense of belonging to a larger culture by bringing them physically into contact with one another, by calling forth three or four times a week all the subconscious emotional messages that music and rhythm always summon. These traditional dances — men playing crack-the-whip or hunched women clapping hands in unison — pushed to its highest point the interaction with others that the veillée helped create for the little community.

Sexual segregation and collective entertainment were variable features of the veillée, present in some places, absent in others. Yet virtually all veillées had common characteristics as well, and in reviewing these we see to what extent the custom served generally to hold the traditional community together.

The rock quarries of the Gâtine have given us one hint: courtship. The veillée was an ideal arena for exposing marriageable girls to the inspection of young men because mothers could so easily supervise the proceedings. And the sources almost invariably refer to the *magnats* (suitors) and the fallen spindles they were supposed to scoop up to signify matrimonial interest. In the Mâconnais, suitors would get leave from farm duties on Tuesday, Thursday and Saturday nights in order to make the rounds of the veillées, "where they idle away their time [*musarder*] aside the young girls who are spinning with their distaffs."[23] These visits would, presuma-

---

[21] Dupin, *Mémoire statistique du département des Deux-Sèvres* (Paris, 1804), p. 211; the author was departmental prefect.

[22] "Modernization and Dancing in Rural France: from *La Bourrée* to *Le Fox-Trot*," paper prepared for the 1975 meeting of the American Historical Association, Pacific Coast Branch, now published in the present volume.

[23] Gabriel Jeanton, *Le Mâconnais traditionaliste et populaire*, 4 vols. (Macon, 1920-23), III, p. 18.

bly, soon lead to an agreement, and thereafter at the veillées these lads would nestle against their *jeunes amies* or *blondes* (as girlfriends were called in that region), "a little embarrassed by the presence of so many people and by the quips which were occasionally tossed at them, having the courage to exchange in a low voice some sweet words only when the general conversation became so animated and noisy that they could spend a second unobserved."[24]

In addition to these routine work bees, special veillées were often held for the express purpose of courtship. Most frequent at carnival time, they would be staged at home by the parents of a marriageable daughter or by some other acceptable adult, such as a widow. In the standard scenario the fellows arrive in a group, dance around burning bales of straw or some similar folkloric decoration, and then drift home late at night yodelling.[25] Around Neuchâtel, where the boys' drinking and the host's lax supervision scandalized the local pastor, such courtship veillées went on year round.[26] During the first half of the nineteenth century such veillées attracted up to seventy guests in the upland hills of Remiremont canton (Vosges): ". . . the *grande lourre*, composed of all the young people of both sexes of the same hillside or valley, took place each evening towards ten o'clock in someone's house, where people had come to do spinning. They would jump around, dance, play games and laugh until midnight. A fiddler, who knew well the importance of his mission, would turn up towards nine, ordinarily bringing with him reinforcements of dancers. With his arrival the kitchen or barn would be cleared; he would hop on top of a table or barrel and for two or three hours people danced to the sound of his violin." The fellows would then escort the girls home, yodelling noisily.[27]

Bear in mind that both specialized courtship veillées and the general work-bee variety represented one of the major occasions for young people to get together. Other courtship opportunities tended to come mainly on the festival days, such as carnival, the hiring fair of St. John's Day, or the autumn harvesthome, which were frenetic experiences but relatively few in number. So the bulk of acquaintanceship activity would take place in these barns on winter nights. Despite the laments of conser-

[24] Emile Violet, *Les veillées en commun et les réunions d'hiver* (Macon, 1942); F. Daniel Fabre and Jacques Lacroix claim that such goings on were more explicitly sexual, *La vie quotidienne des paysans du Languedoc au XIXe siècle* (Paris, 1973), p. 123.

[25] See, for example, Deribier-du-Châtelet, *Dictionnaire statistique ou histoire . . . du département du Cantal* 5 vols. (Aurillac, 1852-57), II, p. 133.

[26] Pierre Caspard, "Conceptions prénuptiales et développement du capitalisme dans la Principauté de Neuchâtel (1678-1820)," *Annales, économies, sociétés, civilisations*, 29 (1974), p. 994.

[27] Xavier Thiriat, *La vallée de Cleurie: Statistique, topographie, histoire, moeurs et idiomes* (Mirecourt, 1869), p. 332.

vative clerics, the pairing-off was subject to all kinds of supervision, the parents and stablehands watching from the sides at the dances, the knitting mothers scrutinizing with eagle eyes the timid caresses and embarrassed giggling of the evening work-bees. Marital alliances of which the community approved could be subtly encouraged by this throng of onlookers. Misalliances could be sharply rebuked. The point is that the whole courtship process was highly visible. Who-marries-whom acquired major importance for the larger social order, and the veillée played a crucial role.

A final common element in these veillées is the talk, because there was always something said. People didn't just sit in silence. And talk is important in evaluating the cohesiveness of these little villages because it reminds people of the rules of the game: the more telling of the Old Tales, the stronger the reminder of past generations to whose model the present one is obliged to adhere. The more "gossip," the stronger the obligation to conform to the expectations of others.

So the rumor mills ground. In the Vosges, "The village also has its chronicle of scandal, and slander is delected by all. Thus people talk about those who aren't there and all their missteps, the planned matches, the troubled marriages, the quarrels of the day. . . . It is [the men] who bring the most elevated tone to the conversation. [Note how impenetrably sexist these sources are.] Almost all have been soldiers or travelled, some of them quite far, and they love to tell about their trips and battles. . . . The daily newspaper, which nowadays is penetrating everywhere, slides as well into these evenings. People read it, but not so much the political analysis as the amusing or tragic stories. Et les faits divers ont les honneurs de la soirée."[28]

Most of the time was likely taken up with gossip and chit-chat, as the above account suggests. But enough authors comment upon the Old Tales as stuff for an evening's entertainment that we might briefly consider what manner of story they represented and how they figured in the community's life. The Old Tales appear not to have been "oral history," in the manner that African tribes, let us say, hand down their collective exploits from generation to generation. "Heroic peasant" is almost a contradiction in terms. Rather these were fanciful stories, fairy tales from the cultural inheritance of myth. Some literate person was usually present, "a curé, a beadle, a returned soldier," to read out sagas from such penny dreadfuls as the *Bibliothèque bleue*, a cheap paperback series printed in Troyes and sold by traveling colporteurs.[29] But even if the popular almanacs or the published adventures of Pierre de Provence were not on

[28] Gazin, "Usages locaux," p. 564.
[29] See Robert Mandrou, *De la culture populaire aux 17e et 18e siècles: La Bibliothèque bleue de Troyes* (Paris, 1964), p. 18 and passim.

hand to be read, people remembered stories told to them as children, "histories of devils and ghosts, of soothsayers, or sorcery and the sabbath, of *bigoures*, and werewolves and *galipodes* who change their form at will by means of a magical potion mysteriously closed away in a small wooden pot."[30] And then there were historical tales of Richard The Lion-Hearted and Red Riding Hood, and the centuries of Nostradamus, "which are more believed and excite greater attention than the treatises of modern philosophy in our academic assemblies."[31] Pious tales, with morals to edify the listener, were often spun forth, after which, according to one author, a "philosophical" discussion would take place.[32] In the Rouergue region, "the old folks retell the simple tales from the Roman de la Rose; they portray Ysengrin the wolf, Chanteclair the rooster, or perhaps master Renard the fox, who let the partridge escape from his jaws. They also speak of the times when queens would spin flax into linen and kings married shepherdesses. . . . They tell about the priest who would advance into the driving rain when it stormed, prayer book in hand, untouched by the drops that fell from the black clouds. . . . And, the oldsters add, as long as that priest lived, hail never destroyed the crops of the parish."[33]

Who told the tales? The elders had first right to speak.[34] And the children were supposed to be completely silent while aged veterans recited the Emperor's Hundred Days or while someone's brother-in-law told about his grandfather who had "killed eleven bears."[35] One writer suggests that it was more often the women than the men who recounted the Old Stories.[36] There were outsiders too. Overnight guests in these big farmhouses helped pay their lodging by bringing news from afar, "with ten or fifteen days delay." ". . . The beggars, the colporteurs, the glaziers, the tinkers . . . all these visitors had dinner with the family and then served as a *journal parlé* during the veillée."[37]

The participants hung upon these stories with rapt attention. Discussions of the Dreyfus Affair were suspended. You weren't permitted to talk at all during the tale-telling in Lorraine. The children were pushed up

[30] J.-L.-M. Noguès, *Les moeurs d'autrefois en Saintonge et en Aunis* (Saintes, 1891), p. 91; the author was the curé of Dampierre.
[31] Amans-Alexis Monteil, *Description du département de l'Aveiron* (Rodez, 1802), I, p. 27; the author was a history teacher at the departmental *école centrale*.
[32] Marin, *Contes traditionnels*, pp. 105-106.
[33] F. Galabert, "Coutumes et veillées du Rouergue quercyois," *Revue des Pyrénées*, 15 (1903), p. 10.
[34] See, for example, Marin, *Contes traditionnels*, p. 106.
[35] Auguste Grise, *Coutumes du Trièves au XIXe siècle: Souvenirs de ma jeunesse* (Grenoble, 1939), p. 23.
[36] Marin, *Contes traditionnels*, p. 116.
[37] Ibid., p. 23.

front around the raconteur who was giving the account,[38] and the Italian workers who were making noise down the street with their accordions might have to be shushed up.[39] These Lorraine veillées sound like pretty sober affairs (no drinking, no cardplaying, etc.), but elsewhere too, even when the rules about merriment were more relaxed, the Old Tales figured importantly in the evening's program.

We must not attach too much importance to the retelling of these myths: rules of the game derived from the adventures of Saint Innocence or Fairy Fanfreluche could not have been all that applicable to village society. Yet entwined in all the gossip and magical accounts were a set of assumptions about how you were supposed to get on with other people: in choosing a marriage partner, in managing your fieldhands, in disciplining your children. The ensemble of these rules provided the moral carapace of traditional society, and people learned them most frequently in the veillées.

The veillée died out between 1870 and 1914. Before the Franco-Prussian War almost no observer suggested that it was weakening. Thereafter a stream of laments begins to flow from conservative antiquarians. Even when nostalgia is discounted, it is apparent that by the interwar years few farm families were continuing to see one another regularly in the evening. The First World War seems to have been the terminal break, according to Suzanne Tardieu, who has studied the Mâconnais quite carefully.[40] And a host of *érudits locaux* confirm this judgment. "Today people go to veillées less and less. . . . [Now it's] reading a newspaper or playing cards that they like with a bottle of red wine."[41] In the 1930's neighbors continued in a few places to gather from time to time, veillée-style. "Entertainment is rare in the countryside," a team of public-health specialists reported of the Tarn department. "There's hunting, the fairs and markets, the winter veillées, and, recently, the radio."[42] Laurence Wylie found that just after the Second World War in the village of Roussillon (Vaucluse) families still assembled in the evening to roast chestnuts (*faire la castagnade*), but that the custom was dying out.[43] The evening spent with neighbors was turning into the evening spent with family.

Why? Under what circumstances did this traditional pattern of sociability perish, to be replaced with the modern pattern in which people stay

[38] Ibid., pp. 65-66.
[39] Ibid., p. 115.
[40] Tardieu, *La vie domestique dans le Mâconnais*, p. 161.
[41] Alfred Durand, *Le vie rurale dans les Massifs volcaniques* (Aurillac, 1946), p. 346.
[42] *Enquête sur l'habitation rurale en France*, 2 vols. (Paris, 1939), II, p. 276.
[43] *Village in the Vaucluse: An Account of Life in a French Village*, rev. ed. (New York, 1964), p. 276.

home at night, relishing the intimacy of the family circle rather than the communal gathering? The antiquarians tend to prefer "technological" explanations:

—According to one writer, the veillée in the Bourbonnais went out once the heating problem was solved, and once news of the world started coming by newspaper and radio rather than by word of mouth.[44]

—Another antiquarian suggested that technical progress in textiles was at fault. Peasants around Nantes no longer had to spin their own thread once machine-spun wool and linen became available. "With the rise of the spinning industry the veillées disappeared, these happy get-togethers in the long winter evening." Nowadays, ". . . instead of talking with their neighbors, people talk about them."[45]

—In many places it was the diffusion of cabarets which by the 1920's had dispersed the veillées. Georges Risler argued that the "bond" which had once existed among the residents of the villages was now no more.[46]

—Oil and gasoline lanterns killed off the veillée elsewhere, it was thought, because the fire danger in the straw-filled barns became too great. And even though the custom may have continued for a while in the kitchens, the number of people who could be assembled there was much smaller.[47]

These accounts are "true" but incomplete. I am unattached to "technological" explanations in general, because people don't abandon some practice that has a purpose in their lives just because a new invention opens up alternatives. Something about how they think (what the French would call their *mentalités*) and how they perceive their needs must change as well.

The mechanism of the decline may give us a clue to the larger forces behind it. We have a detailed view from the Vosges, where, if Xavier Thiriat is right, the decline began after the Revolution of 1848. (It may be that eastern France was an early-decline area, or that the author was simply peddling a political message.) In the Good Old Days the veillées in the hill farms would attract ten or twelve people, who would often plow through several kilometers of "waist-deep" snow to attend. The participants would finish off liters of eau-de-vie while working, and break up towards midnight after agreeing upon where to gather the next time.

[44] Camille Gagnon, *Le folklore bourbonnais*, 2 vols. (Moulins, 1947-48), II, p. 301; see also Grise, *Coutumes du Trièves*, p. 24.
[45] Eugène Bonnemère, *Les paysans au dix-neuvième siècle* (Nantes, 1847), pp. 18-19.
[46] *Le travailleur agricole français* (Paris, 1923), p. 124.
[47] Raymond Billiard, for example, discusses the adoption of oil lamps, *Vieilles coutumes, vieilles traditions, vieux souvenirs beaujolais* (Villefranche-en-Beaujolais, 1941), p. 20. Michael Marrus tells me he has seen a number of texts that say the fire danger of new modes of lighting was sufficient to banish people from the barn.

Then the better-off peasants began to change things, starting to serve wine rather than brandy, and "beef or ham, a salad, some pastry, and coffee afterwards rather than rye bread and cheese. This custom shows that prosperity and a taste for a better diet are penetrating the countryside. But because a large number of families are not sufficiently favored by fortune to adopt this mode of partying, the moment that white bread, wine and meat appear on the table, they stop going to the veillées. This is one of the causes of the rarity of these gatherings since some little time."[48] Among prosperous peasants in the Vosges the veillée had thus changed from a frequent, informal meeting of all the families on the hillside to a modern party: infrequent, elaborate and with a selective guest list. Note that this change was associated not with technology, but with the differentiation of rural social classes.

The antiquarians' analysis was, inevitably, too simple. It was not merely that "egoism and pridefulness" were taking over, making villagers newly indifferent to collective joys. A whole way of life was changing. Traditional village society was breaking up.

Now, we've known about this for a long time. Generations of scholars have speculated on what difference the arrival of the railroad or the primary school made to village culture. But among this great swirl of social changes that swept over the world we have lost, what specifically was responsible for the decline of the veillée? I shall tentatively argue that a new attitude towards family life, one treasuring intimacy and family privacy, as opposed to the formerly rich interaction with the surrounding community, caused these villagers to withdraw deliberately from outside sociability into the family circle.

This is a huge subject. A brief paper can scarcely do justice even to the argument, let alone present the evidence. But in general, we can say that early in the nineteenth century rural attitudes towards two matters began to change: (1) mothers started to become more sentimental about infant life, and were thus willing to breastfeed their infants and care generally better for them than previously. And (2) couples started to feel more sentimental about domestic life as a whole, cherishing family moments over collective occasions simply because conjugal togetherness was becoming something to be valued for itself. If I am right about this shift in *mentalités* — I ask the reader's indulgence to pass in silence over why it may have happened — we have an explanation of the veillée's decline which is intellectually more satisfying than the technological or moral-decay arguments.[49]

---

[48] Thiriat, *La vallée de Cleurie*, p. 331.
[49] I have spelled out this case in detail in *The Making of the Modern Family* (New York, 1975), pp. 255-268.

The model is this: as domesticity crystallized, the adults decided to no longer spend their evenings jammed together with hordes of non-family. And teenagers decided to do their courting in private, where sentiment could rush forth unconstrained by community control. Listening to the radio gave all these newly domesticated couples something to do while at home. And dancing in the local tavern gave all these newly sentimental adolescents a means to escape adult surveillance while rubbing bodies together in a socially acceptable manner. The veillée declined not because it was destroyed by the spinning mill or the gasoline lantern but because rural society decided it was no longer necessary. New ways were being devised to transmit tradition, get work done and bring couples together, and so the institutions which served the old ways were abandoned.

A new appreciation of family intimacy was cloistering the household away from the village community all along the line. In these years the family withdrew from the village festivals, from collective harvesting, from pilgrimages, and from the youth group. The veillée was merely one of the victims. But it's of special interest in this context because we see so clearly the devastating consequences of family intimacy: the veillée had, after all, consumed an enormous amount of time, and these hours and hours spent in cow-barns would now be available for the cozy fireside.

August Grise, in the way of misty-eyed old men, *suspected* that these new attitudes had doomed the veillée in his native Isère: "Because in those days [the 1880's of his youth] people were more open, more frank, less egotistical and self-centered than today, because there was more cordiality and less jealousy, neighbors got together a lot. . . . Nowadays everybody reads his newspaper, in the event that he doesn't have a radio, and *chacun reste chez soi*."[50]

Whether he was right about "egoism," and whether egoism adds up to what I have called "family domesticity," should become part of our new research agenda on the end of peasant France.

[50] Grise, *Coutumes du Trièves*, pp. 23-24.

9

Modernization and Dancing in Rural France: From "La Bourrée" to "Le Fox-Trot"*

MICHAEL R. MARRUS

I

Social history picks up the drumbeat of dancing in both the condemnation and the celebration of popular culture. Listen to the *curé* of Savigny (Rhône) in 1821, worrying about the peasants' overindulgence: "since they are full of passions, and dancing only enflames these passions, since these meetings never finish without crime, since a single debauched person can infect those who watch him, and since things are said [at dances] which should not be heard, and things are done which should not be seen, it is prudent for priests to oppose dances altogether."[1] A century later this was the *mot d'ordre* of his eminence the Cardinal-Archbishop of Paris, who proscribed modern dancing, and also that of the moral pundit of *Le Peuple*, who called the tango, the fox trot and the shimmy "une sorte de précoce et dangereuse défloration virginale."[2]

In the dappled shadows of Renoir's *Au Moulin de la Galette* we see the second theme: the popular pursuit of pleasure. Here is a picture painted in 1876, in the full tide of the *ordre moral*; in it we see a significantly mixed social scene, in which dancing is a center of attention. These relaxed and dapper figures, revelling on Sundays at the top of Montmartre, stood for good comfort, good company, good manners and good fun — the positive spirit of the *belle époque*. And dancing, classically accepted as a popular expression of gaiety, conveys this spirit well.[3]

Historians have picked up these themes, but have not lingered long over the dance itself. Their rivals the folklorists have done little better.

* An earlier version of this paper was read at the Pacific Coast Branch meeting of the American Historical Association held in Berkeley, California, in August 1975. I am grateful for the comments of Judith L. Hanna, Harriet Rosenberg, Ned Shorter, Eugen Weber, and Dianne L. Woodruff, and for the financial assistance of the Canada Council.

[1] [Louis Gauthier], *Traités contre les danses et les mauvaises chansons* (Lyon, 1821), p. xxxiv.

[2] [José Germain], *Danseront-elles? Enquête sur les danses modernes* (Paris, 1921), pp. 12-14.

[3] See Raymond Rudorff, *Belle Epoque: Paris in the Nineties* (London, 1972), ch. 2.

141

Never disposed to ignore any other artifacts of popular life, folklorists left the dance alone until well into the twentieth century. To be sure, they commented upon the fact of dancing, its occasions and its accompaniment, but the folklorists' picture of what actually went on is a blur.[4] The reason for this, I think, is that unlike other forms, such as stories, legends, myths, or songs, dancing cannot be easily recorded, or at least could not until the invention of motion pictures. Relatively few written documents carried the dance between performances, or beyond, to the historian attempting to recreate the past. Instead, as Jean-Michel Guilcher has observed, the forms which dances took were re-created every time they were danced, and at any given moment these forms existed only in the minds of the dancers.[5] Consequently, the best studies we have of the phenomenon, and sometimes the only studies, derive from observation and interview — notoriously unavailable to the historian.

Yet this inaccessibility points to another aspect of dance which is worth considering. Dancing was highly vulnerable to change. Communicated by habit and example more than by written direction, dancing was at the mercy of popular memory. Forms did not depend upon recorded instruction for their continuity, and might be altered in passing from generation to generation. If a style of dance were to lapse for a few years, it would be forgotten; if a dance were seen as no longer appropriate, or uninteresting, or whatever, it could be discontinued with little trace of what once had been. In a society where dancing was an important part of social life it was a direct expression of popular consciousness, not mediated by those who had the power of the pen.[6]

But let us leave popular *mentalités* for a moment, to approach the dancers' performance. We will have to look through bourgeois glasses, at least in part. And we will have to focus on the recent past, for which material exists in abundance — the late eighteenth through the twentieth

[4] Van Gennep observes that choreographic technique scarcely interested the folklorists, at least until the 1920's. See Arnold Van Gennep, *Manuel de folklore français contemporain*, 9 vols. (Paris, 1937-58), I², p. 544. See also the similar comments of Marcelle Mourgues, *La danse provençale* (Cannes, 1956), pp. 25-26, and Jean Baumel, *Les danses populaires, les farandoles, les rondes, les jeux choréographiques et les ballets du Languedoc méditerranéen* (Paris, 1958), p. 13. There is sometimes mention of dancing in the *topographies médicales*, surveys written by doctors in the eighteenth and early nineteenth centuries. See, for example, Jean-Philippe Graffenaver, *Topographie physique et médicale de la ville de Strasbourg* (Strasbourg, 1816), pp. 78-79; and Menuret De Chambaud, *Essais sur l'histoire médico-topographie de Paris* (Paris, 1786), pp. 103-104.

[5] Jean-Michel Guilcher, "Aspects et problèmes de la danse populaire traditionnelle," *Ethnologie française*, 1 (1971), p. 8. Guilcher is the outstanding French authority on this subject.

[6] Idem, "Conservation et renouvellement dans la culture paysanne ancienne de Basse-Bretagne," *Arts et traditions populaires*, 15 (1967), p. 1. idem, *La tradition populaire de danse en Basse-Bretagne* (Paris, 1963), p. 51.

centuries. Dramatic changes occurred in French rural dancing over this period, and in part these will be our concern. This paper attempts both to describe and to explain, and to relate the dance to the larger process of modernization.

II

More perhaps in dancing than in other visible activities, peasant villagers conveyed to their bourgeois observers in the nineteenth century that they were different. What struck the visitors who dared to approach the locals, as opposed to throwing moral dicta from afar, was the sheer strangeness of it all. In the valley of the Loire, during the Second Empire, the peasants danced to the sound of a flute or bagpipes; their arms hung limp at their sides; their eyes cast down. "One could really say that they were working and not enjoying themselves; they turned and jumped alternatively on each foot, and carried on like this for hours on end."[7] The monotonous solemnity drew frequent comment from travellers, for it was in such marked contrast with the boisterous tumult of Parisian dance halls. Abel Hugo noted this for the Haute-Loire in the 1840's, as did others for a later period in Brittany or the Valley of the Ossau, in the far south.[8] Dancing to the sound of locally-made string or wind instruments was bizarre enough; it was positively outlandish when the air was pierced with *huchements*–cries which suggested the neighing of a horse or the wail of some unearthly creature.[9] Sometimes an old woman chanted mournfully in *patois* along

[7] A. Bernard-Langlois, *Etudes topographiques, historiques, hygiéniques, morales, géologiques, agricoles, industrielles et commerciales sur le canton de Bourbon-Lancy (arrondissement de Charolles, département de Saône-et-Loire)*, 2 vols. (Moulins, 1865), I, p. 119.

[8] Abel Hugo, *France pittoresque, ou description pittoresque, topographique et statistique des départements et colonies de la France*, 2 vols. (Paris, 1835), II, p. 147; Olivier Perrin and Alexandre Bouët, *Breiz izel, ou vie des Bretons dans l'Armorique*, new ed. (Quimper, 1918), p. 287; Fernand Butel, *Une vallée pyrénéenne: la vallée d'Ossau* (Paris, 1894), p. 102; and Guilcher, *Tradition populaire de la danse*, p. 60. On this frequently observed gravity of expression, Guilcher notes: "Une danse à contenu dramatique, conçue pour le spectacle ou les échanges mondains, ferait participer le visage à l'expression. Non cette [danse pure], où le danseur n'a souci ni de représenter ni de plaire. Il vit sa danse intensément, et il l'éprouve au plus profond de son être. Elle le re-centre sur lui-même, en même temps qu'elle l'absorbe dans le groupe" (ibid.).

[9] Jean Drouillet, *Folklore du Nivernais et du Morvan*, 3 vols. (La Charité-sur-Loire, 1959-62), III, p. 154; Bernard-Langlois, *Etudes topographiques*, I, p. 119; and Hugo, *France pittoresque*, II, p. 122. One interesting traveller's account from the end of the nineteenth century contains the following observation in a similar vein: ". . . J'ai vu danser une bien gracieuse Ronde chez les paysans de la Sardaigne: ils accompagnaient leur danse d'un chant rythmé à la manière sarde et qui constituait la plus étonnante musique qu'on pût entendre. Ce n'est point vraiment le son de la voix humaine, mais un bourdonnement musical qui s'enfle, puis décroît, pour s'enfler encore. Par instants, les voix donnent à l'unisson en formant une sorte d'accompagnement en sourdine, sur lequel un soliste brode des phrases de mélopée. Ce

with the skirl of the bagpipes; sometimes the young men whistled, clapped their hands or snapped their fingers; and sometimes the entire company sang together.[10]

Moreover, the visitors were bewildered with a tremendous variety of dances and their accompaniment. A survey made in the Nivernais in the early years of the Third Republic found eighty different types which recent memory identified in the vicinity of two communes alone.[11] And the variety was not as rich there as in other regions, such as Provence, for example. In some areas, such as the Basque country, villagers so valued the dance that accomplished male soloists had extraordinary prestige. Here the technical level bordered on the acrobatic, and outsiders were dazzled by the *sauts* of champions or the elaborate ceremonial of a well-drilled group of young men. On the other hand, in a village in the Creuse in mid-century, peasants and migratory workers jammed into a barn on wintry nights, dancing with a much less educated step. Their attention, described by the stonemason Martin Nadaud, was only partially on the dance itself and much more on the local girls. There was also a related but not unimportant objective in the cold and draughty buildings — keeping warm.[12]

Three dance traditions encompass this wide variation.[13] The first of these, and in all likelihood the oldest, is the simple communal dance, in which virtually an entire village took part, moving together in a great circle or line. In areas of Basse-Bretagne this was the rule: villagers met on specified occasions, usually Sundays, weddings, or local festivals, and danced the *bourrée* or other collective dances. There was no division of the

chant particulier, étrange, qu'il est difficile d'analyser, pourrait se comparer à des cantilènes arabes, auxquelles les bourdonnements graves de l'orgue et quelque chant sacré lointain serviraient d'accompagnement. . . . Au son de cet musique singulière, jetée aux vents du soir par ces musiciens des montagnes, se tenant debout, enlacés presque, les jeunes hommes et les jeunes filles se sont avancés pour former un cercle autour d'eux. Puis les jeunes filles se sont prises par la main et se sont serrées les unes contre les autres; le jeunes gens ont fait comme elles, les deux groupes se sont unis par un côté, et, doucement, cette sorte de ronde enveloppant les danseurs a tourné, avançant et reculant, réglant la cadence suivant la mélodie des voix" (Gaston Vuillier, *La danse* [Paris, 1898], pp. 207-208).

[10] See Henri Baudrillart, *Les populations agricoles de la France*, 3 vols. (Paris, 1885-93), III, p. 357; Emile Guillaumin, *La vie d'un simple: mémoires d'un métayer*, 2nd ed. (Paris, 1905), p. 65; Drouillet, *Folklore du Nivernais*, III, pp. 137-138; Felix Arnaudin, *Chants populaires de la Grande-Lande et des régions voisines* (Paris, 1912), p. xxvii; and René Nelli, *Le Languedoc et le Comté de Foix, le Roussillon* (Paris, 1958), p. 236.

[11] Drouillet, *Folklore du Nivernais*, III, pp. 131, 143.

[12] Martin Nadaud, *Mémoires de Léonard, ancien garçon maçon*, 2nd ed. (Paris, n.d.), pp. 86-87.

[13] For an extremely interesting piece of research which relates to this discussion, see Jean-Michel Guilcher and Hélène Guilcher, "L'enseignement militaire de la danse et les traditions populaires," *Arts et traditions populaires*, 18 (1970), pp. 273-328, and especially pp. 299 ff.

company into spectators and dancers, for the dance was itself an expression of the collectivity:

> At least in the time and space that we have studied [writes Guilcher], the dance is an amusement for all ages. It unites generations more than it separates them. Everyone takes part according to his disposition and ability. . . . From [this] derives the important consequence, that the dancing population of a village or a group of villages changes only slowly, and in a very imperceptible way. . . . The physiognomy of the group is not visibly modified. Its total transformation happens only after a good deal of time. . . .[14]

Dancing in this tradition was a celebration of village solidarity, a visible demonstration of unity. Along with the pleasure and recreation more directly involved, each dancer derived a sense of participation, security, and communion.[15] The absence of serious surveys prevents an assessment of how prevalent was this mode in the eighteenth and nineteenth centuries. It would obviously be interesting to know something about this, for the presence of village communal dancing might well correlate with other evidence of village cohesion. However, it does seem likely that communal dancing of this sort existed elsewhere than in the Basse-Bretagne — for example, in parts of Languedoc, Béarn, and the Bigorre.

A second tradition is a variation on the first, for in it the dancers were a local sub-community. Most often they were the young unmarried of a village, or perhaps of the entire parish or commune, assembled together. Here the dance took the guise of an elaborate mating ritual, in which recently marrieds were feted and new matches were devised.[16] Here especially, however, the concerns of the wider community were manifest, for the parents of the young people hovered nearby, both as spectators and as referees, on hand to enforce propriety.[17]

Sometimes the dancing concerned other groups within localities. Work parties during the harvest season danced together in the evenings, as did those who pruned vines or beat sheaves of grain. One woman, born in 1866, told the folklorist Paul Delarue that dancing was one of the principal attractions of the grape harvest about Beaune. Such comments are

[14] Guilcher, *Tradition populaire de la danse*, pp. 50-51.

[15] Ibid., p. 57.

[16] See, for example, Dupin, *Mémoire statistique du département des Deux-Sèvres* (Paris, An XII), pp. 211-212.

[17] André Varagnac, *Civilisation traditionnelle et genres de vie* (Paris, 1948), p. 338; G. de Charville, "La vie à la campagne," *Le Temps*, 4 January 1885. For an important discussion of the significance of community control, see Edward Shorter, "Différences de classe et sentiment depuis 1750: l'exemple de la France," *Annales: économies, sociétés, civilisations*, 29 (1974), pp. 1034-1057.

frequent in the folklorist literature.[18] Shepherds danced in the mountains during the transhumance, while women who worked together spinning or making cheese did the same. All of these dances limited the active participants in some way, either by professional activity, social standing, sex, or marital status.

These group dances were generally more complex than those involving an entire village; the steps were more difficult to learn, and the movements required more skill. The entire genre is extremely rich, but the overall style may be illustrated by a single example, the *bourrée*, perhaps the most common traditional French dance, and frequently associated with its *pays d'origine*, the Auvergne. "This choral dance," says the ethnomusicologist Curt Sachs, "is performed by a file of men and a file of women facing each other. As the two lines dance repeatedly forward and back, the leader on the right and the dancer opposite him break from their lines and change places, and one after another their neighbours follow their example, until all have left their original places."[19] Van Gennep refers to the many varieties of *bourrées*, in which the dance was given special character by virtue of occasion, season, or the particular group which executed it.[20]

More elaborate still was the third dance tradition, in which an individual or a specially designed group performed some dance for the rest of the community. The community usually accompanied the dancers by clapping, singing, or a wordless chant. The *farandole*, a chain dance in which as many as a hundred or more snaked through a town or village, usually in Provence, was sometimes of this character, a necessary accompaniment of local celebration, often at Carnaval. In one variant, the *danse des fileuses*, young men dressed up as spinning women, with ribbons in their bonnets and candles affixed to decorated distaffs. Preceded by a masked clown they wound about, singing "le jugement des fileuses," a sustained criticism or praise of local authorities. Having arrived at the home of a *notable* the "fileuses" formed two concentric circles turning in opposite directions, while a couple carrying a spinning wheel with candles and a reeling machine occupied the centre. The dancers in the exterior circle danced towards the centre while those in the interior fell back, changing places

[18]   Cited in Drouillet, *Folklore du Nivernais*, III, p. 141. See also Baumel, *Danses populaires*, pp. 44 ff; and Guilcher, "Aspects et problèmes de la danse populaire traditionnelle," p. 39.

[19]   Curt Sachs, *World History of the Dance*, trans. by Bessie Schonberg (New York, 1963), pp. 408-409. See also Vuillier, *Danse*, pp. 214-220; and Pierre Charrie, *Le folklore du Bas Vivarais* (Paris, n.d.), p. 270. Sach's work, once widely considered a reliable authority, is now questioned in a number of respects by dance historians. For a useful critique, see Suzanne Youngerman, "Curt Sachs and His Heritage: A Critical Review of *World History of the Dance* With a Survey of Recent Studies That Perpetuate His Ideas," *Committee on Research in Dance News*, 1 (July 1974), pp. 6-19.

[20]   Van Gennep, *Manuel de folklore*, I², pp. 546-547.

with the former. A new movement formed a single circle. Each dancer then separated from the group to say his piece, and the clown finally concluded the satire with a wide-ranging *exposé* on "les personnalités du pays."[21] Dances like these required careful preparation, and were normally undertaken by the *Jeunesse*, who were the organized unmarried men of the village, by a religious fraternity or *confrérie*, or by some other corporate group. Such dances had special meaning in each locality, both by virtue of content (in this case the *critique des moeurs*) and also by their well-worn place in the rhythms of local festivity.[22]

Now in all of these instances, the moving feet were guided by the chart of communal custom. Even when the entire village community was not dancing together, the individuals who participated did so under a wide-ranging system of collective control. Looking at the entire corpus of traditional dancing, André Varagnac used the word *ritual*, implying a network of regulation with moral imperatives for certain actions, rendering them predictable to a high degree.[23] These dances appear to us as a ritualistic expression, directed by a series of customary rules. Participation itself was not a matter of taste, but a question of where one stood in the social system.[24] Custom dictated the occasions for dancing, the choice of partners, and the order of the dances. And to sustain these rules and give them meaning was the group authority which everyone recognized. Into the 1890's such authority still made itself felt — as in the *Règlement des danses au pardon de Saint-Mathurin*, which codified, for the Breton commune, the *usages du pays*. Proper clothing had to be worn, and it was expressly forbidden to dance in ordinary work clothes (*en blouse*). In what was possibly a concession to modernity the rules permitted a chain of dancers "par choix de société," but preference clearly went to "forming a

---

[21] Mourgues, *Danse provençale*, pp. 78-80.

[22] See the description of related dances in Madame Clément-Hémery, *Histoire des fêtes civiles et religieuses, usages anciens et modernes de la Flandre et d'un grand nombre de villes de France* (Avesnes, 1845), pp. 468-470. See also the hilarious description of the "danse du feu aux fesses," performed on Ash Wednesday in the Hérault as late as 1935, in Van Gennep, *Manuel de folklore*, I³, pp. 1059-1060.

[23] André Varagnac, *De la préhistoire au monde moderne: essai d'une anthropodynamique* (Paris, 1954), p. 88. On peasant ritual and ceremony I draw here upon Eric R. Wolf, *Peasants* (Englewood Cliffs, N.J., 1966), p. 99.

[24] See Butel, *Vallée pyrénéenne*, p. 116. Another study of this locality sheds similar light on dancing: F. Capdeville, *La vallée d'Ossau: l'état social de la vallée d'Ossau avec quelques détails sur les eaux thermales, l'archéologie et les montagnes* (Paris, 1891), p. 128. For an excellent description of how the choice of partners could be dictated by social standing within a village, see Pierre Bourdieu, "Célibat et condition paysanne," *Etudes rurales*, nos. 5-6 (1962), p. 55 and passim. For other discussions of dance as a rite, duty or obligation see, for example, Drouillet, *Folklore du Nivernais*, III, p. 135; Perrin and Bouët, *Breiz izel*, pp. 241-242; and Gabriel Jeanton, *Le Mâconnais traditionaliste et populaire*, 4 vols. (Macon, 1920-23), IV, pp. 20-21.

chain with neighbours, according to local custom."[25] This document is a survival, of course, of a time when such rules needed no such codification. It does reflect, however, the spirit of group regulation which permeated the proceedings.

Rules such as these were part of the community's consciousness, and were extended beyond this easily observed protocol to cover aspects of dance composition. In fifteen years of research on the subject, Guilcher could not report ever having heard of an author of a dance. It was the collectivity rather, whether the whole village or some smaller corporate group, guided by some wider tradition, which tested, selected or adapted some given repertoire.[26] Change had occurred, but within the framework of communally-determined limits. Persistence was more generally the rule because the fundamental communal structures had a glacial stability. The dances which seemed so strange to urban and middle-class visitors, therefore, derived from a peasant way of life which had endured for generations; the steps, the cries, the instruments, the music had all some service to perform in the life of the community.

III

This idea of service clashes sharply with our contemporary, popular view of dance, conditioned as most of us are by a society in which the pursuit of individual pleasure embraces almost every nonessential activity. But for the villagers we have been discussing, the recreative function may not have loomed so large. For them dancing helped the community to discharge its business and minister to its well-being. None of this precluded enjoyment, of course, but this was less important than the various ways in which dancing served collective needs. Let us look at some of these in turn.

One has already been mentioned in the context of community dances: the dance articulated the existence of a group, defined its membership, and celebrated its being. Almost all traditional dances served the community in this way. Most vivid, in this connection, are the dances in which body movements pantomimed work — shoemaking, weaving, or whatever — while the dancers themselves, all members of the same corporation, followed the lead of the most prestigious among them.[27] Such dances

---

[25] Quoted in Louis Tiercelin, *La Bretagne qui croit: pardons et pèlerinages* (Paris, 1894), p. 134, n. 1. See also Guilcher, *Tradition populaire de la danse*, p. 44; and Van Gennep, *Manuel de folklore*, I¹, pp. 256-257.

[26] Guilcher, *Tradition populaire de la danse*, pp. 567-568.

[27] See, for example, Mourgues, *Danse provençale*, p. 94 and passim; Van Gennep, *Manuel de folklore*, I³, p. 1112; and Baumel, *Danses populaires*, pp. 44 ff.

could be held at important punctuation points in the life of the group — harvest time for agricultural labourers, *rites de passage* for artisans passing through stages in the craft hierarchy, or the arrival or embarkation of fishermen. Wedding dances in a similar way involved communal groups in some ritualistic expression of the group's identity. This is why custom sometimes prescribed in such elaborate detail with whom the bride or groom should dance, the place of outsiders, the role of invited guests. Wedding dances helped to symbolize the establishment of a new household within the community, an important event of obvious public concern.[28] In all these cases it was crucial to control the dance company; the active participation of outsiders could weaken the symbolic significance and dilute the statement which the dance implicitly made. Hence the innumerable accounts of the group's efforts to achieve this control, often at the cost of considerable violence.[29]

Dancing also served the collective purpose in courtship. Here too the need for control was paramount; it was in the collective interest to regulate the marriage market, and prevent the exchanges between the sexes from being guided by passion or inclination. Sex, as a result, was the enemy. No meddling *curés* were necessary to enforce the strictures against self-indulgence. Most accounts of peasant dancing — the real thing, that is, and not the modernized versions we shall examine in a few moments — report that the proceedings were extremely unerotic. Even the occasional sexual encounter was in the open, stylized and *au fond* rather tame: "at each refrain a fierce and strident *iou! iou!* was heard, and the dancer, in an off handed way [*sans façon*], but also without resistance, planted a rough and heavy kiss on the cheek of his partner."[30] As we have seen, the dances were often with members of the same sex. And when they were not, parental supervision of the unmarried, especially the girls, was constant. Courtship here involved little touching beyond the occasional pinch, or squeeze of a hand, and of course nothing like close embraces. Couples danced by themselves in very few of the dances we have mentioned, and even when they did rapidly changing partners was the rule. Moreover, the couples maintained an "open" position — with both partners facing in the same direction. Courtship was a highly regulated, public encounter, in which the rules set clear limits on sexual contact.

[28] Guilcher, *Tradition populaire de la danse*, pp. 24 ff.; and Van Gennep, *Manuel de folklore*, I², pp. 542-544.
[29] J.-A. Delpon, *Statistique du département du Lot*, 2 vols. (Paris, 1831), I, p. 206; Henri Raulin, "La communauté villageoise en Châtillonnais," *Etudes rurales*, 48 (1972), p. 64; Hugo, *France pittoresque*, I, p. 154; Van Gennep, *Manuel de folklore*, I¹, p. 256; and Jean-Michel Guilcher, "Les derniers branles de Béarn et Bigorre," *Arts et traditions populaires*, 16 (1968), p. 262.
[30] Bernard-Langlois, *Etudes topographiques*, I, p. 119. See also Dupin, *Statistique du département des Deux-Sèvres* (Paris, An X), p. 77.

Dances for magical or religious purposes had apparently existed from time immemorial, but only a vestige persisted into the eighteenth and nineteenth centuries. The Breton folklorist Paul Sébillot once described a special dance performed on the eve of Shrove Tuesday to facilitate the growth of turnips; and there are numerous accounts of peasants who danced around the ritual bonfires kindled before the *fête de Saint-Jean*, in the expectation of healing or other good fortune.[31] As late as the beginning of the twentieth century certain *rondes* were danced in various regions of France during Carnaval to stimulate the hatching of eggs or the growth of hemp.[32] And on other festivals too, dancing was intended, at least in part, to contribute to the fertility of men, beasts, or the soil.[33] Related to these were the *danses pieuses*, executed in times past as part of a religious procession, or after celebration of mass, in which the dancers commemorated the day of a patron saint in some traditional rite.[34]

In the curious working dances, the collectivity harnessed dancing to its common benefit in the performance of some necessary task. In Brittany, an entire parish would assemble annually to beat down the village threshing floor, pounding the earth with wooden shoes; in the valley of the Ossau the task was "rippling" — separating the grain from sheaves of flax in the preparation of fibre.[35] Such cases were classic traditional mixtures of heavy work and what we might call recreation.

Finally, the dance could be geared to public statements about the community's way of life. We have seen one such example in the *danse des fileuses* of Provence. Another would be the charivari — itself often in the form of a dance — when villagers engaged in collective rebuke of local deviants through some ritualized procedure.[36] Dancing frequently followed charivaris, in which case the dance itself constituted a communal

---

[31] Paul Sébillot, "Superstitions agricoles," *Revue des traditions populaires*, 18 (1903), p. 69; Dupin, *Mémoire statistique*, p. 214; Emile Souvestre, *Les derniers Bretons*, 3rd ed., 4 vols. (Paris, 1854), I, p. 12; and Delpon, *Statistique du département du Lot*, I, p. 208.

[32] Guilcher, "Aspects et problèmes de la danse," p. 48, n. 23.

[33] Mourgues, *Danse provençale*, pp. 93, 108; Emile Maussenet, *Recherches statistiques et historiques sur le village de Châlons-sur Vesle* (Reims, 1898), p. 99; Charles Dard, "La fête des brandons," *Mémoires de la société d'histoire et d'archéologie de Châlons-sur-Saône*, XVIII (1934-35), p. 141; and Nelli, *Languedoc*, p. 204.

[34] L.-J.-B. Béranger-Feraud, *Superstitions et survivances étudiées au point de vue de leur origine et de leurs transformations*, 5 vols. (Paris, 1896), III, pp. 409-426; J.-A. Durbec, *Notes historiques sur quelques pèlerinages, processions, fêtes et jeux de Provence* (Paris, 1952), pp. 268-278; and Mourgues, *Danse provençale*, p. 60.

[35] Perrin and Bouët, *Breizizel*, pp. 241-242; and Butel, *Vallée pyrénéenne*, p. 102.

[36] On the subject of charivaris, see especially Natalie Z. Davis, "The Reasons of Misrule: Youth-Groups and Charivaris in Sixteenth-Century France," *Past and Present*, 50 (February 1971), pp. 41-75; E.P. Thompson, "Rough Music': le charivari anglais," *Annales: économies, sociétés, civilisations*, 27 (1972), pp. 285-312; Claude Gauvard and Altan Gokalp, "Les conduites de bruit et leur signification à la fin du Moyen Age: le charivari," *Annales: économies,*

celebration of its own sense of justice.[37] During the French Revolution the *farandole* drew upon the tradition of these danced charivaris, blending with the times. Once devoted to more innocent purposes, the dance became heavily politicized, its targets now those who in some way were identified with the *ancien régime*. Before long the dance lost all association with remarried widows, beaten husbands, or the other violators of local custom. By the time of the Restoration, politics had absorbed all. As one popular jingle put it:

> Nous danserons la farandole,
> En dépit de Charles X . . .[38]

IV

During the nineteenth and early twentieth centuries a modern, urban, national and capitalistic society launched a series of attacks upon the culture of the French village. Villagers were drilled by the military, taught by the *instituteur*, exploited by the merchant, healed by the doctor, employed by the civil service, poisoned by alcohol, and shipped out on the train. For those who were left behind in the *exode rural* a continuous and growing exposure to new cultural influences helped transform village life. The cumulative effect of these developments was to destroy the cohesion of the village community, which had been the generator of a culture all its own. The villages themselves remained, of course, and some of the villagers are still around. But the culture, for the most part, was gone. The communal rites, the *fêtes patronales*, the pilgrimages, the collective decision-making, the sociability patterns — all these were no more.

Dancing, I have argued, reflected the life of rural communities of traditional France. It was fitting, therefore, that the process just men-

sociétés, civilisations, 29 (1974), pp. 693-704; and Roger Pinon, "Qu'est-ce qu'un charivari: essai en vue d'une définition opératoire," in *Kontakte und Grenzen: Probleme der Volkskultur und Sozialforschung: Festschrift G. Heilfwith* (Göttingen, 1969), pp. 393-405.

[37] Abel Hugo gives the following description for the department of the Ain: "Un charivari attend les nouveaux époux lorsqu'un est un *veuf*: mais, en donnant un bal public, ils peuvent éviter ce désagrément. Le bal même s'appelle alors *charivar*; il est d'usage que l'ouverture en soit fait par les deux mariés, qui se retirent ensuite s'il leur plaît" (Hugo, *France pittoresque*, I, p. 122).

[38] Mourgues, *Danse provençale*, p. 148. Ned Shorter reminds me of the words of the *Carmagnole*:

> Dansons la carmagnole
> Rata la tan, Rata la tan,
> Dansons la carmagnole
> Vive le son du canon!

tioned should have eliminated the traditional dance, and replaced it with a modern version. This last reflected the social standards of another world and the cultural ideal of a new way of life. Let us consider, for a moment, the emergence of the new, city styles of dancing which stood in such marked contrast to those just examined.

The urban-rural contrast, it should be noted, may not always have been so great as it was in the modern period. For while there had been longstanding differences between the dances of rural folk and those of the urban upper classes, there was also a network of communication which dance historians have never completely understood. In 1565 there was a famous encounter between the two: at a great feast given by Catherine de Medici at Bayonne the courtiers enjoyed samples of local dances performed by troupes of girls from the provinces — each, sup-posedly, *à la façon de son pays*. Folk dancing here was a curiosity; yet if the historians are correct the courtiers copied the rustics liberally in their *branles*, *contredances* and many others.[39] Borrowing the adaptation may also have occurred in the opposite direction: travelling acrobats, jugglers and other performers may well have offered aristocratic models to peas-ants, leaving some trace in village dancing.[40] But these delicate and obscure exchanges still left two distinct cultural forms.

In the early nineteenth century a veritable revolution in the dancing habits of the upper classes transformed this pattern. In little more than a generation or two the new dances absorbed or displaced those of the lower orders. The steam engine of this revolution was the couple dance, espe-cially the waltz and the polka, setting the process in motion; the "second wave," beginning at the end of the nineteenth century, came with the evanescent fashions of the enormously popular *bals publics* — the *maxixe*, the cakewalk, the tango, and, in 1912, that famous French dance, *le fox-trot*.

One obvious sign of the waltz's importance in the world of dance was the effort of French masters to establish that it was made in France. The author of one manual dismissed Vienna, Johann Strauss and the Austrian connection with a whiff of historical grapeshot — the waltz's beginning lay in the sixteenth century, with the court of Henri III.[41] At stake in this search for pedigree was the honour of having swept Europe off its feet —

---

[39] Sachs, *World History*, p. 348.

[40] See Sachs, *World History*, ch. 7, passim; Maurice A.-L. Louis, *Le folklore et la danse* (Paris, 1963), p. 309; Guilcher and Guilcher, "Enseignement militaire de la danse," p. 319, n. 79; Guilcher, *Tradition populaire de la danse*, pp. 557-558. On cultural borrowing in general, see the stimulating paper "Proverbial Wisdom and Popular Errors," by Natalie Zemon Davis, *Society and Culture in Early Modern France: Eight Essays* (Stanford, 1975), pp. 227-267.

[41] Desrat, *Traité de la danse*, 2nd ed. (Paris, [1900]), pp. 73 ff.

quite literally for upper-class Europe — in the form of a dance whose pre-eminence was unchallenged in the first part of the nineteenth century. With the waltz, fashionable Europeans danced in couples, whirling quickly and at their own direction. Without exaggerating more than a bit it is probably true to say, with one author, that "the waltz permitted . . . the kind of sexual contact which had heretofore been unthinkable."[42] In the salons of the aristocracy or the urban bourgeoisie the old choral dances like the minuet or the *quadrille* were dethroned, and an era of couples began. According to Curt Sachs the change signalled the arrival of a new society. "The decline of the choral dance is a cause and an indication of the social development. The choral dance, communal dances, demand a compact social order; they require an association in the dance which is something more than the mere execution of a series of figures and movements. . . . The triumph of the individual in the nineteenth century inevitably raises the couple dance to the new leading position and allows the choral dance to fall back."[43]

In contrast to the dim changes mainly discussed in this paper, we can trace the advent of the polka with draftsmanlike precision. It came to Paris in the second week of March 1844, brought by an entrepreneur, rather than by a mutation of the collective *mentalité*. Its principal promoter was a dancing master known as the Great Cellarius, whose salon was at 41,rue Vivienne.[44] All authorities agree that the effect of the new import was extraordinary, and however suspicious we may be of such *petite histoire événementalle*, we can read in these accounts of the rapid popularization of a new dancing style. In quick succession came the mazurka, the redowa, the *scottisch*, and others, regarded by one critic "comme de véritables actes de prostitution . . . des danses aphrodisiaques."[45]

It was not only sexual contact which alarmed the moralizers; it was also that the new dances emerged from the closet of private salons and draw-

---

[42] Ruth Katz, "The Egalitarian Waltz," *Comparative Studies in Society and History*, 15 (1973), pp. 368-377.

[43] Sachs, *World History*, p. 437.

[44] Vuillier, *Danse*, pp. 233-242. On March 14, 1844, the London *Times* correspondent observed: "The Paris papers of Monday are destitute of news. Our private letters state, that politics are for the moment suspended in public regard by the new and all-absorbing pursuit— the polka — a dance recently imported from Bohemia, and which embraces in its qualities the intimacy of the waltz, with the vivacity of the Irish jig. You may conceive how completely is 'the Polka' the rage for the (I am assured) fact that the lady of a celebrated ex-minister desiring to figure in it at a *soirée dansante*, monopolized the professor *par excellence* of that *specialité* for three hours on Wednesday, at 200 francs the hour." Quoted in Frances Rust, *Dance in Society* (London, 1969), p. 73. The professor, of course, was Cellarius.

[45] Brieux Saint-Laurent, *Quelques mots sur les danses modernes*, 2nd ed. (Paris, 1856), pp. 10, 20. See also N.-C. de Charlemagne, *Le polka et la mazurka, quadrilles historiques et fantastiques* (Paris, 1844); and Un Observateur, *Les danses des salons* (Paris, 1855).

ing rooms to vast public halls, or even the streets. For it was one thing for the upper classes to clutch each other and spin about the floor in couples; it was another for ordinary folk to do so, and in commercial establishments. Victor Fournel noted that the *hatitués* of the *bals publics* of the 1850's included clerks, *garçons de boutiques*, nannies and cooks; by the 1880's, in Lille, as many as 12,000 workers crowded into the Alcazar on Saint Anne's day to dance until morning.[46] In most places the *salles de danse* of the early nineteenth century — invariably reserved for the *gens du bien* — gave way by the Second Empire to more common people, with little money but a great deal of energy to spend.[47] And in comparison with times past, noted one old Rouennais in 1853, the popular classes did not seem to need a "caller" — they danced the new dances without direction, and they seemed to him at least to know what they were doing.[48]

At the turn of the century, when another series of new dances stimulated the dancing industry, as it now had become, there were hundreds of *bals publics* in Paris, catering to all tastes and social classes.[49] Along with the famous names of Bullier, Salle Wagram, and Tivoli-Vaux-Hall, were the smaller and more modest *bals-musettes* and the *bals de barrière*, on the outskirts of the city. The *Baedeker* of 1898 warned tourists to stay away from these, without bothering to explain; a word to the wise was sufficient.[50] According to Sachs the dances of this time produced a near

[46] Victor Fournel, *Ce qu'on voit dans les rues de Paris*, 2nd ed. (Paris, 1867), pp. 393-399. The first edition of this work was in 1855. A. Desrousseaux, *Moeurs populaires de la Flandre française*, 2 vols. (Lille, 1889), I, p. 53.

[47] See J.J. Juge, *Changemens survenus dans les moeurs des habitans de Limoges depuis une cinquantaine d'années*, 2nd ed. (Limoges, 1817), pp. 92-93; Graeffner, *Topographie physique et médicale*, pp. 75, 78; Marquis, *Mémoire statistique du département de la Meurthe* (Paris, An XIII), p. 139; and J.-B. C. de D., *Moeurs des habitans de Charleville* (Charleville, 1846), pp. 68-71. Desrat summarized the general impression: "A partir de 1830 nous assistons à un changement complet dans la danse et les danseurs. Les bals jusqu'alors étaient restés l'appanage de la haute société. La bourgeoisie allait prendre sa revanche et Paris allait compter autant de bals privés que de bals publics. Ne pouvant se réunir dans leurs salons trop éxigus, les danseurs affluèrent dans les bals publics, établissements splendidement organisés au milieu des jardins. . . . A côté de ces bals vinrent s'ajouter ceux que nous devons regarder comme les prémisses de la Chaumière, du Prado, de la Closerie des Lilas, en un mot des bals d'étudiants et de grisettes. Pendant que dans les uns les familles honnêtes se livraient au seul plaisir de la danse, dans les autres le cancan et le chahut, sorte de danse libre, étourdissaient une jeunesse avide de séductions. Peu à peu on voit disparaître les premiers et arriver les seconds à un chiffre qui nous étonnera quand on le connaîtra" (*Traité de la danse*, pp. 63-65).

[48] E. de La Quérière, *Revue rétrospective rouennaise: coup d'oeil sur les usages, les habitudes et les moeurs de nos pères* (Rouen, 1853), p. 35. For a good survey of the history of *bals publics*, see Vuillier, *Danse*, pp. 256-270.

[49] André Warnod, *Les bals de Paris* (Paris, 1922), passim; *Guide des plaisirs à Paris* (Paris, [1900]), pp. 97 ff., 142-144; and Rudolphe Darzens, *Nuits à Paris* (Paris, 1889), pp. 207-210.

[50] K. Baedeker, *Paris et ses environs: manuel du voyageur*, 13th ed. (Leipzig and Paris, 1898), p. 33; *Guide des plaisirs*, p. 142; and Jean Richepin, "Petites chroniques," *Gil Blas*, 28 October 1882.

anarchy of style, the only common thrust being eroticism and the end of the choral dance:

> Since the Brazilian *maxixe* of 1890 and the *cakewalk* of 1903 broke up the pattern of turns and glides that dominated European round dances, our generation has adopted with disquieting rapidity a succession of Central American dances, in an effort to replace what has been lost to modern Europe: multiplicity, power, and expressiveness of movement to the point of grotesque distortion of the entire body. We have shortly after 1900 the *one-step* or *turkey-trot*; in 1910, inspired by the Cuban *habanera*, the so-called "Argentine" *tango* with its measured crossing and flexing steps and the dramatic pauses in the midst of the glide; and in 1912 the *fox trot* with its wealth of figures. After the war we take over its offspring, the *shimmy*, which with toes together and heels apart contradicts all the rules of post-minnesinger Europe; the grotesquely distorted *Charleston*; in 1926 the *black-bottom* with its lively mixture of side turns, stamps, skating glides, skips and leaps; and finally the rocking *rumba* — all compressed into even movement, all emphasizing strongly the erotic element, and all in that glittering rhythm of syncopated four-four measures classified as *ragtime*. One can hardly imagine a greater contrast to the monotony of steps and melody of the latter part of the nineteenth century.[51]

Dancing could thus no longer be a visible sign of class and good breeding. In dance, as in many aspects of life, there were obvious signs of an aristocratic society in ruin. Not only had high society girls forgotten how to curtsy, as one manual observed, but even *grisettes* could fox trot, and do it well.[52] The new form of dancing had conquered them all, and its effects did not stop here. At the other end of the social scale dance also lost its power to denote cultural distinction; here, however, it was village culture which was in decay, and peasants who were no longer kept apart.

V

Clerical authorities or local officials can always be counted on to view dancing with a *mauvais oeil*; what drew special fire in the French countryside during the nineteenth century was the heavy importation of novelty from the cities. Consider, for example, the week-end threat posed

---

[51] Sachs, *World History*, pp. 444-445.
[52] Desrat, *Traité de la danse*, p. 141. "Ennemies de toute contrainte, les parisiennes saluent à la façon cavalière et masculine, qui consiste en un coup sec de la tête, légèrement penchée pendant que le buste reste droit et que le regard dévisage. Rien de plus insolent. Cela va de pair avec le *Shake-Hand* à l'américaine, qui a remplacé le baise-main galant des cours disparues, avec le galop barbare successeur de la valse harmonieuse" (ibid., pp. 141-142).

in the immediate vicinity of towns and cities, when the *banlieuesards* had to brace themselves for the assaults of *bals de plaisance*.[53] During the Second Empire the *maire* of a commune not far from Noyon laid down the law: musicians and organizers of dances had to make sure that only half the dancers danced at one time; waltzes and galops were expressly forbidden without written authorization; dancing had to be done out of doors; and unless they observed strict decorum, couples were not allowed to dance together ("il est défendu aux danseuses de danser en même temps que leurs cavaliers, et réciproquement, à moins qu'il y ait impassibilité").[54] Dance halls crept closer to rural parishes, laying siege to their inhabitants; in 1866 one archdeacon reported in alarm to the Bishop of Orleans that there were 104 *salles de danse* in the 93 parishes of his *arrondissement*.[55] By the First World War, to take another case, Breton *curés* had turned against the dance on the *aire neuve*, one of the earth-stomping dances referred to before. The reason was that this apparently benign exercise had been transformed by the *aubergistes*, who set up their stands, sold *eau-de-vie*, and established a café atmosphere by the new threshing floor.[56]

In all of these instances one gets the impression of modernity on the march, sweeping village culture before its path, dance and all. Generally speaking, I believe that this is the way it happened. But it was never quite so simple, and by a close examination of some part . of the process, such as dancing, we can see the source of variation as well as exceptional circumstances. The latter too are significant, for they indicate that in dance, as in everything else, the old culture was sometimes a tough nut to crack.

One sign of this was the way in which communities could adapt new styles to the old repertoire. During the 1840's the waltz, *scottisch*, and polka made their appearance at many *fêtes patronales*. But often they coexisted with traditional dances, and sometimes the old styles maintained the *place d'honneur* at the end of the *bal*.[57] In the Nivernais and in other places, the new steps were stripped of some of their form and grafted on to the choral

[53] Jean Belfond, *Vieux carnavals nantais* (Nantes, 1930), pp. 112-114.

[54] Charles Sauvestre, *Mes lundis* (Paris, 1864), p. 180. See also the "Pétition pour les villageois que l'on empêche de danser," in Paul-Louis Courier, *Collection complète des pamphlets politiques et opuscules littéraires* (Brussels, 1826), pp. 289-301.

[55] Christianne Marcilhacy, *Le diocèse d'Orléans sous l'episcopat de Mgr. Dupanloup (1849-1878): sociologie religieuse et mentalités collectives* (Paris, 1962), p. 384. See also Theodore Zeldin, "The Conflict of Moralities: Confession, Sin and Pleasure in the Nineteenth Century," in Zeldin, ed., *Conflicts in French Society: Anticlericalism, Education and Morals in the Nineteenth Century* (London, 1970), p. 13.

[56] See Frédéric Le Guyader's comments (1917) on Alexandre Bouët's 1835 text, in Perrin and Bouët, *Briez izel*, p. 244.

[57] Drouillet, *Folklore du Nivernais*, III, pp. 141-142; Ovide de Valgorge, *Souvenirs de l'Ardèche*, 2 vols. (Paris, 1846), I, p. 341; and Charles Ribault de Laugarderie, *Les noces de campagne en Berry, et principalement à Bengy-sur-Craon* (Bourges, [1855]), p. 17.

traditions of the Centre.[58] When this happened, according to Guilcher, the result was to reduce involvement — from chains or circles of hundreds, to twenty, to eight, and sometimes to couples.[59] It seems likely that adaptation occurred most easily where entire communities were unused to dancing together, and where specialized groups, more inclined to experimentation, could take the initiative.[60] Here the object was to achieve the most decorative or artistically satisfying performance. This process would be quickened occasionally by dance competitions, pitting one *société de danse* against another before the judgment of the local *maire*, whose criteria of excellence might not be that of the Moulin Rouge.

In any event, there could be no modernization of dance without wooden floors. These came rather late to rural France, as an 1894 *enquête* into housing conditions sadly pointed out. The new dances were simply not appropriate to grassy fields or the beaten earth, where a waltz or polka would be incongrous and physically difficult.[61] Dancers had therefore to rely upon the facilities of the cabaret, whose presence only became extensive in the countryside in the early Third Republic. Eventually portable stages made their appearance, set up for special occasions in a village square.[62]

According to a number of personal accounts, it was not until the 1870's or 1880's, a generation or so after their first appearance in Paris, that the new couple dances came to rural France. While they obviously appeared much earlier in some localities in the later period the novelty of the new forms seems almost universal. This was so in the Landes, for example, where couple dances were known before then, but had been considered "tout à fait exotiques," the property of a few bourgeois families with relations outside the *pays*.[63] And in the Bourbonnais, or Provence, or the

---

[58] Drouillet, *Folklore du Nivernais*, III, pp. 167 ff. See also Guilcher, "Aspects et problèmes de la danse," p. 32; and idem, "Conservation et renouvellement dans la culture paysanne ancienne de Basse-Bretagne," *Arts et traditions populaires*, 15 (1967), pp. 1-18.

[59] Guilcher, "Aspects et problèmes de la danse," p. 45.

[60] See Guilcher and Guilcher, "Enseignement militaire de la danse," pp. 304, 307-308.

[61] Some kind of wooden floor, it was observed in this report, is "partout un signe de civilisation, comme c'est partout une condition de propriété et de salubrité. Nous regrettons d'avoir à constater que, dans nos villages, au nord comme au sud, les rez-de-chaussée dallés, carrelés ou parquetés sont encore rares." Alfred de Foville, introduction to Ministère de l'Instruction Publique, des Beaux-Arts et des Cultes, *Enquête sur les conditions de l'habitation en France*, 2 vols. (Paris, 1894), I, pp. xxix-xxx.

[62] On cabarets in the French countryside, see Michael R. Marrus, "Social Drinking in the Belle Epoque," *Journal of Social History*, 7 (1974), pp. 129-131. See also Augustin Bernard and Camille Gagnon, *Le Bourbonnais* (Paris, 1954), p. 229; Charles-Bernard Donnedevie, *Histoire de la commune de Ligardes de 1700 à 1925* (Agen, 1926), p. 126; and Marcel Maget, "Les ruraux," *Esprit*, 27 (June 1959), p. 929.

[63] Arnaudin, *Chants populaires*, p. xiii; G. Langlet, *Le village de Montagne-Fayel à la fin du XIXe siècle* (Amiens, 1964), pp. 22-23; A. Dujarric-Descombes, *La danse en Périgord* (Périgueux, 1913), p. 8.

Dauphiné it was the same, with new styles crowding out the old in the first decades of the Third Republic.[64]

Simultaneously, the railway was sending out secondary lines of communication, and roads, a national market and a national educational system began to draw the country into a unified cultural pattern. Differences remained, but these were vastly reduced. Dancing may not have been on the minds of the engineers of unification — Gambetta, Freycinet, Ferry, and the other bourgeois founders of the modern French state. But the end of traditional, communal dancing was a tiny measure of their success, and one small indication of the unified society they were building.[65]

If the chronology of this process is necessarily unclear, its social significance is more obvious. Behind the transformation of dance we can see the decline of the village as a cohesive social unit. As we have noted, village dancing served as a vehicle for group expression; dancing in the modern style was inclined to do the opposite, to articulate the needs and feelings of individuals. For example, dancing had always been an activity which the entire community could monitor; one aspect of the newer mode was that the proceedings escaped this surveillance. Dances were now held at night; the parents stayed away; and the young people went out in packs, or even in couples. As a result, dances became notorious occasions for sexual encounters, which had previously been regulated by communal custom and public scrutiny.[66] Where tradition had once prescribed dancing in the

[64] Bernard and Gagnon, *Bourbonnais*, p. 229; J.-A. Pilot de Thorey, *Usages, fêtes et coutumes existant ou ayant existé en Dauphiné*, 2 vols. (Grenoble, 1885), II, p. 238; and Henri Meynard, *Lourmarain à la belle époque* (Aix-en-Provence, 1968), p. 101.

[65] For an excellent description of this process, see Eugen Weber, "'Fin-de-siècle': The Third Republic Makes a Modern Nation," in Mathé Allain and Glen Conrad, eds., *France and North America: Over Three Hundred Years of Dialogue* (Lafayette, La., 1973), pp. 87-101. A recent Marxist analysis, focusing on the statebuilders, is Sanford Elwitt, *The Making of the Third Republic: Class and Politics in France, 1868-1884* (Baton Rouge, La., 1975).

[66] Describing this "relâchement de la surveillance paternelle," one *feuilletoniste* gave this racy account: "Nous vous avons montré des enfants de treize à quatorze ans, et très souvent moins, figurant dans toutes les contredanses, au bras de leur préféré, car ces demoiselles en ont déjà un. Sans cesser d'être grand, le mal serait moindre si ces ébats précoces avaient uniquement le bal local pour théâtre; mais [la jeunesse] est assidue à toutes les fêtes patronales, à toutes les assemblées du voisinage; comme c'est surtout lorsque le droit peut vous en être discuté, que l'on tient à marcher avec [la jeunesse], les aspirantes ne manquent jamais d'aller à ces fêtes. On s'y rend par bandes de filles et par bandes de garçons; de minuit à deux heures du matin, on en reviendra avec son *rameneux*, par couples, volontairement isolés, et à distance respectable les uns des autres. Les deux jeunes gens, échauffés par la danse et par les [rafraîchissements], cheminent dans les demi-ténèbres d'une nuit d'été, tantôt par le sentier perdu, entre la double haie d'épis qui ondulent avec un murmure amoureux, tantôt dans les grands bois, où les molles clartés de la lune, qui en argentent la voûte feuillue, laissent les dessous dans une obscurité autorisant toutes les audaces. La situation se passe de commentaires, vous le reconnaîtrez" (G. de Cherville, "La vie à la campagne," *Le Temps*, 4 January 1885).

place du village, or in some other local meeting place, some dancers now preferred to travel — perhaps to a nearby cabaret, perhaps to the region's nearest dance hall, or perhaps to the closest big town.[67] People left the village for amusement, signifying the new kind of activity which dance represented. Dancing no longer spoke to communal needs or wider village concerns; it was rather *une distraction* — activity connoting a separation from *la vie quotidienne*. Obviously, the dancers left in search of better facilities. But there is evidence too of repulsion.

Boredom now stalked the village — unthinkable at the time of Arthur Young. When the old culture lost its meaning, it was not always replaced by satisfactory alternatives. Some villages were left culturally undeveloped, suspended between the collective activities of the past and the individualized recreation of the present. But until cinemas, sporting events or television could do their job, mopping up non-work time, and slowly winning the locals back from drink, dancing provided something to do.[68] Nothing fancy, of course. Villagers who danced no longer had in mind the fate of their turnips, a parody of the local *notables*, or felt the embrace of the village collectivity. Consequently, the *branle*, the *bourrée*, or the *farandole* became extinct, or almost so. The shimmy, the one-step, the fox trot better met village needs, as individuals embarked upon their leisure without the restraining hand of the community.[69]

[67] See, for example, Henri Pourrat, *Ceux d'Auvergne: types et coutumes* (Paris, 1928), p. 81; Joseph Garavel, *Les paysans de Morette: un siècle de vie rurale dans une communauté de Dauphiné* (Paris, 1948), p. 88; and Rayna Reiter, "Modernization in the South of France: The Village and Beyond," *Anthropological Quarterly* 45 (1972), p. 47. For a superb description of the new situation and its implications for modernization, see Bourdieu, "Célibat et condition paysanne," *Etudes rurales*, pp. 32-134, esp. pp. 97-103 (cited in note 24, above).

[68] M. Jollivet and H. Mendras, *Les collectivités rurales françaises: étude comparative de changement social* (Paris, 1971), p. 86, passim; André Ramus, *Vie paysanne et technique agricole: exemple de la Bresse louhannaise* (Paris, 1952), p. 131; Donnedevie, *Histoire de la commune de Ligardes*, p. 37; Pilot de Thorey, *Usages, fêtes et coutumes*, II, pp. 238-239; and Meynard, *Lourmarain*, pp. 58-60.

[69] I have discussed the problem of leisure in a general way in *The Rise of Leisure in Industrial Society*, Forums in History (St. Charles, Mo., 1974).

10

Who Sang the Marseillaise?

EUGEN WEBER

The battle song of the Army of the Rhine was born at Strasburg, on April 25, 1792, from a suggestion that mayor Dietrich made to a young officer among his guests, Captain Rouget de Lisle.[1] The song Rouget composed was sung in Dietrich's salon the following evening; and three days later, on Sunday, April 29, it was played by the band of the National Guard and sung for the Lyons volunteers of the first Rhône-et-Loire Battalion,[2] who paraded that day on the Place d'armes in Strasburg. It was a great success: Mrs. Dietrich, the mayor's wife, wrote to her brother about it, describing it as "*du Gluck en mieux*," and within a few days it had been put into print — which facilitated its distribution throughout the land.

Quite what happened after that we do not really know: but on June 17 it is sung at Montpellier; and within a few days a delegate of the Constitutional Society (that is, of the Girondists) of Montpellier carries it to Marseille. The delegate was Mireur, who was destined to become a general of the Republic; for the moment, he was trying to encourage the Marseillais to respond to a Paris appeal for 500 men "qui sachent mourir"; and, since he was not beyond using audio-visual aids in a tricky task, on June 22 he sang the new song at the end of a Constitutional banquet.

People sang a lot in those days — popular deputations would visit the Convention and sing patriotic songs of their own composing, which rather hampered proceedings; and Danton had to intervene several times to establish that the Convention was *not* a place for singing songs.[3] But banquets were, and this one met with great enthusiasm.

The very next day, the new song was printed in the local press, and also

---

[1] For historical details, see Julien Tiersot, *Les fêtes et le chants de la Révolution française* (Paris, 1908); Maurice Dommanget, *De la Marseillaise de Rouget de l'Isle à l'Internationale d'Eugène Pottier* (Paris, 1938); Alfred Chabaud, "La Marseillaise: chant patriotique Girondin," *Annales historiques de la Révolution française*, September-October 1936, pp. 460-467; and Pierre Cavard, *L'Abbé Pessonneaux et la Marseillaise* (Vienne, 1954).

[2] Loire and Rhône became separate departments only one year later, in 1793.

[3] Tiersot, *Les fêtes*, p. 101.

on a separate broadsheet of which the volunteers of the Marseille Battalion, then being raised with some difficulty, received several copies each. They would sing the song and distribute copies of it, on their march to Paris, which took all of July. They may also have shouted snatches of it when they helped to storm the Tuileries, on August 10. At any rate, the song became known as the hymn or the air of the Marseillais.

This raises an intriguing question: who sang the *Marseillaise*? Or, to put it differently: how was it that the *Marseillaise* was sung in French? In 1792, by all accounts, French was as foreign to most provençaux as to Senegalese a century later. As a matter of fact, it was unfamiliar to most people within the borders of France. The abbé Grégoire, who undertook a vast official survey of the question in 1790, concluded rather hopefully that three-quarters of the people of France knew *some* French. On the other hand, he admitted that only a *portion* of these could actually sustain a conversation in it, and he estimated that only about 3 million could speak it properly — while fewer still, of course, could put their French in writing.[4]

We can take this as a rough guide, although I think Grégoire was a bit sanguine. But it is well to remember that, south of the magic line that runs from Saint-Malo to Geneva and divides northern, francophone, developed France from the rest of the country, the non-French speakers were much more concentrated than Grégoire's estimates suggest. In 1824, a third of a century after the *Marseillaise* was born, the official *Statistique des Bouches-du-Rhône* recognized that the normal speech of the middle and lower classes was Provençal, and added: "il s'écoulera encore bien d'années et peut-être des siècles avant que la langue française ne devienne populaire. . . ."

Just as most Neapolitans nowadays can produce some English if they have to, the ordinary people of Marseille understood enough French for whatever aspects of their business would call for it, but they seldom spoke the language. This suggests that the volunteers were a bit exceptional — which they must have been, since they numbered a little less than 500 out of a population well over 100,000, and had to pay their own way! We do not know how many of them really did pay it, or had it paid for them; and really precise information about them is oddly hard to get. But we do know that they were led by young men of the upper classes — who would be, by definition, bilingual; and we know that they included a good few people whose trade edged them towards a knowledge of French: ex-soldiers, journalists, port workers and artisans, or simply drifters.

A writer of the 1840's claims that true Marseillais were few among a

---

[4] For further details and references, see Eugen Weber, *Peasants into Frenchmen* (Stanford, 1976), especially ch. 6.

rabble of foreign elements; and while he is a hostile witness, it is certain that Marseille itself had become a foreign element in its region — a great, cosmopolitan trade center. Outsiders and other mobile types would be more likely recruits for the Battalion: they would be more available mentally and physically, they would be more likely to know or understand French, and it is significant that Michelet wrote about them as "alliés et amis du parti français. . . ."[5]

However, Michelet recognized that the battalion included also "rude men of the people," and this may account for Lamartine's remark that the masses of people who saw them on their march to Paris were struck by "leurs langages étrangers mêlés de jurements."[6] They also improved on Rouget de Lisle by producing a provençal verse of their own, which was pretty strong stuff:

> March on, God's arse
> March on, God's fart
> The emigres, by God
> Have no more idea of God
> Than old monarchist priests.[7]

But obviously what was remembered and noted wherever they passed were the words in French.

By autumn of 1792 the hymn created in the far north-east, disseminated from the south, was sung throughout France — "by all the troops and by the children," specified a report of October 1792, which pointed to the chief agents of its penetration. When Kellerman wanted a *Te Deum* sung on the battlefield at Valmy, to celebrate his victory, the Minister of War wrote back prescribing instead the *Hymne des Marseillais*, "que je joins ici à cet effet." This was certainly connected with other political considerations, but it also reflected the official campaign of frenchification. In 1790, the famous *fête de la Féderation* had included a *Te Deum* sung in Latin, with the responses provided by "the people." This had produced criticism of such official use of Latin: "Parlons en français."[8] "Chantons en français" was the same thing, and the *Marseillaise* was used to that purpose. But the circumstance also suggests that for populations traditionally used to singing canticles or responses in Latin (or dog Latin) which they could

---

[5] Laurent Lautard, *Marseille depuis 1789 jusqu'en 1815, par un vieux Marseillais* (Paris, 1844), I, p. 134; Jules Michelet, *Histoire de la Révolution française* (Paris, 1869), III, pp. 238-239; and Joseph Pollio and Adrien Marcel, *Le Bataillon du 10 août* (Paris, 1881), p. 389.

[6] Alphonse de Lamartine, *Histoire des Girondins*, book I, ch. xvi.

[7] François Mazuy, *Essai historique sur les moeurs et coutumes de Marseille au 19e siècle* (Marseille, 1854), p. 32.

[8] Tiersot, *Les fêtes*, pp. 38, 42.

not understand, a French refrain to a much livelier tune would present no greater problem.

The paradox, of course, was that the new national hymn (as it became in 1795) was linked to a city whose people did not speak French nor, in the case of many of them, feel themselves to be French. But even those who did not speak French could sing it, and singing endowed them with the gift of tongues.

For example, here is a true scene which took place at Bellegarde, between Nîmes and Arles, one day in the 1850's. The poor of a whole parish go off to glean at the break of dawn, and as they go they are singing their own songs. Then, in the midst of this unschooled, thoroughly *patoisant* mass, one man starts to sing *Partant pour la Syrie*, in French; and the whole crowd, we are told, joins in the culminating verse of this song that Queen Hortense had composed at the first Napoleon's court:

> Faites, reine immortelle,
> Lui dit-il en partant,
> Que j'aime la plus belle
> Et sois le plus vaillant![9]

And yet, the man, Batista Bonnet, who tells us this and who tells us how as a little boy he joined in the singing, would go off to be a soldier and serve for six years until wounded in the Franco-Prussian War; and he would know French so little at the end of this, at age twenty-seven, that when he decided to stay on in Paris and try to work there, he had to take French lessons "à 40 sous l'heure."[10]

Bonnet was no exception, and in a way that is what I want to stress. In 1893, according to official figures, about a quarter of the 37,000-odd communes in France spoke no French. Their population accounted for seven and a half million out of the thirty million souls in France. About half a million out of four million children between seven and thirteen spoke no French; another million and a half could speak or understand but could not write it — a strong suggestion that they knew it badly. And the reports of Academy Inspectors inspecting Teachers' Normal Schools through the 1870's and 1880's show that the children's teachers and apprentice teachers knew it badly too.

To put this differently: French was a foreign language for a large minority of the country's inhabitants. And almost half of the children who would reach adulthood in the last quarter of the nineteenth century were taught French, if and when they were taught it, as a foreign language.

[9] A perfect parallel to the stories Robert Mandrou reveals in his study of the *bibliothèque bleue*: as far away as possible from the *concret vécu*, from the *expérience vécue*, of its singers.
[10] Batista Bonnet, *Vie d'enfant* (Paris, 1968), pp. 16, 61.

The Revolution and the Empire had perfected the administrative and legal unity of French territory; but cultural integration, cultural unity, still had to be imposed on a vast and stubborn (or, rather, indifferent) diversity. My reference to the *Marseillaise* was intended to stress the superficiality of certain symbols, the relatively narrow range of their effects, and the depths still unplumbed where everyday life went on, where the *pays* or *patrie* still stood for a limited valley or parish or land, and where it would take a long time before symbols like the *Marseillaise* reflected any real identification with a wider culture — the culture of France as we read and learn about it, the culture of French, of Paris, of the schools.

The subject is immense and few have bothered to scratch at it. The accepted dogma has France forged by the *quarante rois qui en mille ans ont fait la France*, or struck out at a heat in the furnace of the 1790's. A variant of this prefers 1848, or '49, or '51. And yet Jacques Duclos, born in Béarn in 1896, only learnt French after he went to school. And when he was called up for military service there were peasants around him who did not speak French at all. Around 1903, just when Duclos was going off to school, a travel writer called Ardouin-Dumazet was trying to find his way in a village in the monts d'Ambazac, not far from Limoges. He could not find a single person who could understand him (or who would, which culturally amounts to the same thing). So he went on and, outside the village, in the fields, he found the men at work — and they could speak in French, having learnt enough of it at school or in the army to get by.

I mention this story because it is not about the Pyrenees; or about Flanders, where under the Third Republic priests like the Abbé Lemire had to learn Flemish in order to exercise their ministry; or about Brittany, where in the 1880's the Rector of the Academy of Rennes suggested in an official report that the French should do what the Germans were doing to "our poor Alsace-Lorraine." The monts d'Ambazac are in the very center of France, and their speech is the speech of Languedoc. But I mention the story also because what schooling there was in country places until the 1880's was directed to the boys, and was therefore bound to have only superficial effects in societies where women and older people were left outside its ken, and where the business of life outside school, in the home, in the streets, was necessarily conducted in the local speech.

Clearly language, the form of speech in which we conduct our transactions, in which we enshrine our wisdom or speculate about our experience, is crucial to culture and to mentality. Those for whom their speech (and hence their thoughts) was something else than French, could never be really French, could not be (as long as this state lasted) really thoroughly part of the modern nation: France. At least no more, or little more or more significantly, beyond the level of taxes and conscription, than they were part of humanity.

Now, it is fairly clear that they aspired to participate in French culture, at least in terms of what they saw of its external expressions. French was a Sunday language, just as meat (for those lucky enough to have it) was a Sunday dish. *Habits mangeant viande* and *habits de messe* are both terms for a Sunday suit. French, remarked an officer riding through Hérault in 1828, was a *language de parure et de cérémonie*. And there is a lot to show that he was right. Thus, until the end of the century, peasants addressed their betters in French. At dances, the invitation and the first approach are still made in French. In old *noëls*, the shepherds speak dialect, but the angels speak French. And Agricol Perdiguier tells us that at Morière, near Avignon, in the 1820's, the peasants who spoke only *patois* nevertheless resented being given a sermon in *patois* and not in French at a First Communion ceremony: "It struck us as common, trivial, unworthy of so great a ceremony."[11] As with the songs, as with the Mass, how much you understand is secondary. What matters is the melody, the sense of the act.

Speaking French, or giving oneself French airs, was a symbol of social promotion — or at least of aspirations in this direction. And this was understood by village society that both mocked and envied the *Franciot*, the *Franchiman* — or whatever he was called in various places. French reflected a superior other-ness, like that of squire or priest or teacher; and so it was perceived by them, as can be seen from a story that Albert Dauzat told about the peasants in Puy-de-Dôme who got uppity as the nineteenth century dawned and began to give their children French names, in imitation of their local squires. Around 1820, the priest of Vic-le-Comte asked a little girl her name: "Marie," she said. "Marie! But that is a young lady's name, not a name for a peasant. You must be called Miyette or Mayon." And the little girl answered: "I'm as entitled to bear the Holy Virgin's name as any lady."[12]

French was dignified, suspect and superior. It was also urban, modern, "civilized." It provided the terminology of innovation and modernity, and it provided certain more or less abstract notions for which traditional language had not catered. So that little *Janed* of the Breton song, who is tired of service and wants her freedom, sings:

Mé zo skuiz o servicha
La mé houl và *liberté*!

[11] Agricol Perdiguier, *Mémoires d'un compagnon* (Paris, 1964), p. 45.
[12] Albert Dauzat, *Glossaire étymologique du patois de Vinzelles* (Montpellier, 1915), pp. 18-19. The Virgin, incidentally, also spoke French as a rule, until asked to express herself in more comprehensible terms, as she was by the shepherd children to whom she appeared at La Salette in 1846.

But French provided or helped provide something else as well; and this was an image or self-image that I can best describe by referring to a new book by an ex-colleague of mine, the English Africanist Terry Ranger.[13] The book is devoted to the history of a dance mode called *Beni*, which had developed on the Swahili coast of East Africa, in places like Mombassa and Dar-es-Salaam. As *Beni* progressed into the interior, into the back country, it carried with it the aura of Swahili civilization. It was sung in Swahili, it came from the great Swahili urban centers, and Ranger quotes a local informant: "People who could sing in such a dance were esteemed very highly as Swahili, even though his or her spoken Swahili was very poor."

French songs, city songs, were similarly regarded. And, in a period of national integration, when public policy and private interest seem to coincide, at least on this score, songs (like those of Béranger, immensely popular in the 1830's) helped the singers pick up elementary notions of the national language, perhaps encouraged them to learn more of it, but also bolstered their self-esteem. In the small urban centers of Provence workingmen had their own singing societies, where they made up their own songs in local dialect. But we are told that they avoided public performance of "songs in the vulgar tongue."[14] Thus, when the Prince-President, Louis-Napoleon, visited Aix in 1852, the local authorities tried to organize a performance of Provençal songs for his benefit. But they could not. The choirs sang fragments from operas and comic operas (very likely they sang *Partant pour la Syrie*), and they sang original French songs by local composers. But they would not sing in Provençal. It may have been cultural snobbery. But it was probably also a refusal to be cast into an exotic and implicitly demeaning role.

This *mimétisme*, this socio-cultural mimicry that affected many more realms beside that of song, could also be used to didactic ends — not only to spread the use of French, but to spread the mentality approved by official culture: to moralize, to civilize, to soothe the savage breast. So national integration also involved a war of songs. Before they turned to collecting popular songs, like butterflies on pins and just as dead, educated men pursued them with their ire. In the 1860's an excellent folklorist of Lorraine, Xavier Thiriat, wrote about the Vosges, insisting on the vulgar character of native songs (in dialect of course!) as opposed to "those coming from big cities and written in our time," which he found "well-inspired and true expressions of noble sentiments."[15]

Feelings like this were strongest among professional carriers of civiliza-

---

[13] *Dance and Society in Eastern Africa* (Berkeley, 1975), p. 129.
[14] Armand Audiganne, *Les populations ouvrières et les industries de la France* (Paris, 1860), II, p. 253. Further details and references in Weber, *Peasants into Frenchmen*, ch. 26.
[15] *La Vallée de Cleurie* (Remiremont, 1869), p. 381.

tion and literacy: the teachers. Popular songs, like other forms of popular culture, were best the soonest shed and replaced by something finer. And one of the first ways in which teachers intervened as publicists for noble sentiments would be in the realm of conscription — which normal people loathed, and which called forth popular comment that was either tearful, or bitterly satirical and sarcastic, like the well-known product of three stocking-makers from Languedoc:

> Monsieur le Maire et le Préfêt
> Ce sont deux jolis cadets.
> Ils nous font tirer au sort
> Pour nous conduire à la mort.[16]

This sort of thing had to be countered, and it is interesting that about the only songs in French that became part of the village *répertoire* after the 1850's were patriotic conscript songs like:

> Partons, partons, vaillants conscrits,
> Partons, la fleur de la jeunesse!

produced by *instituteurs* and such like propagandists. The next step would be moralistic. In the 1860's, we find a Pyrenean schoolteacher, in Ariège, complaining that all one hears in the countryside are coarse and impure songs: the singing that would improve morals, refine feelings, enoble the spirit, develop intellect, was completely ignored. Schoolteachers, he said, must realize that it is their duty, nay their mission, to propagate such songs. They did.

In 1864, the department of Aude reported with pride that "the lewd songs that wounded even the least modest ears have been replaced by the religious and patriotic choirs of numerous *orphéons* . . . due to schools and to the initiative of teachers."[17] Under the Republic, virtuous but isolated efforts of this sort turned into a nationwide campaign. Jules Simon, who was Minister of Public Instruction in 1872, had often been struck, he wrote to Ambroise Thomas, the composer, "de n'entendre chanter dans les réunions d'ouvriers et de paysans que des airs très vulgaires." He and others set out to provide remedies on the model of German ones, because they had noticed that in 1870 the Germans, whatever region they came from, could join in song, and they wanted to "teach little French children this means of uniting and of glorifying their fatherland," sentiments which, incidentally, most little Frenchmen ignored — at

[16] Albert Dauzat, *Le Village et le paysan de France* (Paris, 1941), p. 162.
[17] *Etat de l'instruction primaire en 1864, d'après les rapports officiels des inspecteurs d'académie* (Paris, 1866), II, p. 37.

least in the areas I am talking about.[18]

In 1864, a school-inspector in Lozère had expressed indignation after visiting schools where he could not find a single child to answer questions like: "Are you English or Russian?" or "What country is Lozère in?" And he added bitterly that, in most of the children, "thought does not go beyond the limits of the poor parish in which they live." The great educational campaigns of the 1880's were directed against this sort of thing, and among their more effective armaments were new songbooks that followed German models for school use. Lay elementary schools put great stress on singing lessons which could inculcate a sense of the father-land, of civilization, and of moral ideals. And the effects of this become clear when, by the mid-eighties, we hear the hills of backcountry Cantal echoing no longer with lewd ditties, but with the songs of Déroulède, yelled out by enthusiastic schoolboys. In 1894, one of the great educa-tional apostles of the day, Félix Pécaut, noted that songs learnt at school were beginning to replace (*sometimes*, he added cautiously) among adult youth "the bad songs that had been too current in France." This was terribly important: "C'est la patrie, c'est la civilisation, c'est aussi un certain idéal moral. . . ."[19] In other words, we are talking about culture and about the process of replacing one culture, one set of cultural equipment, by another.

The *Marseillaise*, with which I started, plays only a marginal role in all this. But it does provide a symbol of the process, and a special case. At Jemappes, it played the soldiers of Dumouriez to victory, and after that it became associated with the great battles of the Republic: Hoche had it sung at Wissemburg, Bonaparte crossed the Saint Bernard with it, and in 1795, after Thermidor had delivered Rouget de Lisle from prison, an official decree made it the national anthem.

Under the Consulate and the Empire, the *Marseillaise* seems to ebb, although it reappeared at the Berezina, at Waterloo, and above all during the Hundred Days. After that, it went underground, of course, but it rose again in 1828, in Auber's opera, *La Muette de Portici*; and it marked the revolutions of 1830, not only in Paris but in Brussels too. But Louis-Philippe (although he provided a pension for Rouget de Lisle, who was old and ill) did not really like it very much. It was too closely associated with *cannibales*,[20] and this was confirmed in 1834, when the insurgents of

---

[18] Amédée Reuchsel, *L'Education musicale populaire* (Paris, 1906), p. 91. In 1887, Thomas would be commissioned to establish the final official version of the national anthem.

[19] "Notes d'inspection," *Revue pédagogique*, October 1894, p. 307.

[20] In 1848, when the peasants of Oyonnax (Ain) heard it sung, they barricaded themselves: "Fremin neutre peurte, y canton la Marseilloise, recha la terreur!" Louis Bollé, *Histoire et folklore du Haut-Bugey* (Bellegarde, 1954), p. 80. ("Close the doors, they're singing the *Marseillaise*, here's the Terror!")

the rue Transnonain adopted it, after which it was largely suppressed until 1840, when, at the height of the Orient Crisis, the government permitted its singing, thus providing the cities of France with a perfect way to express their chauvinism.[21]

War and Revolution, War *or* Revolution, was what the *Marseillaise* represented. And in 1848, naturally, Rachel brought down the house every time she sang it wrapped in a *tricolore*. Just as on March 28, 1871, the Commune would be proclaimed at the Hôtel de Ville to the strains of the *Marseillaise*.

So the song was loaded with political implications, and it was a party song. We read about a bloody political riot at Tarascon in 1850, where the Reds, says the police report, cried out ferociously (no doubt in dialect!) while singing the *Marseillaise*. It was banned under the Second Empire, but an Ardennes workers' song, which represents the journeymen going off for a Monday's drinking in the country, also called for it:

> And if one of us should know it,
> Let him sing the *Marseillaise!*[22]

Obviously some people did know it, because in 1858, when the garbled news of Orsini's attempt to murder the Emperor reached a little village in the Pyrenees, and people thought the Emperor was dead, the deputy mayor sang the *Marseillaise*, because "now we are all free."[23]

It was difficult to build up the myth of Napoleonic glory and stifle its most rousing battle song. Around 1865, in far-off Aurillac, Frère Hilarion, who taught History in the local high school, communicated his own enthusiasms to his students. "One day, as he was telling us about the volunteers of 1792, he was carried away by his enthusiasm into singing us a verse of the *Marseillaise*. Suddenly, we were all on our feet, pale and shivering, drunk with the glory of our forefathers. We took it up, in full voice. . . ." Arsène Vermenouze, the royalist poet who recalled the scene many years later, had learnt to play the trumpet then, simply in order to play the hymn.[24] So, when the Empire fell, and especially during the siege of Paris, the *Marseillaise* was back very quickly,[25] often with new verses.

[21] Note that when it did not suit the government's purpose, the song could still get one into trouble. In a pamphlet of 1844, Claude Tillier denounced the government for celebrating the Revolution on July 14, yet setting the gendarmes on anyone who dared to sing the *Marseillaise* during the festive hubbub. See Henry Leslie Maple, *Claude Tillier* (Geneve, 1957), p. 54.

[22] Archives nationales, BB 30 370 (Aix, October 16, 1850); Eugène Baillet, *Chansons* (Paris, 1867).

[23] Archives départementales, Ariège, 5M3 (April, 1858).

[24] Arsène Vermenouze, "Discours," *La Croix cantalienne*, July 30, 1903.

[25] Note also the equivocal German attitude to the hymn. When on September 19, 1870, the Fifth Prussian Army Corps entered Versailles, its bands played it "pour insulter le vaincu."

The Commune would also have its own version, written by the wife of Jules Fauré, herself born a Castellane, which did not prevent her from writing:

> Chantons la liberté,
> Défendons la cité,
> Marchons, marchons!
> Sans souverain
> Le peuple aura du pain.

Down again, up again. . . . The *Marseillaise* could not be the hymn of the *ordre moral*. Indeed, it was the symbol of opposition to it; in 1877, when Marshal MacMahon visited Roanne between the 16 May and the October elections, his reception would be troubled by a crowd of workingmen belting out the subversive song.[26] But the Republican political victory in 1879 once more reinstated it as the national anthem. And by 1900 or so, that is what it had fully become, with even the band of the *Ecole des Frères* at Pont l'Abbé, in darkest Brittany, concluding their program with it, and having to repeat it to public acclaim.[27]

By that time, too, the workers whose fathers had sung the *Marseillaise* were learning to sing the *Internationale*. The general acceptance of what had long been prized as a fighting song had softened its implications. As late as 1880, the *Marseillaise* was still the favorite song of striking workmen. After 1884, Michelle Perrot tells us, the *Carmagnole* began to offer it serious competition.[28] By 1890 it had overtaken it among working people, and the first strains of the *Internationale* were being heard in Socialist meetings. A new factional song had replaced the old one that was now recognized as a symbol of national unity.

Before that happened, however, the song had to cover some ground. Not only in terms of politics, where the Right took a very long time to accept it (we know all about that!), but in terms of culture, of significance: because you will have noticed that, like most expressions of the official culture, the *Marseillaise* remained an urban affair, and that even when "the people" sang it, it was in towns that they sang.

Gustave Desjardins, *Tableau de la guerre des Allemands dans le département de Seine-et-Oise* (Paris, 1882), p. 11.

[26] *Journal de Montbrison*, September 9, 1877.

[27] Similarly symbolic of the ralliement, and more visible, was the occasion in 1904 when the leaders of the *Action libérale populaire* (Albert de Mun and Jacques Piou) entered the grand banquet of their annual party congress to the strains of the *Marseillaise*.

[28] Michelle Perrot, *Les ouvriers en grève* (Paris, 1974), II, pp. 549, 562-563; Leo Loubère, *Radicalism in Mediterranean France, 1848-1914* (Albany, 1974), p. 220; and Roger Béteille, *La vie quotidienne en Rouergue avant 1914* (Paris, 1973), p. 201. Note that the *Carmagnole*, though its tune came from Provence, was also endowed with Parisian lyrics, like the *Internationale*, set to music in Lille in 1888.

Perhaps I can best make the point with one of the mass of popular patriotic songs that blossomed with the *République des républicains*. In 1882, a ditty called *Le fils de l'Allemand* represented a German officer in Lorraine asking a peasant woman to nurse his baby.[29] And the woman proudly answered:

> Và, passe ton chemin, ma mamelle est française.
> N'entre pas sous mon toît, emporte ton enfant.
> Mes garçons chanteront plus tard la *Marseillaise*,
> Je ne vends pas mon lait au fils d'un Allemand!

The point here is not only the reference to the *Marseillaise*, but the fact that, at that time, the countrywoman would most probably express herself in *patois* — something that the Parisian author of the song ignored, of course. And, as long as she did, French could hardly be a *langue maternelle*, with all that this implies for the sort of patriotism our *chansonnier* was interested in. Identification could only shift from the familiar community to a broader one, the cult of the local fatherland could only be transferred to more abstract entities, when speech confirmed and suggested new values and new identities.

Of course, this is not what the song was about. We know that the *chansonnier* wanted to make the point that Lorrainers continued to feel more French than German — and very possibly he was right. He would certainly be right in suggesting (but it never occurred to him that the issue arose!) that the generation born around 1880 would indeed sing the *Marseillaise*, and that they would find in it a meaning as great as the songs of their own *pays*, or perhaps greater. But my point has been to suggest that such feelings were *not* there, in much of the countryside, in 1882, any more than they had been in 1792. Both the French language and French sentiments had to be inculcated. They had to be taught. In January 1884, a teacher's magazine called *L'Ecole* recommended that teachers should teach their students the *Marseillaise*, "whose words are as ignored as its music is famous." And it would be the schools that taught both the French words of the *Marseillaise*, and the French sentiments — the French identity it stands for.

By the end of the century, the warlike, patriotic, revolutionary song of one political faction had, in effect, become the song of France. And it carried not only the language of its lyrics, but a potent identity. "One sings the *Marseillaise* for its words, of course," said Maurice Barrès in 1902, "but one sings it especially for the mass of emotions that it stirs in our subcon-

[29] Pierre Barbier and France Vernillat, *Histoire de France par les chansons* (Paris, 1961), VIII, pp. 38-39.

scious."[30] In an age of oral culture, it is unlikely that anything but a song could have wrought so much.

[30] *Scènes et doctrines du nationalisme français* (Paris, 1902), I, p. 3.

11

The Moralization of Society: The Enemies of Popular Culture in the Nineteenth Century*

ROBERT J. BEZUCHA

In 1824 a promoter from Arles sought permission to build a bullfight ring in La Guillotière, a suburb of Lyon. The only protest came from neighborhood residents, who were concerned about the noise of trumpets and crowds and who suggested that the arena be built on an island in the Saône River where even larger contests might be staged without creating a public nuisance. The Prefect of the Rhône authorized the project after being assured that the spectators would be protected from the animals.[1] Such a decision would have been unthinkable half a century later. Not only would the *Société Protectrice des Animaux* have lobbied government ministers and organized a public campaign against it,[2] but the Prefect himself would probably have inquired how the animals were to be protected from the spectators. In a larger sense, the arena would have been unthinkable because it would have offended an ideal by now cherished among the French elites: the moralization of society. The purpose of this essay is to discuss some of the reasons for the emergence of this ideal and some of the ways in which it took root in French sensibilities.

"In these turbulent times," wrote W.H. Riehl in Germany in 1848, "new things appear daily and new words as well, and when we cannot find a new word we give an old one new meaning."[3] *Moralisation* was such a word in France. By the publication of Larousse's *Grand Dictionnaire universel du XIXe siècle* (1866-1876), the standard definition, "*Rendre moral,*" with its

---

* The research on which this essay is based was made possible by a grant from the National Endowment for the Humanities.

[1] Archives Départementales du Rhône: M 1824.

[2] For an example of pressure to halt bullfighting in the Gard, see *Bulletin de la Société Protectrice des Animaux*, 1876, p. 352.

[3] "Die Arbeiter: Eine Volksrade aus dem Jahre 1848," in C. Jantke and D. Hilger, eds., *Die Eigentumlosen* (Munich, 1965), p. 394.

175

religious connotations, had been joined by a new one, *"régler les moeurs de
. . .,"* implying discipline and control. Durkheim would later describe
moralité as "that capacity of restraint or . . . inhibition, which allows us to
contain our passions, desires, habits, and subject them to law."[4] Those
who warned against the *démoralisation* of society were employing the old
meaning, while those who championed its *moralisation* were usually using
the new one.[5] The challenge they had taken up was epitomized in the
Bulletin of the *Société Franklin* in 1868: "The life of the worker is over-
whelmed with temptations, and we often find that . . . he submits to
them. Why is this true? [Is it] because he does not know the consequences
of his weakness, or because even when he knows them he is powerless
against himself and against dangerous suggestions? We must enlighten
and arm him."[6]

The motto of the *Société Protectrice des Animaux* — "For the moralization
of the laboring classes, for social progress, and for international union" —
reminds us that those who sought to enlighten and arm the common man
considered themselves part of an international crusade. What the French
called *moralisation* was called "the reform of manners" in England and
Bildung in Germany. That nexus of nineteenth-century voluntary effort
known as the "Reform Movement" has best been described by Robert
Malcomson as "a closer regulation of popular behavior, an improvement
in the common people's tastes and morals, a reform of their habitual vices,
the instilling in them of discipline and orderliness. . . ."[7] In every nation
of Western Europe, the Reform Movement coincided with the break-up
of traditional society: it was one of the agencies by which "the variety of
local, traditional, popular cultures inherited from the past gave way
before an official . . . national culture . . ."[8]

Norbert Elias has brilliantly demonstrated that there is a fundamental
relationship between the distribution of power in society and the development [*processus*] of civilization.[9] By the end of the nineteenth century, the normative mode of behavior in Western Europe, the measure of
each nation's "civilization," the "official culture," was no longer grounded
in aristocratic values. It was recognizably bourgeois. Bourgeois percep-
tions dictated the Reform Movement's attack on popular culture, and

[4] Cited in Steven Lukes, *Emile Durkheim, His Life and Works* (London, 1973), p. 113.
[5] Robert R. Locke, *French Legitimists and the Politics of Moral Order* (Princeton, 1974), pp. 180
and 185.
[6] *Bulletin de la Société Franklin*, 1868-1869, p. 177.
[7] *Popular Recreations in English Society, 1700-1850* (Cambridge, 1973), p. 169.
[8] Eugen Weber, "Fin-de-Siècle: The Third Republic Makes a Modern Nation," in Mathé
Allain and Glenn Conrad, eds., *France and North America: Over Three Hundred Years of Dialogue*
(Lafayette, La., 1973), p. 91.
[9] *La civilisation des moeurs*, trans. from the German by Pierre Kamnitzer (Paris, 1973).

bourgeois tastes and organizational methods dictated its manifestations. Variations in the timing, form, and emphasis of the Reform Movement in the individual nations can be explained by the different ways each achieved its transition to modernity.

Although the "reform of manners" began in England in the eighteenth century, associations for the *moralisation* of French society did not appear until the mid-nineteenth century. The English set about these civilizing tasks before their neighbors not because of some imagined Anglo-Saxon genius for volunteerism, but because English society was the first to modernize. The way the English pursued reform, however, *was* related to England's legal and political institutions, the composition of her elites, and her cultural traditions, principally the conflict between the established and dissenting churches. The French reform movement lagged behind England's for structural reasons. Nevertheless, it is inescapable that French reformers thought their *confrères* across the Channel were not merely advanced but innately superior, and this for at least five reasons.

The first was English national character. The secretary-general of the *Société Protectrice de l'Enfance* considered "enthusiasm without persistence, a kind of platonic generosity" to be "one of the great flaws of the French spirit."[10] "England, country of individual liberty," he added, "does not wait for official notice to search for a remedy. . . . Ah, those English! any pretext to humiliate us."[11] Jean Macé, whose *Ligue de l'enseignement* gathered more than a million signatures on petitions for free, compulsory, public education, constantly admonished his followers to "imitate the English."[12]

The second reason was the requirement in French law that all associations of more than twenty members seek a revocable authorization from the State. Its consequences were profound for the formation of public life. In January 1867, for example, the Minister of Public Instruction, Victor Duruy, advised the Minister of the Interior that he had read the application of an educational group and approved its program. Nevertheless, he went on, when "a Society seeks to manifest itself, with a head, a central council, a budget, and agents obeying orders from on high, I have a rule, in spite of my taste for individual action, to oppose such projects with an energetic veto."[13] In France it was difficult or impossible to build what Duruy called "a vertibrate association," that is, a truly centralized, national organization.

The third impediment, the Roman Catholic church, was an institution

[10] *Bulletin de la Société Protectrice de l'Enfance*, 1872, p. 55.
[11] *Bull. S.P.E.*, 1869, pp. 3, 19.
[12] *La ligue de l'enseignement à Beblenheim, 1862-1870* (Paris, 1890), p. 399.
[13] Archives Nationales de la France, F[17] 12542: report of January 1867.

which could be neither enlisted nor ignored. Most French reformers, whether they were Voltarians, Protestants, Jews, or even Catholics, accepted Jules Simon's distinction between religious, state, and private "propaganda" and generally preferred the latter.[14] The secretary-general of the *Société Protectrice de l'Enfance* described his organization with pride as ". . . a Society owed to private initiative, independent of all authority and of any religious or political coterie."[15] Moreover, even those associations which solicited the Church's support (such as the *Société Protectrice des Animaux* in its early years) lamented that if a few bishops recognized "the essential relationship between religion, sociability, and public morality," French parish priests still thought *moralisation* meant saving souls. Unlike English country parsons, they were unsympathetic to the cause of mere secular improvement.[16]

A fourth problem was the status of local government. Paul Leroy-Beaulieu's *L'Administration locale en France et en Angleterre* (1872) made a painful comparison: "French communes are treated as minors (*en mineurs*) against whom there is a presumption of ignorance in all deliberations. . . . English communes are . . . considered mature and virile persons in full possession of their rights and judgements. . . ."[17] This fact had an enormous effect on provincial reform associations because it drove all initiative toward the capital where Parisian reformers negotiated with the government.

Finally, reform-minded Frenchmen found that ministerial patronage was indispensable to the success of their programs. A recent student of her administration remarks that: "In France the importance of the [central] bureaucracy, insofar as interest groups are concerned, is probably greater than that of any other branch of government activity."[18] January 1 was an important day each year for the *Société Protectrice des Animaux* because that was when the ministries held their annual public receptions. As its secretary-general reported in 1875: ". . . these efforts [to persuade Prefects and *Procureurs* to enforce the animal protection laws] will be struck with sterility . . . if the agents of the administrative and judicial authority do not receive a sovereign impulsion from the ministers."[19] Faced with the government's monopoly in the sale of tobacco, the *Société Contre l'Abus du Tabac* counted it a triumph when *No Smoking* signs were ordered displayed in French post offices.[20]

[14] "L'Instruction et les bibliothèques populaires," *Revue des Deux Mondes*, 1863, p. 352.
[15] *Bull. S.P.E.*, 1872, p. 55.
[16] *Bull. S.P.A.*, 1858, p. 49.
[17] (Paris, 1872), p. 110.
[18] Ezra N. Suleiman, *Politics, Power, and Bureaucracy in France: The Administrative Elite* (Princeton, 1974), p. 223.
[19] *Bull. S.P.A.*, 1875, p. 150.
[20] *Bulletin de la Société Contre l'Abus du Tabac*, 1878, p. 45.

For all these reasons, French reformers accurately perceived that they were incapable of creating a grass-roots movement on the English model. But it is far from certain that their influence on government policy was therefore weakened. On the contrary: the way to get results in France was to lobby at the top. In 1877, for example, the *Société Protectrice des Animaux* exploited the fact that the Minister of Public Instruction had been a student of the Society's president at the Ecole de Droit.[21] But its low membership did inhibit the reform movement's ability to moralize popular behavior without resort to state intervention. Consequently, the reformers had to develop some new standards of action for their societies. They drew a clear distinction between their own work and that of traditional charity associations which, as the secretary-general of the *Société Protectrice des Animaux* put it, "are by their essence modest and discrete, seek to avoid noise and ostentation. . . . Our Society has the duty to show itself as much as possible, to assert its existence . . . because it is only under such conditions that it can gradually substitute more tolerant and milder [*douce*] manners for the rude manners of certain classes . . . ."[22]

The moralization which these men and women envisaged would be "one of those revolutions which take from no one and give . . . to everyone."[23] But there were other, less amiable revolutions in nineteenth-century France. When Jean Macé saw an *affiche* announcing universal male suffrage in 1848, he experienced "a mixture of wild joy and secret terror."[24] A similar ambivalence pervaded the motives of the reformers. In their effort to "civilize" their fellow-citizens, they inevitably became the enemies of popular culture — without, however, being quite able to admit that class differences separated them from most other Frenchmen. "In our country, where all class distinction has disappeared, where all are reunited and mixed as a single class which is called the *Nation*," asked the Marquis de Chasseloup-Laubat, president of the *Société Franklin* in 1868, "who can say where the application of the word *popular* begins or ends?"[25] The moralization of French society began as a way of ensuring domestic order and later (principally after 1870) became a means of national regeneration, as a comparison of the fortunes of the *Société Protectrice des Animaux* and the *Société Protectrice de l'Enfance* will illustrate.

The animal protection movement in France was deeply marked at its start by the reaction of notables against the experience of the Second

[21] *Bull. S.P.A.*, 1877, p. 154.
[22] Ibid., 1860, p. 186.
[23] Ibid., p. 187.
[24] Gabriel Compayré, *Les grands éducateurs: Jean Macé et l'instruction obligatoire* (Paris, 1902), p. 17.
[25] *Bull. S.F.*, 1868-1869, p. 177.

Republic. Consciously modeling itself on the Societies of London and Munich, the *Société Protectrice des Animaux* held its first public meeting in the Hôtel-de-Ville in Paris in early February 1848. Although the Revolution sparked an explosion of *associationisme* in other spheres, it halted the Society's activities for four years. When it was re-organized in April 1852 — after the "re-establishment of order," as its *Bulletin* put it — it was armed with a ready-made program: the enforcement of the *loi Grammont*.[26]

Passed a short time after the *loi Falloux*, the law of 2 July 1850 imposed fines of from five to fifteen francs for the public mistreatment of domestic animals. Its sponsor, General Delmas de Grammont, stated: "The law, in rendering barbarous acts more rare, will ameliorate manners and little by little cause to disappear the revolting spectacles which familiarize men with the sight of blood and strongly implant habits of cruelty in children which will later influence their destiny . . . ."[27] When the deputies condemned the way Parisian butchers slaughtered cattle, in other words, the barricades of the June Days were in their minds. As Maurice Agulhon has noted, the *loi Grammont* offers an insight to the *mentalité* of the men of Order.[28] General Grammont served as the Honorary President of the *Société Protectrice des Animaux* until his death in 1862.

During the Second Empire the *Société Protectrice des Animaux* measured its progress by the rising number of prosecutions under the *loi Grammont*. In Paris and Lyon, the urban poles of its activity, members inspected slaughterhouses, awarded prizes to humane coach drivers, distributed handbills with the text of the *loi Grammont*, and debated such issues as vivisection (condemning only its *abuses* in 1860), the licensing of France's two to three million dogs, and the question of whether luxury fashions contributed to civilization or to the abuse of animals.[29] As its provincial membership grew the Society's attention was drawn outside the cities toward cruelty in the traditional economy of the countryside. Brutal methods of transport to village markets, the mistreatment of working animals on farms, the suffocation of bees, and slow bleeding to produce better *boudin*: all called for the application of the *loi Grammont*.[30] By publishing letters from throughout France the Society's *Bulletin* exposed a world of rural behavior previously unknown: readers who had never been to the Gironde, for example, learned that peasants there drove old horses into the swamps as food for leeches, which they collected and sold to medical suppliers.[31]

[26] *Bull. S.P.A.*, 1855, pp. 4-6.
[27] Quoted in *Bull. S.P.A.*, 1859, p. 109.
[28] *1848 ou l'apprentissage de la République, 1848-1852* (Paris, 1973), p. 120.
[29] *Bull. S.P.A.*, 1860, p. 387; 1855, pp. 61-63, 101.
[30] Ibid., 1855, pp. 36, 106, 166.
[31] Ibid., p. 209.

The historian of the temperance movement in England, Brian Harrison, has noted: ". . . the twin response which the rough aroused in the respectable: disgust at a whole complex of behavior — swearing, cruelty, drunkenness, vulgarity, and violence; and an authoritarianism inspired by fear at the fragility of civilization."[32] The *Société Protectrice des Animaux* linked the two in seeking ". . . to enlighten ignorance and refine barbarity, . . . to pursue the progress of manners which will render repression unnecessary."[33] Picturing itself as "a vigilant sentinel and always at the breach,"[34] it had a clear idea of the new world for which it labored: "In inspiring men to be more generous . . . to creatures of the second order, our Societies . . . continue to hope to ameliorate the manners of the people . . ., for if brutality leads to crime, gentleness of character leads to virtue, resignation, fraternity. . . ."[35] "Resignation" was a kind of code-word for "order" at a time when, as the secretary-general stated in 1858, "our libraries, our theatres, our walls can sow such errors in minds, such corruption in hearts. . . ."[36] The Paris Commune, during which the *fédérés* actually invaded the Society's headquarters in the rue de Lille, intensified this conviction: ". . . there was no place for our work of peace and civilization," reported the secretary-general.[37]

Membership in the *Société Protectrice des Animaux* tripled between the Liberal Empire (1,165 members in 1865) and the moment when the Republicans inherited the Third Republic (3,432 members in 1880).[38] By that date the State had recognized its *utilité publique*, thereby conferring on it the legal status of a *personne civile* and the right to own and inherit property. It had developed a number of expert committees: an 1876 Senate bill to protect useful birds, for example, was based on the work of the Society's commission on birds.[39] The annual number of prosecutions under the *loi Grammont* in Paris alone equaled that for all of France twenty years earlier.[40] The challenge, however, was no longer in the protection of domestic animals used for work or food: it now lay in curbing cruelty toward "our inferior brothers" in popular recreation. As members were told during the annual meeting in 1870: "The foundations are laid, the building completed. . . . Now we must convince the masses of its advantages and its beauty. . . . [T]he work of vulgarization and propaganda begins."[41]

[32] *Drink and the Victorians: The Temperance Question in England, 1815-1872* (London, 1971), p. 24.
[33] *Bull. S.P.A.*, 1855, p. 5.
[34] Ibid., 1860, p. 186.
[35] Ibid., 1856, p. 78. [36] Ibid., 1858, p. 8.
[37] Ibid., 1870-1871, p. 331.
[38] Ibid., 1880, p. 5.
[39] Ibid., 1876, p. 199.
[40] Ibid., p. 144.
[41] Ibid., 1870-1871, p. 214.

It was relatively easy to attack popular amusements in the cities. When members learned of dog fights, cock fights, or observed rabbits being thrown to "wild beasts" on the streets, they could find a policeman, identify themselves as belonging to the Society, and ask him to intervene (an urban officer usually would).[42] The proper authorities could be notified about public behavior at zoos and the condition of the caged animals. And attempts by Spanish promoters to re-introduce bullfighting as a blood-sport in Toulouse or Bordeaux could be blocked by public protests. The reform of rural leisure customs, however, was more difficult.

The issue of hunting plagued the animal protection movement in all nations. The delegates to the 5th International Congress in Zurich in 1869 adopted a resolution condemning its "abuses . . . without hiding the difficulty of assuring the triumph of these principles among hunters and persons of the upper class [*la classe élevée*].[43] What Brian Harrison has found for England was also true for France: the animal protection society "had to tread carefully, for it depended heavily on support from aristocratic lovers of field sports."[44] The French directed their attention to hunting abuses committed by the lower classes out of sheer ignorance or cruelty: for example, the blinding of finches for use as lures and the destruction of rare or ecologically valuable species. One correspondent to the *Bulletin* blamed the *phylloxéra* epidemic on the peasants' shooting of insect-catchers.[45]

A concerted campaign was launched against the violent games involving animals which accompanied fair days and the celebration of *fêtes patronales*. In 1876, for example, the Society succeeded in pressuring the mayor of one village to substitute clay pigeons for live birds in the annual *tir aux pigeons* and was assured by another mayor that the *course aux canards* involved no cruelty to the ducks.[46] Other games, such as *tir à l'oie* (where a goose was hung by its neck and battered with sticks) or setting fire to dogs and shooting at them as they ran, were suppressed by demanding that the Prefect enforce the *loi Grammont*. By the end of the 1870's, the Society was lobbying for a *code rural* and distributing copies of the *loi Grammont* in villages. The chapter in Algiers had them printed in Arabic.[47]

In 1877, the secretary-general reported: "The battle has not yet been won, but we are already able to hope that in the future we can plant the

---

[42] Ibid., 1876, p. 308.
[43] Ibid., 1869, p. 55.
[44] "Animals and the State in Nineteenth Century England," *English Historical Review*, October 1973, p. 792.
[45] *Bull. S.P.A.*, 1876, p. 64.
[46] Ibid., pp. 364-365.
[47] Ibid., p. 282; ibid., 1875, p. 152.

flag of protection in the smallest hamlets as well as the largest cities."[48] The "missionaries of modern urban culture" (as Michael Marrus calls them) on whom the Society depended were the *instituteurs*. Already it had created *Sociétés scolaires pour la protection des animaux*, clubs for schoolchildren under the direction of their teachers. In the 1880's, classroom discussion of the *loi Grammont* and the animal protection movement became part of the required program of moral instruction.[49]

In his popular *Malt Lecture* the English reformer Joseph Liversey extolled the virtues of "good roast beef and barley pudding" over beer. According to Brian Harrison, the temperance movement was "above all designed to alter public opinion to diet. . . ."[50] Some French moralizers had a different menu in mind for the worker's table: horsemeat.

As early as 1856, a vice-president of the *Société Protectrice des Animaux* explained to the annual meeting that killing horses humanely for food before they reached the age when their owners would beat them brought "humanity into accord with economic doctrine."[51] There were many vegetarians in the animal protection movement, however, and it took a decade of often angry debate before the Society voted to support "*la voie de l'hippophagie.*" In 1869, the French delegation convinced the 5th International Congress in Zurich to adopt a resolution in favor of the establishment of horsemeat butcheries.[52] The task of persuading people to eat horsemeat was undertaken by a group calling itself the *Comité de l'hippophagie*. By 1878, a speaker reported to an audience of four or five thousand persons at the Trocadéro Palace: "Before the foundation of the Propaganda Committee savants had spoken . . . of the nutritious quality of the flesh of our *solipèdes*, but without beginning to convert the masses." Now sixty horsemeat shops had been opened in Paris.[53]

The members of the *Comité de l'hippophagie*, "always wanting to be useful," were so impressed with their own ability to change popular habits that they launched yet another voluntary association, the *Société Contre l'Abus du Tabac*.[54] Among its initial activities was the establishment of a *prix des instituteurs* for the best essay on how to alert schoolchildren to the dangers of smoking and a joint campaign with the *Société Protectrice de l'Enfance* to warn of its effects during pregnancy. Among the men who served as vice-presidents of the new organization were vice-presidents of

---

[48] Ibid., 1877, p. 191.
[49] Ibid., 1876, p. 167; David Thomson, *France: Empire and Republic, 1850-1940* (New York, 1968), pp. 235-238.
[50] *Drink and the Victorians*, p. 33.
[51] *Bull. S.P.A.*, 1856, p. 265.
[52] Ibid., 1869, p. 350.
[53] *Bull. S.C.A.T.*, 1878, pp. 220, 242-244.
[54] Ibid.

the *Société Protectrice des Animaux* and the *Société Protectrice de l'Enfance*, the secretary-general of the *Société Philotechnique* and the director of the *Association Philotechnique*.[55] Eighteen hundred invited guests to the first annual meeting of the *Société Contre l'Abus du Tabac* heard its president cite these groups and others for their mutual concern for the creation of "moral order."[56]

The *Société Protectrice de l'Enfance* was established in 1866 as "a crusade . . . against an . . . absurd, barbarous custom, that of abandoning . . . a small being a few hours after birth . . . to a fat peasant woman . . . whose character and morality are unknown. . . ." The association's concern for "the culture of new generations" was hedged, however, by a peculiar class-laden view of the limits of reform. Its secretary-general, a health inspector named Dr. Alexandre Mayer, incorrectly believed that wet-nursing was "an industry which our fathers never knew and which is a totally modern invention." He further thought it was "indispensible in the present state of society. . . ." The Society's goal, therefore, was not so much to convince working class parents to keep their babies at home as "to moralize, by . . . regulating" the wet-nurses themselves.[57]

Dr. Mayer, along with the Society's first president, a retired Lyonnais surgeon and professor of medicine named Barrier, had been a youthful disciple of Fourier. The *Société Protectrice de l'Enfance* was initially pledged to establish *colonies maternelles* near France's major cities. There peasant husbands could practice modern farming methods while their wives wove cloth and nursed babies in "model cottages" and enjoyed regular health inspections. Restaurants and shops operated by *Sociétés de consommation* would serve the urban workers, who combined Sunday trips to the countryside with a visit to their children.[58] These plans were dropped from the Society's *statuts* when it gained the status of *utilité publique* in 1869. If the English reformers often carried with them the baggage of evangelicalism, the French sometimes bore that of utopian socialism.

Their flirtation with *colonies maternelles* notwithstanding, the members of the *Société Protectrice de l'Enfance* were practical men and women who got results. In its first year the Society sent 835 Parisian infants to approved wet-nurses through the placement bureau of Madame Lobel in the rue de la Harpe. By 1872, it had 383 volunteer inspectors at work in thirty-five departments.[59] As one of them reported from the Loiret: ". . . medical inspection has produced . . . excellent results with a certain

[55] *Association française contre l'abus du tabac: liste générale alphabétique* (Paris, 1868).
[56] *Bull. S.C.A.T.*, 1868, p. 160.
[57] *Bull. S.P.E.*, 1866, pp. 10-35, passim.
[58] Ibid.
[59] Ibid., 1872, p. 43.

number of wet-nurses. Finding themselves under the surveillance of the doctor-inspectors, they are making efforts to keep their nurseries clean. One no longer sees at Ladon wet-nurses who allow *seven* new-borns die, as did one unfortunate woman who has ceased her trade since I became the inspector."[60]

By 1872, there were Societies in six major cities and *comités de patronage* in 150 towns and villages. The latter contributed funds to support the inspectors, helped them to intervene with the authorities, and distributed medals with the figures of Romulus, Remus, and the She-wolf to selected wet-nurses. The parent organization in Paris helped to found local associations by sending out copies of its statutes and advising that *comités de patronage* be composed of "a certain number of persons well known in the locality, and who, by their position, will exercise an influence which will facilitate the success of the enterprise." Among the occupations suggested were "doctors, lawyers, notaries, and merchants. . . the principal professions. . . ."[61] Membership rose from 864 in 1869, and 2,712 in 1878, to 3,486 in 1882.[62] Perhaps it was a type of reform which appealed to Gambetta's *nouvelles couches sociales*.

Perhaps the Society's growth was also encouraged by the defeat in the Franco-Prussian war. As its *Bulletin* stated in 1872: "It has been demonstrated that the present generation is powerless to save France and that our children alone can come to her aid. To form a generation better than ours, to make . . . true citizens should be the first, the unique preoccupation of all. . . ." If France had had a child protection law, the article concluded, she might not have lost Alsace and Lorraine.[63]

In fact the State had been reluctant to help the *Société Protectrice de l'Enfance* openly for fear of invading parents' legal rights over their children. The Prefect of the Seine did contribute 2,000 francs to support the wet-nurse placement office in Paris, but when the Minister of the Interior offered a direct allocation of 1,000 francs to the Society in 1867, he cautioned: "In a matter this delicate a great reserve imposes itself."[64] On the eve of the war Dr. Mayer described the association's work to the annual meeting as "a task even more delicate than public instruction, and for which governmental action . . . even in our country where for centuries one has habitually surrendered to it, will certainly remain weak or incomplete if . . . it is not supported by the forces of private initiative."[65]

[60] Ibid., p. 38.
[61] Ibid., 1866, pp. 259-262.
[62] Ibid., 1882, p. 42.
[63] Ibid., 1872, p. 30.
[64] Ibid., 1869, p. 27; ibid., 1868, pp. 157-158.
[65] Ibid., 1870-1871, p. 153.

Matters changed once the issue had become "the revenge of our national honor."[66] The *Société Protectrice de l'Enfance* was able to tap a powerful source of wealth and influence in the capital by sponsoring the more fashionable *Société Nationale des Amis de l'Enfance*, where names such as Ferry, Cambon, Engel-Dollfus, and Schoelcher soon appeared on the list of subscribers. At its first *soirée littéraire et musicale*, Dr. Mayer spoke of the "need to repair the misfortune of our country, to fortify its strength, to augment its prosperity, and to regenerate its morals."[67] The parent organization also found a new president, Dr. J.-B. Roussel, a Republican deputy (first elected in 1849 and again in 1871) and later a senator from the Lozère, who led its successful political campaign for State inspection of the wet-nurse industry. There was an air of triumph at the annual meeting following the passage of the *loi Roussel*. "Listen to the pessimists," a speaker stated, "they will tell you that the French are incapable of creating anything by their private initiative, that they need the State, and without it they can achieve nothing." The *Société Protectrice de l'Enfance* now saw itself as "a truly national work [*oeuvre*] which touches the welfare of thousands of little beings, who are one day destined to become soldiers of France."[68]

We should not conclude that the French cared more about animals than about their children, although a law protecting the former preceded a more limited law protecting the latter by thirty years. The *loi Grammont* and the *loi Roussel* do reveal, however, the way changes in the political climate affect the success or failure of reform legislation. Yet those engaged in the moralization of society did not believe that laws were their only weapons: to cite the *Société Protectrice des Animaux* again, they sought "the progress of manners which will render repression unnecessary."

Following the passage of the Ferry laws, the public school became the principal vehicle for this *mission civilisatrice de l'intérieur*. "Without the school to mold the future citizen," admitted the president of the *Sociétés fédérées contre l'usage des boissons spiriteuses*, ". . . our League would not amount to much." He described the *instituteur* as a "militant" who "indirectly molests" the father by "moralizing the child."[69] In his autobiographical account collected by Jacques Ozouf, a teacher from the *bocage* of the Vendée described the "special duties" which his role in the village imposed on him at the turn of the century as "collaboration" with the voluntary forces of Republican reform.[70] And Roger Thabault, in his

---

[66]   Ibid., 1872, p. 55.
[67]   *Bulletin de la Société Nationale des Amis de l'Enfance*, 1876, p. 14.
[68]   *Bull. S.P.E.*, 1883, pp. 49-53.
[69]   *L'Alcool*, July 1898, p. 108.
[70]   *Nous les maîtres d'école* (Paris, 1967), p. 28.

evocative study of the modernization of his own village, Mazières-en-Gâtine, refers to the school between 1882 and 1914 as "the cause of economic, social, and moral development."[71] The State itself was now the leading enemy of popular culture in France, but there were new worlds to moralize: chapters of the *Société Protectrice de l'Enfance* were organized in Phnom-Penh in 1904 and in Saigon a few years later.

[71] *Education and Change in a Village Community, Mazières-en-Gâtine, 1848-1914*, trans. Peter Tregear (London, 1971).

12

The Village Schoolmaster
as Outsider

BARNETT SINGER

The Third Republic suffers in scholarship from a tone of stolidity, a permanent sort of Méline look that, apart from the Dreyfus Affair, only seems to change with the 1930's. Watershed status has been claimed for the era of the French Revolution and for the Second Empire, saliency attributed to "days" and strikes of the July Monarchy, and primordial importance given to the Commune of 1870. The pre-1914 Third Republic bumps along, but we may soon get the study it deserves as the seedtime of contemporary France.

Certainly the school laws of Jules Ferry, passed in the 1880's and creating one of the republic's key institutions, have received attention.[1] Balzac-like we swoop down from Paris to prefecture to *bled perdu* and find the *instituteur* — the Republic's personification — in the villages of France, spreading the new Gospel. The theme is known. What has not been sufficiently detailed is the teacher's village position, the constraints of life he endured, not only in the West but everywhere. In him there was something of the Republic: both were bringing outside ideals to particularist, sometimes stubborn, rural nuclei; both seem like myths agreed upon. We know of the Republic's iconography — the flag, Marianne, the patriotic fêtes. The teacher in his stern black coat is almost an icon as well. Many indeed remember the schoolmaster as a *chose sacrée*: from Marcel Pagnol's *La Gloire de mon père* we get saint; from Péguy's *De 'Jean Coste'* saints; from Georges Duveau "saints" (*sans espérance*); from Jean Boorsch "lay saints"; and Professor Pierre Goubert recalled his childhood teachers

---

[1] See Evelyn M. Acomb, *The French Laic Laws (1879-1880)* (New York, 1941) and my own "Jules Ferry and the Laic Revolution in French Primary Education," *Paedagogica Historica*, December 1975. The best history of French education is Antoine Prost, *Histoire de l'enseignement en France 1800-1967* (Paris, 1968). Also worth consulting are Maurice Debesse's and Gaston Mialeret's recent *Histoire de la pédagogie*, Vol. II of *Traité des sciences pédagogiques* (Paris, 1971), and R. Deldime, "Aux sources de la laïcité (XIII): Jules Ferry ou l'école de la République," *Tribume laïque*, 110 (1973), pp. 21-16.

in identical terms: saints.[2] Obviously not all were; obviously Marianne was not the great civilizing force she desired to be. Myths are easily discredited, but that is not my intention here.

Rather, I wish to make an argument along the lines of the old Roman proverb — *per ardua ad astra*. Only by transcending an insecure village position — which meant accommodation to daily difficulties — did teachers become a collective myth agreed upon before 1914.

The bulk of this essay outlines those daily difficulties and, tangentially, treats the quality of all village life before 1914. The teacher's problem in essence was this: better-off financially than most peasants he was yet too ill-paid to meet bourgeois standards; supposed to be a bridge to commoners (and usually of common origin himself) the teacher had yet to subscribe to an uncommon moral standard that separated him from the people; supposed to be a pillar of the coming order — "va, petit esprit des idées modernes," said Ferdinand Buisson — he never entirely abandoned his ties with the *pays* of his birth.

Fundamental to the teacher's ambivalent status was money, or the lack of it. Jules Ferry had said that his school laws would not only make primary education free, secular, and compulsory but would also emancipate the teacher, make him materially comfortable, a bourgeois at last.[3] Needless to say this did not occur; and Antonin Lavergne's novel *Jean Coste* (1901) only capped a wave of protest initiated by disgruntled teachers themselves. Objectively we now know how correct Ferry's critics were. The basic salary scale, which, with a slight increase in 1905 and additions for outside work, obtained before 1914,[4] is given in Table I.

TABLE I

	Instituteurs	*Institutrices*
Fifth Class	1000 fr.	1000 fr.
Fourth Class	1200 fr.	1200 fr.
Third Class	1500 fr.	1400 fr.
Second Class	1800 fr.	1500 fr.
First Class	2000 fr.	1600 fr.

---

[2] Pagnol, *La gloire de mon père* (Paris, 1957), p. 28; Péguy, "De *Jean Coste*" in *Oeuvres complètes* (Paris: Nouvelle revue française edition, 1920), II, pp. 62-63; Georges Duveau, *Les instituteurs* (Paris, 1966), ch. 5; and Jean Boorsch, "Primary Education," *Yale French Studies*, 22 (1959), p. 22. Professor Goubert's remark appears in a letter to the author.

[3] Ferry's rhetoric was conveniently general. In a speech to the teachers in 1881 he said: "You have been freed as citizens by the French Revolution, you are going to be emancipated as *instituteurs* by the Republic of 1880" (*Revue pédagogique*, [1881] pt. I, p. 581).

[4] *Annales . . . deputés. Docs. parls. (Sess. ord.)*, II (1889, du quatorze mai au quinze juillet), p. 306.

In theory communes of a certain size had to provide the teacher either lodging or an indemnity for lodging. Despite that, the salary scale was woefully inadequate and unjust, not only because of its low stipends but because of its system of promotions. The system was based upon percentages: 35 percent of teaching effectives had to be in the fifth class; 25 percent in the fourth; 15 percent in the third; 5 percent in the second and in the first together. To accede to the top salaries — the liveable salaries — could take a lifetime, and indeed, many teachers never reached the upper two classes. The remaining 20 percent of teachers were *stagiaires*, untenured novice teachers whose salary was a pitiful 800 francs without any other benefits. Until they passed an examination conferring the *Certificat d'Aptitude pédagogique (C.A.P.)* they were doomed to remain in this servile state, and *stagiaires* of five years experience were not uncommon. The system of advancement was modified in 1902, but on balance teachers' salaries remained a scandal.[5] The experienced German schoolmaster, for instance, received almost twice as much as his French counterpart in 1913; and the average *instituteur's* salary, even after 1905, amounted to little more than the average French industrial worker's wages and was below that of all other functionaries.[6]

What did this do for the teacher's village position? It obviously placed his income well beneath that of the bourgeois, and denied him social equality with the notables of his commune. And if the bourgeois skimped for puritanical reasons the teacher skimped out of degrading necessity. "The purchase of a pair of shoes is a catastrophe," as one wit put it":[7]

[5] For information on salaries I have used Octave Gréard's compendium, *La législation de l'instruction primaire en France depuis 1789 jusqu'à nos jours* (Paris, 1898-1900), VI and VII. Gréard was one of the most important men in primary education in France in this period, holding several high posts. For the period after 1900, Prost's *Enseignement en France* is a reliable source. I have also used departmental files such as Archives départementales (hereafter, A.D.) Loire-Atlantique 26-T-4: Traitement des instituteurs et institutrices — affaires diverses 1881-1927.

[6] Peter Sandiford, ed., *Comparative Education* (London, 1918), pp. 324-327. The experienced German teacher's salary cited for 1913 is 3700 marks (4125 francs). The average industrial worker's wage for 1906, according to Jacques Chastenet, was roughly 1350 francs a year. Chastenet, *La France de M. Fallières* (Paris, 1949), p. 172. A good table comparing teachers' salaries to those of other functionaries for 1907 appears in Ida Berger and Roger Benjamin, *L'Univers des instituteurs* (Paris, 1964), p. 143:

Bank of France	1800-4800 [francs]
Customs clerks	1700-4000
Clerks for indirect taxes	1500-3300
Postal clerks	1500-4000
. . .	. . .
Tenured clerks	1100-2200

[7] J. Arren, *L'Eclair* (October 24, 1905), cited by Berger and Benjamin, *Univers des instituteurs*, p. 142.

when a decent pair of shoes cost 15 francs he wasn't joking. Beginning
teachers were worst off — one whom I interviewed in Brittany earned 65
francs 30 centimes a month in 1912, of which an incredible 60 francs was
allotted for *pension*. Extra income for luxuries like a bicycle, indispensable
for a daily seven kilometer trip, was just unavailable, given the fact that a
used bicycle cost 90 francs.[8]

As if financial embarrassment were not problem enough, there were
limits as to what one could or should do with the money one had. Peasants,
who called teachers "mangeurs de fricot" — roughly, earners of easy pay
— did not want to see them surrounded with comforts. The bias against
conspicuous consumption ran deep in France, in part due to a heritage of
taxation upon visible signs of wealth, in part due to scorn of *dérogement* up
or down. And yet, peasants expected the teacher's belongings to be in
impeccable order. These included garden, house, tea service, and
clothes.[9] Such expectations were particularly high for a married schoolmaster who was a permanent fixture in the commune. But yet another
paradox: teachers must absolutely not incur debts. According to both
academy and villagers, indebtedness — always a stigma in France — was
doubly unacceptable for this important public servant. Files I have seen
for Brittany are filled with angry and often petty letters taking indebted
instituteurs and *institutrices* to task. Butchers, bakers, grocery-store owners
would not hesitate to write the teacher's superiors when he owed a few
francs at the store — you almost sense the pleasure they got from doing so.
Relaxed village camaraderie did not extend in such matters to the
teachers. In 1893 the manager of the Paris department store, *Aux Classes
Laborieuses*, informed the inspector of the academy of the Côtes-du-Nord
that one of his *institutrices* owed twelve francs there.[10] More representative
of village vernacular is the following letter:

> bain, 12 juin 1892
>
> Messiu, je vous declare qu'y a a noblanche un instituteur qui est si endête que
> il doit à tout le monde. Ca fais jolimant murmerer. . . . Si vous le nomié
> aieur, ca feré plaisi à tous les republicain.[11]

---

[8] Interview with H.L., Nantes, May 15, 1970. Because of its price (compounded by a tax),
the bicycle was a luxury item for teachers right up to the war. See Eugen Weber, "Gymnastics
and Sports in Fin-de-Siècle France: Opium of the Classes," *American Historical Review*, 76
(February 1971), pp. 80-81.

[9] In this regard teachers were sometimes models to be emulated. One from the Nièvre
wrote: "At Montauban the country folk came to visit my garden and experiment field, and
tried afterwards to do better than I. Now there is great competition in the village to see who
will have the finest garden." Autobiographical sketch, 1911-12, in Ferdinand Buisson and
F.E. Farrington, eds., *French Educational Ideals of Today* (New York, 1919), p. 203.

[10] A.D. Côtes-du-Nord. T: Dossiers par communes. Letter, February 16, 1898, about
institutrice of Saint-Fiacre. Many other letters of this sort are found in the dossiers.

[11] Anonymous letter in A.D. Ille-et-Vilaine. T: Dossiers individuels du personnel: instituteurs.

Letters of this sort were conducive neither to a teacher's advancement nor to his village position. And when a teacher was in debt everyone knew it. The nature of the debt — whether medical expenses for children, books from Paris, or clothes — mattered little to the peasant.

Now the very fact that teachers owed money not only in villages but also in Paris stores indicates how far the communications revolution had come in France. Zola in his *Au Bonheur des dames* had first seen the implications of democratic buying under the Second Empire. Came mail order catalogues, advertisements in the newspapers, and other enticements, dangled before teachers who, much more than most rural people, valued fine things and looked outward for their values, and the difficulty is obvious. You feel that teachers were confined in a rural world and prevented from adequately connecting with the urban world they knew outside. A teacher's daughter in Savoie recalls her young life as "le strict nécessaire, sans jamais de gâteries": when her uncle sent chocolates from Chambéry it was a great occasion.[12] So that even when the teacher had an extra stipend as secretary to the mayor, even if his wife taught and added her income to the household, the strict rules emanating from villagers and more, from those great Protestant masters of the *écoles normales*, Pécaut, Buisson, and Steeg, dictated monetary sobriety.

Teachers, however, were criticized for the very aloofness which their financial circumstances imposed on them. Why would they never relax, go on a spree? Aloofness indeed was immediately connoted by the very clothes the teachers wore — crisp frock coat and bourgeois hat, pinned hair in the case of ladies. As Stendhal had called women's clothes "the artillery of love" so he might have seen teachers' vestments as moral artillery, even class artillery. And clothes were differentiators, as will be elaborated further on; classes were perhaps more reliably indicated by clothing during the early Third Republic than in the era when Père Grandet's bourgeois advisors all wore greasy, sloppy clothes. Add to this the fact that teachers were bookish, and that books, too, meant snobbery. Of course, teachers in self-defense might have asked: how else may I spend my discretionary income [when it existed]? With the café closed to them on moral grounds, with its homely diversions (smoking, cards, bowling, dancing) forbidden, what recreation was left, besides gardening and reading? But books were definitely abnormal. They lent the teacher an air of subversion.[13]

[12] Jacques Ozouf, *Nous les maîtres d'école: Autobiographies d'instituteurs de la Belle Epoque* (Paris, 1967), p. 155.

[13] A teacher of the Department of Vienne noted that "since I read late into the night I am judged eccentric." Buisson and Farrington, *French Educational Ideals*, p. 198. (The autobiographical sketches collected here are all from the *Manuel général de l'instruction primaire*, 1911-1912.) H.L. also remembers his teacher's taste for books as abnormal in the village of Guénouvry (Loire-Atlantique). Interview, Nantes, May 15, 1970.

So the teacher was neither bourgeois nor proletarian nor peasant. Mona Ozouf and Jacques Ozouf both devote space to the problem and reduce it to this: lack of money kept the teacher out of the bourgeoisie; too much learning put him above the peasantry.[14] My view, as has been seen, follows that of the Ozoufs, but their analysis needs to be greatly nuanced. First, other village figures were similarly caught between these poles — for example, the *pharmacien*, according to Pierre Sorlin.[15] And what of the various functionaries — in what slot should we place them? Was not the teacher's outsider status in part due to his government post? Not only was he being paid for non-manual labor, but the pay came from Paris, which made him in village eyes a sort of *demi-rentier*. And everyone knew that the strings were pulled from elsewhere, that the teacher could not be his own person. The petitions and anonymous letters that inundated the files of prefectures and academies before 1914 were obviously sent in the conviction that the authorities would punish teachers who offended local opinion.

And if teachers were neither bourgeois nor proletarians, what the Ozoufs fail to emphasize is that the education ministry wanted it that way. The myriad articles in education journals not only gave counsel on appearance — keep your hair trimmed; don't slouch — but also recommended insistently that teachers keep apart.[16] *Instituteurs* must not become too friendly with anyone in the village, for they must preserve their special, unsullied status as guardians of future French citizens. Affiliation with any subgroup was suspect. An adjunct at La Rouexière (Loire-Atlantique) was chastized by the inspector of Ancénis for being too close to a group of young workers, thereby losing "the dignity and the consideration which an *instituteur* needs in order to succeed . . . in his task."[17] Similarly, the teaching father of one of my interviewees, though very well-liked at Plounévez-Lochrist (Finistère), would have been, in the estimation of his inspector, "better respected if he showed himself to be less familiar with everybody."[18] This last statement gives a good indication of how teachers were forced by superiors to walk the tightrope between over-cultivation and under-cultivation of villagers' friendship.

[14] Mona Ozouf, *L'Ecole, L'Eglise, et la République 1871-1914* (Paris, 1963), pp. 151-155; Jacques Ozouf, *Nous les maîtres d'école*, pp. 132-134.

[15] Pierre Sorlin, *La société française*, Vol. I, *1840-1914* (Paris, 1969), p. 91.

[16] Good examples: A. Richard, "Conseils pratiques aux instituteurs," *Revue pédagogique*, pt. I (1881), pp. 394-407; Cazès (inspector of the Department of the Aube), "Conseils aux instituteurs sur la conduite à tenir dans la vie," *Revue pédagogique*, (1886) pt. I , pp. 88-94.

[17] A.D. Loire-Atlantique. sTi220: Dossiers individuels des instituteurs et institutrices, ayant cessé leurs fonctions, de 1870 à 1948. Primary inspector, Ancénis, to inspector, of academy, August 7, 1886.

[18] A.D. Finistère. T: Instituteurs — 1901-1919. Primary inspector, Morlaix, to academy, December 11, 1893.

Perhaps it is only by your acquaintances that you can ultimately be classed. But the teacher had no stable group of associates: he flitted from sub-group to sub-group, or perhaps over them, and in turn was viewed differently by each. When Theodore Zeldin noticed that the bourgeois was what you made of him, he could have transferred that theme to the teacher, who himself was a Pirandellian animal.[19] *Ni bourgeois ni prolétaire* of course: but to a *métayer* he might be a *monsieur* while to a *fermier* merely *maître d'école*; even to a city colleague he would be of a different taint than to a country colleague. When all is said and done, the Ozoufs are correct: the teacher was an in-betweener. More research, however, will be needed to elucidate the varying nature of his rural marginality, the different points of view that made of him different people at different times.

When one talks of teachers caught between peasantry and bourgeoisie a corollary problem is the important question of *déclassement*. This theme, with variations, has received much attention in our own time — witness George Orwell on deproletarianized worker politicians or Vance Packard on rootless America[20] — but in nineteenth century France it was a hot political issue with its own peculiar flavor. The problem needs its separate historian. *Déclassement* was a central rallying point for Legitimists and the Right generally,[21] and also part of the nationalist propaganda of a Barrès, whose favored word was *déracinement*.[22] Education was considered the prime instrument of *déclassement* and on it many an article was written, the best by Emmanuel Labat in the *Revue des deux mondes* for 1912.[23] Labat painted a touching picture of Gascon peasant children, forced to go to school, told about foreign lands like Korea or America, given rationalist ideals made in Paris, and thus inoculated with scorn for their own tiny corner of earth. To this sort of criticism the *laïc* side felt compelled to reply; Félix Pécaut, grand master of Fontenay-aux-Roses, acknowledged the problem but believed the school could blunt its impact by more attention to agricultural and rural matters; and anyway, other forces in society were drawing young people to towns, school or no school.[24]

In this debate few people stopped to consider the teachers himself as

[19] See Zeldin, *France 1848-1945: Vol. I, Ambition, Love, and Politics* (Oxford, 1973), pp. 12-22.

[20] Orwell *Road to Wigan Pier* (New York, 1958), pp. 174-179; Packard, *A Nation of Strangers* (New York, 1970), passim.

[21] See Robert Locke, *French Legitimists and the Politics of Moral Order in the Early Third Republic* (Princeton, N.J., 1974), p. 177.

[22] In Barrès' *Les déracinés* it is a Kantian professor who woos the hero from his native Lorraine.

[23] Emmanuel Labat, "L'Instruction primaire au point de vue psychologique," *Revue des deux mondes*, 82 (July 1912), 135-172.

[24] Félix Pécaut, *Quinze ans d'éducation* (Paris, n.d.), pp. 70-74; also important, G. Tarde, "L'Instituteur et la désertion des campagnes," *Manuel général de l'instruction primaire* (June 17, 1899).

déclassé, except those writers who used the term in its most pejorative and partisan sense. But the schoolmaster, often *fraîchement issue de la classe paysanne*, was deloused of his heritage much like an immigrant to America. The process was rigorous. Even before normal school, that "laic seminary" as some called it (notice the element of religious conversion), prospective teachers were marked out by their brilliance at the village school. Like privileged eighteenth-century Court Jews, teachers were offered a bargain: you, sir, may escape by virtue of your brains the burden of peasantry and become an *instituteur*. Take M. Auguste Bouet who became head teacher at Roger Thabault's village of Mazières-en-Gâtine in 1881. Bouet's teacher had entered him for the *lycée* scholarship examination at age twelve. He failed because his peasant French made the word "*vipère*" masculine, not feminine, in an era when country people still said "un gros (grou) *vipère*." This error, says Thabault, really cost Bouet a university career. Instead, he took the primary route, ended up in Mazières, fifteen kilometers from home, and taught there from 1881 to 1925. Now the attachment to one area indicates at least some residual peasant identification, and undoubtedly that was a major part of his notability. Bouet wrote the local monograph, gave courses in agriculture, was secretary to the mayor, and ultimately became mayor of the village itself.[25] But only by divesting himself of a good deal of his heritage.

France is now rethinking its peasant past, its lurching into modernity, and remarkable books like Claude Duneton's *Parler Croquant* frankly treat the linguistic and spiritual impoverishment wrought by the nationalizing, anti-local Third Republic. The teacher comes off very badly; in this book on Corrèze as in Lebesque's *Comment peut-on être Breton?* he is an agent of cultural genocide.[26] Duneton remembers:

> As for the teacher Bordas, the "Monsieur", he was something different. Very simply he represented France, culture, power, in a word civilization, and he put his conduct on a footing with his very high functions. Although of modest origins and unavoidably a maternal speaker of Occitane, he refused with hauteur and a certain scorn to use that plebian language.[27]

Again, no one really looks at the teacher himself as victim. Why should they? The person had won social promotion — what more is there? And look at the letters of the inspectors, the optimism, the faith in the coming

[25] Roger Thabault, *Education and Change in a Village Community: Mazières-en-Gâtine 1848-1914*, trans. by Peter Treager (New York, 1971), pp. 207-211. I have studied the teachers as notables in Brittany in an article to appear in *French Historical Studies*.

[26] Duneton, *Parler Croquant* (Paris, 1973), passim; Lebesque, *Comment peut-on être Breton* (Paris, 1970), pp. 96-99.

[27] Duneton, *Parler Croquant*, p. 20.

eradication of illiteracy and error, the bright forward-looking faith of mental *défricheurs*: to paraphrase Auden, had there been a problem we should have known. Well we do know there was another reality beneath this Ferryite one, perhaps not the ultimate reality, but nonetheless another level. Teachers in their polished and urbane French did try to grope back to what they had lost. Even in the 1960's Huguette Bastide, in her best-selling account of an *institutrice's* life in Lozère, writes plaintively: "Je ne sais pas me dégeler, je réponds, mes phrases figées m'énervent. J'aimerais leur parler patois, je ne sais pas, m'asseoir avec eux et manger un morceau de lard ou de fromage. . . ."[28]

Now language is obviously the key differentiator here between teacher and peasant. The gulf of language can easily cause trepidation in those who find it hard to switch idioms. Schoolmasters, bearers of good grammar, could never descend into the abyss of slangy French for that would be *dérogement* of the worst sort. Yet for schoolmasters in an area like Alsace or Armorican Brittany the problem of speaking irreproachable French had as its mirror image a second obligation. A primary inspector discussing a successor to the esteemed teacher of Lannion in the Côtes-du-Nord recommended that the new teacher there have absolute command of Breton. Almost all the inhabitants could understand and speak Franch, but in 1901 Breton was still preferred among the lower orders. "The Breton, the *homme du peuple*, of course, is by his nature timid, not very expansive, purposely distrustful. How can his reserve be conquered . . . if one is, so to speak, a foreigner to him?"[29] Here is the crux of the matter: even in a rural area where only French was spoken, the teacher, by virtue of his urbane language, was still set off as a kind of foreigner. And yet he was a half-peasant, frequently devoted to his natal area, but linguistically isolated in his own *pays*.

A final note on *déclassement*: teachers normally taught their entire careers in a *petit pays*, but their sons and daughters, I would speculate, often migrated elsewhere. This problem of social mobility requires much more research, yet there are straws in the wind which suggest that the ultimate defeat of the teacher's peasanthood was in his progeny. Three village teachers I interviewed chanced to mention their children. One couple, both teachers, had an only son, now a high functionary in the finance administration in Paris — a bourgeois in income and life-style. The granddaughter, also *fille unique*, is finding herself. Another teacher

[28] Huguette Bastide, *Institutrice de village* (Paris, 1969), p. 55.
[29] A.D. Côtes-du-Nord. T: Dossiers par communes. Primary inspector, Lannion, to academy, January 6, 1901. Marc Bloch wrote in 1940 of ". . . une opinion villageoise, comme la nôtre, volontiers méfiante de l'étranger et un peu repliée sur elle-même." *L'Etrange défaite* (Paris, 1957), p. 101.

had a child who became an engineer in a big town. A third's daughter emulated her mother by teaching in the Girls' Normal School, Saint-Brieuc.[30] I would also imagine that a substantial number of teachers' male offspring rose into the ranks of *professeurs*. Jacques Ozouf referred to a recent colloquium at the Ecole Normale Supérieure (Paris) where one university professor affected to apologize to his confrères for not being the son of an *instituteur*, as most there were.[31] The generational ooze is universal, of course, and democratized avenues of advancement have changed the status of teachers in any event during our century. It is hard to know whether a grandson teaching at Nanterre in the 1960's has any more status than his grandfather at Nanterre-sur-Chantepie. But the point is the loosening from the land: uprootedness.

To return to the major theme of teachers' difficulties: John Cuddihy, in his new book *The Ordeal of Civility*, defines modernization as "refinement."[32] For village teachers, refinement in language and comportment was a daily must. Even the *instituteurs'* dwellings had to be *comme il faut*, a reflection of their self-discipline. The teacher, you feel, was almost a new *curé* and indeed one finds, in a report as early as Victor Duruy's time, concrete evidence to that effect: "The teacher's house, as with that of the *curé*, should be the model house of the village: well-developed construction of course; sobriety, elegance, windows; and everywhere that cleanliness which is the poor man's luxury. . . ."[33] In fact, we easily forget that rural notables were all to some degree surrogate religious figures and, as in early nineteenth century New England, "acted not as individuals, but as though they were clergymen and each profession were a church."[34] Teachers were as well the representatives of a new secular morality on trial, agents of a civic culture getting established at the grassroots. No wonder they acted like the saints people now remember them to have been. Directives from the academies or politicians in Paris repeatedly drove the point home lest they forget: for example, this circular of the inspector of Bouches-du-Rhône for 1882: "Our teachers must not forget it: teaching of morals imposes upon them, in turn, a moral obligation, that of putting their conduct in accord with their teaching. . . . The master is

---

[30] Interviews: the F.T.'s, Saint-Anne-La-Palud, August 9, 1970; Mme. C.L., Châteaugiron, January 31, 1970; and L.L., Saint-Brieuc, February 24, 1970.

[31] Jacques Ozouf, *Nous les maîtres d'école*, pp. 7-8. On teachers' social mobility, see also Ida Berger, "Contribution à l'étude de la mobilité sociale en France: les instituteurs," *Transactions of the Third World Congress of Sociology* (New York, 1956), pp. 45-50.

[32] John Murray Cuddihy, *The Ordeal of Civility: Freud, Marx, Levi-Strauss, and the Jewish Struggle with Modernity* (New York, 1974), p. 11.

[33] Duruy's report quoted in Jean Rohr, *Victor Duruy, Ministre de Napoléon III: Essai sur la politique de l'instruction publique au temps de l'Empire libéral* (Paris, 1967), p. 157.

[34] Henry Adams, *The Education of Henry Adams* (New York, 1939), p. 32.

the example."[35] The example could never swear, never exclaim (the hottest kind of exclamation my interviewees used was *ma foi*), never verbally let go. And of course if the teacher was forbidden from being one of the boys in talk and action, he was also blocked in another way — blocked in his intellectual aspirations. Gore Vidal complains that writers like himself never have anyone to talk to, and I suppose that some degree of isolation is common to all thinkers. But for the teacher fresh out of normal school, debouched into a spanking new world of ideas, the problem was acute: who was there in the village who could seriously discuss Hugo or positivism or even French foreign policy? Certainly those who came nearest to his station in life — the rural postman, the road surveyor (*agent voyer*), the mayor — were at the same time usually inferior to him in intellectual attainments. The young *stagiaire* or unmarried woman teacher hadn't even a literate spouse with whom to mull over matters. An *institutrice* of the Sologne, the type who seems to have been susceptible to depression, scratched in her diary January 4, 1893: "Solitude, a black cold, the humid walls in my room — nothing to read."[36] And Jean Guéhenno, a lifetime laicist of distinction, gives us a similar passage, striking off the intellectual isolation that at least some teachers of the pre-World War I era experienced:

> On les laisse dans un isolement intellectuel affreux. Je pense à ce qu'est un jeune instituteur à vingt ans, quand il sort de l'Ecole Normale, si avide de savoir, si magnifiquement curieux, éveillé à tous les problèmes. Il rejoint son poste, le plus petit hameau le plus éloigné. Et soudain c'est le silence autour de lui. Un océan de terre! Rien que l'inertie de la terre! L'inquiétude se meurt devant tant de sérénité. Et pas un livre! La paye est trop maigre qui permettrait d'en acheter. Personne à qui parler. Quelle volontè est nécessaire pour demeurer alors préoccupé de vivre comme un esprit. Il n'est guère pour l'intelligence d'adventure plus tragique.[37]

Now from all of the foregoing it should be clear that intellectual, social, and moral isolation were inextricably mixed. And yet, simultaneously, teachers could attain the status of notables, be invited to every village marriage and funeral, and be consulted in every touchy dispute, as was the case with a teaching couple in Saône-et-Loire and many others.[38] Notability and isolation were not mutually exclusive. The teacher who

---

[35] Circular in *Revue pédagogique*, (1882) pt. I, p. 223.

[36] Ida Berger, ed., *Lettres d'institutrices rurales d'autrefois: Rédigées à la suite de l'enquête de Francisque Sarcey en 1897* (Paris, n.d. [1964]), pp. 7-8.

[37] Jean Guéhenno, *Sur le chemin des hommes* (Paris, 1959), pp. 152-153.

[38] Teaching couple, Saône-et-Loire, in Jacques Ozouf, *Nous les maîtres d'école*, pp. 130-131; for other indices of notability see my article on the subject, forthcoming in *French Historical Studies*.

coined the phrase "bien avec tout le monde, très bien avec personne" was probably describing the outer limit of acceptance.[39]

But the boundaries for manoeuvre, the tolerance for error, were very slight, and particularly was this so in the case of village *institutrices*. For one thing, women were sometimes replacements for nuns, and since mothers worried more about their little girls' morals than about those of boys, their expectations of schoolmistresses, who usually taught girls, were higher than for schoolmasters. Then there was the Church itself, whose press at its worst caricatured *institutrices* as billiard-playing, cigarette-smoking, atheistic modern women.[40] And some male teachers, too, set impossible standards for their female colleagues to follow. A lady teacher of the Vosges in 1897 complained that the *instituteur* there (Rouvre-en-Xantois) could stomach neither her seriousness — "c'est une prétention" — nor her relaxed moods — "il ne fera qu'en rire." She ended her memoir philosophically, with the consoling reflection that all social positions require a "thousand daily renunciations."[41]

Among those thousand daily renunciations was dress. I have already touched upon this matter, but I stress here the special sort of sumptuary repression that was applied to women. Like males they could not condescend to casual attire; nor, like all women, could they adopt anything provocative — witness the scandal of Emma Bovary in pants. But neither could they soar into the realm of elegance. When a woman teacher wore a feathered hat or a lorgnon she ran the risk of appearing a social climber, of trying to be bourgeoise. As an *instituteur* of the Centre direly warned: "Daughters of peasants or of workers, the *institutrices* too often forget their origins, and want to ape women of the world in their clothes and bearing."[42] Look at the old photographs: the women teachers seem nothing less than dignified. Their long dresses are of conservative color, their hair is done in a neat bun (inspectors referred several times to the lascivious effect of hair "falling on the shoulders"), and they are groomed impeccably.[43] On the other hand, however, *institutrices* must avoid stiffness, nascent masculinity. The term *bas bleus*, conventionalized by Barbey d'Aurevilly's novel of that title (1878), was the term of reproach for unfeminity, too much learning, and lack of give all in one.[44] Dress, like language, was

---

[39] Quoted in Jacques Ozouf, *Nous les maîtres d'école*, p. 134.

[40] See Mona Ozouf, *Ecole, Eglise, République*, pp. 104-106.

[41] Berger, ed., *Lettres d'institutrices rurales*, p. 37.

[42] Ibid., p. 55.

[43] There are good photographs in Jacques Ozouf, *Nous les maîtres d'école* and Mona Ozouf, *Ecole, Eglise, République*. See also the description of the male teacher, Tafardel, in Gabriel Chevallier, *Clochemerle* (Paris, 1934), p. 9. A film made on the basis of Alain-Fournier's *Le Grande Meaulnes*, and with the same title, skillfully depicted teachers of the Belle Epoque.

[44] C.f. also Albert Duruy, who wrote contemptuously of the "*bas bleus* that are being *manufactured* [my italics] today in primary normal schools and in the girls' lycées." Duruy, "L'Instruction publique et la démocratie," *Revue des deux mondes*, 75 (May 1886), p. 187.

at once a great differentiator and a critical part of image — a tight-fitting thing both literally and figuratively.

Marriage, probably as important as dress, presented similar constraints. Finding a suitable spouse helped raise your legitimacy quotient in a village, for the French were then hard on celibacy, but how to find that spouse? Male teachers could rarely marry into the bourgeoisie and at best might envision a match with a functionary's daughter or the offspring of a small shopkeeper. Peasant wives were also of course a possibility. But for women teachers finding a partner was infinitely harder, in part because their opportunities for courtship were more restricted, in part because of their learning, in part because of economic reasons. Peasants in certain areas looked on the *institutrice* as a *poupée*, afraid to get her hands wet; and *commerçants* required a dowry, *rentiers* a goodly sum to make a match worthwhile.[45] On the other hand, the single *institutrice* was probably more common before the turn of the century than after. Jacques Ozouf's study of the Manche indicated that the percentage of married *institutrices* in that department more than tripled between 1897 and 1922.[46] After 1900, too, the administration and teachers at normal schools began vigorously to preach the virtues of marriages within the teaching community. Madame C.L. remembered how her headmistress at the Rennes Normal School warned the girls to keep themselves attractive in order to marry someone worthwhile, preferably a male teacher, and above all not to succumb to the blandishments of shiftless *coqs de village* for whom a young *institutrice* was a prized marriage prospect.[47]

When it comes finally to sexual constraints we enter terra incognita only beginning to be mapped by the likes of Professor Zeldin. Neither peasants nor rural bourgeois notables were as sexually free as the urban working class or the dying Paris aristocracy — this we can say for sure. Peasants were constrained mainly by village gossip or, in areas like the West, by Church doctrine. Bourgeois morality is harder to capsulize; but I would say that one ingredient was the puritanism that went along with making money and keeping it. Central was the maintenance of family, if guides like Henri Baudrillart's *La famille et l'éducation en France* (1874) are to be trusted. Immorality would strike at the tight control of father over son and daughter, and destroy that well-ordered devolution of property for which the bourgeoisie has always striven. As for teachers, they had enough injunctions to last a lifetime, going beyond both peasant and bourgeois in this respect. There was, for one thing, the *Académie* sitting

[45] See testimony of *institutrice* at Evian-les-Bains, 1897, in Ida Berger, ed., *Lettres d'institutrices rurales*, p. 58.

[46] Jacques Ozouf, "Les instituteurs de la Manche et leurs associations au début du XXe siècle," *Revue d'histoire moderne et contemporaine*, 13 (January-March 1966), pp. 98-99.

[47] Interview, Madame C.L., Châteaugiron, January 31, 1970. She married a railway worker.

over them, and we know from Zeldin that the *laic* establishment, perhaps due to Protestant evangelical influence, was at least as puritanical as the Catholic one.[48] Dancing and smoking were doubly taboo — both because they were immoral and also because they showed the pillar of the Republic with his guard down. Villagers reinforced these standards, for they concurred with inspectors: teachers who took children from the fields had better be upright. Peasants permitted the teacher little deviation from the moral norm; moreover, scandal-hungry themselves, they were prone to spreading rumors about this vulnerable paragon of virtue just to liven up a mundane existence. So even a wayward glance was open to much interpretation. How many teachers must have dreamed, like Zola's bourgeois Hennebeau in *Germinal*, of being for one day as sexually autonomous as a worker? This we will never know.

Since none of the standard authorities touch this subject I will have to use my own Breton sources for solid examples. The trouble is that this sort of history easily descends into *petite histoire*. One thing we can say is that women teachers bore the brunt of morals charges more often than did males. Just as they had to be prudent in their relations with the Church so also did they have to be careful to lead exemplary private lives. A lady teacher of Ille-et-Vilaine, though excellent in the classroom, was considered anathema at the village of Lillemer because she had had a baby too soon after her marriage before coming there. For the first year she was snubbed by most people, and right up until she left the commune three years later she was slandered in numerous anonymous letters.[49] Another woman teacher came to the reactionary village of Marsac (Loire-Atlantique) from the Department of Gers in 1907. When the people heard that she had married a defrocked *curé*, their venom was unbridled. One of the anonymous letters in her file is a shameless castigation of her morals and gives an indication of village pettiness at its worst, partly a reaction to "foreigners."

> Depuis l'an dernier, on a comme maîtresse d'école une vrai coureuse, elle a été chassée de son pays car elle vivait avec son curé — ils sont parti ensemble depuis qu'elle est arrivez ici il était lui a St. Nazaire elle allait couchez avec lui tous les dimanches et des fois plus souvent ils sont mariés à présent mais ils ont une petite fille qui avait 3 ans avant qu'ils sont mariés et tout le monde sait cela, il ne faut toute de même pas se moquer de nous nos filles ne vont plus à l'ecole on aime mieux qu'elle save pas lire que d'aller chez une femme de mauvaise vie. . . .

[48] Theodore Zeldin, "The Conflict of Moralities: Confession, Sin and Pleasure in the Nineteenth Century," in Zeldin, ed., *Conflicts in French Society: Anticlericalism, Education and Morals in the 19th Century* (London, 1970), pp. 36-45.
[49] A.D. Ille-et-Vilaine. T: Instituteurs. Doss. inds. Primary inspector, Fougeres, to academy, September 28, 1911. The anonymous letters are in this dossier. The woman died soon after

An investigation by the inspector found this letter to be a complete prevarication but by the end of the year the highly-rated *institutrice* had to leave the commune, transferred to the city of Saint-Nazaire, where she taught from 1907 to 1936.[50]

In some other cases sex scandals did have an adverse effect upon teachers' careers. An *instituteur* of the Loire-Atlantique had been doing well at Le Pellerin from 1886 until 1897, when his wife's love affair behind his back came to the attention of the villagers. The French traditionally have made the *cocu* an object of their mirth — the rural classic *Clochemerle* revolves around that theme — and this teacher was hastily sent to Touvois, an inferior post.[51] Another teacher, a young *stagiaire* at Saint-Ouen-La-Rouerie (Ille-et-Vilaine), was sent to the Department of the Nord after two people spied him in the house of a thirty-eight-year-old woman "who is weak-minded." Their description of what they saw through a hole in the shutters, certified by M. le maire as honorable testimony, was sufficient evidence for the inspector.[52] The most spectacular case of this sort that I came upon involved an *institutrice* who was caught embracing a man on a beach near Saint-Nazaire in 1887. The detailed police investigation for "Outrages publics à la pudeur" contains more than a dozen testimonies of people who watched them from behind the trees on a hill overlooking the beach. An old man with a pair of binoculars called some youths to the spot to take a look and then more observers came over. The *institutrice* was forced to resign soon after.[53] She was eighty-odd years too early for sainthood.

In the latter two instances it is certain that the *stagiaire* and the *institutrice* had actually engaged in activities providing grist for snoopers' mills. The *institutrice* made no attempt to recant when confronted with evidence against her. At other times, however, *institutrices* or *instituteurs* were un-

departing the commune at age thirty-one, partly from unhealthy conditions there and perhaps also due to the hate campaign.

[50] A.D. Loire-Atlantique. sTi105: Doss. inds. . . . instituteurs et institutrices. Anonymous letter with original punctuation and spelling to academy, March 2, 1907; primary inspector, Châteaubriant, to academy, March 17, 1907. A recent film highly acclaimed in France, *La fiancée du pirate*, concerns an illegitimate girl growing up in a village. She is continually reminded of her fallen state — like this *institutrice* — but ultimately takes revenge on the whole village by becoming a prostitute, tape-recording compromising words spoken by her clients (including the *curé*), and playing the tapes from behind a pillar in Church one Sunday. The movie illuminates the worst aspects of village mentality in France.

[51] A.D. Loire-Atlantique. sTi144: Doss. inds. . . . instituteurs et institutrices. Primary inspector, Paimboeuf, to academy, February 18, 1897.

[52] A.D. Ille-et-Vilaine. T: Instituteurs. Doss. inds. Primary inspector, Fougeres, to academy, October 31, 1891.

[53] A.D. Loire-Atlantique. sT24: Enseignement primaire. Personnel: plaintes, affaires diverses mettant en cause les instituteurs (publics et privés) 1887-1945. Copies of all the testimonies are in the file and are very precise.

justly involved in sex scandals. A major affair of this sort took place in the Finistère in 1907. A fifty-four-year-old father of two had been teaching at Gouesnou since 1880. From about 1900 he had fallen out with the mayor, who fired him from his post as secretary and accused him successively of brutality to students, drunkenness, and exploitation of children in the classroom — charges thoroughly investigated by the inspector and found to be unsupported by evidence. Meanwhile, the mayor had roused groups of *pères de famille* against the teacher, a prelude to the scandal that followed. On August 13, 1907, the teacher (this is his version) was reading a newspaper in his favorite field near the village. Three young girls, two of them sisters, aged eight, eleven, and twelve years old, asked him if he could see their cow, and one had him lift her up in order to gaze over the field. They went away shortly afterward. Late in the day their mothers charged him with serious sexual offences. The full report of the inspector of Brest, relating the detailed investigations he undertook, reveals to us the gravity of the affair. The story he heard from the girls and their mothers was that the teacher had called them over, encouraged them to do somersaults, and began to commit certain perverse acts with them. The girls returned home crying. The primary inspector noted that the mother of the two sisters modified her story several times. She was also known as a drinker and, being very poor, was dependent on charity administered by the mayor and a noble landowner of the area. Furthermore, the inspector noticed that the field was very close to a main road, making such escapades difficult to conceal. Finally, all three girls were pupils at the rival Catholic school. On the other hand, the girls sounded sincere to him, and the mayor supported them although he was certainly not an impartial bystander. This report, a model of clarity and balance, ended: "It is difficult to conclude; but I am rather disposed to conclude that the teacher is innocent." The dimensions of the affair quickly widened. On August 31, the influential daily, *La Dépêche de Brest*, carried a long article entitled "Gros scandale en perspective," which sided with the mayor and his whole *conseil municipal* against the teacher. Other newspapers took up the case soon after. On September 10 a huge petition with 100 signatures of *pères de famille*, validated by the mayor, was sent to the prefect asking that the teacher be sent out of the village for "immoral acts." The *instituteur* did not resume his duties in the new school year, and everybody waited for the outcome of his trial at the *Cour d'assises* of the Finistère at Quimper. The verdict came on April 4, 1908, after a long closed-door trial, that is, with no minutes available as befitted an affair of this genre: the teacher was acquitted. He retired in August, at a plausible age for retirement, but blackened for life.[54]

[54] A.D. Finistère. T: Instituteurs — 1901-1919. Teacher's letter August 25, 1907; primary inspector, Brest, to academy, August 28, 1907 and March 2, 1907 (most important reports).

One should not think that the academy blindly protected the teacher even in such ambiguous cases. Though less capricious than villagers, inspectors, as I have said, enforced the same moral standards and continually warned teachers not to give occasion for gossip, even going so far, in several cases, as to censure women teachers for bicycle-riding through villages! The most closely-watched teachers were those who could get into the most trouble, youthful *stagiaires* and adjunct teachers. Inspectors used the directors to inform them of the whereabouts and particularly the nocturnal habits of their young subordinates.[55]

Besides sex the other great moral pitfall for teachers was obviously alcohol. In France a necessary concomitant of social intercourse has always been the *coup de rouge* (in the South pastis; in Normandy Calvados), but for teachers it was forbidden fruit. Use of spirits was damaging to the reputation of *instituteurs* who, themselves, taught courses on the evils of alcoholism. Marcel Pagnol describes the central position of "Alcool" in his father's normal school in the Midi. On the walls you saw livers colored a sickening green or purple, herniated aortas, a twisted pancreas. Teachers strode forth, he says, anxious to fight the *trinité atroce* of Church, Royalty . . . and Alcohol.[56] Of course they had read *The Assommoir*, great anti-alcohol document of the century, if not Pierre Loti's *Mon Frère Yves* (1883) on the ravages of eau-de-vie in Brittany. Yet to eschew the friendly drink was once again to isolate oneself. The pressure was very strong — particularly when the teacher had become somewhat accepted — to have a drink with the boys. Nothing was more socially central to village life. When a teacher did succumb too often the academy pounced; a schoolmaster at Leuhan (Finistère) was transferred out of the commune in 1912 after twenty-five successful years there just because he was too fond of going to the bar with mayor and *conseil* after meetings where he was the secretary.[57] There were teachers who drank on the sly, usually out of anxiety; and generally, in Brittany at least, young teachers and *institutrices* were most

The verdict is in the *Dépêche de Brest* of April 4, 1908 (the archives lacked papers of the *Cours d'assises* for 1908). The petition — for which some of the signatures do not appear authentic — is also in this file. If acquitted the teacher was undoubtedly innocent. According to M. Jacques Leonard, an assistant professor at Rennes, French judicial authorities then were very stringent in morals affairs and made painstaking investigations of them.

[55] For censure of bicycle-riding, see, for example, A.D. Loire-Atlantique. sTi139: Doss. inds. . . . instituteurs et institutrices. Primary inspector, Saint-Nazaire, to academy, June 14, 1884, on institutrice at Saint-Nazaire. A teacher at Scrignac (Finistère) to primary inspector, Châteaulin, January 1, 1900, told of his adjunct's nights out in Brest. A.D. Finistère. T: Instituteurs — 1800-1899.

[56] Marcel Pagnol, *La gloire de mon père*, p. 23.

[57] A.D. Finistère. T: Instituteurs — 1901-1919. Primary inspector, Châteaulin, to academy, October 24, 1912. In my interview with H.L. (Nantes, May 15, 1970), he also spoke of his teacher at Guenouvry as a teetotaler (by necessity).

prone to depression.[58] Crack-ups there must have been; space forbids review of the kinds of evidence I have.

But teachers possessed great self-discipline, indeed cultivated it, and that, finally, is what I wish to stress. "Il faut savoir se dominer," "le maître c'est l'exemple" — these aphorisms really meant something to schoolmasters holding forth before the partly-draped map, a *Tour de France* in their hands. It is easy of course to sentimentalize; but it seems to me that today's reverse Whiggery, making history's progression a vale of tears, can be silly as well. Bergson thought that the sense of religion was inherent: it prevented man from caving in at the sight of himself. With teachers, however, those positive doctrines were learned elements of faith that worked like the real thing. This acquired capacity for internal resistance to village problems made teachers the *instituteurs de la République*. No problems to overcome, no sainthood.

How then was the teacher a paradigm for the pre-1914 Republic? First, he symbolized the period in microcosm, poised, as he was, between local and national Frenchness. Instrument of the latter, in the period when according to Professor Weber France really became French for the first time,[59] the teacher yet remembered the soil whence he had come. When I interviewed a now-deceased teacher at Ste-Anne-La-Palud in Brittany I noticed this ambivalence: the man could converse eloquently about universal ideals dating from the Ferry era and to which he still subscribed; but when he brought out a map to make a particular point, I knew he was a Breton through and through. On that map the village of Quéménéven appeared in great bloc letters, and Quéménéven is a hole-in-the-wall! I won't forget that moment, hunched over those village names which actually meant something.[60]

The period 1870-1914 was also the great intermediary time in intellectual history when positive morality, having replaced Church morality, had yet to be deposed by twentieth century relativism. It was the last period, too, of rural notabilities, of tutelage. The organs of mass diffusion had not yet triumphed; but, given the literacy teachers provided one and all, it was

---

[58] Generalizing for his district in an unusually sensitive report of 1903, the primary inspector of Vannes noted: "The life of the *laïc Institutrice* is often very painful; the unfortunate *Institutrice* is, in most rural areas, often kept apart and I wonder how, in many cases, she does not become totally discouraged." A.D. Morbihan. T1049: Instruction primaire. Statistiques — 1903-1908, "Rapport sur la situation de l'enseignement primaire dans l'arrondissement." Clerical pressure was undoubtedly stronger in Brittany than in most regions, but the Sarcey *enquête* for 1897 shows that *institutrices* were prone to depression in all rural areas.

[59] Eugen Weber, "Fin-de-Siècle: The Third Republic Makes a Modern Nation," in G.R. Conrad and M. Allain, eds., *Proceedings of the First Symposium of French-American Studies* (Lafayette, La., 1973), pp. 87-101.

[60] Interview, F.T., August 9, 1970.

only a matter of time. Then the choices of urban existence would beckon — choice-agony, we might now say.

Perhaps we don't realize how unsure of itself the pre-World War I Republic actually was. We sometimes see the teacher descending from the train and making the country a Gambetta land at one stroke. In fact the period shows the Republic in the process of national conquest using symbols of which it was not yet sure. When *Le Correspondant* (March 10, 1886) attacked the teacher as a parvenu it was also attacking the government's whole legitimating apparatus, "the dithyrambs with which the Republic celebrates its modest functions."[61] Indeed the Republic's fragility was there for all to see. Its real strength came from rallying against remembered foreign invasion and particularly against contemporary clerical enemies. These enemies helped cement ideals; and like the ancient Egyptians who sprang into consciousness by expelling the Hyksos, the Republic illustrates my own historical law — you are what you oppose. Without demeaning the Republic's positive philosophies, such as positivism itself, we should realize that these were far less clear-cut than they seemed on paper. Even what looks like one hundred percent patriotism was actually bought at the price of tension, by the union of opposites. This is what Duneton means when he says that peasants fought in 1914 for national ideals but as rural people.[62] Once complete, the national revolution would make such local patriotism, and perhaps all patriotism, a thing of the past. In our own country it is no accident that sons of the immigrants were the most fervent supporters of the American Way of Life.

The Republic, like its teacher, was an outsider trying to get inside (as Louis XIV got inside, as Napoleon did). Already by 1910 Charles Péguy was taxing the regime for having arrived. Its stability was boring. (Needless to say, that stability would appear as a *Belle Epoque* to a future generation.)[63] But was Péguy's aphorism — *toute mystique finit en politique* — ill-considered? Certainly he was correct in assuming, as I think he did, that a solid franc was no guarantee of happiness or longevity. The myth was vital when being fought for. Become glaciated, as all myths do, into outworn dogma, it began to show its age. As Joseph Schumpeter pointed

---

[61] Abbé A. Sicard, "Les Deux Maîtres de l'enfance: le prêtre et l'instituteur," pt. 8, *Le Correspondant*, 142 (March 10, 1886), p. 899. The article goes on to describe the teacher as "nine times out of ten" a discontented person, "if not one in revolt."

[62] Duneton, *Parler Croquant*, pp. 141-148.

[63] Péguy's book referred to here is obviously *Notre jeunesse*. C.f. also Nadezhda Mandelstam: "At the beginning of the thirties M. once said to me: 'You know, if ever there was a golden age, it was the nineteenth century. Only we didn't know.'" Nadezhda Mandelstam, *Hope against Hope*, trans. by Max Hayward (New York, 1970), p. 253.

out perceptively back in the 1930's, systems do choke on success.[64]

We have heard a number of explanations for the Republic's decline after 1918, many of them reasonable. We know, too, that the teachers progressively lost their force as linch-pins of a regime. Urbanization, material uncertainty, the rise of Socialism, the huge effect of World War I — all undoubtedly figure in both phenomena. But perhaps we should also emphasize, more than has been done, the evaporation of a clerical opposition. The battle was pretty well won. The Republic and the teacher lost not only their raison d'être but also that insecure, grappling, marginal status that always marks the healthy period of life. The *instituteur*, even more than the Republic he served, had had to steer between many shoals; and it was his own resistance that staked out his position and endowed him and her with a fundamental greatness before 1914. That is why so many remember these village black-coats as saints. Saints are not made in heaven.

[64] See Schumpeter, *Capitalism, Socialism, and Democracy* (New York, 1962), passim.

13

"Atala" in the Arts

SUSAN J. DELANEY

Atala devint si populaire qu'elle alla grossir, avec la Brinvilliers, la collection de Curtius. Les auberges de rouliers étaient ornées de gravures rouges, vertes et bleues, représentant Chactas, le père Aubry et la fille de Simaghan. Dans des boîtes de bois, sur les quais, on montrait mes personnages en cire, comme on montre des images de Vierge et de saints à la foire. . . . Parodies, caricatures, moqueries m'accablaient.[1]

When François-René de Chateaubriand published his novel *Atala* in 1801, he was astounded at its amazing success. New editions were issued rapidly and sold out immediately. The story was borrowed by contemporary playwrights, poets, and artists. As early as 1802 Pierre Gautherot, a student of Jacques-Louis David, sent *The Funeral Procession of Atala* (Fig. 1) to the salon. Many other painters followed suit. The most famous was Anne-Louis Girodet, whose *Death of Atala* (Fig. 4) combines romantic sensuality and neo-classical severity in the manner characteristic of French painting in the early years of the century. *Atala* also provided subjects for decorative artists: scenes from the novel appeared on vases, plates, upholstery fabrics and clocks. And the theme was common in popular graphic arts. Printmakers stamped Atala's image on cheap, garishly-colored engravings meant for unsophisticated people who had nothing in common with the aristocratic Chateaubriand but their pleasure in the love story he wrote.

This essay began as an investigation of the specific examples of the Atala story within the arts. The quest seemed necessary because Atala's popularity had been often cited, but never fully documented.[2] Prelimi-

---

[1] François-René de Chateaubriand, *Mémoires d'outre-tombe*, ed. by M. Levaillant (Paris, 1948), II, p. 21.

[2] Girodet's *Death of Atala* is the example most frequently given of the impact of the novel. John Canaday, *Mainstreams of Modern Art* (New York, 1959), pp. 31-32, discusses the emotional, Christian, and exotic elements in the painting which led to its success in the salon. Jacques de Caso, "Girodet," *Art Bulletin*, 51 (1969), p. 87, describes the painting as a "puritanical image that emphasized the melancholic aspects of the story." Frederick Antal,

nary research has permitted me to compile a catalogue of over forty works of art from the first half of the nineteenth century.[3] Since the most fascinating example of *Atala's* diversified appeal is its appearance in popular graphics, Part I of this paper is a brief discussion of the methodology involved in the study of popular art. In Part II the task is one of analysis. We study the specific works thematically, determining how the general topics of (1) Christian martyrdom; (2) the Noble Savage and exotic America; and (3) eroticism are expressed. These areas have been chosen because they encompass the primary romantic interests that made the novel so famous: "Ainsi, le caractère poétique d'*Atala*, l'exotisme et l'amour, la thèse et le style, voilà ce qui a intéressé les gens de 1801."[4] We hope to verify this more fully as we proceed. An awareness of how the three categories of artistic production (fine arts, decorative arts, popular arts) do or do not differ in content has been a constant factor.

At this point, let us review the plot of *Atala*. The story takes place along the Mississippi. Chactas, a Natchez Indian, had been orphaned early in life and raised by a Spaniard, Lopez. As a youth he had spent some time in France. Upon reaching manhood Chactas returns to the Indian life he remembers only dimly. He is soon captured by an enemy tribe, but is set free by the chief's daughter, Atala. She has fallen in love with him. They escape and hide in the forest. As their mutual love grows, Atala becomes increasingly depressed. Chactas tries in vain to cheer her. He tries to make love to her, but she refuses. Finally, she tells him she is only part Indian, that her real father was a Spaniard named Lopez. The revelation that Atala is his "sister" overwhelms Chactas. He embraces her passionately and this time she is willing, too. But at that moment a lightening bolt strikes the ground and a Capuchin monk arrives on the scene. He is Père

Classicism and Romanticism (New York, 1973), pp. 22-23, relates the work to the romantic revival of Catholicism after the Concordat. For bibliography on this painting, see the entry by Jacqueline Pruvost-Auzas in Musée de Montargis, *Girodet 1767-1824* (exhibition catalogue; Paris, 1967), no. 38.

[3] No fewer than thirteen academic painters submitted *Atala* canvasses to the salons. Several sculptures, some by Italian artists, were also admitted to the salons and to mid-century expositions. Over ten graphic artists from St.-Aubin to Doré illustrated the story. Nine objects (or sets of objects) remain as a sampling of *Atala* in the decorative arts. And the popular arts category includes several different series of prints, and some illustrations for inexpensive editions of the novel. The most helpful sources in composing our catalogue have been the partial lists of art works in the following: Henri Lemonnier, "L'*Atala* de Chateaubriand et l'*Atala* de Girodet," *Gazette des Beaux-Arts*, 11 (1914), pp. 365-371; François-René de Chateaubriand, *Atala*, ed. by A. Weil (Paris, 1950), hereafter referred to as Weil, *Atala*; and Paris, Bibliothèque nationale, *Chateaubriand (1768-1848): Exposition du centenaire* (exhibition catalogue; Paris, 1948), hereafter referred to as BN, *Centenaire*. The bicentennial exhibition catalogue [Paris, Bibliothèque nationale, *Chateaubriand, le voyageur et l'homme politique* (Paris, 1969)] is less complete.

[4] Louis Hogu, "La Publication d'*Atala* et l'opinion des contemporains," *Revue des facultés catholiques de l'Ouest*, 21 (1913), p. 466.

Aubry and he has been searching for them for some time. Atala and Chactas follow the priest to the mission where he ministers to a host of happy, converted Indians. There Atala begins to die from the poison she took just before her near-surrender to Chactas. And she tells the two men her sad tale. As an infant, she had been dedicated to a life of Christian virginity by her mother. As a child Atala respected the vow, finding it easy to keep. But as a woman her love for Chactas threatened to destroy her Christian resolve, and finding the conflict unbearable, she has committed suicide. There is nothing for the men to do now but mourn. Père Aubry gives her communion. And they bury her with many tears. Chactas goes away and grows old with his melancholy memories.

I

The study of popular art presents many problems with which scholars have been intrigued for more than a century. The pioneering work in the area is *L'Histoire de l'imagerie populaire*, published in 1869 by Jules Champfleury. Champfleury concentrated his research on two representative themes that appeared in popular prints, *Le Juif errant* and *Le bonhomme misère*. He urged that images like these be conserved and studied with as much respect as is accorded the works of established graphic artists. Moreover, popular prints could be of social benefit. Because they often bore captions, they encouraged literacy. And they expressed traditional values that Champfleury felt could help alleviate the turmoil within contemporary France: "La philosophie de nos pères est inscrite à chaque page . . . et il serait à regretter qu'elle ne restât pas la philosophie de nos jours."[5] T.J. Clark indicates the distance that often separates the scholar from his/her interests when he remarks that Champfleury, afraid of the people, "began to study the popular."[6] But romantic nostalgia provided only part of the impetus for Champfleury, who recognized the historical value of this study:

de l'imagerie découlent encore divers enseignements historiques, et si on ne juge pas digne de faire entrer, même au dernier rang, l'image dans l'histoire de l'art, elle tiendra sa place au premier dans l'histoire des moeurs.[7]

Contemporary scholars concur that popular imagery reveals the customs and values of the society from which it comes. They have offered

[5] Jules Champfleury, *L'Histoire de l'imagerie populaire* (Paris, 1869), p. 179.
[6] Timothy J. Clark, *Image of the People* (London, 1973), p. 66.
[7] Champfleury, *L'Histoire de l'imagerie*, p. xiii.

definitions of popular art, in terms of its association with social class. Pierre-Louis Duchartre and René Saulnier state that:

> on peut dire qu'une oeuvre est cent pour cent populaire quand son auteur est un homme du peuple, non dégagé de son milieu, non formé par l'école, que cette oeuvre est non seulement destinée à des milieux populaires, mais préférée par eux.[8]

Jean Mistler adds the qualification that the sources of popular art are not necessarily found in "l'âme profonde des peuples," but that the images spread by *colporteurs* and sold "à bas prix à la foule" are often based on subjects drawn from elite culture.[9]

Robert Mandrou defines popular art as that which nourishes the masses because it is formed from their own traditions and not from those of the elite (though the subject matter may have originally come from the elite). Popular art is part of "la culture créée par le peuple, dans un sens actif en quelque sorte . . . la culture est l'oeuvre du peuple: s'appuyant sur la richesse des arts et traditions populaires."[10]

Closely connected to the problem of defining popular art is the difficulty of identifying certain works as popular. There are several criteria that can be applied. Popular prints are generally recognizable on stylistic grounds, since they differ in expression from both salon art and advanced movements. This is not to say that the popular image fails by comparison, but that it quite logically seeks another audience.[11] It is also helpful to know the means of production — usually a specialized publications shop. And the expected market for the popular works can be determined by their cost, the means of distribution, and the usual locations in which they appeared. It is not possible to recover all of this information, since it

---

[8] Pierre-Louis Duchartre and René Saulnier, *L'Imagerie parisienne (l'imagerie de la rue St.-Jacques)* (Paris, 1944), p. 6.

[9] Jean Mistler, François Blaudez, and André Jacquemin, *Epinal et l'imagerie populaire* (Paris, 1961), pp. 7-8.

[10] Robert Mandrou, *De la culture populaire aux XVIIe et XVIIIe siècles* (Paris, 1964), p. 9.

[11] In some cases the disparity between elite standards and an actual work can pose problems of classification. For instance, a number of the scenes on the plates from Choisy-le-Roi (Figs. 13a-1) are awkwardly designed. Were they to be judged on stylistic grounds they would certainly fare poorly. Yet we cannot call them popular art because they were produced by the Royal Manufactory, are made of fine faience, and have little utilitarian value. They must have been too expensive to be popular. Now, in contrast, a plate in the Le Savoureux collection [reproduced in Henri Le Savoureux, *Chateaubriand* (Paris, 1930), pl. XI] bears the same scene as one from Choisy-le-Roi, but it was produced in a manner "plus commune" (Weil, *Atala*, p. 1). Because the technique involved was even less expert, does the latter plate then qualify as popular art? There can be no answer until the stylistic evaluation is supplemented by other, as yet unavailable, information, such as the provenance and cost of the Le Savoureux plate.

concerns the art forms of "ce petit peuple qu'il est si difficile de tirer de l'ombre où il a vécu."[12] But we can try to discover whatever remains.

Several centers, particularly in eastern France, specialized in the production of popular prints. The Pellerin family of Epinal built such a successful organization that the term *images d'Epinal* became a generic name for nineteenth-century popular prints, whether or not they were actually produced in Epinal. In addition to Epinal, printing houses flourished in Metz, Nancy, Strasbourg, and elsewhere.[13] Although most artists in these shops were "anonymous," it is often possible to identify a given print as having issued from a certain center, because the printer's name and city (not the artist's) are generally stamped on the image. If the print has come from Paris, the artist may also have signed his name. Paris, "la Ville des villes," was unique, and her art forms differed from those in the provinces. Most of her known graphic artists set up shop in the rue St.-Jacques, which gave its name to Parisian imagery in general.[14]

A third means of identifying popular art is to determine for what art market the objects (plates, prints, figurines) were produced. It can be assumed that high prices signify a wealthy clientele, and that very low prices are not only directed at those in low socioeconomic levels, but also effectively prevent the bourgeoisie from purchasing the works, since that act would imply unacceptable contact with *le peuple*.[15] Some prints sold for as low as one sou. An English traveller in France in 1818 reported on his visit to a shop from which:

sortent les milliers et dizaines de milliers d'estampes, de livres à bon marché, etc., dont la basse Normandie est inondée. Ces objets coûtent depuis un sou jusqu'à trois selon que le sujet est simple ou composé, gravé sur bois ou sur cuivre.[16]

[12] André Latreille, "Pratique, piété, et foi populaire dans la France moderne au XIXe et XXe siècles," *Ecclesiastical History Society: Studies in Church History*, 8 (1972), p. 279.
[13] Among the studies dealing with regional popular arts are the following: Pierre-Louis Duchartre and René Saulnier, *L'Imagerie Populaire: les images de toutes les provinces françaises du XVe siècle au Deuxième Empire* (Paris, 1925); Duchartre and Saulnier, *L'Imagerie parisienne*; Jean-Julien Barbé, *L'Imagerie de Metz* (Metz, 1950); J.-M. Dumont, *La Vie et l'oeuvre de Jean-Charles Pellerin* (Epinal, 1956); J. Mistler, et al., *Epinal: Art populaire de la France de l'Est*, ed. by Adolphe Riff (Strasbourg, 1969); and George Klein, *Arts et traditions populaires d'Alsace* (Colmar, 1973). A most valuable resource on popular prints in general is Louis Ferrand and Edmond Magnac, *Guide bibliographique de l'imagerie populaire* (Auxerre, 1956).
[14] Biographical information on Parisian printers is available in Duchartre and Saulnier, *L'Imagerie parisienne*, pp. 189-243.
[15] Mandrou, *Culture populaire*, p. 170, records Stendahl's revealing comments on his bourgeois friends' fascination with cheap novels and their embarrassment at being caught reading such books.
[16] Mistler, *Epinal*, p. 62.

The implication is that everyone could afford them.[17]

The distributors of popular images were itinerant peddlars called *colporteurs*. Often whole families were involved; many came from the Lorraine. François Blaudez provides a revealing description of their life:

> cette localité . . . était habitée par une pauvre population agricole qui avait peine à vivre sur un sol ingrat. Aussi, chaque année, à l'automne, bon nombre de familles quittaient le village. Avant de s'égailler à travers la France et les pays limitrophes, elles faisaient provision d'une pacotille composée de menus objets de piété, de livres de la "Bibliothèque bleue" et d'images. Le chef de famille portait sur son dos une petite armoire en sapin qui, lorsqu'elle était ouverte, formait une sorte de triptyque. Le fond était garni par une image représentant la Sainte Vierge ou le plus souvent une Crucifixion. La femme et les enfants portaient les ballots de marchandise. Le groupe s'installait sur la place du village. Une petite table était dressée, recouverte d'un linge blanc. On y posait l'armoire ouverte et on étalait médailles, chapelets, fleurs artificielles, livres et images. . . . Le marchand, en même temps qu'il montrait avec une baguette les objets et les images, récitait une mélopée monotone.[18]

In 1854 Charles Nisard was the director of a governmental inquiry into *colportage*, charged with reporting on its subject matter in order to facilitate regulation and censorship.[19] He succeeded in demonstrating the widespread popularity and scope of the material that the peddlars sold. Robert Mandrou, in his book on the *Bibliothèque bleue* of Troyes, further specified how *colportage* provided the rural French with a choice of visual and literary materials.[20] The peddlar was often allied with a certain printing firm. The objects he sold at provincial fairs and on village squares can be securely classified as very basic popular art.

A related area of investigation involves discovering in what places popular art works were likely to be found. The interiors of lower class homes have only recently begun to be studied.[21] Considerably more work needs to be done. In terms of our project, we know only that images of Atala found their way into farm houses and country inns because Armand

---

[17] Similar information is available concerning mid-century editions of Chateaubriand's works that were sold *à bon marché*. The appearance of *Atala* and other novels for as little as 20 sous is heralded as a *fait sociologique* by Roger Dévigne: "l'imprimerie cessait d'être le privilège d'une caste" [Les éditions populaires de Chateaubriand," *Courrier graphique*, no. 36 (1948), p. 18].

[18] François Blaudez, "L'histoire de l'imagerie d'Epinal," in Mistler, *Epinal*, p. 133.

[19] Charles Nisard, *Histoire des livres populaires ou de la littérature de colportage depuis le XVe siècle*, 2 vols. (Paris, 1854).

[20] Mandrou, *Culture populaire*, pp. 36-41.

[21] See, for example, articles by E. Georges, M. Stahl-Weber, C. Voegelé, and A. Jacquemin, in Riff, ed., *Art populaire*.

Weil recorded the former[22] and Chateaubriand, in Salzburg in 1833, remembered the latter:

> je me trouvai en famille dans la chambre de l'auberge: les aventures d'Atala, en six gravures, tapissaient le mur. . . . Elle était bien laide, bien vieillie, bien changée, la pauvre Atala![23]

We have discussed the problem of defining and identifying the popular arts because, as Champfleury realized, such study is an invaluable part of cultural history. It reveals information not available through other means. As André Latreille warns, statistics are but exterior facts and should be supplemented by a subjective analysis of the literature and arts of a people.[24] In addition, Maurice Crubellier stresses the significance of those elements that are *not* borrowed by the people from the art of the elite, because both the adoption and the exclusion provide insights into the collective attitude of the class:

> Même lorsque le peuple emprunte à l'élite, faisons bien attention qu'il n'incorpore pas telle quelle la matière de ses emprunts, il la modifie pour la faire mieux sienne, la digère en quelque sorte. Il ne reçoit pas la parole ou l'image comme fait le lettré: son choix, toujours restreint par nécessité, s'accompagne d'une forte valorisation.[25]

In a related vein, T.J. Clark maintains the importance of determining what factors prevent an artist from seeing. One studies "blindness as much as vision."[26] The historian, then, looks to the popular arts in order to gather their special contributions, and must be particularly attentive to the message of these forms and attempt to draw conclusions from them.

Before proceeding to our thematic analysis of *Atala* in the arts in general, it might be helpful to indicate the various forms in which the story appeared in popular art. Chateaubriand recalled that wax figures of his characters were sold on the quais like the statuettes of the Virgin Mary. Little plaster replicas of Atala were also peddled. A hawker of such objects is the subject of an engraving by Karl Giradet in the *Magasin pittoresque*. The commentator reports that the plaster modeller "adopte l'oeuvre en vogue, il la popularise," and he mentions busts of Paul and

---

[22] Weil, *Atala*, p. xlix.
[23] Ibid., p. 1. Also, Alphonse de Lamartine (see below) enjoyed the prints of *Atala* that he saw in the village inn and in the home of the parish priest.
[24] Latreille, "Pratique, piété," p. 287.
[25] Crubellier, *Histoire culturelle*, p. 69.
[26] Clark, *Image*, p. 15.

Virginie (though not of Atala and Chactas): "plupart des célébrités lit-téraires et politiques, des fantaisies de l'art . . . ont paru là, à leur tour."[27] But the popularity of any one character was of brief duration. There seem to be no extant examples of Chateaubriand's characters in wax or plaster. It is conceivable that, in the space of a century, such temporary and inexpensive trifles have all been destroyed, whereas porcelain objects bearing Atala's image, which belonged to the wealthier classes, have been passed on through the generations and can still be found.[28]

Chateaubriand also commented that representations of Atala, her lover, and her priest had enlarged the Curtius collection. Philippe Cur-tius, a Swiss physician, fashioned and exhibited full-size wax models of famous personages in his *Cabinet de cire* at the Palais Royal . His establish-ment on the Boulevard du Temple featured notorious criminals.[29] He was out of business by 1847, after having taught his trade to his niece, Mme. Tussaud.[30] But there is no record, aside from Chateaubriand's note in his *Mémoires*, that Curtius' oeuvre included fictive characters. (The Biblical villain Holofernes did have a place among the criminals.) Leading figures in French politics and society, for example, Voltaire, Robespierre, and Napoleon, dominated the collection. Was Chateaubriand recording a fact of which the substantiation has disappeared with time? Or was he, twenty years after the novel's publication, exhibiting some confusion brought on by fame and vanity? The answer is not apparent, but since no wax figures of Atala are known to survive, we will have to exclude them, for the present, from our study. The same situation exists concerning marionettes of Chactas, Atala, and Père Aubry, which have been recorded but evidently not preserved.[31]

Atala found her way into popular literature. Mandrou has shown that the commercial activity of the *Bibliothèque bleue* of Troyes increased in the first half of the nineteenth century due to higher levels of literacy, and that a significantly greater number of love stories were published at this time. Distributed by *colporteurs*, the romantic novels were read in the

[27] "Le marchand de figures de plâtre," *Magasin pittoresque*, 18 (1850), p. 389.

[28] There are two vases (ca. 1820) in the Roger Imbert collection which feature two detacha-ble medallions picturing: (a) *Atala Freeing Chactas*, and *Natural Bridge*; and (b) *Père Aubry Discovers the Lovers*, and *Rapids in the Mountains* (BN, *Centenaire*, no. 104). The Musée céramique in Sèvres has a porcelain plaque (inv. no. 7658) on which Victoire Jacquotot (1772-1855), in 1829, painted a *Death of Atala* based on Girodet's composition [see A. Brogniart and D. Riocreaux, *Musée céramique* (Paris, 1845)].

[29] Jacques Hillairet, *Dictionnaire historique des rues de Paris* (Paris, 1957-61), II, p. 222.

[30] E. Pyke, *A Biographical Dictionary of Wax Modellers* (Oxford, 1973), pp. 34-35.

[31] Hogu, "La Publication," p. 461.

·*veillée.* Mandrou's description of the usual subject matter of mid-century popular novels reveals why *Atala* was so eagerly received:

> forêts sombres, médaillons, serments, larmes et baisers, nacelles, jeunes fiancés plus courageux que des lions, doux comme des agneaux, suicides par délicatesse, dévouements à tous les degrés.[32]

As we have stated, the presence of *Atala* scenes in popular graphics provides strong testimony to the wide dissemination of Chateaubriand's story. Wherever a printseller set up his display, "ce sera toujours un groupe d'Atala."[33] In discussing the relationship between literature and the visual arts of the people, Duchartre and Saulnier maintain that:

> l'aurore du XIXe siècle est illuminée par la gloire retentissante de Chateaubriand. *Atala* . . . ne manqua pas d'inspirer aussi peintres, graveurs, sculpteurs . . . pendant plus de 50 ans, et à la suite de ces artistes, l'imagerie s'empara du sujet, suivant le processus habituel. Ces petites estampes s'inspirent souvent du tableau de Girodet, ou de l'oeuvre gravée d'après lui, et les légendes, du texte original; mais par un naïf pathos elles en exagérent les défauts du maître.[34]

Alphonse de Lamartine believed Chateaubriand to have been a formative influence upon him, and he recalled his childhood delight in the simple poetry of naively-done images:

> Je me souviendrai toujours des premières gravures de poèmes qui frappèrent mes regards d'enfant. C'étaient Paul et Virginie, Atala, René. La gravure n'était pas parvenue alors à ce degré de perfection qui la fait admirer aujourd'hui indépendamment du sujet. Ces images, tirées de ces charmants poèmes, étaient grossières et coloriées avec toute la rudesse des couleurs les plus heurtées. . . . Je ne me lassais pas de la contempler sur les murs du vieux curé de mon village et dans les salles d'auberges de campagne, où les colporteurs avaient popularisé Bernardin et Chateaubriand.[35]

Among the most common subject matter in popular art were themes of morality and crime, love, dreams, merrymaking, and quasi-historical legends.[36] Women were depicted as either faithful or fallen. Exotic set-

---

[32] Mandrou, *Culture populaire*, p. 166.
[33] "Le marchand de gravures," *Magasin pittoresque*, 19 (1851), p. 321.
[34] Duchartre and Saulnier, *Imagerie parisienne*, p. 130.
[35] Alphonse de Lamartine, *Jocelyn* (Paris, 1925), nouvelle préface, pp. xxv-xxvi.
[36] Crubellier, *Histoire culturelle*, p. 74.

tings and improbable coincidences permitted temporary escape from the constraints of real life. Atala's tale includes several of these elements and so it appealed to the masses for many reasons. The virgin's commitment to her Christian vow produces intolerable conflict, ending in suicide; the lovers' idyll in the benevolent wilderness is never marred by mundane problems of what to eat or how to stay warm. Atala becomes a *vedette*, an example of the virtuous female. For over five decades her image is carried throughout the provinces and printers add multilingual captions in response to her widespread popularity.

II

Three major themes appear in the art work derived from *Atala*: Christian martyrdom, the Noble Savage in exotic America, and eroticism. The following analysis of these themes centers around those illustrations that are presently available (Figs. 1-17), although references are made to the subject matter of lost or as yet unpublished material.

The situation in which Atala finds herself is a fundamentally romantic predicament, because reason is paralyzed. Either way she decides it is wrong. Her choice between the fulfillment of a Christian vow and a normal life including sexual expression belongs to a tradition far older than romanticism. Within Christian teaching, the exaltation of the chaste life finds its origin in St. Paul, who was convinced that the celibate person could better devote him/herself to preparing for the Kingdom of God. He urged those who could to abstain from sex (I Cor. 7:8-9), and he even cautioned against marriage: "the unmarried woman or virgin is interested in the Lord's affairs . . . but the married woman is concerned . . . with how she may please her husband" (I Cor. 7:34).

The early Fathers of the Church elaborated upon the preferred state of virginity. It is outside the scope of this essay to present an outline of medieval thought on the matter. Let it suffice to mention Christendom's deep attachment to the saints known as virgin martyrs. Legends emphasized the ordeals these women endured for Christian conviction. St. Agatha and St. Agnes lost their lives but not their virginity. St. Lucy poked out her own eyes, rather than be tempted by the physical beauty of her fiancé (whom she eventually abandoned). St. Margaret succeeded in escaping an undesirable suitor, but she was swallowed by a dragon. (She escaped the dragon, too). Medieval legends such as these were part of the basic folklore in eighteenth-century France. Mandrou demonstrates their persistence in popular literature: the fame of SS. Barbara and Margaret "a passé les siècles."[37]

[37] Mandrou, *Culture populaire*, p. 92.

Chateaubriand's position within this tradition is clear. *Atala* was intended as part of *Le Génie du Christianisme*, an exposition of the richness of Christianity as a thematic source for literature, poetry, and art. In his view, it is beautiful to contemplate the sacrifice of a young girl who dies for her Christian virginity. Contemporary critics did not always agree. A satirical (and censored) poem from 1802 included the lines:

> Ci-gît la chrétienne Atala
> Qui _____
> Très moralement préféra
> Le suicide au mariage.[38]

It is, of course, obvious, that when the conflict of faith versus sex involves fatal results, it is a female dilemma. Celibate male saints, like SS. Augustine, Jerome, or Francis, waged internal struggles to conquer physical desire for women. "Dans nos vies de saints la femme est d'abord l'occasion du péché."[39] But, had they lost the battle, the consequence would not have been death. This points out the polarized view of women in traditional Christian thought. Atala is symbolic of both extremes: she is the faithful virgin, but she is sorely tempted to fall. And there is no middle ground.

The appearance of the theme in art in the early nineteenth century is particularly appropriate. Atala's story coincided with the romantic vogue for death and suicide. Northern gloominess was a prevalent malaise. Goethe's Werther read Ossianic poetry on the eve of his suicide. Byronic tragedies were subjects for salon paintings. The classically-trained Delacroix painted himself in the guise of Hamlet.

Among all the art works based on *Atala*, the heroine's death is the episode most commonly represented. It is safe to say that all the salon paintings depict the events surrounding her death — last rites, burials, funeral processions. The title of Henriette Lorimier's work, *Jeune fille près d'une fenêtre pleurant sur une page d'Atala*,[40] implies that Atala's fated demise has caused the tears. It is noteworthy that only Louis Hersent (Fig. 2) reminds us that Atala took her own life. This is possibly because, for all its morbid popularity, suicide was still a touchy subject. Chateaubriand had been severely attacked for his unorthodox theology: even an Indian Christian should know that suicide is a sin.[41]

---

[38] Hogu, "La Publication," p. 463, deleted the second line in this poem. It originally appeared as "Epitaphe d'Atala" in the *Journal de Paris*, 26 messidor, an IX. ·

[39] Mandrou, *Culture populaire*, p. 152.

[40] Lemonnier, "L'*Atala*," p. 365, mentions this apparently lost painting.

[41] For contemporary critical opinion on the novel, see Hogu, "La Publication," and H. Chatelain, "Les critiques d'*Atala* et les corrections de Chateaubriand," *Revue d'histoire littéraire de la France*, 9 (1902), pp. 414-440.

Generalizations are difficult in the decorative arts since the sampling is, at present, quite small. But among the objects we have catalogued it seems that there is less emphasis placed on death than in the fine arts. Events surrounding the maiden's death account for only four of the scenes on the plates from Choisy-le-Roi (Figs. 13 a-l). (Would it be offensive to find a funeral beneath your strawberry tart?) With the exception of Victoire Jacquotot's tribute to Girodet on the Sèvres plaque (see note 28), most of the porcelain objects, upholstery fabrics, and clocks that employ *Atala* motifs feature more pleasant episodes, such as *Atala Freeing Chactas* (Fig. 14).

In the popular arts, *Atala* prints were frequently issued in series of four. The common formula comprised the following events: (1) *Atala Freeing Chactas*; (2) *Flight of Atala and Chactas*; (3) *Père Aubry Finds the Lovers*; and (4) *Death of Atala*.[42] Thus Atala's death is only one scene out of four. This is interesting. The percentage of death scenes decreases from 100 percent in the salon art to as low as 25 percent in popular prints, a drop suggesting less fascination with idealized death on the part of *le peuple*.

In all the works Atala peacefully accepts death. She shows no regrets. François Grenier (1793-1867), in his *Death of Atala* of 1810, reportedly depicted Atala trying to remove her crucifix,[43] not in denial of her faith, but in order to leave it with Chactas as an aid to his conversion.

Chactas' reaction to Atala's death varies somewhat among the artistic representations. Being male and pagan, he was not a victim of conflict. In the novel he at first rages against the injustice of it all: "Périsse le Dieu qui contrarie la Nature!"[44] Only Ferdinand Delannoy hints of the lover's protest in his *Death of Atala* (Fig. 11). In the novel, Atala and Père Aubry are able to calm the Indian's passionate outbursts and he subsides into melancholy and grief. Chactas is usually depicted in this state. He crouches at Atala's feet, often bent over so that his face is hidden.

An anonymous print from Metz (Fig. 17) is, so far, our only available illustration of how Atala's death is presented in the popular arts. In this example the tragedy is de-emphasized. Chactas suffers from a headache, not from grief. Is this because the artist was relatively unsophisticated or is it deliberate? Do other popular prints show Atala's death the same way? The attitudes of the people toward a martyr's death could be deciphered from a deeper study of this material.

Père Aubry's role in Atala's death cannot be overlooked. In the novel, Chateaubriand assigns the priest several pages of impromptu homily,

---

[42] For lists of the usual subjects, see Weil, *Atala*, p. xlix; BN, *Centenaire*, nos. 97-98; and Savigny-sur-Orge, Syndicat d'initiatives, *Exposition Chateaubriand* (exhibition catalogue; Savigny-sur-Orge, 1952), nos. 113-116.

[43] BN, *Centenaire*, no. 84; the present location of Grenier's work is unknown.

[44] Weil, *Atala*, p. 96.

part of which involves telling Atala that the Bishop of Quebec could have released her from her mother's vow.[45] For the most part, though, he praises the beauties of a Christian death. In the arts, Père Aubry is often presented as the major figure. He takes over the scene because, in giving communion, he is the only active member. That is the case in the paintings by Mallet (Fig. 3), Lordon (Fig. 5), and in the Metz print (Fig. 17). Père Aubry leads the procession in Gautherot's work (Fig. 1). In the Delannoy illustration (Fig. 11) he is a benign God-the-Father figure. Due to this dominant role, he seems to approve her death.

Père Aubry on occasion looks strange, sometimes frightening, sometimes absurd. Girodet's priest, with his scowling face and overly-large hood, is an unnerving image. Père Aubry in Fig. 17 resembles a gnome with a "Santa Claus" face, and is too big in relation to the Indians. In Mallet's painting (Fig. 3) his intent expression borders on the deranged. Most disturbing, however, is the close physical relationship between Atala and the priest. Clad in flimsy gauze, she dies in his arms. Salon visitors were not upset by this, but similar popular prints circulating in Spain in 1818 were condemned by the reinstated Inquisition. According to one report, they showed Atala, "presque nue," attended by "un anachorète ou frère capuchin, dont l'attitude, bien que toujours convenable, pouvait être mal interprétée."[46]

It is also instructive to observe some of the stylistic characteristics which reinforce the theme of Christian martyrdom. In most of the death scenes one of the men supports the limp Atala by holding her shoulders. Often Chactas throws himself at her feet, like a Mary Magdalene at the feet of the dead Christ. These compositions are similar to traditional representations of the Lamentation or the Entombment of Christ.[47] The principle at work here is termed associative composition: by structuring a painting so that it recalls the compositions of other known works, the artist borrows some of the content of the other paintings and thereby adds deeper meaning to his own subject.

The same principle applies to Atala's facial expressions. Her upturned eyes and partly open mouth have their source in Baroque depictions of the martyrdom of saints. The best example of this type of work (though the subject is not a martyrdom, exactly) is Gianlorenzo Bernini's

[45] Richard Switzer, *Chateaubriand* (New York, 1971), p. 17, notes that this motif is rooted in the author's childhood. Once when he was seriously ill, his nurse vowed to the Virgin Mary that, if he recovered, she would always dress him in blue. He recovered, and the nurse kept the vow until it was revoked by a local priest.

[46] Jean Sarrailh, *Enquêtes romantiques* (Paris, 1933), p. 80.

[47] This comparison was first made by Antal, *Classicism*, p. 23; it was elaborated upon by George Levitine, "Some Unexplored Aspects of the Illustrations of *Atala*: the *surrenchères visuelles* of Girodet and Hersent," in R. Switzer, ed., *Chateaubriand Today* (Madison, Wisconsin, 1970), pp. 139-146.

sculpture, *The Ecstasy of St. Theresa* (S.M. della Vittoria, Rome; 1645-52). Her experience is a mixture of pain and pleasure. In like manner, Atala, though dying, registers the pleasures of martyrdom on her face.

Can some tentative conclusions be drawn about the theme of Christian martyrdom in the arts of *Atala*? It does seem that the emphasis on conflict and suicide was concentrated in, if not limited to, the upper classes who patronized the salons. It was the educated elite who contemplated melancholy. The religious dimension is more difficult to assess. Can we assume that the diffusion of *Atala* indicates a revived interest in Catholicism, as Antal suggests?[48] Christian themes began to appear in the salons with greater frequency after the Concordat of 1802. Is this also true for popular prints? Mistler notes that religious images reappeared after 1802, but that "l'imagerie populaire du XIXe siècle n'a réservé qu'une part de son activité aux gravures religieuses."[49] How do those prints that were religious in content relate to *Atala* prints? How do popular prints showing Atala's martyrdom differ from salon paintings of the same scene? Are any of the popular prints of *Atala* anti-clerical in content? Latreille discusses the difficulties in ascertaining the collective religious mentality of a people, and he suggests that their art forms could provide answers. The analysis of popular *Atala* prints might therefore be quite helpful. Clearly it is one area where additional visual material is necessary before our questions can be answered and our conclusions made.

The cult of the Noble Savage was basically an eighteenth-century French variation on the recurring human dream of an Earthly Paradise inhabited by naturally good people.[50] Ancient Greek poets wove tales about life in Arcadia, the Golden Age before worry and want afflicted mankind. In the Judeo-Christian tradition, history began with Eden and would end with a second and more permanent paradise. Medieval and Renaissance poetry and legends were dominated by this theme. Similar dreams affected the New World explorers. When the Spanish and Portuguese put out to sea they expected to find the Earthly Paradise still

[48] Antal, *Classicism*, p. 22.
[49] Mistler, *Epinal*, p. 61, continues: "c'est le culte de la gloire militaire, c'est la célébration de Napoléon qui a été sa source majeure d'inspiration."
[50] Bibliography on the theme of Paradise and on the cult of the Noble Savage is extensive. Some of the sources that have shaped our awareness of the topic include: Hoxie Neal Fairchild, *The Noble Savage: Study in Romantic Naturalism* (New York, 1928); Robert Beetem, "George Catlin in France: His Relationship to Delacroix and Baudelaire," *Art Quarterly*, 24 (1961), pp. 129-145; George Williams, *Wilderness and Paradise in Christian Thought* (New York, 1962); Henri Baudet, *Paradise on Earth: Some Thoughts on European Images of Non-European Man*, trans. by E. Wentholt (New Haven, 1965); Harry Levin, *The Myth of the Golden Age in the Renaissance* (Bloomington and London, 1969); and Frank E. and Fritzie P. Manuel, "Sketch for a Natural History of Paradise," *Daedalus*, Winter 1972, pp. 83-128.

flourishing. Naturally it would be peopled by a simple race much like the early Greeks or Hebrews. Columbus, for instance, had come prepared to communicate with the kind of natives he was sure he would find: his crew included a Jewish scholar who spoke Arabic and Chaldaic.[51] And when he reached the mouth of the Orinoco River, he was convinced that it was the boundary of the Earthly Paradise. In mortal fear of trespassing on holy ground, he fled back to Spain.[52] So it is not surprising that the actual inhabitants of the New World were identified with the mythical peoples of the old legends, likened to the wise Hebrew patriarchs, and hailed as the heirs of the Golden Age. Their primitive life style became an outward sign of their inward nobility. As Harry Levin comments, "life at its barest was somehow decked out with a set of trappings inherited from the learned conventions of literature."[53]

The cult of the wise and Noble Savage was enthusiastically embraced by French intellectuals. As early as 1580 Montaigne was insisting that Brazilian Indians be judged in their own context, and expounding his theory of the natural goodness of man, which he felt was more apparent in primitive peoples.[54] And, of course, there was Rousseau. His ideal of the primitive life, uncorrupted by civilization, had its affect on Chateaubriand. He revered Rousseau, who had shown the world a better way, who had put "parmi ses contemporains abâtardis l'homme vierge de la nature."[55] But in 1791, when Chateaubriand was confronted with the realities of Indian life in America, he was greatly disillusioned. The novel he wrote ten years later represents his fantasy of how it ought to have been.[56] The contrast between contemporary man and natural man is present throughout *Atala*. Chactas' initial conversation with René begins:

> C'est une singulière destinée, mon cher fils, que celle qui nous réunit. Je vois en toi l'homme civilisé qui s'est fait sauvage; tu vois en moi l'homme sauvage, que le grand Esprit (j'ignore pour quel dessein) a voulu civiliser. Entrés l'un et l'autre dans la carrière de la vie, par les deux bouts opposés, tu es venu te reposer à ma place, et j'ai été m'asseoir à la tienne: ainsi nous avons dû avoir des objets une vue totalement différente. Qui de toi ou de moi, a le plus gagné ou le plus perdu à ce changement de position? C'est ce que savent les Génies, dont le moins savant a plus de sagesse que tous les hommes ensemble.[57]

[51] Baudet, *Paradise*, p. 26.
[52] Manuel, "Sketch," pp. 118-119.
[53] Levin, *Myth*, p. 60.
[54] Baudet, *Paradise*, p. 29.
[55] Jean Mourot, *Etudes sur les premières oeuvres de Chateaubriand* (Paris, 1962), p. 207. I would like to thank Ms. Louise Scott for this reference.
[56] Switzer, *Chateaubriand*, p. 98.
[57] Weil, *Atala*, p. 35.

The diffusion of the cult of the Noble Savage in the visual arts is of great importance to our study of *Atala* paintings and prints. In the last two decades of the eighteenth century, European and American artists alike depicted primitive people as neoclassical heroes. In other words, the Indian was made to look just like Poussinesque Arcadian shepherds.[58] Wright of Derby, an English painter, gave an *Indian Widow* (Derby Museum and Art Gallery; 1875) Caucasian features and draped her in a loose flowing robe with one breast bared.[59] The American painter Benjamin West set a Michelangelesque Indian in the contemplative pose of a classical philosopher in his *Death of General Wolfe* (National Gallery of Canada; 1770). This same artist delighted his European companions in Rome when, upon seeing the Apollo Belvedere, he exclaimed, "My God, how like a Mohawk warrior!"[60] French artists shared the passion. They painted characters from Marmontel's *Les Incas* as classically-built Amazons, and they showed Chateaubriand's three protagonists in the same way, as we shall soon demonstrate.

At this point, however, someone like T.J. Clark would ask what forces prevented artists from using other racial types (for instance, Turks, Arabs, or Blacks) to portray American Indians? Why did Benjamin West, who knew what American Indians looked like, enlarge the physical size and alter the color of his figures? And none of the European painters had, as yet, even seen an Indian. Most would not have that opportunity until 1845 when the American painter George Catlin brought some Iowa Indians to France. Their visit reinforced the strength of the cult of the Noble Savage.[61] An answer to the quandry would probably be based on three factors: namely, (1) the undeniable tenacity of the classical tradition in French painting; (2) the existence of the Black slave trade; and (3) the Islamic faith of Turks and Arabs. The first factor is obvious. The second factor dates back to the age of exploration when Indians, in contrast to Black Africans, were considered amenable to Christian conversion and also lacking in the strength and stamina necessary for heavy labor.[62] Thus the stereotypes already built up about Blacks preserved for the Indians a more noble future. As for the Moslems, the European Christian had been

[58] A similar process occurred with heroes from Ossian. Girodet's *Death of Comala* is one of the many examples given by Henry Okun, "Ossian in Painting," *Journal of the Warburg and Courtauld Institutes*, 30 (1967), pp. 327-356. Okun, p. 329, states that Ossian paralleled Rousseau and preceded *Atala*: "His warriors are the northern counterparts of the noble savage. Fingal, the leader, is brave, noble, loyal. . . . His maidens are virginal."

[59] A reproduction of *Indian Widow* is available in Robert Rosenblum, *Transformations in Late 18th-Century Art* (Princeton, 1967), fig. 42.

[60] James T. Flexner, *History of American Painting, II (1760-1835): The Light of Distant Skies* (New York, 1954), p. 7.

[61] Beetem, "Catlin," p. 130.

[62] Baudet, *Paradise*, p. 30.

Fig. 1

C. Normand, engraving after Pierre Gautherot, *Funeral Procession of Atala*, 1802 (photo: H. Lemonnier, "L'*Atala* de Chateaubriand et l'*Atala* de Girodet," *Gazette des Beaux-Arts*, 11 [1914], 366).

Fig. 2
C. Normand, engraving after Louis Hersent, *Atala Committing Suicide in Chactas'*
Arms, 1806 (photo: C.-P. Landon, *Annales du Musée* [Paris, 1806], pl. 43).

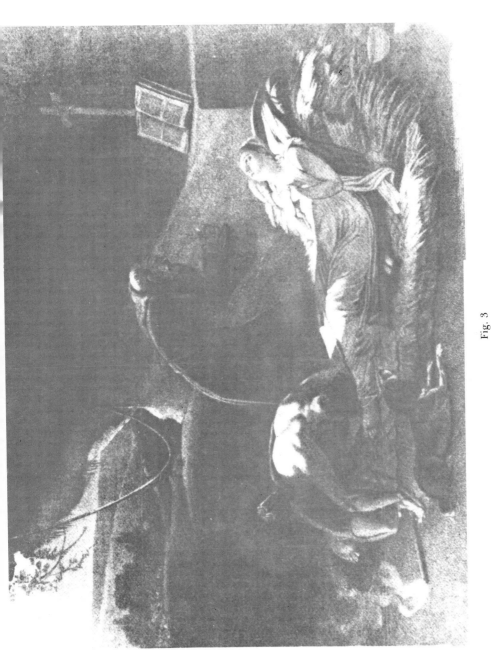

Fig. 3

Engraving after Jean-Baptiste Mallet, *Last Communion of Atala*, before 1808
(photo: Lemonnier, "*L'Atala*," p. 367).

Fig. 4

Anne-Louis Girodet, *Death of Atala*, 1808, Louvre (photo: Musée de national).

Fig. 5

E. Lingée, engraving after Jérôme Lordon, *Last Communion of Atala*, 1808, Villa Carlotta, Tremezzo (photo: C.-P. Landon, *Annales du Musée* [Paris, 1808], I, pl. 43).

Fig. 6

Auguste de St.-Aubin, *Chactas Leaving Lopez*, engraving from Le Normant edition of *Atala*, 1805 (photo: Letessier edition, *Atala, René, les aventures du dernier Abencérage* [Paris, 1958]).

Fig. 7

Auguste de St.-Aubin, *The Maiden of Last Love*, engraving from LeNormant
edition of *Atala*, 1805 (photo: Letessier edition, *Atala*).

Fig. 8

Auguste de St.-Aubin, *Père Aubry Discovers the Lovers*, engraving from LeNormant
edition of *Atala*, 1805 (photo: Letessier edition, *Atala*).

Fig. 9

Ferdinand Delannoy, *Atala Freeing Chactas*, engraving from Lecou edition, François-René de Chateaubriand, *Oeuvres complètes* (Paris, 1850), IV, facing p. 544.

Fig. 10

Ferdinand Delannoy, *Death of Atala*, engraving from Lecou edition, *Oeuvres complètes*, IV, facing p. 608.

Fig. 11
Ferdinand Delannoy, *Death of Atala*, engraving from Garnier edition, François-René de Chateaubriand, *Oeuvres complètes* (Paris, 1859), III, facing p. 60.

Fig. 12

Charles Geoffroy, *Atala*, engraving from Lecou edition, *Oeuvres complètes*, **IV**,
facing p. 472.

Fig. 13a

Fig. 13b

Fig. 13c

Fig. 13d

Fig 13e

Fig 13f

Fig. 13 (a)-(f)

Octagonal dessert plates from the imperial factory at Choisy-le-Roi, ca. 1808-10, now in J.-P. Dauriac collection (photo: J.-P. Dauriac, "*Atala* in Choisy-le-Roi: A Novel Illustrated on French Plates," *Gebrauchsgraphik*, 41 [1970], 48-51): reading left to right, top to bottom — (a) *Chactas Leaving Lopez*; (b) *Atala Freeing Chactas*; (c) *Atala and Chactas in the Forest*; (d) *Atala Prays Not To Succumb*; (e) *Atala and Chactas on the River*; (f) *Père Aubry Discovers the Lovers*.

Fig. 13g

Fig. 13h

Fig. 13i

Fig. 13j

Fig 13k

Fig 13l

Fig. 13 (g)-(l)

(g) *Chactas Puts the Rose of Fertility on Atala's Forehead*; (h) *Atala Tells Her Story*; (i) *Last Communion of Atala*; (j) *Chactas Carrying Atala to the Grave*; (k) *Burial of Atala*; (l) *Chactas Mourning at Atala's Grave*.

Fig. 14

Bronze mantle clock, *Atala Freeing Chactas*, ca. 1815, now in Roger Imbert collection (photo: S. Faniel, *Le XIXe siècle français* [Paris, 1957], p. 137).

Fig. 15

Anonymous color engraving, *Atala and Chactas on the River*, now in Le Savoureux

ATTALA DÉLIVRE CHACTAS.

Chactas était fils du Guerrier Outalissi, chef de la nation des Natchez qui habitaient le beau pays des Florides. Il fut prisonnier dans un combat contre les Muscogulges en suivant l'usage il devait être brulé lorsqu'Attala fille du galant Simaghan touchée de la jeunesse et de la beauté du jeune sauvage profita des ombres de la nuit pour le dégager de ses liens, lui donne des armes & s'enfonce avec lui dans le désert et le soustrait à la mort.

ATALA LIBERTA CHACTAS.

Chactas hijo del guerrero Otalisi, Gefe de la nacion de los Nachetes que habitaban el buen pais de los Floridos, fue prisionero en una batalla contra los Muscogales; el cual segun costumbre debia ser quemado, cuando Atala hija del valiente Simaghan, movida de la hermosura del joven salvage, valiose de las tinieblas de la noche para soltarle los lazos; le da armas, y se oculta con el en el desierto, librandole la vida.

Atala befreit Chactas. Chactas war der Sohn des Kriegers Utalisses, Anführer Natchez, Bewohner der schönen Florida. Er wurde in einem Treffen gegen die Muscogulen gefangen und gemäß der Sitte sollte er verbrannt werden, als Attala, die Tochter des tapfern Simoauken; aber von der Schönheit des jungen Wilden, das Dunkel der Nacht benutzte, um ihn aus seinen Banden zu befreien, ihm Waffen verschaffte und sie mit in die Wüste hineinbringt und ihn dem Tode entzieht.

Fig. 16

Anonymous color engraving, *Atala Freeing Chactas*, ca. 1840-52, from Fabrique d'estampes de Gangel, Metz, now in Armand Weil collection (photo: A. Weil, "Chateaubriand à l'étranger, ou le rayonnement du génie français au début du XIXe siècle," *L'Information littéraire*, 1 [1949], p. 184).

MORT D'ATTALA.

Le lendemain Attala ouvrit ses beaux yeux, en tendit une main défaillante à son bien aimé qui était à genoux près d'elle. puis d'une voix faible elle lui dit: ami je vais mourir. Bon Père je vais vous avouer mon fatal secret. Prête à succomber à mon amour pour Chactas, j'ai pris un poison violent, je vais rendre mon ame à Dieu, qu'il ait pitié de moi. Attala vécut encore un jour, elle reçut la S.te Hostie en s'endormit dans le Seigneur.

MUERTE DE ATALA.

El dia siguiente despertandose Atala, extendio su debilitado brazo hacia su amante arrodillado à su lado en seguida le dice con una voz debil; amigo, voy à morir. Padre mio. quisiera confesarle un fatal secreto mui cerca de sucumbir à mi amor para con Chactas, he bebido un veneno violento voy à entregar mi alma à Dios. que tenga piedad de mi. Atala vivio aun un dia; recibio la sagrada Comunion y dio su alma al Redentor.

Tod Attala's. Am andern Morgen, als sie ihre schöne Augen öffnete, reichte sie ihre bebende Hand ihrem Geliebten, welcher vor ihr kniete und sagte zu ihm mit schwacher Stimme; Freund, ich bin meinem Ende nahe;" "Guter Vater, ich will Ihnen mein verhängnißvolles Geheimniß bekennen ... eine Liebe für Chactas beherrschte mich, ich habe ein wüthendes Gift genommen und will dem Herrn meine Seele empfehlen, daß er sich meiner erbarme;" Attala lebte noch einen Tag, empfing die h. Wegzehrung und entschlief im Herrn.

Fig. 17

Anonymous color engraving, *Death of Atala*, ca. 1840-52, from Fabrique d'estampes de Gangel, Metz, now in Armand Weil collection (photo: Weil, "Chateaubriand à l'étranger," p. 185).

convinced for centuries that they were his enemies. The Arabs and the Turks, although certainly savage, had too often been the villains to now be considered wise, benevolent, or noble.

In our analysis of the Noble Savage theme in the arts of *Atala*, we concentrate on stylistic characteristics, because the use of the neoclassical mode in these works indicates the application of the cult to American Indians. Chactas is a perfect example. In nearly all the works he is Caucasian. He is only a little darker in the Delannoy print (Fig. 10). Lemonnier commented that Dugorc, in his *Death of Atala* (no reproduction available), "parait avoir confondu, à propos de Chactas, le type nègre avec le type indien."[63] Actually, no one at that time painted "le type indien."

Chactas is nearly nude in many of the works, completely nude in St.-Aubin's engraving (Fig. 7). In the works by Girodet (Fig. 4), Hersent (Fig. 2), and Delannoy (Fig. 10), Chactas has insecurely-anchored loin draperies. A slight variation on classical nudity is the short cloth or feather skirt that Chactas wears in most of the other works.

The muscular torso of this Noble Savage is generally emphasized by his positioning. He crouches or kneels so that his shoulders are prominent. Girodet's Chactas has rippling shoulder muscles that are worthy of a Hercules. St.-Aubin's Chactas, too, is of sculptural proportions. The anonymous bronze caster who formed Chactas' body on Imbert's mantle clock (Fig. 14) created a sensuous finish reminiscent of the Renaissance master, Donatello. The popular printmakers were less interested in giving Chactas the body of an Olympian. Instead, in Figs. 15, 16, and 17, the Noble Savage has an unarticulated chest. His body is too smooth, and by classical standards a bit paunchy.

Classical artists rarely showed a female entirely nude. Instead they teased their public by using the "wet drapery" technique. That is, a woman's clothing is sculpted or painted so thin and transparent that it clings to the body as if wet. This is the procedure used for Atala. Imbert's clock (Fig. 14) provides a good example of "wet drapery" possibly because the device is predominantly sculptural. Atala's diaphanous peplum features tassles, the artist's way of indicating her exotic origin. Girodet's Atala is so thinly covered that her nipples are visible. And following the best eighteenth-century tradition, Auguste de St.-Aubin leaves her breasts bare (Figs. 7-8). St.-Aubin was the oldest of the artists who used the *Atala* theme. He had studied under the Rococo master François Boucher, who delighted in cotton-candy nymphs. The billowing drapery that emphasizes Atala's rounded forms is quite within that manner. Drapery

[63] Lemonnier, *L'Atala*, p. 368.

blown around by a wind that affects nothing else was a classical device used to add dramatic movement. It is found in the Choisy-le-Roi plate that is taken from St.-Aubin (Fig. 13f) and is also employed by Hersent (Fig. 2). His *Atala Committing Suicide* is the most dramatic of all these paintings, objects, and prints, because Atala is in movement.

The only departures from the Greek mode of showing Atala are found in popular prints. In Le Savoureux's (Fig. 15) she wears a fashionable gown, gathered under the breasts in what is still known as an "empire waistline." Of course its source is basically Greek, but its appearance here suggests contemporary fashion. The elaborate coiffures worn by both Atala and Chactas in the print reinforce this impression. In Fig. 16 Atala wears a large bow at her waist — a decorative addition that would never be tolerated on the image of a Greek maiden because it violates the law of simplicity.

The poses in which Atala and Chactas are presented are also common in classical art. Chactas often stands in *contrapposto* (Figs. 8, 13d, 13f, 13h). He kneels like a Roman soldier before a commander in Figs. 6 and 13a. In the plate of "Atala praying not to succumb" (Fig. 13d) they assume *Noli me tangere* positions: Atala kneels and prays as if she were Mary Magdalene reaching out for the Christ who forbids her to come closer. In our example, Chactas raises a cautionary hand. The content has been garbled, in respect to both the *Noli me tangere* message and the novel, in which Chactas hopes she will succumb. Nevertheless the reference remains as another suggestion of Atala's conflict.

A final indication of neo-classical aesthetics within the arts of *Atala* is that the scenes chosen for representation generally involve controlled emotions and refined thought. The mutual respect the savages accord each other is emphasized. Chateaubriand's novel includes violent and exciting events: Indian warfare, electrical storms, young people about to make love. But the early romantic artists were still bound by the strict conventions of academic propriety and limited their content accordingly.

In surveying the image of the Noble Savage in the arts of *Atala*, one finds that the Greek ideal is less apparent in popular prints. In these examples Chactas is soft and tender, lacking in tragic nobility. Atala wears fancy dresses, more like a fashion model than a goddess. The classical mode suggests a utopian, unspoiled civilization. Is it replaced in popular imagery by the vision of a society in which lovely clothes and elegant coiffures suggest the affluent life? Whether or not additional representations will bear this out remains to be seen.

Closely tied to the cult of the Noble Savage was the fascination with exotic lands on the part of many artists in the early nineteenth century.

Faraway countries with strange people and natural features unknown in France were places to which one's imagination could escape. America's vast size and variety made her a perfect setting. Chateaubriand visited America in 1791, having prepared beforehand by studying itineraries and journals written by previous European travellers in the New World. He never saw the Mississippi. The rich natural description in *Atala* comes primarily from his reading:

> Suspendus sur le cours des eaux, groupes sur les rochers et sur les montagnes, dispersés dans les vallées, des arbres de toutes les formes, de toutes les couleurs, de tous les parfums, se mêlent, croissent ensemble, montent dans les airs à des hauteurs qui fatiguent les regards. Les vignes sauvages, les bignonias, les coloquintes, s'entrelacent au pied de ces arbres, escaladent leurs rameaux, grimpent à l'extrémité des branches, s'élancent de l'érable au tulipier, du tulipier à l'alcée, en formant mille grottes, mille voûtes, mille portiques.[64]

The artists responded to this view of America. And though their Indians were all Greek, their landscapes were not. Girodet set the standard in his carefully planned painting (Fig. 4). Atala dies in a dark gothic cave whose otherwise bare walls are inscribed with Père Aubry's meditational verse from Job: "J'ai passé comme une fleur; j'ai séché comme l'herbe des champs." Outside the cave grow a profusion of bushes, trees, ferns, and flowers, parting near the top to reveal a lone cross. This formula was followed by Mallet (Fig. 3), Lordon (Fig. 5), the designer of the Choisy-le-Roi plates (Figs. 13g, 13i) and by the Metz engraver (Fig. 17).

A second interpretation of America's exotic landscape focused on mountainous terrain. The natural rock bridge, under which Atala was buried, was a particularly impressive image. This environment is presented by Gautherot, the earliest artist to be inspired by the novel. He illustrates the episode in which Chactas and Père Aubry carry the virgin's body down to her grave:

> Je chargeai le corps sur mes épaules; l'hermite marchoit devant moi, une bêche à la main. Nous commençâmes à descendre de rochers en rochers, la vieillesse et la mort ralentissoient également nos pas.[65]

---

[64] Weil, *Atala*, p. 29. Many scholars have attempted to determine the accuracy of Chateaubriand's writings on America. Foremost among them is Gilbert Chinard, *L'exotisme américain dans l'oeuvre de Chateaubriand* (Paris, 1918). See also J.-M. Gautier, *L'exotisme américain dans l'oeuvre de Chateaubriand: Etude de vocabulaire* (Manchester, 1951); and Switzer, *Chateaubriand*, pp. 89-104, who provides a good summary of the problem.

[65] Weil, *Atala*, p. 116.

"From rock to rock" becomes a descent of the Grand Canyon. A similar presentation is Delannoy's (Fig. 10). And the rocky terrain appears in the Choisy-le-Roi plates (Figs. 13j, 13l). In this case, the small format requires that a few boulders serve to suggest mountains.

The third interpretation of the exotic American wilderness comes closer to the actual terrain of Florida (Chateaubriand implied that the foliage of the entire east bank of the Mississippi was of an Evergladian density). Charles Geoffroy (Fig. 12) shows Atala demurely sitting in a lush grove whose cave-like form also recalls Girodet. St.-Aubin fills every corner of Figs. 7 and 8 with foliage. Deciduous trees have been inappropriately added to the jungle, but they do not detract from the total effect. His engraving of Chactas asking Lopez' permission to return to the forest (Fig. 6) includes palm trees that are convincing (and distant mountains that are not).

The popular prints each follow this third interpretation. In Le Savoureux's print (Fig. 15), ferns and branches encroach upon the river from three sides. It is dark and crowded, but not particularly frightening. The engravings from Metz (Figs. 16 and 17) are both lush, flower-filled. Odd plants grow in every available location. A banana tree rises behind Atala in Fig. 16. The flatness of the image and the presence of the two pudgy natives bear resemblance to later works by Paul Gaugin and "Douanier" Rousseau. The relationships between the paintings of well-known "primitive" artists and the popular prints merit further exploration.[66]

So it could be said that book illustrators and popular engravers produce scenes that more successfully evoke the exotic Florida jungle. Is this never-never land of Atala and Chactas another example of escapism that, according to Mandrou, pervades the popular arts?[67] Coming to some conclusions will involve investigating sources available to the artists, such as travel books and journals like the *Magasin pittoresque* (founded in 1833), and other interpretations of America, the New Eden, home of the Noble Savage.

The third theme to be traced throughout the art devoted to Atala's story is that of eroticism. Of course, individual reactions to particular scenes may vary — eroticism is in the eye of the beholder. Our primary intention here is to note when and how the artists intended their images to be suggestive, and what implications may be involved in those presentations.

Chateaubriand may be compared to the English author Richardson

[66] Switzer, *Chateaubriand*, p. 42, compares the plot and organization of the novel *Atala* to the work of "Douanier" Rousseau.

[67] Mandrou, *Culture populaire*, p. 163: "La *Bibliothèque bleue*, pour ses lecteurs et auditeurs à la veillée, c'est d'abord d'une évasion."

(*Pamela, Clarissa*) and to the French artist Greuze (*Broken Eggs, The Morning Prayer*). His story, like their novels and paintings, pretends to set a moral example for young girls, but instead, sensuality abounds. Some critics were offended. They claimed that telling a love story of a woman who commits suicide because she cannot have intercourse with her lover is a strange way of evangelizing for the Christian faith.[68] Throughout the novel Atala admits her physical desires: "Si je me penche sur toi, je frémis."[69] Yet she is torn by conflict. The contradictions come to a climax when, during a spectacular cloudburst, and at the very moment preceding intimate contact, Atala drinks the poison she had hidden within her clothing. Chateaubriand's language leaves no doubt that the storm reflects the sexual agitation of the lovers:

> Désormais les combats d'Atala alloient devenir inutiles: en vain je la sentis porter une main à son sein, et faire un mouvement extraordinaire; déjà je l'avois saisie, déjà je m'étois enivré de son souffle, déjà j'avois bu toute la magie de l'amour sur ses lèvres. Les yeux levés vers le ciel, à la lueur des éclairs, je tenois mon épouse dans mes bras, en présence de l'Eternel . . . je touchois au moment du bonheur, quand tout-à-coup un impétueux éclair, suivi d'un éclat de la foudre, sillonne l'épaisseur des ombres, remplit la forêt de soufre et de lumière, et brise un arbre à nos pieds.[70]

An artistic prototype for this combination of physical pleaure and religious intensity has already been mentioned: it is Bernini's *St. Theresa*. Theresa's vision of a heavenly visitor who pierced her innermost depths with his flaming golden arrow is translated into visible form. The angel stands above her. She is limp, her head is thrown back, eyes upturned (and closed), and her mouth open. Bernini's statue was an influence on Baroque and eighteenth-century artists, and the motif persisted into the nineteenth century. It is found in the expression on Atala's face as she prepares for her last communion in the paintings by Mallet and Lordon. Salon visitors would have recognized the motif due to their awareness of ecstatic martyrdoms in other paintings. This, again, is associative composition. The convention is also at work in Delannoy's *Death of Atala* (Fig. 10) where her euphoric expression refers to the pleasure she has found in martyrdom.

We noticed in discussing Atala as a Grecian savage that her breasts were sometimes bare and that her clothing was minimal, even transparent.

---

[68] Sarrailh, *Enquêtes*, p. 69.
[69] Weil, *Atala*, pp. 65-66.
[70] Ibid., p. 75.

Such classical modes may also serve to increase the erotic content of the works. Girodet offers the most subtle touch in this regard. He paints Atala's drapery so thin that the contours of her breasts are clearly marked. Then he has allowed the top of the crucifix she holds to rest just behind her right breast, so that its light brown color and its texture emphasize the shape of her erect nipple.[71] In addition to drawing one's eyes to Atala's bosom, this device reasserts the body/soul conflict that caused her death.

An analysis of eroticism in Chactas alone would, to some extent, duplicate the comments already made concerning his classical physique. One additional point might be made. In Fig. 7 Chactas is tied to a tree by a rope around his waist. As he hears Atala approach he twists around to see her, thereby assuming a more modest position. The crucial manoeuver causes the viewer's imagination to draw the scene as it might have been a moment before. A similar phenomenon nearly occurs in Fig. 13b, in which, due to poor technical ability, the designer has made Chactas' torso too long.

There are basically three ways the artists present erotic content when showing Atala and Chactas together. The first is the familiar manner in which she is held in her dying scenes. In the paintings by Lordon and Girodet, Chactas embraces her with abandon. Père Aubry in the Girodet (and in those works influenced by it) supports her under the arms, his fingers pressing against her breast.[72] We recall that prints with passages like this were condemned in Spain. Atala and Chactas are also shown standing in an embrace. The scene represented in Figs. 8 and 13f is the same one quoted just above, but St.-Aubin is somewhat restrained. He gives only a little hint of the emotional storm that Père Aubry has just interrupted. Louis Hersent (Fig. 2) is more explicit. The lovers are wound together in a spiral, Chactas' legs enfolding the lower half of Atala's body. The convention employed here is an old one; when sexual intimacy was the subject matter, Renaissance and Baroque artists implied it by placing one lover's leg over the other's. It was a discreet symbol that all understood.[73]

A third example of eroticism in these works is found in the plates from Choisy-le-Roi. Atala puts her hand on Chactas' knee as they float down the river (Fig. 13e). In another scene, as she tells her story (Fig. 13h), she gestures with her hand aiming under his thigh. These gestures implying

[71] This may be difficult to see in our reproduction. Consult Marcel Brion, *Romantic Art* (London, 1960), pl. LI.

[72] An identical motif is present in Henri-Pierre Danloux's *Deluge of 1802* (reproduced in *The Detroit Institute of Arts, French Painting 1774-1830: The Age of Revolution* [exhibition catalogue; Detroit, 1975], pl. 184): a man holds his drowned wife with his left hand near her breast. Since Girodet could have seen this painting in the salon of that year, it may have been an influence on his *Atala* of 1808.

[73] Leo Steinberg, "Michelangelo's Florentine *Pietà*: The Missing Leg," *Art Bulletin*, 50 (1968), pp. 343-353, traces this convention.

possession are less obvious than Hersent's intertwined bodies because it is a good woman (not a fallen one) who is making them, almost by accident.

In conclusion, then, the salon paintings include a certain amount of erotic content through their references to traditional devices. Examples from the decorative arts and in the expensive LeNormant edition of *Atala* (illustrated by St.-Aubin) contain passages that are more explicitly sexual, possibly due to a more intimate nature of their audience, i.e., only a small number of people can admire a book or a plate at any one time. These art forms appealed, in large part, to the same *haute bourgeoisie* and elite classes which patronized the salons. Examples of popular art are noticeably absent from my discussion of the theme of eroticism. It does not appear that any of the prints currently available contains suggestive elements, unless the gentle embrace in Fig. 15 could be so interpreted. Other surviving prints need to be found and studied. It would be fascinating to discover if they differ from the upper class works in which sexual references play a large role, because it might indicate some of the attitudes toward sex on the part of *le peuple*. A more thorough analysis of *Atala* in the popular arts may help determine why the novel had such great appeal, and why so many "auberges de rouliers étaient ornées de gravures rouges, vertes et bleues" that presented Chateaubriand's story to a wider audience.[74]

[74] *Atala* in the popular arts is part of my doctoral dissertation, which is being written at the University of Wisconsin-Madison, under the direction of Professor Robert Beetem. I have also received valuable assistance from Professor Edward Gargan and Professor Lorin Uffenbeck.

Hugh Honour's *The European Vision of America* (exhibition catalogue; Cleveland, 1975), which features a chapter on *Atala*, unfortunately appeared too late to be consulted for this article.

14

The Bar at the Folies-Bergères*

TIMOTHY J. CLARK

In the Salon of 1882 Manet put on show a big picture, more than three feet high and four feet wide, of a bar at the Folies-Bergères. It was his last large-scale painting of Parisian life, and the last painting he sent to the Salon; he died in April 1883 at the age of 51. The *Bar* was shown again in the Manet memorial exhibition the following year, and it very soon came to seem a satisfactory last painting, a summing-up of Manet's strategies and preoccupations for two decades. It fetched the highest price in the sale of Manet's pictures in February 1884 — 5,850 francs, paid by Emmanuel Chabrier.[1]

The *Bar* will do as a final painting. It harks back to the pictures Manet did in the 1860's, pictures like *Olympia* or the two *Déjeuners*, in the studio or on the grass. The same dead-pan face confronts us, the same frozen posture, the same compacted space; and, as the mark of the *Bar's* finality, all these old materials are arranged here without striking us as strange, as somehow dislocated. That is the difference from the pictures of the 1860's. The order of the *Bar* — the first order, the immediate arrangement of the thing — is almost stately. It has the quality of a proof, a demonstration. And perhaps that is partly a question of subject-matter. The subject here is thick with meanings. It is a subject that the avant-garde had already spent a decade describing. The *Bar* is a picture of the café-concert of the early 1880's.

We can ask two kinds of question about the *Bar aux Folies-Bergères*. Questions about its order, its arrangement of people and things. And questions about how that order and this subject-matter are articulated. How much are they part of each other? How much does it matter that

* The research for this article was financed in part by a Research Fellowship from the Leverhulme Trust. The argument altered under pressure from various people I worked with at U.C.L.A. in 1974-76. In particular I am grateful for the criticism of Karl Werckmeister, Tom Crow and Julius Kaplan.
1 See J. Meier-Graefe, *Edouard Manet* (Munich, 1912), pp. 317-331, for list of paintings in sale, with prices and purchasers. Cited in G.H. Hamilton, *Manet and His Critics* (Norton edition, New York, 1969), p. 271, n. 2.

Manet chose this peculiar location? Why did he make it the site of his last investigation of *modernité*? It seems as though in the years round 1880 Manet was gearing himself to deal once again with modern life, with the ordinary imagery of modernity, I mean, the banalities of the *faits divers* and the *roman feuilleton*. In April 1879 he wrote a formal letter to the prefect of the Seine, asking to paint a series of murals for the new Hôtel-de-Ville, "une série de compositions représentant, pour me servir d'une expression d'aujourd'hui consacrée et qui peint bien ma pensée, le *Ventre de Paris*, avec les diverses corporations se mouvant dans leur milieu, la vie publique et commerciale de nos jours. J'aurais Paris-Halles, Paris-Chemins de fer, Paris-Port, Paris-Souterrains, Paris-Courses et jardins."[2] In 1880 the chief engineer of the Compagnie de Chemins de Fer de l'Ouest gave Manet permission to make studies in one of the company's depots for a painting of "une machine-locomotive montée par son mécanicien et son chauffeur."[3]

Neither of these projects came to anything. The prefect did not even reply, and the close-up study of stoker and engine-driver at work was never done. But the projects themselves are evidence, and what is unexpected here is the directness — the *naïveté*, the crudity almost — of the imagery Manet is proposing. What did he mean by the invocation of Emile Zola, just two years after the scandal of *L'Assommoir*? And what did the promise to paint *Paris-Souterrains* signify, if not some kind of ironic response to the cartoonists' reference, year-in year-out, to Monsieur Manet's predilection for sewer-workers and degenerates recruited from some *dépot de mendicité*?[4] Part of this may have been provocation, but part at least was in earnest, right down to the engine sheds. It was time to look at Paris again head-on, time to try once more for "some new imagery . . . something long hidden, but suddenly revealed. Captivating and repulsive at the same time, eccentric, and new, such types as he gave us were needed in our ambient life." The phrases are Mallarmé's, looking back to Manet's work of the 1860's.[5] They apply again, to *Un Bar aux Folies-Bergères*.

[2] Cited in E. Moreau-Nelaton, *Manet raconté par lui-même* (Paris, 1926), II, p. 97.
[3] Letter from Ernest Mayer, cited in *Manet raconté par lui-même et par ses amis*, ed. by P. Cailler (Lausanne, 1953), I, pp. 200-201.
[4] I am thinking, for instance, of Bertall's caricature in *Le Journal Amusant*, 27 May 1865; of Manet's *Jésus insulté par les soldats*, the picture that accompanied *Olympia* in the 1865 Salon. The caption reads: "*Le Bain des Pieds*, par M. Manet. Quatre employés du grand égout collecteur se proposant de faire prendre un bain de pieds à un vieux chiffonnier de leurs amis qui n'en avait jamais pris. — Etonnement du chiffonnier." Compare Félix Deriège, writing in *Le Siècle* on 2 June 1865: "J'imaginé que l'artiste est allé choisir ses types dans un dépot de mendicité, et qu'il a cherché dans la hotte d'un chiffonnier les guenilles dont il les a vêtus." Such as it was, the joke went on being repeated through the 1870's.
[5] In an article entitled "The Impressionists and Edouard Manet," in the *Art Monthly Review*, 30 September 1876. Even in the courageous, but tortured, hopeless English translation, which is all we have, the article is fundamental: the only adequate writing on the subject done

The *Bar* is a painting of surfaces: that is the first and last thing we notice about it. It begins as a painted surface, as something literally flat, seeded with signatures of its own flatness: the thick-painted, pasty circles of the hanging lamps, the neat intersection of woman's head and halo of chandelier at top right, the knowing way the red triangle on the obligatory bottle of Bass at the right is turned just a little too much towards us, so that it lifts off on to the painted surface. Even a device which does most to establish the picture's strange, unfolding spaces — I mean the dry, scumbled marks which register dazzle or discoloration on the glass of the mirror behind the girl, and which conjure up the mirror and its spaces for us — even this indicator of depth is treated in a way which makes it at the same time so much pigment, calling attention back to its own depth, or lack of it. And that in turn, we shall see, becomes part of a complex dialectic. The surface of the mirror is and has to be the surface of the picture. That is basic to the insistence with which it — what we find it contains — pulls apart our sense of what we see. If we could make the mirror *not* the painting — if we could make it a part of the painting, something that is painted rather than the reality *of* the painting — we could bracket off its interference with our gaze and our appetites. (Compare, for example, Magritte's mirror-pictures: the essentially harmless strangeness of all these mis-reflections which are merely in a mirror, not in the painting, not in seeing itself.)

The *Bar* is a surface, and yet of course the *Bar* is not flat. It is full, first of all, of a greasy fatness of form, a putting down of substance and texture, particularly in the objects lined up on the counter under our noses. How the bourgeois critics, robbed of their barmaid, lap up the oranges and the silver paper on the champagne! And in answer to their naive consumption of the still life, does not the most cogent kind of dissatisfaction with the *Bar* fasten on the pulpy self-consciousness of the painting here and elsewhere in the picture, the quality of performance?[6] It is a cogent objection, especially in view of Manet's painting in the 1860's: the kinds of harsh conciseness in the brushwork there, the refusal of fullness, the pressing out of everything flat and even.[7] And if the over-ripeness has a function in the *Bar* — I think it has — it can only be grasped as part of the whole picture's mis-matching of parts, its different ways of seeing and painting what is seen. This is a picture where *continuity* of surface — the kind you

in the nineteenth century, and in many ways the strangest piece of prose Mallarmé ever wrote. In the course of feeling for an appropriate explanation of the avant-garde achievement in his time, Mallarmé seems to sabotage — deliberately? — all his most carefully preserved "positions" on art.

[6] Best expressed to me in conversation by Jonathon Adamson.

[7] Looking for ways to convey this central characteristic of Manet's work in the 1860's, Zola oscillated in an arbitrary way between *acre* and *âpre* and their cognates. The typographical monotone works, oddly: it gets across something of the insistence of the style it describes.

find in *Olympia*, for instance — would be out of place, a reassurance.

But what breaks the surface completely is not the stuff on the counter but the realisation of how shallow the "real" space of the picture is. The mirror appears, and with it a space in which we ought to be included. The mirror is an invitation *into* the picture, a way we can enter the picture's space — with our eyes simply, standing firm. We accept the invitation, and the difficulties begin.

If that is a mirror behind the girl, then what exactly is being reflected in it? If it is a mirror, then that second woman on the right, seen from behind, must be the mirror-image of the girl who looks out at us. She must be, and yet she cannot be. She clearly does correspond, she could be the back view of the girl who confronts us. And yet how could the reflection be there, that much to the right? Does it mean — it must mean — that the whole mirror surface is at an angle to us, quite a sharp angle, receding into the distance from right to left? That could be so, there is nothing that precisely contradicts it: and yet it cannot be so, since everything else about the picture does contradict it, imprecisely. Everything about the picture is frontal, face-on to us, arranged in layers aligned to the picture surface. (And the mirror itself, to say it again, *is* the picture surface; and so *a fortiori* part of that plain arrangement.) Are we expected to insert, somehow, in this orderly set of spaces *another* space, a contrary diagonal? We cannot do it, in fact; or not in any way we can sustain, make part of one convenient "picture": that sloping mirror will not ever stay in place, it keeps lining up parallel to the surface; the reflection escapes from the person it belongs to. And that is not just because of contrary spaces: it is just as much a matter of contradictory images, views that do not quite match. Looking out at us, the girl is inviolate, upright, symmetrical, *recueillie*; but looking in at him, the man in the mirror, she leans forward too much, too close, the unbroken oval of the head sprouts a wispy hairdo; she is plumper, maybe; she is certainly deferential, she is "at your service." The girl who looks out at us is at nobody's service, least of all ours.

And then of course, final uncertainty, there is a gentleman in the mirror, standing in the top right-hand corner. Who is he? Where is he? Where does he stand in relation to her, in relation to us? I wrote already "looking out at us, looking in at him," but the problem is that she must be doing both at once, that *we* must be where he is. And yet we cannot be: not anyway if we are to remain what that "we" implies, all through the discourse so far — the single viewer of the painting, ourselves, myself, the subject for whom the picture exists and makes sense, by whom the whole thing is seen.[8] "We" are at the centre, he is squeezed out, cut off by the

[8] The notion of the subject as the cornerstone category of all ideologies has its roots in Hegelian and Marxist theory: one might say, in the critique of one by the other. (By subject is meant a "given" unity of consciousness, a subjectivity which is conceived as "fundamental"

edge of the canvas. His transaction with the girl who leans towards him taking his order cannot be the same as our transaction with the girl who gazes back at us, the girl who appropriates our stare. She is impassive and self-contained; her gaze resists interpretation; her expression is impenetrable: it is the face, to paraphrase a remark of Michael Fried's, of the painting itself, in which the painting stares at us.[9] All these things — and I am casting around, as Fried was, for words to suggest the complex, shifting relationship we have with that face, that pose, that expression — cannot simply be a matter of buying and selling, the mere professional impassivity of the barmaid.

What I have been describing is a texture of uncertainties. And the special force of the picture's uncertainty is the way in which what begins as doubt about relationships in space ends by being doubt about relationship in general. Little by little we lose our location in the *Bar aux Folies-Bergères*. And if we want to push the exploration a bit further — too far, in fact, because this last is an interval which appears only fitfully, as background to the images that cannot be avoided — we end up teetering on the edge of an unlikely abyss, a great space above the stalls which seems to be there, between the customer in the top hat and the ladies on the balcony far behind. Over the abyss is balanced the only performer in the picture, the solitary trapeze artist appearing for a moment at top left.

We lose our location in space, and because of that — as part of that — our first straightforward exchange of glances with another person is made into a problem. Here, too, in the matter of persons and expressions, we begin to struggle for a reading, to include in the transaction all that the reflection contains and disallows. And we *cannot do it*, the equation will not

and *always the same*, not something constructed and reconstructed in changing, specific social and ideological structures: the family, motherhood, fatherhood, childhood, etc.) The notion has more recently been revived and refined in the psychoanalytic work of J. Lacan. The most interesting and accessible current development of Lacan's ideas in the context of the study of artistic production can be found in recent issues of the magazine *Screen* (London, published by the Society for Education in Film and Television). See especially Vol. 16, no. 2, for some basic explanatory texts.

[9] The phrases come in the context of a different argument, one about Manet's stress in the 1860's on the *painting* as a unity. Not that this is necessarily in conflict with what I am arguing here: it might be said, and sometimes I believe Fried is saying, that in order to confront "the beholder" with the unity of the picture *as painted surface* all the other kinds of unity which are built into our normal appropriation of the work of art — including the unity of ourselves, the "beholder" — have to be deconstituted. Fried's text: "Manet seems to have wanted to establish a particular kind of relationship between the beholder and the painting *as a whole*, in its essential unity *as a painting*. In this sense it is as though the *painting itself* looks or gazes or stares at one — it is as though it confronts, fixes, even *freezes* one — through the eyes of the Old Musician, or through those of Victorine Meurend in the *Déjeuner sur l'herbe*, or through those of the soldier holding a cloak in the *Christ Scourged* . . . and as though this was an essential source of Manet's conviction, that the pictures in question really *were paintings*." In "Manet's Sources, Aspects of His Art, 1859-1865," *Artforum*, March 1969, p. 69, n. 27.

be resolved. We cannot, we will not occupy the place of the gentleman in the top hat clasping a cane; but there is no other place to occupy; we are left in a kind of suspended relation — to the girl, to ourselves, to the painting itself.

It is hard to put a name to what has happened. Have we gained or lost knowledge in the process I have described? We started out from a normal world, the world of subjects, a double unquestioned illusion: the open, unavoidable unity of the look, which confirms *us* as the person looked at, and conjures her as another of us. By the end we have all but lost that illusion; but in place of illusion is simply a shifting of places; we have not gained any *other* access to that face and that interior. And of course the illusion does not disappear: it would be absurd to claim that it does. "She" is still present, if we want her; the woman and her look still dominate our doubts, if we look in a certain way — the way that desire dictates, for instance. After all we *want* that barmaid to stay in position, to end up as one substance still open for "understanding." The shadow of the subject remains. It is the persistence of ideology in us, in our curious role of beholder (holding on to the image, and yet beholden to it); in Manet, if you want to psychologise the whole thing; in artistic production in 1882.

It seems clear that the *Bar's* elaborate structure was contrived with a great deal of care.[10] You have only to put the finished picture side by side with the preliminary oil sketch to see how much Manet worked to get rid of in the final painting. He had to dispose of any clear, readable relation between barmaid and customer: he had to obliterate the simple, almost caricatural relationship in the sketch, with its more or less blowsy *madame* lording it over the midget customer. He had to prize apart barmaid and reflection, and call back the mirror from its place between one and the other. In the process the painting turned into a restatement of an old theme in Manet's art. It referred back to those paintings from the 1860's, like the *Déjeuner sur l'herbe* and the *Olympia*, in which a seemingly unqualified gaze, a frank and free staring out at us, is counterpointed by the presence — real or implied by flowers — of owners of that liberty and that frankness.

But that does not help us to pose, or to answer, the question that is left, the questions imposed by the reading we have given. What does this texture of uncertainties signify? Why are we placed in this state of sus-

[10] Do not ask, finally, how much of this Manet *intended*. That would be to bring in wholeness by the back door: if we are robbed of the subject behind the bar, let us have the subject who made the bar and the barmaid. Let us have "the painter." Several arguments could be deployed against this fiction, some of them Freudian, some of them not. See, for instance, the arguments, which seem to me convincing, used by N. Hadjinicolau in "Premier obstacle: l'histoire de l'art comme histoire des artistes," ch. 2 of *Histoire de l'art et lutte de classes* (Paris, 1973), pp. 27-50; also pp. 90-95.

pended relationship? What kind of consciousness is being portrayed — or rather enforced, recreated? Where and how did the subject become, for once, unavailable?

Those are questions about the Folies-Bergères, and about the café-concert.[11]

*   *   *

At one level — let us say the economic level — there was nothing mysterious about the café-concert. It was a form of speculation, a café with a stage, floodlights, a lead singer and a couple of third-rate comedians: it was a way to sell more lukewarm beer at more exorbitant prices. And the café-concert had a rather special location in Paris: though the form began on the Champs-Elysées, and spread north beyond the *barrières*, it had its base in the new Paris of Baron Haussmann. It occupied, positively invaded, the great spaces Haussmann created in the 1850's and 1860's, the sidewalks and squares of a city built for trade, traffic and swift movement of troops. And as one kind of private enterprise among others, the café-concert was at first sight a perfectly appropriate form of life to be spawned in Haussmann's boulevards.

But the writers of the time — the journalists, the guidebook writers, the producers of *études de moeurs* — were not so sure. The cafés-concerts "ont fini par exercer une influence incontestable sur l'état d'esprit des nouvel-

[11] Note that there was some uncertainty in the early 1880's as to whether, or how, the Folies-Bergères *was* a café-concert. It was almost always classified as such, but it was clearly a special case of the breed — though its emphasis on spectacle and decor was only an extension of something that had always been central to the form. (So that Pissarro, for instance, talking of architecture in 1896, could write naturally: "c'est café-concert, c'est Julian, école etc." Letter to Lucien Pissarro, 3 January 1896.)

Maupassant, describing the Folies in *Bel-ami* in 1885, seems to start with a distinction between Folies-Bergères and café-concert proper. The jounalist Forestier says, "les cafés-concerts peuvent distraire mon pharmacien et son épouse, mais pas moi . . ." [*Bel-ami*, ed. by G. Delaisement (Paris, 1959), p. 13], but he troops off with the hero to the Folies. Yet when the Folies themselves are described, the initial distinction (pharmacien/Forestier: petit bourgeois/homme du monde) breaks down. The Folies do have a bourgeois clientele, which is placed initially in the stalls. But any imagery of class segregation soon breaks down: in the *promenoirs* there is an extraordinary mixture of classes, a mixture that defies analysis beyond a certain point (see passage cited in text, below).

In terms of its audience, then, the Folies-Bergères seems distinct from the café-concert only in the *intensity* of its mixing of classes. And in this, as I am arguing, it once again only exaggerated something basic to the whole world of the café-concert.

Incidentally, one feature of the *Bar's* spatial oddity — the way the bar seems perched on the edge of empty space — may be partly explained by the Folies' architecture. The bars were situated on the high-level *promenoirs* above the stalls. But this does not touch the question of Manet's exploitation of this fact, the deliberate unclarity of his depiction of it.

les générations."[12] Most critics agreed with that judgment, but most critics seemed alarmed or uneasy about it. They did not understand the café-concert, and they did not approve of its power.

The first sign of that uncertainty was the way the café-concert was seen — still seen after it had dominated central Paris for 30 or 40 years — as an accidental phenomenon. For some reason it failed to take on the appearance of permanence that usually goes with success; it never looked like a "natural" part of the social order. Commentators went on wondering where the cafés-concerts had come from and how long they would last. And one or two of these myths of origin are instructive: they point to the sources of the critics' unease. One, for instance, Pierre Véron in 1861,[13] claimed that the café-concert was born on the Champs Elysées in the 1840's, in the course of a contest between a solitary *saltimbanque*, "un énorme poussah . . . hissé sur deux planches soutenues par deux chaises boiteuses" outside the *Café du Midi*, and a whole *parade* of down-at-heel rivals outside the *Ambassadeurs*.[14] Some clients brought chairs on to the terrace to watch; others joined them, half-laughing, half-incredulous; the cafés did good business and paid the grotesques to come back; the crowd

[12] E. Drumont, *Mon vieux Paris*, 2e série (Paris, 1897), p. 212. Figures on the cafés-concerts are sparse. Maxime du Camp, *Paris, ses organes, ses fonctions, et sa vie dans la seconde moitié du XIXe siècle*, (Paris, 1875) VI, p. 327, gives the number of cafés-concerts as 180. (He is probably using the 1872 census. Cf. 238 *bals publics*, 424 registered street entertainers, this last figure on p. 315.) V. Fournel, *Esquisses et croquis parisiens* (Paris, 1876), p. 40, gives the popularly-cited figure as 117 (this was in 1874), but argues that this excluded a vast number of weekend and part-time cafés-concerts, and a mass of transient cafés-concerts on the working-class outskirts of the city.
    The present essay deals with the first hey-day of the café-concert, from the mid-1860's to the mid-1880's. In the later 1880's, a new more literary, more *avant-garde* café-concert grew up alongside the remnants of the primitive type: this was the café-concert of Yvette Guilbert, Lautrec and Bruant. It was immediately recognised as a different kind of phenomenon from the café-concert I am describing. See, e.g., G. Montorgueil, *Le café-concert, lithographies de H.-G. Ibels et de H. de Toulouse-Lautrec* (Paris, 1893), p. 9, for a discussion of the differences between Thérésa and Yvette Guilbert. "La chanson de l'empire débraillée et canotière, qui avait été bâtarde et chahuteuse avec Thérésa — tout en gueule, elle musclée, solide, hanchée crânement, vivandière du dernier bataillon impérial — se transmuait. . . ."
[13] P. Véron, *Paris s'amuse* (Paris, 1861), pp. 84-85. He gives the date of invention as 1844; others favoured the aftermath of 1848.
[14] Various other details make Véron's insistence on the "popular" origins of the café-concert clear. The *parade* is led by "un aimable faubourien, affublé d'un costume grec. . . ." "Depuis . . . j'ai rencontré l'aimable faubourien dans la rue d'Amsterdam. Il avait troqué le costume grec de la prospérité contre une blouse bleue qui lui allait infiniment mieux que son travestissement héroïque, et aboyait aux gros sons la complainte des *Feuilles Mortes*."
    In the early 1860's it was still possible for café-concert performers to fear a return to the ranks of the *saltimbanques*. See, e.g., Emile Mathieu, *Les cafés-concerts* (Paris, 1863). This is a description of the form before its hey-day — Thérésa is listed on p. 44 as just one of 40 women singers — and it is throughout a *defence* of the cafés-concerts by "un artiste des cafés-concerts." The threat is suppression by the government, and in 1863 it still seemed real: "Les cafés-concerts n'étant qu'une tolérance, ils peuvent être biffés d'un trait de plume,

E. Manet, *The Bar at the Folies-Bergères*, 1881. Courtauld Institute Galleries, London.

grew, other cafés were forced to compete. "Quoiqu'il en soit, le tréteau a fait souche. Un gland contient le chêne, un oeuf l'aiglon; la parade de 1844 contenait le café chantant de 1861. Fauteuils de velours, gaz coquet et enguirlandé, dames en robe de bal, orchestre complet."

What does it tell us when a form of life as firmly entrenched as the café-concert goes on being seen as an aberration? And why — the second, explicit sign of uncertainty — is there such persistent distaste at what went on in the *Alcazar* or the *Eldorado*? Here, for example, is a description of the greatest café-concert performer, the immortal Thérésa, who ruled the *Alcazar-Lyrique* in the 1860's.[15] It is a description by Louis Veuillot, who is vitriolic as usual, but in this case the viciousness is typical of one whole strain of comment.

Elle allait paraître, un tonnerre d'applaudissements l'annonça.

Je ne la trouvai point si hideuse que l'on m'avait dit. C'est une fille assez grande, assez découplée, sans nul charme que sa gloire, qui en est un, il est vrai, du premier ordre. Elle a, je crois, quelques cheveux; sa bouche semble faire le tour de la tête; pour lèvres, des bourrelets comme un nègre; des dents de requin. . . .

Elle sait chanter. Quant à son chant, il est indescriptible, comme ce qu'elle chante. Il faut être Parisien pour en saisir l'attrait, Français raffiné pour en savourer la profonde et parfaite ineptie. Cela n'est d'aucune langue, d'aucun art, d'aucune vérité. Cela se ramasse dans le ruisseau; mais il y a le goût du ruisseau, et il faut trouver dans le ruisseau le produit qui a bien le goût du ruisseau. . . .

La musique a le même caractère que les paroles; un caractère de charge corrompue et canaille, et d'ailleurs morne comme la face narquoise du voyou. Le voyou, le Parisien naturel, ne pleure pas, il pleurniche; il ne rit pas, il ricane; il ne plaisante pas, il *blague*; il ne danse pas, il chahute; il n'est pas amoureux, il est libertin. L'art consiste à ramasser des ingrédients dans une chanson, et les auteurs y arrivent neuf fois sur dix, la chanteuse aidant. Le succès est en rapport avec la dose.

---

et rentrer dans le néant: que feraient les artistes qui exercent leur profession depuis 12 ou 15 ans? . . ." (Ibid., p. 14). Mathieu is also aware of the beginning of a change in status: the audiences, he says, are becoming less noisy and uninterested; and already a new class of customer is appearing. "Cette classe d'abonnés dont je parle, est composée de presque tous rentiers, j'en connais qui sont même plusieurs fois millionnaires, et qui viennent au café-concert par goût." (Ibid., pp. 25-26.)

[15] Thérésa provided one of the natural points of comparison for critics confronted by Manet's *Olympia* in 1865. The cartoonist Bertall imagined Manet repenting of *Olympia* in these terms: "M. Manet nettoie la place de son chat, envoie son bouquet à Thérésa, et sa charbonnière aux Batignolles. Le tour est fait. S'il lui prend l'idée de faire un chef-d'oeuvre l'année prochaine, on en parlera.dans Landernau." (*L'Illustration*, 17 June 1865, p. 389.) Oliver Merson, in *L'Opinion Nationale* of 29 May, called *Olympia* "l'enseigne de la *Femme à Barbe*,". which was the song that had made Thérésa's name.

Tout cela sent la vieille pipe, la fuite de gaz, la vapeur de boisson fermen-tée; et la tristesse réside au fond, cette tristesse diserte et plate qu'on appelle l'ennui. La physionomie générale de l'auditoire est une sorte de torpeur troublée. Ces gens-là ne vivent plus que des secousses; et la grande raison du succès de certains "artistes," c'est qu'ils donnent la secousse plus forte. Elle passe vite, l'habitué retombe dans sa torpeur.[16]

Two things trigger Veuillot's sarcasm: the performance on stage and the public in the hall. What offended Veuillot first of all — and here he is hardly modifying the common refrain — was the style of Thérésa's performance, the vulgar, violent, proletarian songs, the slang, the obscene gestures, the lavatorial humour.[17] And beyond that, the terrible *rapport* between singer and audience, intoxicated by Thérésa like Alsa-ciens by the smell of sauerkraut (that is another of Veuillot's similes). What takes place on the stage of the café-concert is an art of the streets, the gutter, the *canaille*: *le petit chic canaille*, another writer called it.[18] It is an art designed for another public, the public that crowds to the edge of the stage and shouts, "ce public en veste, en casquette et en pipe" which, when the tenor comes on in evening dress, "exige aussi que l'acteur en habit noir

---

[16] Collected in L. Veuillot, *Les odeurs de Paris* (Paris, 1867), pp. 149-150. Of course Thérésa had plenty of defenders and enthusiasts in the press. Her memoirs of 1865, ghosted by a leading boulevard journalist, thanked her various literary defenders. But the strength and persistence of the opposition — the kind of writing I have cited — is the remarkable thing, I believe.

[17] "Hélas! qu'est devenu le bon goût, la délicatesse de nos pères! Voulez-vous connaître les titres de quelques-unes des oeuvres qui se chantent dans les cafés-concerts? Oyez et jugez:

   — Où qu'il est que je lui retire ma casquette.
   — Je renfonce mon chapeau.
   — J'vous conseille pas d'fourrer vot'nez là-dedans.
   — Ça presse. - Balayez-moi ça.
   — Soufflez dessus. - Quel barbottage!
   — Faut avaler ça, Verpillon.
   — Ote donc tes pieds d'là, ça sent la trichine.
   — J'ai tapé dans le tas!
   — Asseyez-vous d'ssus!
   — Je t'enlève le ballon, etc. etc."

Marc-Constantin, *Histoire des cafés-concerts et des cafés de Paris*, nlle. ed. (Paris, 1872), pp. 93-94.

   The verdict of the one-time Realist Champfleury is of interest. "Sans doute, dans les cafés, de choquantes individualités jouent un rôle un peu trop considérable. Qui les met à la mode, qui les acclame, qui reçoit dans l'intimité ces chanteuses qu'un Ribeira seul pourrait idéaliser, lui le grand idéalisateur des idiots et des pouilleux?" "Bals et Concerts," *Paris Guide par les principaux écrivains et artistes de France* (Paris, 1867), II, p. 997.

[18] A. Delvau, *Plaisirs de Paris* (Paris, 1867), p. 181 (on Thérésa's rival, Suzanne Lagier: "quoique passablement délurée et même grivoise, il lui manque le petit chic canaille qui donnait un si violent relief aux chansons de Thérésa . . .").

'courbe son échine'; et l'acteur n'a garde d'y manquer."[19]

Thérésa was conscious of her power. She dedicated her *Mémoires* of 1865 *Au Peuple de Paris*. She seemed to be, or she claimed to be, the voice of that *peuple*, their life, their language, their values; and that fact was resented by many of those who wrote about her. She had enemies on the Right and the Left. The Right, naturally, saw the café-concert as little more than an outpost of socialism. They quoted the words of one favourite café-concert song, *La Canaille*, with its chorus, *J'en suis! J'en suis!*[20] Or occasionally they were more circumstantial. This, for instance, is Victor Fournel, writing in *L'Ordre* on 24 April 1874:

> On m'avait dit que les chanteuses, après leurs morceaux, venaient se mêler au public et boire dans la salle. Je n'ai rien vu de pareil. La police y a mis ordre, à ce qu'il paraît. Aussi ces dames des cafés-concerts ont-elles cela de commun avec le *Rappel* et la *République française*, qu'elles n'aiment point *l'ordre moral*. Ce n'est pas la seule concession qu'on ait faite à la police. La premiere partie de la soirée s'est terminée par une chanson très-résolûment antisocialiste dont j'ai retenu ces quatre vers:
>
> > "Puisque tous les hommes sont frères,
> > J'demand' que les ceuss qu'a pas l'sou
> > Reçoiv't des rentes viagères
> > De ceuss qui couch't dans l'acajou.
>
> Les blouses blanches elles-mêmes riaient à ventre éboutonné, et je me suis levé alors, pour partir sur la bonne bouche.[21]

Part of this is fantasy of course. Fournel is disturbed not so much by the cod-socialist songs as by the whole assertive culture of the *café-concert de la pègre*.[22] (He is all the more angry because in another guise he posed as the

---

[19] L. Veuillot on the *Bataclan, Les odeurs de Paris*, p. 155.

[20] Marc-Constantin describes the vehemence with which that chorus was sung in *Le Grand Café Parisien* (the date is 1872): "les poings crispés et l'oeil hagard, elle préconisait *la Canaille*, dont le refrain était: J'en suis! J'en suis!" *Histoire des cafés-concerts*, p. 98.

[21] Collected in *Esquisses et croquis parisiens*, pp. 44-45. Fournel writes here under the pseudonym Bernadille. He was a constant opponent of the café-concert, partly for reasons of politics, partly because of his attachment to what he believed to be an earlier, truly "popular," picturesque street culture. See, e.g., Fournel, *Ce qu'on voit dans les rues de Paris* (Paris, 1858), pp. 29-32, or Fournel, "Etablissements de plaisir," in *Paris dans sa splendeur* (Paris, 1861), II, pp. 23-24 (a more guarded guide-book account).

[22] The title of another Bernadille *esquisse*, dated 2 August 1872, collected op. cit., pp. 46-51. "Les piliers d'estaminets borgnes, les rôdeurs de barrière, les ouvriers qui ne travaillent pas et les *retour de pontons* composaient toute la partie mâle du public" (p. 47). "J'ai retenu les titres des principales chansons: *Je n'comprends pas ça — Je suis tout chose. — Complet partout. — La Vénus au battoir. — Comment qu'ça s'fait? — La calotte de velours. — Je n'suis pas préparé.* . . . Est-il besoin de dire que toutes les chansons dont je viens de transcrire les titres ne sont que des tissus d'allusions et d'équivoques ordurières, bien dignes d'un tel public!" (p. 50).

champion of "popular" culture, the chronicler of the *saltimbanque* and the sideshow.) But the government was at least as nervous as Fournel. A circular sent out to all cafés-concerts late in November 1872 decreed, or rather repeated an old decree, that political allusions were "absolument interdites."[23]

The Left was not much more enthusiastic. It saw the café-concert as one more diversion from working-class struggle, and it pined for the old tradition of militant popular song — the tradition still represented in the 1860's by Darcier. The cover of *Le Hanneton* in 1867, with a giant Darcier stifling Thérésa in mid-verse, summed up the Left's feelings. And *La Rive gauche* — published in Belgium to avoid the censors, and already in contact with the First International[24] — had this to say on the subject of Thérésa in 1865:

> Dernièrement, une rixe dont elle était le sujet, a eu lieu aux Champs-Elysées entre la police et la foule de badauds et de gandins venus pour l'entendre. Quelques sergents de ville ont reçu des horions, paraît-il, et ont dû dégaîner, mais le sang n'a pas été répandu.
>
> Quel grand peuple que celui qui sait se battre pour une chanteuse de brasserie, et ne sait rien faire pour conquérir sa liberté![25]

That is interesting in two respects. First, because it tells something — maybe nothing new — about the inflexible reflexes of the Left. Second, because it indicates a little of the tension that existed within the café-concert, the constant danger that violence would spill over from the stage to the tables. When Veuillot said that the shock-treatment of Thérésa's songs was momentary, and that the *habitué* fell back immediately into his usual torpor, he was, among other things, reassuring himself.

All the same, this is only one aspect of the critics' uneasiness. They may have hated and feared Thérésa, but that hatred and fear was partly a game, partly a received manoeuvre of class society — the name of Veuillot's and Fournel's game, after all, is snobbery. Or it ought to be. But what they produce is not snobbery exactly: it is snobbery gone haywire. And what *interferes* with the ordinary procedures for placing and containing the people and the "popular" is, I believe, the nature of the public which went to the café-concert. Look at the people who listen, or do not listen, in the margins of Degas' studies of the café-concert, or in the foreground of

---

[23] Cited in J. Parain, "Censure, Théâtre et Commune 1871-1914," *Le mouvement social* (April-June 1972), p. 330.

[24] The first French translation of Marx's Inaugural Address of the International Working Men's Association was published in the paper in 1865. Charles Longuet was the editor.

[25] Impavidus, "Correspondance Parisienne," *La Rive gauche*, 18 June 1865, pp. 5-6.

Manet's café-concert paintings from the late 1870's, or in the blurred spaces of one or two drawings by Seurat, of the *Eden-Concert* in the 1880's. What disturbed critics about this audience was the way it refused to be classified, to be "classed," the way it did not fit into the normal categories of social perception.[26]

The *Murray Guide for English Visitors to Paris* had this to say of the café-concert in its 1872 edition: "The company is not the most select, and the performance tends to the immoral; respectable people keep aloof."[27] But the trouble — the problem for social perception — was that Murray's *Guide* was wrong. Respectable people did not keep aloof.

There were cafés-concerts with an exclusively working-class clientele, out on the northern boulevards, on the slopes of Montrouge or Belleville. And there the tourist and the bourgeois did not go. Fournel was describing a place like this, and occasionally Degas drew them — spit and sawdust decor, whores, absinthe, *chapeaux moux*.[28]

But the cafés of the centre and the Champs-Elysées were different. The public there was a mixture of *bourgeois* and *populaire*, a mixture in which the boundaries of class identity, the very existence of class divisions, seemed to blur and disappear. It was not just a matter of a *double* public, though many writers indicated that some such dual public did exist. "Trois mille personnes au moins étaient entassées là," this is Victor Four-

[26] For all Theodore Zeldin's efforts to dismantle the notions of "class" in his *France 1848-1945* (Oxford, 1973), it still seems to me unavoidable, from the body of evidence I know, that as far as *social identity* was concerned in 19th-century France — and particularly in 19th-century Paris — the distinctions between *bourgeois* and *populaire* (and later, between *bourgeois* and *prolétaire*) are fundamental. We may want to show that what they designated was a shifting, ambiguous set of professions and allegiances: but they did designate, and there were no other designations available. It is the moment when the normal categories of social perception are interfered with that fascinates me — and which links this study with previous work on the unstable nature of *bourgeoisie* in 1850. But the thoroughgoing perceptual panic that results from these interferences only confirms my sense of how fundamental — how necessary to knowledge — a consciousness of class was in the 19th century.

[27] *Murray Guide* (1872), p. 32. Interesting variations from the 1867 edition, which noted: "The company is not aristocratic, but the visitor need not be afraid of annoyance or unbecoming conduct" (p. 34). And cf. the 1882 edition, where an English term of comparison is available: "*Cafés-concerts* or *Chantants*. These are all of the "Music-hall" order, both in the style of their entertainment and in the class of their frequenters" (p. 109). The parallel with music-hall could be pursued, as Murray says, on the level of performance and public. The analogies between Thérésa and Marie Lloyd are irresistible, and the terms of T.S. Eliot's obituary discussion of Marie Lloyd's "popularity" work well: "popularity in her case was not merely evidence of her accomplishment; it was something more than success. It is evidence of the extent to which she represented and expressed that part of the English nation which has perhaps the greatest vitality and interest."

[28] Notably the pastel on monotype done around 1882, P.A. Lemoisne, *Degas et son oeuvre* (Paris, 1946-49), n. 688. There is a description of the special character of the "café-concert of the Barrier" in l'Anglo-Parisian, *Paris by Day and Night* (Paris, 1880), pp. 227-229.

nel on the *Alcazar*, "bourgeois, petits commercants, quelques ouvriers endimanchés, familles entières en partie de plaisir, provinciaux et étrangers."[29] Even though the *ouvriers* are *endimanchés*, that is still a list of separate elements. And sometimes the separation was absolute: one writer described the outskirts of the *Ambassadeurs* in the Champs-Elysées, where a second public sauntered endlessly by the tables, craning their necks for a sight of Thérésa, straining to hear and memorise the words of the latest song.[30] They were excluded for the simplest of reasons: they could not afford the price of a beer.

But these were exceptional images. The distinctive imagery of the café-concert was of the public inside the *Ambassadeurs*, a public playing at the dissolution of class distinctions. "Les commis-voyageurs en bordée et les grandes dames en débauche": that was a writer describing the *Mirliton*.[31] "Ces bourgeois, calicots, et gommeux très peu dignes";[32] "des *calicots* dont le magasin ferme de bonne heure, des clercs de notaire qui font l'étude buissonnière, des hommes mariés — qui soi-disant vont au Cercle."[33] Maupassant only elaborated this imagery when he pointed out the crowd on the *promenoirs* of the Folies-Bergères: ". . . derrière nous, le plus drôle de mélange qui soit dans Paris. . . . Il y a de tout, de toutes les professions et de toutes les castes, mais la crapule domine. Voici des employés, employés de banque, de magasin, de ministère, des reporters, des souteneurs, des officiers en bourgeois, des gommeux en habit, qui viennent de dîner au cabaret et qui sortent de l'Opéra avant d'entrer aux Italiens, et puis encore tout un monde d'hommes suspects qui défient l'analyse."[34]

The café-concert, said one Walter Francis Lonergan in 1880, masquerading under the (improbable) title Anglo-Parisian, "is the Elysium of

---

[29] *Esquisses*, p. 35.

[30] Drumont, *Mon vieux Paris*, p. 213. Later in the century, in a way that is typical of one kind of *Symboliste* writing, attention sometimes focused on the penumbra of figures — seated and on the move — which existed *Autour du Café-Concert d'Eté*. See the essay-cum-prose-poem of this name by Thadée Natanson in *Badauderies Parisiennes: Les rassemblements, physiologies de la rue* (Paris, 1896) (various authors, including Paul Adam, Félix Fénéon, Gustave Kahn; illustrated by Felix Vallotton).

  Thérésa in her *Mémoires* has a passage in which she claims to sing above all for "les gamins parisiens qui comprennent, eux!" who listen "au dehors, groupés autour des massifs de verdure qui nous servent d'enceinte" (op. cit., pp. 233-234).

[31] G. Montorgueil, *Le café-concert*, p. 11. The date is rather too late, and the *Mirliton* rather too "literary," for this to be treated as hard evidence, but it is corroborated by witnesses of the kind of café-concert that interests me.

[32] A line from a poem by M. Vaucaire, "Café-chantant — A J.M. de Hérédia," in *Effets de théâtre* (Paris, 1886), pp. 105-106.

[33] P. Véron, *Paris s'amuse*, p. 87.

[34] *Bel-ami*, p. 16.

the emancipated *calicot*, or apprentice."[35] In other words, the public in these places played out a charade of classlessness. The *calicot* played at being a dandy, the dandy pretended to be a *calicot*. They all tried to hide in the same troubled torpor, the same collective enthusiasm, the same "débraillement social."[36]

It was this above all that interfered with description. In its strongest form, the café-concert produced a kind of social vertigo, as if here nothing was stable any longer, as if the most basic categories of experience — interior and exterior, public and private — were about to dissolve in a total loss of classes. It was this that Edmond and Jules de Goncourt feared, one evening in 1860:

> Je vais ce soir à l'*Eldorado*, un café-concert du boulevard de Strasbourg, une salle à colonnes d'un grand luxe de décor et de peintures.
>
> Mon Paris, le Paris où je suis né, le Paris des moeurs de 1830 à 1848 s'en va. Il s'en va par le matériel, il s'en va par le moral. Le vie sociale y fait une grande évolution qui commence. Je vois des femmes, des enfants, des ménages, des familles dans ce café. L'intérieur va mourir. La vie menace de devenir publique. Le cercle pour le haut, le café pour le bas, voilà où aboutiront la société et le peuple. . . . De là une impression de passer là dedans, ainsi qu'un voyageur. Je suis étranger à ce qui vient, à ce qui est, comme à ces boulevards nouveaux sans tournant, sans aventures de perspective, implacables de ligne droite, qui ne sentent plus le monde de Balzac, qui font penser à quelque Babylone américaine de l'avenir.[37]

It is a dense text, and it points to the heart of the matter. In the café-concert the interior was dying. Private life — all that protected, bourgeois reality, the hidden but most real part of life, family, home, wife,

---

[35] *Paris by Day and Night*, p. 221. Guide books cannot make up their minds about the public of the cafés-concerts. Baedeker's 1872 guide says that the Champs-Elysées cafés-chantants "afford unbounded delight to the middling and lower classes of Parisians" (p. 17). Galignani in 1879 says: "Cafés-concerts or chantants are the favourite evening lounge of the Parisian *bourgeois*, who does not object to hearing favourite songs and other music, while regaling himself" (p. 236). Gustave Geffroy, writing about Yvette Guilbert in 1894 wants, from his moderate socialist perspective, somehow to conjure away the fact of class mixing: "La vérité, c'est qu'il n'y a pas, dans une grande ville telle que Paris, de si grandes différences de public. Ou plutôt, la grande différence crée une infime minorité et une immense majorité," *Yvette Guilbert* (Paris, 1894), n.p. It is a curious way of dealing with the fact that in certain places class did disappear.

[36] Veuillot, *Les odeurs de Paris*, p. 147.

[37] E. and J. de Goncourt, *Journal des Goncourt* (Paris, 1891), I, pp. 345-346. I first encountered the second paragraph in R. Wollheim's article, "Babylon, Babylone," *Encounter*, May 1962, p. 25, though only discovered later that it was a response to the café-concert in particular.

children — was spilling out on to Haussmann's sidewalks and into the *Eldorado*. In the *Eldorado*, as other writers show us, the bourgeois adopted the style of the *populaire*. It seems as though one class, the dominant class, was obliged to exploit the forms of another, the class it dominated. In the process it was forced to include and imitate *too much* of the culture it aimed to domesticate.

I believe that tells us something important about the whole nature of bourgeois culture, or at least the culture of the bourgeoisie as it became the ruling class of a capitalist society. That becoming was necessarily a painful, fragmentary process, and particularly so for the nineteenth-century bourgeoisie. First of all, because of the speed with which it was forced to take on a dominant political role. Secondly, because in the centuries of its prehistory — its history as *part* of the social order, as masters of the mere "economy" of things — it had built itself a culture which was massively instrumental, tied to the particulars of making and doing. The other dimension of any culture — the devising of specific patterns of being and feeling, the construction of a more-or-less coherent sense of self, the business of bringing up one's children to be one of "us" — all that had been left for later, tentatively sketched. The relationship of bourgeoisie to aristocracy was unresolved. (Not that one would expect any sudden magic demarcation. Any class builds its identity out of the bits and pieces of previous cultures: the relationship of peasant culture to the remnant languages of feudalism is a case in point. But bourgeois culture is peculiarly incoherent. The peasantry quickly digested and reordered the debris of feudalism; the aristocratic heroes, costumes, preferences were transformed, often beyond recognition. In contrast, the bourgeois flinched from appropriation; he either copied or ignored. The *Bourgeois gentilhomme* describes one stage of the process; the signs of another, in the later 18th century, are the frantic yet essentially half-hearted attempts to revise the notion of "nobility" so as to include some of the bourgeois virtues.)[38]

What bourgeois culture lacked was any real sense of identity: a sense of what was different in its whole relation to the world. An identity is made

[38] See the account of this process, and its implications for the visual art of the time, in T. Crow, "Connoisseurs and Men of Good Sense, the Reaction against the Rococo" (unpublished M.A. thesis, U.C.L.A., 1976).

The obvious counter-example to this argument — particularly as stated in the next paragraph — is the 19th-century novel. This is too big an issue to broach here, but let me indicate the lines that the reply might take. The novel, when it does describe the bourgeoisie, has as one of its central subjects the very lack of bourgeois identity I have been describing. The make-shift and incoherent nature of bourgeois self-consciousness is, for instance, the crucial subject of *Madame Bovary*. And secondly, the novel is a much less bourgeois form than we (or the text-books) tend to think. Tolstoy, after all, was a count writing about princes. I exaggerate, but I believe the argument could be pursued along these lines.

out of modes of feeling, speaking, understanding; finding some things funny, some tragic, others in bad taste; having your own criteria for pity, forgiveness, disbelief. Alongside its aristocratic rivals, what stands out about the bourgeoisie is its lack of these modes and criteria — it is almost as if its identity *depended* on not having time for feeling. ("Our aristocrats can do that for us.")

In the nineteenth century, there was one more constraint on bourgeois culture. Perhaps the bourgeoisie did not devise itself an identity because it was never allowed to; because its rule was immediately contested, and not just by the class it had defeated but by the class its industry had brought into being — a class which soon elaborated its own militant sense of "us" and "them." "The bourgeoisie is defined," wrote Roland Barthes, "as the *social class which does not want to be named.*"[39] I believe that is largely true. But part of the reason why it cannot and must not name itself is simply a lack of vocabulary: it is no good calling oneself bourgeois if that concept, at the level of the *self*, is such an empty one.

For all these reasons, bourgeois culture in the nineteenth century was specially make-shift, marked and misshapen by its own heterogeneity. It cobbled together its travesties of aristocratic style, and its covert, envious imitations of the "popular"; and the patchwork almost always showed; the materials rarely took on a new order of their own. Shuttling between aristocrat and *populaire*, the bourgeois maintained his sense of identity only by never standing still; the *bourgeois gentilhomme* modulated into the *bourgeois calicot* — in the course of a day, or an hour, or a single sequence of word and gesture.

The café-concert was the perfect place for this. Two forms of life were held in permanent tension there: in a kind of double masquerade, the bourgeois behaving as part of "ce public en veste, en casquette et en pipe," and the apprentice decked out in *habit noir*. The café-concert was a place of exchange: exchanging selves, shifting identities. That produced in the Goncourts a sort of perceptual panic, a sense that nothing any longer could be identified. And it produced in the ordinary public of the café-concert a style of behaviour — a certain presentation of self — which seemed designed to cope with this openness. Most of the writers felt for words to describe the style, the state of troubled torpor, the indifference, the *ennui*,[40] "la complicité tacite de la foule, des êtres semblables à eux, de

---

39 R. Barthes, *Mythologies*, nlle. ed. (Paris, 1970), p. 225. Again, Barthes' definition applies to the bourgeoisie as ruling class. The self-consciousness of the bourgeoisie before its accession to power is a different matter.

40 Veuillot, *Les odeurs de Paris*; A. Chadourne, *Les cafés-concerts* (Paris, 1889), citing a comment by an unnamed contemporary: "Est-ce désoeuvrement, ennui, indifférence, ou le plaisir de payer trois francs un verre de mauvaise bière qui fait aller la foule dans ces endroits?" (p. 7).

la cohue des ennuyés."[41] Here was an audience which had invented an ineffable dialect of its own, a language of cliches, *blagues*, catchphrases, *idées reçues*.[42] "Ceux-là sont trop ordinaires. Leur satisfaction uniforme empêche qu'on remarque rien d'eux."[43]

That last phrase brings us back to the *Bar aux Folies-Bergères*. The *Bar* is a superficial painting, in the strict meaning of the word. And superficiality had always been at the centre of Manet's sense of *modernité*: the interior was dying, and in its place stared out exteriors, appearances, *maquillage*. Manet, just as much as the brothers Goncourt, insisted on the strain involved in that new order of things. He went to where the new behaviour existed in its purest and most intransigent forms — the picnic, the brothel, and finally the *Folies-Bergères*. And he painted externals, matters of fact; *candour* was a word his first critics applied to his faces and spaces; at first sight, in the *Bar*, things look straightforward.

I described before how that straightforwardness does not last, how surface covers surface instead of revealing it, the card house collapsing, the pieces refusing to fit. And I tried to show how that uncertainty of surface infects our whole relation to the girl, to the exterior that stands there at the centre, offered to us. Everything becomes untrustworthy; everything is a matter of appearances; the poise, the patience, the plainness become instead the empty, the evasive, the noncommittal. Might boredom be a way of putting these attributes together, and making an "emotion" out of them? It is a word we try on for size; but once again it does not fit, it does not stay still. It disperses, migrates to the flat white discs or the turn of the wrists as the hands rest placid (placid?) on the counter.

The truth is external, the interior is dying. So that even the face of the customer takes on a certain pinched intentness, and the patches of scumbled grey condense the picture's uncertainty about seeing: they are all that tell us that the mirror is there, the indices of a certain kind of visibility, and yet interruptions, imperfections of vision, patching the girl's black dress, the man's top hat; they are privileged marks of the *picture's* surface, yet marks of a surface which is nowhere, a fact that will not fit with others.

---

[41] Geffroy, *Yvette Guilbert*, n.p.

[42] P. Véron, for example, has an imaginary dialogue of café-concert habitués, conceived as an exchange of completely ready-made phrases. G. Coquiot, in a pretentious and bizarre book called *Les cafés-concerts* (Paris, 1896), has a theory as to the mechanism of change in the world of the café-concert: it is impossible for the performance to stay at the level of joyless banality which its audience wants and understands, and so eventually each café-concert is deserted by its public. A pretentious theory, but once again the imagery of the public, "si obstinément niais devant la cage ronronnante et piaillante des cabotes et des cabots" (p. 19), agrees with other sources.

[43] T. Natanson, *Badauderies parisiennes*, p. 143, speaking of the public *inside* the *café-concert d'été*.

What is left at the centre is a face which is full but empty, a face which cannot be read as the outside of anything, anybody. It is a place where nothing is expressed, least of all an emotion. It cannot be read because we are left no place to read it from: least of all the place we are allotted in the mirror, the place of the Other, the emancipated *calicot*.

In a pamphlet of 1889 entitled the *Guide secret de l'étranger celibataire à Paris*, the Folies-Bergères has this entry: "Les Folies-Bergères, trente-deux rue Richer; célèbre par ses promenoirs, son jardin, ses attractions toujours nouvelles et son public de jolies femmes."[44] Needless to say, the *Guide secret* was not interested in trapeze artists: it was a list of brothels, of places where the bachelor stranger could buy women. Other evidence tallies with this. Maupassant's Folies-Bergères is swarming with prostitutes. An art critic of 1877, reaching for a rude comparison with which to crush Cabanel's painting of Lucretia, writes without hesitation: "sa Lucrèce ressemble à une habituée du Bois ou des Folies-Bergères."[45]

So perhaps there is one more element in the transaction, or lack of transaction, depicted here. Perhaps this is more than the *ordinary* behaviour of this place — the exchange of disguises, the interruption of class. Is the woman's glance not just the barmaid meeting the customer's gaze, but the whore appraising the client, offering herself for appraisal? Is the look — the famous stare — a commodity?

Of course we cannot be sure. But if prostitution is part of it — part of the relationship — we should not be surprised. The *Bar aux Folies-Bergères* is about the grounds of one kind of consciousness: it is about the way in which, in parts of Paris in the nineteenth century, a certain *modernité* was constituted — a certain mobility, a certain *ennui*, a collective suspension of inquiry into one another's identity. That way of behaving was *play*, of a special kind. It was called leisure or, more strangely, recreation. But play is determined by work; and this recreation was an industry in itself, imitating — putting on display — the ground rules of the new economy. Little wonder that prostitution was the flesh of this *modernité*, indistinguishable from it. The whore is the perfect commodity, "seller and commodity in one," the body congealing into goods for sale.[46]

Being seller and commodity in one is hardly a rarity in the nineteenth century, more like a general condition. But there are always places where what we share is visible suddenly, suddenly obvious. (The freeway as the image of everyone's useless, elating power; smog as the price of freedom.) And perhaps that is why Manet went back and back to the bars and the

---

[44] Op. cit., p. 4.
[45] "Salon de 1877," article 3 in *La Petite république française*, 22 May 1877.
[46] W. Benjamin, "Paris, Capital of the 19th Century," in *Charles Baudelaire: A Lyric Poet in the Era of High Capitalism* (London, 1973), p. 171.

cafés-concerts. In the Folies-Bergères, at the moment the whore accosts the client, you can still *see* alienation — see a face lose its meaning, see a gesture go abstract. Alienation seems special here, almost exotic. What happens when every form of alienation looks alike: ordinary, and therefore invisible? What do painters offer us then? Pictures of everyone's alienation, or mirror-images of their own?

The Contributors

ROBERT J. BEZUCHA is a professor of history at Syracuse University and the author of *The Lyon Uprising of 1834: Social and Political Conflict in the Early Nineteenth Century* (1974).

TIMOTHY J. CLARK is a professor of fine arts at the University of Leeds and the author of *The Absolute Bourgeois: Artists and Politics in France, 1848-1851 (1973), and Image of the People: Gustave Courbet and the Second French Republic, 1848-1851* (1973).

NATALIE ZEMON DAVIS is a professor of history at the University of California, Berkeley, and the author of *Society and Culture in Early Modern France* (1975).

SUSAN J. DELANEY is an art historian at the University of Wisconsin, Madison.

CLARKE GARRETT is chairman of the history department at Dickinson College.

B. ROBERT KREISER is an assistant professor of history at the University of Rochester.

ROBERT MANDROU is a professor at the Université de Paris, X, and director of studies at the Ecole des Hautes Etudes Sociales. His books include *Histoire de la Civilisation française* (1958; nlle ed., 1968); *De la culture populaire en France aux XVIIe et XVIIIe siècles, La bibliothèque bleue de Troyes* (1964, nlle ed., 1975); *Magistrats et sorciers en France au XVIIe siècle* (1968); *Louis XIV en son temps* (1975); *Des humanistes aux hommes de science* (1975); and *Introduction à la France moderne, essai de psychologie historique* (1961; Eng. trans., 1976).

MICHAEL R. MARRUS is a professor of history at the University of Toronto and author of *The Politics of Assimilation* (1971).

LUCIENNE A. ROUBIN is a professor at the Laboratoire d'Ethnologie, Musée de l'Homme, Paris, and author of *Chambrettes des Provençaux* (1970).

EDWARD SHORTER is a professor of history at the University of Toronto and author of *The Making of the Modern Family* (1975).

BARNETT SINGER is a visiting lecturer in history at the University of Alberta.

MARC SORIANO is a professor at the Université de Paris, VII, and director of studies at the Ecole des Hautes Etudes Sociales. He is the author of *Les Contes de Perrault; Culture savante et traditions populaires* (1968).

EUGEN WEBER is a professor of history at U.C.L.A. His most recent book is *Peasants into Frenchmen* (1976).

STANFORD FRENCH AND ITALIAN STUDIES

Editor: Alphonse Juilland – Stanford University

1. **Robert Greer Cohn**. *Modes of Art*. An original aesthetics from the author of *L'Oeuvre de Mallarmé*; topics include the image, the symbol, genre, poetic realism, impressionism, creative temper.

2. **Michele Leone**. *L'industria nella letteratura italiana contemporanea*. The first discussion of industrialization in Italian society on the basis of works by Zolla, Vittorini, Bernari, Micheli, Arpino, Bianciardi, Buzzi, Bigiaretti, Calvino, Mastronardi, Ottieri, etc.

3. Edd. **J. Beauroy, M. Bertrand, J. Gargan**. *Popular Culture in France*. Contributions by leading scholars among whom Mandrou, Soriano, Weber, Roubin.

4. **Jacques Beauroy**. *Vin et société à Bergerac du moyen âge aux temps modernes*. An original and remarkable contribution to the history of French vineyards and of the Gascon wine trade; based on private archives.

5. **Alphonse Juilland**. *Structuralist and Transformationalist Morphology*. Confronts the descriptive and explanatory powers of the structuralist and transformational models in morphology.

6. **William Calin**. *Crown, Cross, and 'Fleur-de-lis'*. The first extended modern critical work devoted to Pierre Le Moyne's 'Saint Louis' deals with influence of Tasso, typology, treatment of women, imagery, elements of the baroque, etc.

7. **John C. Lapp**. *The Brazen Tower: Essays on Mythological Imagery in the French Renaissance and Baroque, 1550-1670*. Studies the impact of Greek and Roman mythology on French poetry, particularly on Pontus de Tyard, Du Bellay, Ronsard, D'Aubigné, Tristan l'Hermite, Corneille and La Fontaine.

Available Fall 1977:

8. **Hélène Fredrickson**. *Baudelaire: Héros et Fils. Dualité et Problèmes du Travail dans les Lettres à sa Mère*.

9. **Charles A. Porter**. *Chateaubriand: Composition, Imagination, and Poetry*.